FREQUENTLY CONSULTED ADVICE

P9-DMK-121

LISTS

The Borzoi Handbook for Writers

SECOND EDITION

Frederick Crews
University of California at Berkeley

Sandra Schor
Queens College
The City University of New York

Alfred A. Knopf   New York

This is a Borzoi book published by Alfred A. Knopf, Inc.

Second Edition
987654321

Copyright © 1985, 1989 by Frederick Crews and Sandra Schor

Library of Congress Cataloging-in-Publication Data

Crews, Frederick C.
    The Borzoi handbook for writers / Frederick Crews, Sandra
    Schor.—2nd ed.
        p.   cm.
    Includes index.
    ISBN 0-394-37270-0 :
    1. English language—Rhetoric.   2. English language—
    Grammar—1950–   I. Schor, Sandra.   II. Title.
    PE1408.C7145   1989
    808'.042—dc19   88–26618
                                CIP

Manufactured in the United States of America

Cover design: Lawrence R. Didona

Page 153: Michael Massing, "Snap Books." *The New Republic,* May 4, 1987. Excerpted by permission of *The New Republic,* © 1987, The New Republic, Inc.

Page 153: Harry F. Waters, "TV's New Racial Hue," *Newsweek,* January 25, 1988.

Page 162: From *The Random House College Dictionary,* Revised Edition. Copyright © 1984 by Random House, Inc. Reprinted by permission.

Page 186: Helen Vendler, "Body Language," Copyright © 1986 by *Harper's Magazine.* All rights reserved. Reprinted from the October issue by special permission.

Page 186: Thomas Geoghegan, "Chicago, Pride of the Rustbelt." *The New Republic,* March 25, 1985. Excerpted by permission of *The New Republic,* © 1985, The New Republic, Inc.

Page 187: Russell Baker, "New England Gray." *The New York Times Magazine,* December 1, 1985. Copyright © 1985 by The New York Times Company. Reprinted by permission.

Page 187: Mick LaSalle, "She's Her Own Best Imitator," *San Francisco Chronicle,* December 14, 1987. © San Francisco Chronicle, 1987. Reprinted by permission.

Page 187: Russell Davies, "A Prodigious One-Man Show." London *Times Literary Supplement,* November 28, 1986. © Times Newspapers Ltd. 1986.

Page 187: From *Herzog* by Saul Bellow. Copyright © 1961, 1963, 1964 by Saul Bellow. All rights reserved. Reprinted by permission of Viking Penguin, Inc.

Page 190: Clifton Daniel, "Presidents I Have Known." *The New York Times,* June 3, 1984. Copyright © 1984 by The New York Times Company. Reprinted by permission.

Page 192: Cynthia Ozick, "On Excellence." Reprinted by permission of Cynthia Ozick and her agents, Raines & Raines, 71 Park Avenue, New York City. Copyright 1985 by Cynthia Ozick.

Pages 192–193: Abigail Zuger, "Acrophobia in the Ivory Tower." Copyright © 1975 by *Harper's Magazine.* All rights reserved. Reprinted from the October issue by special permission.

Page 343: Margot Slade, "Siblings: War and Peace." *The New York Times Magazine,* March 11, 1984. Copyright © 1984 by The New York Times Company. Reprinted by permission.

Page 445: Excerpt from *Reader's Guide to Periodical Literature.* Copyright © 1978, 1979 by The H. W. Wilson Company. Material reproduced by permission of the publisher.

Page 446: Excerpt from *Book Review Digest.* Copyright © 1985, 1976 by the H. W. Wilson Company. Material reproduced by permission of the publisher.

Page 455: From *Modern Times: The World from the Twenties to the Eighties* by Paul Johnson. Copyright © 1983 by Paul Johnson. Reprinted by permission of Harper & Row, Publishers, Inc.

Page 459: J.M. Roberts, *History of the World.* Reprinted by permission of Sterling Lord Literistic, Inc. Copyright © 1976 by J.M. Roberts.

PREFACE

Readers familiar with *The Borzoi Handbook for Writers* ought to feel at home with our second edition, which once again aspires to be a positive, comprehensive, and flexible guide to composition. Thanks to constructive advice from many instructors and students, we have made some notable improvements, including five new chapters and a major reorganization:

1. The text now begins with the set of chapters (1-5) called "Composing Essays," thus underscoring our belief that the real basics of composition are finding a good idea, developing an appropriate structure, and drafting and revising until a thesis has been persuasively supported.
2. Without backing down from our direct and practical advice to the student writer, we have revised our headings, relying less on grammatical terminology and more on examples that make immediate sense.
3. A new chapter (8), "Paragraph Functions," supplements our innovative chapter on paragraph development, offering models for handling narration, description, comparison and contrast, and the like. Instructors can now emphasize either or both of our complementary approaches to paragraph mastery.
4. Another new chapter (3), "Considering the Reader," puts together questions of audience, purpose, voice, stance, and tone, thus stressing the essential importance of rhetorical choices based on anticipation of their effect on the reader.
5. A third new chapter (15), "Figurative Language," greatly expands *Borzoi*'s treatment of imaginative diction.
6. Still another new chapter (42), "Writing with a Word Processor," shows how a computer can become a creative resource in every phase of the composing process.
7. A fifth new chapter (33), on hyphenation, usefully isolates the rules pertaining to that convention.
8. Chapter 21, "Pronoun Agreement and Reference," constitutes

a major expansion of its predecessor, which dealt with pronoun reference alone.

9. *Borzoi* now offers full treatment of both MLA and APA documentation styles, while still covering the "alternative MLA" footnote/endnote style. A new student research paper on U.S.– Chinese joint business ventures is cast in recommended MLA style; it is followed by sample pages illustrating the two other styles as well.

10. With clear cross-referencing, we continue our policy of covering punctuation rules *both* in separate punctuation chapters and in chapters on syntactic elements such as modifiers and parallel constructions. But now Chapter 25, on commas, goes beyond restatement of earlier material. It handily groups all comma rules into three instantly understood charts labeled "Learn where you should include a comma or pair of commas," "Learn where you should omit a comma," and "Learn where a comma is optional."

11. The frequently consulted Index of Usage has been appreciably expanded and moved to the back of the book, where it will be easier to consult.

12. The index has been both expanded and simplified, clarifying where the major discussion of a given problem can be found.

Instructors should know that every new copy of *The Borzoi Handbook* comes shrink-wrapped with the second edition of Michael Hennessy's much-admired *Borzoi Practice Book for Writers,* a uniquely engaging workbook that goes beyond mere drill. In addition, Knopf offers a full range of supplements to *Borzoi.* A word processing program package, two free workbooks with separate answer keys, computerized interactive exercises (IBM and Apple versions), sample syllabi, teaching suggestions, videos, diagnostic tests, CLAST preparation texts, and correction symbol bookmarks are available.

We remain grateful to many colleagues, students, and editors who helped us to shape our first edition, and we hereby thank all the others who showed us how that book could be improved. Student writers whose work is represented include, among others, Jaime Baczkowski, Angela Day, Scott Diamond, Carol Dougherty, John Higgins, Louise

Hope, George McCoy, Alex Melvin, Avi Miller, Stefani Pont, and Ely Tsern.

Within Random House/Knopf, we owe special gratitude to Steve Pensinger, Lauren Shafer, David Morris, and Cynthia Ward. And the following experts on composition, among others, offered invaluable critiques of the first edition: Marlene S. Bosanko, Tacoma Community College; Wayne A. Buchman, Rose State College; Roger Christeck, Belleville Area College; Virgil Cook, Virginia Polytechnic Institute; Barbara Daniels, Camden County College; Gary L. Goodno, Community College of the Finger Lakes; M. Kip Hartvigsen, Ricks College; Mary-Lou Hinman, Plymouth State College; Pat C. Hoy II, United States Military Academy; James L. Johnson, Eastern New Mexico University; William B. Lalicker, Murray State University; Anne Laskaya, University of Oregon; Stuart D. Morton, Macomb Community College; Susan Monroe Nugent, Keene State College; Katherine R. Pluta, Bakersfield College; Jan Zlotnik Schmidt, State University of New York at New Paltz; Joyce G. Smoot, Virginia Polytechnic Institute; Sondra J. Stang, Washington University; Janet Streepey, Indiana University Southeast.

Helpful advice was also received from the following instructors: Craig F. Ash, Sophia B. Blaydes, Phyllis Brooks, Mary Burns, David J. Burt, Christopher L. Couch, Gerald Evans, Philip Greene, Duane A. Grimme, Andrew Halford, Morgan Y. Himelstein, Francis X. Jordan, David Kann, Shelby J. Kipplen, Martin Ley, Mary Meiser, Hazel Pierce, Ruth F. Redel, Donetta Suchon, Barbara Traister, Elaine D. Travenick, Margaret Whitt, Johnny Wink, and Richard Zbaracki.

Frederick Crews
Sandra Schor

TO THE STUDENT WRITER

The *Borzoi Handbook* is at once a reference work and a "rhetoric"—that is, a book of advice about getting ideas for an essay and successfully maneuvering through the whole process of composition, including the constructing of effective sentences and paragraphs. Chapters 1–15 in particular cover rhetorical principles, and you can profitably read those chapters straight through. You may want to consult other chapters more selectively, either to resolve a point of usage or to refresh your memory about the best way to handle quotations, punctuation marks, and the like. If you will be asked to write a research paper, however, you should study Chapters 36–38 as a sequence. And if you are facing a word processor for the first time, Chapter 42 will help you get your bearings.

Any part of this book can be understood independently of the others, and you will find cross references to any unfamiliar terms. But you should also have a general sense of the *Handbook*'s features. Before going further, turn to the following pages:

1. The **inside front cover** contains a Checklist for Revision, a series of questions you can run through before submitting a paper; a guide to Frequently Consulted Advice; and a guide to Useful Lists found throughout the text.
2. The **Table of Contents** (p. xiii) shows how the whole book is organized into parts and chapters.
3. The **inside back cover** provides a list of Symbols for Comment and Revision that your instructor may use in marking your papers. Note that problems such as a comma splice can be marked either by a symbol *(cs)* or by a section number *(17b)*. Since section numbers accompany the symbols on the inside back cover, you can always find the relevant discussion by locating its *thumb index*—the colored box in the margin.
4. The **index** (p. 599) is your surest means of locating any point you need to look up.
5. The **Index of Usage** (p. 540) is a handy alphabetical list that

can help you resolve common problems of word choice—for example, *affect* versus *effect*.

6. The **Glossary of Terms** (p. 567) offers definitions of grammatical and rhetorical terms and indicates where you can find a fuller treatment of each term.

Once you grasp the various ways in which this book can be consulted, you should find it of lasting value to your writing in college and beyond.

CONTENTS

IX APPLIED WRITING 511

X TOOLS 531

I
COMPOSING
ESSAYS

Composing Essays

An **essay** *is a relatively brief piece of nonfictional prose that tries to make a point in an interesting way. To explain:*

1. It is fairly brief. *Some classic essays occupy only a few paragraphs, and in a composition course you may be asked to keep your first essays to 500 words. But an essay generally falls between two and twenty-five typed, double-spaced pages. Under that minimum, the development of thought that typifies an essay would be hard to manage. Above that maximum, people might be tempted to read the piece in installments like a book. A good essay makes an unbroken reading experience.*

2. It is nonfiction. *An essayist tries to tell the truth or to speculate about possible changes in the world we all recognize. If the essay contains a story or a description, we presume that the details have not been made up for effect.*

3. It makes a point. *An essay characteristically tells or explains something, or expresses an attitude toward something, or supports or criticizes something—an opinion, a person or place, a work of art, an institution, a movement. A poem or a novel may also do these things, but it does them incidentally; it appeals above all to the reader's imagination. An essay directly addresses a topic or specific subject, and its usual aim is to win sympathy or agreement to the point or* **thesis** *it is maintaining.*

4. It is meant to be engaging. *An essay should arouse curiosity, convince the reader that the main idea is worth bothering about, and move toward a satisfying conclusive finish.*

To be an effective essayist you must be willing to strike some balances. You will want to tell the truth, but first make people interested in hearing it; write with conviction, but consider whether your ideas and attitudes will stand up under criticism; supply evidence, but not become a bore about it; be purposeful, but not follow such a predictable pattern that your reader's attention slackens.

1 Arriving at a Topic

1a Recognize the flexibility of the writing process.

Some students make things hard for themselves by conceiving of "good writing" as a one-time challenge—a brass ring to be seized or, more probably, missed on their first and only try. In their view the world is already divided into the lucky few who "can write" and all the others who cannot. What they fail to realize is that, by and large, *writing is rewriting*. Even the most accomplished authors start with drafts that would be woefully inadequate except *as* drafts—that is, as means of getting going in an exploratory process that will usually include a good many setbacks and shifts in direction. To feel dissatisfied with a sample of your prose, then, is not a sign of anything about your talent. The "good writer" is the one who can turn such dissatisfaction to a positive end by pressing ahead with the labor of revision, knowing that niceties of style will come more easily once an adequate structure of ideas has been developed.

And how will you arrive at such ideas? Many students believe that sheer inspiration or luck must be the answer; they furrow their brows and hope that a light bulb will flash over their heads. When it does not, they lose heart. But experienced writers know that good ideas, instead of dropping (or not dropping) from the sky, must be generated by activities that place one thought into relation with another. And one of those activities is writing itself. In the labor of writing you will be forced to zero in on connections, comparisons, contrasts, illustrations, contradictions, and objections, any of which may point you toward a central idea or alter the one you began with.

Thus the finding of that idea, or **thesis,** is not a fixed early stage of the composing process, but a concern that is urgent at first and will probably become urgent again when you run into trouble or realize that a better idea has come into view. The sooner you arrive at a thesis—by any means, including random writing—the better; but your choice is being continually tested until you are ready to type up the final copy of your essay. At any moment you may find yourself having to take more notes, argue against a point you favored in an early draft, or throw away whole pages that have been made irrelevant by your improved thesis. Do not imagine that such annoyances set you apart from other writers; they put you in the company of the masters.

So, too, the other "stages of composing" normally leak into one another. Although you cannot complete your organizing, for example, until you have arrived at a thesis, unexpected problems of organization may point the way to a better thesis. Even a simplified diagram of your options at such a moment would look complex:

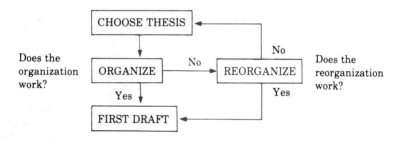

And even the revising of paragraphs for internal unity may prompt a more fundamental change of direction. Writing is almost never a linear process; it typically doubles back on one phase because a later one has opened new perspectives.

Thus, though we will discuss composing as a logical sequence of steps, its actual order in any one instance defies summary. At nearly every point you are free either to move ahead or to reconsider a previous decision. A reasonably ample flow chart for composing, then, would look like this:

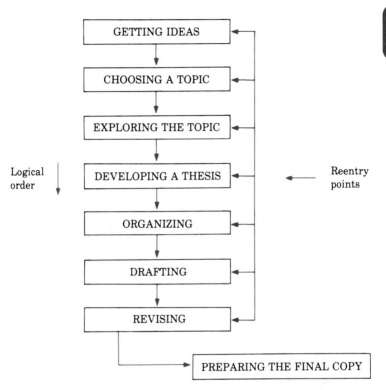

The lesson here is that, wherever your composing hits a snag, it is normal and useful to double back. Such rethinking is nothing to be alarmed about; it is the usual means by which weak ideas and structures give way to stronger ones.

1b Recognize the differences between a subject area, a topic, and a thesis.

The key to writing a successful college essay is a strong and clear *thesis*—that is, a central idea to which everything else in your essay

will contribute. You cannot get by with only a *topic* or, worse, a *subject
area*.

Subject area

A **subject area** is a large category within which you hope to find your
actual topic—the specific question you will address. Thus, if you are
asked to "recount a personal experience" or "discuss open admission to
college" or "write an essay about *Catch-22*," you have been given not
topics but subject areas: a personal experience, open admission to college, *Catch-22*.

Topic

The **topic** of an essay is the particular, focused issue or phenomenon
being addressed. Thus, within the subject area "Open admission to
college," some workable topics might be:

> The effect of open admission on "high potential" students
>
> My debt to the policy of open admission
>
> Why did open admission become popular in the late 1960s?
>
> The success (or failure) of open admission
>
> Is open admission a means to social equality?

Notice that these topics take up considerably more words than "Open
admission to college." Potential "topics" expressed in few words may
be subject areas in disguise.

Thesis

Your **thesis** is the one ruling idea you are going to propose *about* your
topic. Thus a thesis is never material to be investigated. It is always
an *assertion*—an idea you will support in the body of your essay. And
because it always makes a claim, a thesis lends itself to expression in
one clear sentence.

   Here is a chart that illustrates the contrast between a subject
area, a topic, and a thesis. Notice that two possible theses are given for
each topic.

SUBJECT AREA	TOPIC	THESIS
Open admission to college	The success of open admission	1. The success of open admission in my large urban college can be measured by the effectiveness of our basic instruction in reading and writing. 2. Unconventional students admitted under a policy of open admission have had a positive influence on the education of traditional students.
A personal experience	My night in jail	1. After my night in jail I will have more respect for prisoners' rights. 2. My night in jail helped to make me a safer driver.
Agricultural production	The effect of mechanization on farm employment	1. The typical farm employee has changed from a migrant laborer to a sophisticated regular with the skills to operate large machines. 2. Many migrant farm laborers have become the unskilled unemployables of the cities.
Civil liberties	Phone tapping as an issue of civil liberties	1. When government officials place innocent citizens under observation and routinely tap one another's phones, everyone's civil liberties are threatened. 2. Despite its infringement of civil liberties, phone tapping is the most effective device the government has for procuring evidence in criminal cases.

1c Narrow your subject area.

Once you recognize that you have been given a subject area rather than a topic, you can work toward possible topics by dividing and sub-dividing the subject area. That maneuver will not in itself present you with a topic. "Chicago," for instance, is narrower than "Illinois," and "Lakeshore Drive" is narrower still, but all three lack a suitable focus; they remain subject areas because no question has yet been asked about them. Yet the process of breaking a large subject area into several smaller ones may bring such questions into mind.

If all you have to go on is the vast subject area "Education," for example, you can start by noting as many *categories* of education as you can. It may help to think of the categories as sets of opposites:

Education:
    private/public
    religious/secular
    vocational/academic
    lower/higher

Which of these categories do you feel most comfortable with? Write it down and run through the categorizing operation again:

Higher education:
    undergraduate/graduate
    science/humanities/engineering
    privately supported/state-supported/federally supported

Now study each item in your second list and ask what *issues or questions* it raises in your mind. One of them should prove to be an acceptable topic. Thus, if you are looking at *federally supported education,* you might ask these questions:

1. How much influence does the government exercise on admission policies?

2. Do professors in a federally supported institution enjoy greater academic freedom than those in a privately supported institution?

3. Has the program of federal loans to students been cut back too far?

4. To what extent can the government insist that men's and women's athletic programs be equally funded?

5. What is the effect of tying federal aid to student responsibilities, such as registering with Selective Service?

1d   Use notes to develop your thoughts.

You should take notes throughout your composing, raising previously unforeseen questions, commenting on earlier notes, jotting down changes of plan, and reminding yourself of the next two or three points you ought to cover. Even if you are working from an outline (p. 43, 4b), your notes can overrule any segment of it.

When your essay is supposed to deal with an assigned text, your note taking should begin during your reading of the text. Do you own the book? If so, mark it up. Underline passages that look significant and write comments and questions in the margins. Wherever one part of the text helps you to understand another part, make a marginal cross reference such as "see p. 134." And as soon as you have finished reading or, preferably, rereading, get your miscellaneous impressions onto paper so that you can begin dealing with *them* instead of with the whole text. Of course you will need to keep returning to the text, but now you can do so with specific, pointed questions in mind.

Some writers use uniform-sized index cards for all their notes, restricting themselves to one idea per card, but you may prefer full pages of scratch paper. In either case, you can use your notes to quote passages from your reading, record or summarize facts, make comparisons, launch a trial thesis as it occurs to you, express doubts or warnings, or comment on your comments, developing a dialogue of pros and cons.

1e   Get ideas from your experience.

Instructors sometimes assign essays of a certain structural type (for example, comparison and contrast) without specifying a subject area or a topic. When you find yourself thus free to choose a topic, think at once about your own interests and areas of special knowledge—activities, skills, attitudes, problems, and unique or typical experiences. The reason is simple: what doesn't interest you is not likely to engage a reader, whereas it is easy to be convincing when you can draw on firsthand information.

Reviewing course work and recent reading

One source of interest may be your course work in composition or any other discipline. Have you come across a significant problem in the assigned reading? If you have been taking notes during class, do the notes contain questions or observations that could lead to a thesis? Wherever you have recorded doubts or strong agreement or connections with ideas of your own, you may have in hand the beginnings of an essay.

So, too, you can search for topics in the books and magazines that happen to be within easy reach. The goal, of course, is not to copy someone else's words or ideas (see p. 459, 37a), but to find an issue that meets up with experience or knowledge or an opinion of your own.

Keeping a journal

Your search for ideas will be easier if you keep a *journal.* Unlike a diary, which has no restriction of focus, a journal is a daily record of your experience and thoughts within a certain area. A typical journal, for example, might trace your progress in understanding musical theory or mastering computer skills. Alternatively, it could store your reflections about life in general, your plans and ambitions, your ideas for short stories you hope to write, and so forth. You may even be asked to keep a journal about your efforts and problems in this very course. Whatever material it deals with, a journal can point you toward a topic by reminding you of already developed interests and opinions.

1f Try freewriting or brainstorming.

Freewriting

If you have ever told yourself or others, *I don't know what I want to say until I've written it out,* consider yourself normal. Writing *is* a primary way of arriving at ideas, and teachers have increasingly been recognizing that fact. By forcing yourself to hook up nouns and verbs, subjects and predicates, you can draw forth insights that you didn't know you possessed.

You can even begin writing before having any idea of what your topic will be. When you feel stymied, assign yourself a ten- or fifteen-minute stint of **freewriting.** The trick is to put pen to paper at "Go" and to keep writing until "Stop" without pausing between your sentences or fragments of sentences. If you get stuck, just repeat a key word in the last sentence you have written and build a further statement around it. And even if one freewriting session appears to take you nowhere, a second one, started a few minutes later, may pick up on thoughts that were not quite ready for expression in a first effort.

Here, for example, are two passages of freewriting that a student produced in quick succession:

FIRST FREEWRITING:
Well, what do I have to say? Not much it appears! Sitting here "free" writing, so they tell me. How free is freewriting on demand, with the stopwatch ticking? Freedom in general—it always confuses me. I never know whether it's supposed to be freedom to go out and do something you'd like to, or freedom to keep somebody else from doing something mean to you. Anyway, would sure like to be free from freewriting! What is so sacred about exactly ten minutes worth of this stuff? How about nine or eleven? Stuck for ideas—ugh! Well, just keep pushing this pencil until time's up. . . .

SECOND FREEWRITING:
OK, maybe something here after all. Idea of freedom. *Total* freedom is empty, unattractive, boring—we always have something in mind to be free *for*—i.e. something that won't leave us so free any more. E.g., religious freedom usually means spending that freedom on some belief and/

or practice—some "service." Or does it? What about unbelievers? I guess
they have a right to a freedom that stays negative: no, thanks. . . . But
historically, the fighters for freedom have always been people with
strong beliefs of their own. Luther, Jefferson, Lincoln, King . . . Maybe
an essay here? "Freedom For or Freedom From"?

Although neither of these passages has the grammatical completeness
and the logical continuity of finished essay prose, and although the
writer is clearly uncomfortable with an imposed task, his struggle to
keep writing finally yields a likely-looking idea.

Brainstorming

Freewriting teases forth ideas by means of our natural tendency to
link one sentence with the previous one. **Brainstorming,** in contrast,
works by the opposite principle, discontinuity. To brainstorm is to toss
out suggestions without regard for their connections with one another.
Since no development is called for, nothing stands in the way of your
leaping from one notion to a completely unrelated one.

You can brainstorm by yourself, listing random words and
phrases as they occur to you, scribbling across a notepad, or talking
into a tape recorder. Or you can work in a group, either among friends
or in the classroom, where the "notepad" is a shared chalkboard. In
discussion or reflection, certain ideas will begin to look more fruitful
than others—and you are on your way toward a topic.

When brainstorming works, it sometimes evolves naturally into
freewriting as one hastily mentioned idea starts to look more interesting than the others:

> Freedom / freedom fighters / free-for-alls / freed slaves / "free gifts" / I.e.,
> come-ons for renting (or buying) a car, going to grand opening, etc.
> What's really free—nothing! Who pays? The customers, of course; extra
> costs added back into prices. Notice that "free gifts" come only when the
> customers aren't buying. . . .

By this point the writer already has a clear topic in view: the hidden
costs and motives behind "free" merchandise.

1g Test your trial topic.

Once you are sure you have arrived at a topic rather than a subject area, you may feel so relieved that you yearn to start the actual writing of your essay. But that would be a mistake. In the first place, your writing will quickly bog down if you still lack a thesis—a main point that answers the question implied or stated in your topic. And second, how do you know that the first topic to come to mind is the best one for your purpose? Your **trial topic** should stay on probation until you are sure it can pass six tests:

1. Is this trial topic sufficiently focused?
2. Is it likely to sustain my interest?
3. Is it appropriate to my intended audience?
4. Can it lead to a reasonable thesis?
5. Does it involve enough complexity—enough "parts"—for development at essay length?
6. Do I have enough supporting material to work with?

If, without further thought, you can answer all of these questions positively, consider yourself lucky. More probably, you will need to explore your trial topic by one or more of the following means.

Focused freewriting or brainstorming

If freewriting and brainstorming can lead to preliminary ideas for an essay, they can also help you to explore a trial topic. The same rules apply (see pp. 11–12). The only difference is that now you begin with a definite focus and try to keep it—developing, not miscellaneous thoughts about anything, but specific features of the trial topic. As before, the idea is to set aside worries about correctness of organization and expression and to see what happens.

Asking reporters' questions

Another simple yet surprisingly helpful way to expand your view of the trial topic is to run through the standard list of questions reporters are supposed to answer in covering a story: *who? what? when? where? how? why?* Unlike a reporter, of course, you are not trying to make sense of a single event, yet the procedure can work because it keeps returning you to the same material from fresh perspectives.

Suppose your trial topic were the merits of a proposed law that encouraged recycling of glass by requiring a five-cent returnable deposit on all bottles. Asking the six standard reporters' questions, you might come up with answers like these:

Who? The elected officials of your community or state.

What? Pass a law requiring a five-cent deposit on every returnable bottle.

When? At the next session of the city council or legislature; law to take effect at start of next calendar year.

Where? Only within the boundaries of this community or state.

How? Fix penalties for noncompliance by sellers of bottles, give the law wide publicity, warn first offenders, then begin applying penalties.

Why? Reduce waste and pollution; raise public consciousness about conservation; cut prices through use of recycled glass.

Any of these brief notes could carry you beyond your first thoughts and lead to an adequately focused thesis. Given inflation, for example, will a five-cent deposit be large enough to ensure returns? Will there be special problems associated with putting the law into effect so soon? If the law applies only within a small geographic area, will consumers take their business elsewhere? Are the penalties for noncompliance too strict? Not strict enough?

Applying analytic strategies

Whether or not you intend to write a whole essay of analysis, you can explore your trial topic by considering it in the light of classic analytic strategies: *definition, division, illustration, cause and effect, compari-*

son and contrast, and *process analysis.* (For another useful strategy, see the discussion of *analogy,* p. 193, 15d). These maneuvers are so basic that you can hardly fail to stimulate new trains of thought by reviewing them in turn.

topic 1g

Definition: How does a law differ from a regulation? A misdemeanor from a felony? What kinds of containers would be included or excluded?

Division: What are the separate provisions of the bill? What types of stores would be affected?

Illustration: Which communities and states have already established deposit laws? What reports of success or failure are available? Do we have case histories of bottling companies and grocery chains that have accommodated themselves to the law, of individuals who were prosecuted, of others—the homeless—who have made a subsistence living by collecting other people's empty bottles for refund?

Cause and effect: What events and trends have made passage of the law likely or unlikely? What differences in consumers' behavior would the law bring about? Would littering be significantly curtailed? In the long run, would prices of bottled products go up or down?

Comparison and contrast: In what way does this law resemble others that have been enacted elsewhere? How does it differ from them? Are the conditions (commercial, political, environmental) in this community or state like those elsewhere, or must special factors be taken into account? Do young people and older people hold different views of the law?

Process analysis: How will violations of the law come to public notice, arrive at a prosecutor's desk, and be subsequently handled? Does the law allow unknowing violations to be treated differently from outright defiance? If so, at what point would such a difference be recognized? And what flow of payments and reimbursements is expected between the consumer, the grocer, and the distributor?

2 Developing a Reasonable Thesis

2a Write out a one-sentence trial thesis.

Let us assume that, using one or more of the strategies described in the previous chapter, you have arrived at a *trial thesis,* or preliminary idea for your essay. Do not simply mull that thesis over in your head. Write it out in one clear sentence that you can then consider from several angles. That sentence may or may not eventually find its way into the body of your essay. Its function for now is to let you make sure that you have *one* central idea—not zero, not two—and that it looks sufficiently challenging and defensible. To these ends it is important that you keep to the one-statement limitation. Though your trial thesis can contain several considerations, one point should control all the others.

Typical trial theses for an essay about instituting a bottle law (p. 14, 1g) might be these:

ANALYTIC TRIAL THESES (p. 30, 3b):
Increased fear that the environment is becoming polluted and that raw materials are growing scarce has provided broad-based support for laws requiring deposits on returnable bottles.

The passage or failure of bottle-deposit legislation in any given state or community can be directly correlated with the proportion of voters under age thirty.

ARGUMENTATIVE TRIAL THESES (p. 30, 3b):

The minor inconvenience of paying a deposit and having to return empty bottles to a store is far outweighed by the benefits that all citizens would receive from a well-drafted law requiring the deposits.

A deposit law would not only hurt small-business people by adding to their expenses and reducing their sales but also result in more, not less, pollution because of the increased trucking it would require.

thesis
2c

None of these four examples is good or bad in itself; everything would depend on whether the writer had appropriate material on hand to make a convincing case. But all four trial theses meet the requirement of presenting just one main idea.

2b Give your thesis definite content.

To secure your reader's interest, you must propose an idea that will require support and illustration to be made convincing. Avoid the unassertive **weaseling thesis,** which expresses nothing more than a desire to stay out of trouble.

DON'T:
x A deposit law is very controversial.
x Although some people approve of a deposit law, others do not.

Compare these vacant assertions with the "deposit law" theses above, which do take the necessary degree of risk.

2c Limit the scope of your thesis.

A thesis that quickly proves unworkable may suffer from too broad a scope. Remember that you have only a short essay in which to develop your idea successfully. Instead of discarding a thesis that seems to lead nowhere, try recasting it in narrower terms, replacing vague general concepts with more definite ones.

TOPIC	THESIS TOO BROAD	THESIS IMPROVED
The popularity of garage sales	x Garage sales reflect the times we live in.	● Garage sales circulate goods during periods of high inflation and high unemployment. ["The times" are carefully defined.]
A "star wars" missile defense system	x We need to invest in a "star wars" missile defense system.	● Although extremely costly, a "star wars" missile defense system may be our only safeguard against nuclear war. [Considerations of cost and safeguarding our future are both expressed in the thesis.]
Late marriages in relation to careers for women	x Late marriages are creating a different kind of American family life.	● Because marriage is often postponed to accommodate careers, North Americans are creating a new kind of family in which parents are old enough to be their children's grandparents. [Reason for late marriage and a detailed explanation of "different" belong in the thesis.]

Faulty generalization

When you write out a trial thesis, examine it for telltale danger words like *all, none, no, any, always, never, only,* and *everyone.* Such all-inclusive terms usually signal the presence of **faulty generalization,** the illegitimate extension of *some* instances to cover *all* instances of something. Suppose, for example, you want to argue that *There is no reason to delay immediate adoption of a national health insurance pro-*

gram. Ask yourself: no reason at all? Will I be anticipating *all* possible reasons in my essay? Perhaps I can avoid unnecessary trouble by making my thesis more modest: *Adoption of a national health insurance program would answer needs urgently felt by the poor, minorities, and the chronically ill.*

You should be especially wary of faulty generalization if you find that you have written a thesis that covers centuries of history or makes sweeping judgments of right and wrong.

DON'T:

x The decay of our culture has been accelerating every year.

x The West is guided by Christian morals.

x The purpose of evolution is to create a higher form of human being.

Encyclopedias of support could not establish the plausibility of such theses. Consider: (1) What universally recognized indicators of "cultural decay" do we have, and how could anyone show that cultural decay has been "accelerating every year"? (2) Can something as vague and various as "the West" be said to be "guided" by certain "morals"? How will the writer explain away all the brutalities of the past twenty centuries? (3) How has the writer been able to discover a purpose hidden from all professional students of evolution?

DO:

• Describing social problems in terms of general cultural decay often proves to be a veiled means of protest against new groups of immigrants.

• Although governments rarely behave according to strict religious principles, official allegiance to a religion may nevertheless place some restraints on their conduct.

• While it can hardly be considered the fated outcome of evolution, human intelligence could be regarded as the most daring evolutionary experiment in replacing instinct with learning.

Keeping personal experience in perspective

We have said that personal experience can be an important source of ideas for a college essay (p. 10, 1e). Yet you should also recognize the

thesis 2d

risks of generalizing from such experience. If the question, for instance, is whether the human species has an innate aggressive instinct, you may feel inclined to look in your heart and say either yes or no. To do this, however, would be to rely on guesswork and an inadequate sample of just one case. The same lapse occurs when a foreign-born writer asserts, x *The idea that immigrants want to become "Americanized" is contradicted by all experience,* meaning *I, for one, do not want to be "Americanized."* Someone else writes, x *Professors actually enjoy making students suffer,* meaning *I had an ugly experience in History 10.* Personal experience can usefully illustrate a thesis, but the thesis itself should rest on more public grounds.

2d   Be fair to an opposing position.

Just as there is little point in choosing a thesis with which no one could disagree (2b), so it is vital to avoid artificially shielding a *controversial* thesis by trying to shut off the very possibility of disagreement. The best posture to assume is one of inviting fair-minded attention to everything that can be said on both sides of the issue. If, instead, you resort to special pleading or dirty tricks, you are signaling to an astute reader that you lack confidence in the merits of your case.

Classic **fallacies,** or illegitimate shortcuts of reasoning, that you should be alert to in both your writing and your reading include **begging the question,** use of the **straw man, ad hominem reasoning,** and **either-or reasoning.** (For further fallacies, see 2c and 2e.)

Begging the question: reasoning in circles

Technically speaking, to beg the question is to arrive at a conclusion that is essentially the same as a premise used to support it. More informally, you are begging the question, or indulging in *circular reasoning,* whenever you state a point in such "loaded" terms that your language itself prejudges the issue.

DON'T:
  x A. It is inadvisable to let hardened criminals out of prison prematurely so that they can renew their war on society.

x B. Society has no right to lock up the victims of poverty and inequality for indefinite periods, brutalizing them in the name of "rehabilitation."

thesis
2d

Writers A and B are addressing the same issue, but each of them has settled it in advance. The word *prematurely* already contains the idea that many convicts are released too soon, and other terms—*hardened criminals, renew their war*—reinforce the point. For writer B there is no such thing as a criminal in the first place. Prisoners have already been defined as *victims,* and imprisonment is equated with *brutalizing.* Similarly, the quotation marks around *rehabilitation* dismiss the possibility that a criminal might be taught to reform. The trouble here is that both writers A and B, in their eagerness to sweep away objections, are portraying themselves as close-minded. No one will want to read an essay whose very thesis forbids all disagreement.

Of course your thesis should convey an attitude, but it should do so in fair language.

DO:
- A. The policy of releasing prisoners on probation has not justified the social risks it involves.
- B. If the goal of prisons is to rehabilitate, the prison system must be considered on balance to be a failure.

Note that these two versions are just as hard-hitting as the ones they replace; the difference is that their language does not beg the question.

The straw man: misstating the opposing case

In formulating your thesis, be careful not to distort a position contrary to your own. Such distortion creates a so-called **straw man**—that is, an imaginary opponent that can be all too easily knocked over. Thus, if the question is whether students should be allowed to serve on faculty committees, a writer would be creating a straw man with this thesis: x *Faculty efforts to keep the student body in a state of perpetual childhood must be resisted.* Here the specific issue—the pros and cons of student participation—has conveniently disappeared behind the straw man of wicked faculty intentions. A fairer thesis would be *If faculty members really want to make informed judgments about conditions on campus, they ought to welcome student voices on their committees.*

<u>Ad</u> <u>hominem</u> reasoning: attacking personalities

Still another fallacious shortcut is to attack the people who favor a certain position rather than the position itself. This is known as *ad hominem* (Latin, "to the man") reasoning. Sometimes such an argument tells us real or invented things about somebody's character or behavior. The implication is that if we disapprove of certain people, we had better reject the idea that has become linked with them. More often the writer simply mentions that a despised faction such as "Communism" or "big business" supports the other side.

DON'T:

x By now we should all recognize the dangers of national health insurance, a scheme for which subversives have long been agitating.

DO:

• To judge from the British example, national health insurance might impose an intolerable burden on our economy.

DON'T:

x The benefits of home videotaping are obvious to everyone except the money-crazed Hollywood moguls who stand to lose by it.

DO:

• Although movie executives are understandably worried about competition from home videotaping, they would do better to adapt to the new technology instead of trying to have it banned.

As politicians realize, *ad hominem* attacks do often have their desired effect. Because none of us has time to think through the pros and cons of every public issue, we sometimes rely on surface clues; if certain "bad guys" are revealed to be on one side, we automatically favor the other. As citizens, though, we ought to recognize that the *ad hominem* appeal is a form of bullying. And as writers, we ought to get along without the cheap advantage it affords. If you *can* win an argument on its merits, do so; if you cannot, you should change your position or even your whole topic.

thesis 2e

Either-or reasoning: believe it or else

Make sure your thesis does not pull the alarmist trick of **either-or reasoning**—that is, pretending that the only alternative is something awful. Thus a writer favoring legal abortion might claim, x *We must legalize abortion or the world will become disastrously overpopulated,* and a writer on the opposite side might reply, x *We must prevent legal abortion or the family will cease to exist.* Both writers would be delivering an ultimatum. *Which do you choose, overpopulation or legal abortion? What will it be, legal abortion or the survival of the family?* The choice is supposed to be automatic. All a reader must do, however, to escape the bind is to think of one other possibility. Is there no means to control population except through abortion? Might legal abortion have some lesser consequence than the destruction of family life? Your wisest course would be to admit that people favoring an opposite stand from yours have good reasons for their view—reasons that you do not find decisive. If the issue *were* one of total right versus total wrong, you would probably be wasting your time writing about it.

2e Limit your claims about causes and effects.

Bear in mind that two events or conditions can be associated in time without being related as cause and effect. Perhaps this seems obvious, but most of us become superstitious when partisan feelings or pet beliefs are involved. Democrats claim that Republican administrations "cause" economic recessions; Republicans call their rival "the war party" because most wars have erupted when Democrats were in power; and some people support their beliefs by arguing that their dreams were fulfilled or that a certain result followed their witnessing an unusual phenomenon: "I saw a black cat and then lost control of the car"; "I landed my job after I saw a rainbow." This fallacy goes by its Latin name, **post hoc, ergo propter hoc:** "after this, therefore because of it."

POST HOC THESIS:

x Aspirin cures colds, as can be seen from the fact that a cold will disappear just a few days after you begin taking regular doses of aspirin.

REVISED THESIS:

• Though aspirin relieves some cold symptoms, the idea that any currently available medicine "cures" a cold is not supported by evidence.

2f   Try developing your trial thesis into a full thesis statement.

Let us suppose that your thesis is no longer on trial: it has passed the tests of definiteness and reasonable scope, and you are ready to go with it. At this point you would do well to take an extra step that may look unnecessary at first. Cast your thesis into a *full* **thesis statement**—a sentence that not only names your main point but also includes its most important parts, supplies reasons why that point deserves to be believed, and/or meets objections to it. This statement will probably be long and cumbersome. Never mind: it will *not* appear anywhere in the body of your essay. It is simply a private guide which will help you (a) be completely sure that you are in control of your material and (b) choose a sound organization for your essay's parts (p. 41, 4a).

Sometimes your unexpanded thesis will possess the complexity that can carry you into the work of organizing. We have already met one such thesis/thesis statement: *A deposit law would not only hurt small-business people by adding to their expenses and reducing their sales but also would result in more, not less, pollution because of the increased trucking it would require.* Here we see three crucial factors begging to be made structurally prominent: added expense, reduced sales, increased pollution. The writer is ready to decide on an effective order for these main supporting points.

More often than not, though, a thesis will be too simple in form to serve as a thesis statement. The remedy is to spell out some of the large considerations that made you adopt the thesis in the first place. You can add *main details, reasons,* and/or *objections,* all of which will become prominent units of your organization.

Including main details

Suppose your tested and approved thesis is a sentence as plain as this: *Chinese farming methods differ strikingly from American ones.* Fine—but are you sure you know exactly which differences you will be emphasizing in your essay? Now is the time to clear up any lingering doubt by working those differences into a full thesis statement.

Since you will eventually have to choose an order of presentation for your main details, why not decide right now, as you are drawing up your thesis statement? The final position is generally the most emphatic one, whether the unit be a sentence, a paragraph, or a whole essay. Think, then, about the relative importance of your points and arrange them accordingly within your thesis statement:

- Chinese farming differs strikingly from American farming in its greater concern for using all available space, its handling of crop rotation, its higher proportion of natural to manufactured fertilizers, and, above all, its emphasis on mass labor as opposed to advanced machinery.

Here you already have a complete blueprint for a brief essay, which you could begin writing without delay.

Supplying reasons

In some theses the main statement does not lend itself to the kind of expansion we have just considered. Yet you can always find more "parts" for your essay—and thus for your full thesis statement—by listing the reasons why you think the thesis deserves to be believed. Suppose, for example, you intend to maintain that *The first year of college often proves to be a depressing one.* That is a fair beginning, but it tells you only that *x proves to be y.* How is a whole paper going to

thesis
2f

result from such a simple declaration? Ask yourself, then, why or in what ways you find that year typically depressing.

If you tell why in one or more *because* clauses, your thesis statement becomes an organizational blueprint:

- The first year of college often proves to be a depressing one, because many students have moved away from their parents' homes for the first time, because it is painful to be separated from established friends, and because homework and grading are usually more demanding than they were in high school.

Now you have laid out the nature of your explanation: you are reasoning from an effect (depression) to its causes, which you will discuss one by one in your essay.

Meeting objections

If your thesis is controversial—and all argumentative theses and many analytic theses are—you should expect to deal with at least one major objection to it. Typically, you will want to handle that point either through **refutation** or through **concession**—that is, either by showing that the objection is wrong or by granting its truth while showing that it does not overrule your thesis.

Since the objection will be discussed in your essay, it should also appear in your full thesis statement. Include that objection in an *although* clause:

- *Although some students find their freshman year exciting and rewarding,* many others find it depressing, because they have moved away. . . .

Again, suppose you intend to maintain that the government should not insist on equal expenditures for men's and women's athletic programs in college. You know that to be convincing you will have to blunt the force of at least one strong point on the opposing side. Get that point into your full thesis statement, add your positive reasons, and you are ready to go:

- *Although men and women in college should certainly have equal opportunities to participate in sports,* the government should not insist on equal expenditures for men's and women's athletic programs, because in colleges where a football program exists it requires disproportionately high expenditures, and because such a program can produce income to support the entire spectrum of men's and women's athletics.

A mouthful! But, again, a thesis statement is only a road map, not an excerpt from your essay. You need not try to make it concise. It will succeed in its purpose if it allows you to move confidently to the next phase of planning.

3 Considering the Reader

3a Consider your audience.

Even with a full thesis statement in hand, you will not want to begin writing mechanically—just churning out the material you have decided to present. Rather, it is time to focus on your goal: to make a certain kind of impression on a certain reader. Your **rhetoric,** in other words, must be geared to the specific audience and purpose you have in mind.

This advice may leave you uneasy if you think of rhetoric in its casual meaning of insincere, windy language, as in *Oh, that's just a lot of rhetoric.* But in its primary meaning, rhetoric is simply *the strategic placement of ideas and choice of language*—the means of making an intended effect on a reader or listener. Rhetoric need never call for deceptive prose; it calls, rather, for making a strong case by satisfying your audience's legitimate expectations.

General versus specialized audience

The aspect of composing that students are most apt to underrate is *audience expectation.* Experienced professional writers are never really abandoned to the blank page. They begin with a sense of relevant issues and attitudes, and almost from the outset they are mentally formulating patterns of writing that they know will be familiar to their readers. How do they know? Simply by having read a great many pages of the magazines or journals to which they will be submitting their work. Every field of knowledge—medicine, psychology, forestry, and so on—has its specialized vocabulary, its typical way of introducing and concluding a report or article, even its characteristic tone.

You, too, when you write for a specialized audience, will find that many of your composing choices "come naturally" because you are already a member of the community formed by your prospective readers.

When you write for a general audience—and that, by and large, is the role your composition instructor and your classmates expect to play—you cannot take so much for granted. If you are treating, say, bicycle repair or particle physics or the popular music of the 1960s, you need to ask yourself how much background information the general reader is likely to need. And since you are now offering opinions to a stranger rather than advancing the knowledge of a community, you must take greater pains to *interest* that reader by showing that your topic matters. Furthermore, you cannot presume that the general reader agrees with your politics, your religion, or your tastes. Insofar as possible, you will have to appeal to facts and judgments that are widely held to be plausible.

Nevertheless, you and your general reader have a good deal in common. You both value straightforward, honest writing in which shrewd ideas are backed by evidence. You both appreciate freshness of language and point of view. And you both cherish your time. Prose that never gets to the point, or that strays from it, or that takes thirty words to do the work of ten is not going to impress either of you. As a reviser of your drafts, you want to put yourself in the place of that reader and keep applying these common standards of adequacy.

Classmates as audience

Understandably, some students find their inspiration leaking away when they contemplate their instructor as a stand-in for the general reader. But you have to write with *somebody* in mind or you will find yourself paralyzed by indecision. Why not try putting your classmates in the audience's role?

This is not to say that you should now begin writing in chummy slang. It is more a matter of trying to please and convince some people who are much like yourself. To be sure, classmates as critics and peer editors have been known to apply "the rules" with a strictness that may make your instructor look easygoing by comparison. But your classmates share your world in important ways, and you can usually trust their good sense. If the student sitting next to you would choke on some contrived generalization, leave it out. If you suspect that the class as a whole would say *Make that clearer* or *Get to the point,* do so. Your instructor will be delighted by any essay that would impress most of your classmates.

3b   Adapt the modes of writing to your purpose.

Whole essays and parts of essays have traditionally been divided into four basic types, or rhetorical **modes,** according to their varying tasks and purposes.

MODE	TASK	PURPOSE
1. Description	Picture	Make vivid to the reader
2. Narration	Recount	Tell the reader what happened
3. Analysis (Exposition)	Define Divide Illustrate Compare and contrast Show causes and effects Follow a process Analogize	Make the reader understand
4. Argument	Defend a position	Win the reader's agreement

Note that the first two modes, **description** and **narration,** are presentational; they ask the writer to call scenes or episodes to the reader's mind. The third mode, **analysis,** or exposition, characterizes most college writing assignments; the pursuit of knowledge is by and large the pursuit of analyses or explanations. And **argument** appeals to facts, descriptions, narrations, and/or analyses in order to support a position on an issue. An argument typically *rebuts* (gives reasons for rejecting) an opposing position in the hope of *refuting* it (proving it wrong).

To see the logical relations among the four modes, we can locate them on a scale with immediate experience at one end and abstraction from experience at the other:

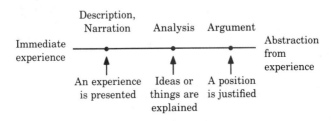

Does a given passage aim chiefly to represent something that can be remembered in its physical actuality? Then it must be either *description* or *narration*.

Does the passage aim chiefly to help us understand the nature or function of something or to see its relation to other things? Then this is a passage of *analysis*.

Does the passage try to convince us that a certain view or policy is preferable to another? Then we are dealing with *argument*—the rhetorical mode that stands at the greatest distance from immediate experience.

Suppose, for example, you were thinking about discussing the subject of bubonic plague, a disease that flourished in the Middle Ages and that remains dangerous today on a smaller scale.

In a *description* you might give your reader a detailed, physically vivid account of the symptoms: fever, boils, discoloration, chills, and so forth.

In a *narration* you might tell how the plague swept through Europe in 1348–49—or, in a personal vein, how you recently had to change your camping plans when health authorities found that rodents were dying from the disease.

In an *analysis* you might show how the plague bacillus is transmitted by rats and their fleas.

And in an *argument* you might support as essential, or oppose as no longer necessary, public health regulations designed to prevent outbreaks of the plague.

Most of your college essays will probably incorporate two or more of the modes—moving, say, from analysis to narration and back again as you seek to influence your reader in different ways. But since analysis and, to a lesser extent, argument are the modes that dominate college writing, we will concentrate below on the devising of essays that call for a strong central idea backed by evidence.

3c   Choose between a personal and an impersonal voice.

Voice refers to the "self" projected by a given piece of writing. The relevant question to ask is not "what am I really like?" but "what is the nature of this occasion?" For certain occasions you will want to maintain a formal, impersonal air, while in others you will want readers to feel much closer to you as an individual.

Consider the following deliberately impersonal paragraph.

IMPERSONAL VOICE:

Asked to compare the benefits of academic jobs with jobs in government or business, over 90% of humanities graduate students cited greater flexibility in the use of time. Two-thirds or more mentioned freedom to do as one wished, opportunities to experiment with differing life-styles, and ability to flout social conventions. On the down side, one-quarter to two-fifths expressed suspicion that a teaching job would carry less social prestige and less job security. They were divided almost evenly on whether teaching would involve less leisure or more. The chief drawback to the academic career identified by the majority was relatively lower earning power.

—ERNEST R. MAY and DOROTHY G. BLANEY,
Careers for Humanists

The authors of this passage want to show a serious, well-informed audience that they are reliable transmitters of information. They do not refer even distantly to their own experiences, opinions, or feelings; nor do they ask their readers for anything beyond attention to the reported results. In this deliberately neutral prose, "the facts speak for themselves." The absence of intimacy is a deliberate stylistic effect, well suited to the businesslike work of conveying information. Whenever that is your chief purpose—as, for example, in a report of facts you have uncovered or of laboratory results you have obtained—you will want to adopt such an **impersonal voice.**

The following student paragraph illustrates an opposite effect.

PERSONAL VOICE:

Eating the catered meals they serve on airplanes is always a memorable experience. In the first place, you have to admit it is exciting to open that little carton of salad oil and find a stream of Thousand Island dressing rocketing onto your blouse. Then, too, where else would you be able to dig into a *perfectly* rectangular chicken? And let's not forget the soggy, lukewarm mushrooms which are accused by the menu of having "smothered" the geometrical bird. They look and taste exactly like the ear jacks that are forever falling off your rented headset. Come to think of it, what *do* they do with those jacks when the flight is over?

This writer, using a **personal voice,** everywhere implies that she is drawing on her private experience, and she insists on an involved response by addressing her reader as an individual: *you have to admit; your blouse; where else would you be able; your rented headset.* Since the "facts" in this passage are not facts at all but witty exaggerations of widely shared inconveniences, the writer wants us to gather that she is saying at least as much about her own wry, mildly cynical attitude toward life as she is about airline food.

By choosing an appropriate voice, you also help to establish the **tone,** or quality of feeling, of your essay, paper, or report. An impersonal voice necessarily carries a dry, factual tone, but a personal voice can be intense, respectful, supportive, fanciful, mocking, worldly, authoritative, and so on, depending on your purpose. Compare the wry tone of the "airline food" passage, for example, with that of the following lines by Martin Luther King, Jr., addressing a "letter" to eight Alabama clergymen who had urged him to proceed cautiously in seeking racial justice. Both voices are personal, but King's tone is noble and angry:

We know through painful experience that freedom is never voluntarily given by the oppressor; it must be demanded by the oppressed. Frankly, I have yet to engage in a direct-action campaign that was "well timed" in

the view of those who have not suffered unduly from the disease of seg-
regation. For years now I have heard the word "Wait!" It rings in the ear
of every Negro with piercing familiarity. This "Wait" has almost always
meant "Never." We must come to see, with one of our distinguished
jurists, that "justice too long delayed is justice denied."
                              —MARTIN LUTHER KING, JR., *Why We Can't Wait*

Here is the rhetoric of a writer who knows that he cannot bank on
much agreement from his immediate readers; after all, they had just
written *him* a highly critical letter. Instead of swallowing his feelings,
King defiantly stands on his own authority: *I have yet to engage in a
direct-action campaign that was "well timed"* . . . ; *for years now I have
heard the word "Wait!"* He and other black activists *know through
painful experience* what the eight timid clergymen will never know
about how freedom is won; and he and *every Negro* have a personal
basis for asserting that *"Wait" has almost always meant "Never."*

Choice of governing pronoun

Notice that the **governing pronoun** you choose for your essay helps
to establish a consistent voice. If you call yourself *I,* you are guaran-
teeing at least a degree of personal emphasis. Even greater intimacy is
implied if, like the "airline food" writer, you presume to call your reader *you.* That pronoun can quickly wear out its welcome, however; a
reader resents being told exactly what to think and feel. If, like King,
you occasionally shift from the personal *I* to the community *we,* you
can imply a sense of shared values between yourself and all fair-
minded readers. And if you want a strictly formal, impersonal point of
view, you should refer to yourself rarely, if at all—and then only as a
member of the indefinite "editorial" *we,* as in *We shall see below.* . . .

3d   Generally prefer a forthright stance.

Most essays and nearly all college papers, like the prose of this present
book, are meant to be taken "straight." Readers sense that the writer
is taking a *forthright stance*—a straightforward, trustworthy rhetorical posture. Thus they assume that the writer is being sincere in

making assertions and in endorsing certain attitudes while disapproving of others.

The following paragraph from a freshman essay shows the usual features of the forthright stance:

> When this University switched from quarters to semesters, my first reaction was dismay over my shortened summer. The last spring quarter ended in mid-June; the first fall semester began in August. Was this what the new order would be like—a general speedup? It took me a while to realize that my lost vacation was not a permanent feature of the semester system but a one-time inconvenience. Now that I have survived nearly two whole semesters, I am ready to admit that there is much to be said for the changed calendar. As for vacations, those five weeks of freedom around Christmas have turned my vanished summer into a trivial, faded memory.

Note how this writer, using middle diction (p. 174, 13g) and maintaining an earnest manner, carefully lays out the reasons why she had first one reaction and then another to the semester system. She gives us no cause to doubt any of her statements.

3e Note the special effect of an ironic stance.

Once in a while, instead of taking the usual forthright stance (3d), a writer may strike an *ironic stance,* saying one thing in such a way as to express a different or even opposite meaning. Irony is delicious when it works and disastrous when it does not. Before practicing it, you should understand what kinds of opportunities and difficulties it typically presents.

Irony can be either subtle or broad and either local or sustained. Local and subtle irony, lasting only for a sentence or two and scarcely striking the reader's attention, can enter into any essay possessing a personal voice (3c). Take, for example, the sentence *Recovery from an all-out nuclear attack would not be quite the routine project that some officials want us to believe.* The irony here, barely noticeable at first, is concentrated on the word *quite.* Taken at face value, the sentence claims that recovery from an all-out nuclear attack would be *almost* routine. But of course the writer means just the reverse—that there would be nothing routine about it. The word *quite* serves two ironic functions, twitting the business-as-usual mentality of the bureaucrats and hinting, through *understatement,* at the unspeakable horror of an actual nuclear attack. After such a sentence, the writer would want to shift to a straightforward stance and paint the gruesome details.

Broad irony, in contrast to the subtle kind, is deliberately outrageous in turning the world upside down to make fun of some disapproved policy or position. The idea is to *pretend to take seriously* a ridiculous extension of that policy or position and to run through its consequences with seeming enthusiasm. Thus, in the most famous example of broad irony, Jonathan Swift's "A Modest Proposal" suggested that the Irish children who were being starved by English absentee landlords could be profitably butchered and sold as meat for their persecutors' tables. Swift was not of course putting forward any such plan; he was ironically exposing the landlords' inhumanity.

For a modern sample of broad irony, consider the following excerpts from an essay mocking the bewildering options faced by consumers after the breakup of the national telephone monopoly in 1984. The writer pretends that gas and electricity, too, are about to be deregulated:

> With the proposed breakup of PG&E, many subscribers have been thrown into confusion over exactly *how* it will work once gas and electricity are distributed according to age, sex and zip code. . . .
>
> Using guidelines established in the recent AT&T breakup, the new PG&E will become Gasco and ElectroCorp, with customers billed for each, either by the month or triannually, depending. Those over sixty-five will be billed weekly. . . .
>
> Subscribers to Gasco will have their choice of gas and, in some cases, meter readers. Those with gas ranges and gas heaters can choose between gas piped in from Alaska (more expensive but hotter) and gas that comes directly from local gas lines (more toxic but cheaper). People who use a lot of gas and not much electricity—or vice versa—will be able to decide which of several smaller gas and electric companies they prefer.
>
> Major gas users may find it more economical to forgo Gasco and subscribe to either Big Boy Gas or FumeCo, "no-frills" companies able to supply low-cost gas on a prorated, per-annum, prix-fixe basis. Those with a greater demand for electricity may decide to go with Specific Gas &

Electric, which has a twenty-four-hour service that provides energy to customers "by the appliance." Here is how it works. Say you have a washing machine, a gas stove, a TV set, two radios and a canary. When your bill arrives, there will be a separate page for each appliance under 540 milliwicks. . . .

It is, of course, still possible to rent a utility pole or gas main by the month, but it's probably cheaper to buy your own, if you're a regular user of either gas or electricity. The average utility pole costs anywhere from $175 to $250, and comes in various sizes and decorator colors; the most popular is the Evergreen, which clamps onto any standard back-fence jack.

"But I never *bought* a gas main before," you may say. You are not alone. Many people have not, so it's going to mean a period of adjustment for many. Tough.

Most neighborhoods have utility pole and gas main boutiques, where one may drop in and ask to look at the various models available. Or you might want to attend a natural gas show at the Civic Auditorium. No one but you can be the ultimate judge of the *kind* of gas main that will best fit your daily needs. . . .

—GERALD NACHMAN,
"Your Home Guide to Energy Divestiture"

If you have a fruitful premise to work with—one like "Let's pretend that Irish children can be sold as table meat" or "Let's pretend that energy is going to be deregulated as the phone business was" — you can build a whole essay upon broad irony, working out the various implications of the absurd situation you have created. But if you are just poking fun at others or yourself, you would do well to keep your irony relatively low-keyed. A whole essay taking the stance of the "airplane food" passage (p. 33), for example, would become tiresome.

By adopting a less blatant ironic stance, one that only gradually becomes apparent to us, another student writer is able to sustain a whimsical effect:

Powerful people never walk aimlessly. You'll never see James Bond stop in the middle of a room and look around, scratching his head. I went directly for the blackjack table because I was aimed for it. I stood behind a woman, maybe my age, waiting for her cards. She got ten more dollars out of the wide-open purse in her lap. In it was her room key chain with

312 embossed in gold. Her nervousness proved her a novice at the game and the casino—she was too well-dressed to be a regular. I smiled at her hand. Too much sophistication won't allow a man to smile at a stranger. "I'll hold." She laid her cards down and lost. "Why didn't you tell me? Didn't you see my hand?" I got the waitress. "Bambi [I saw her name tag], would you be so kind as to send a bottle of champagne to room 312?" I gave her the $25 covering the room service charge. I looked down at the woman still seated at the blackjack table (down is the direction of the most powerful eyes) and explained, "You see, I make it a point not to get involved in the games played. Had I misled you, you might not come back." This stunned her and the dealer. The waitress shuffled off to do as I said. I walked back to the hallway to prove that it wasn't a pick-up. In the elevator up to my room, I finally exhaled, having sucked in my stomach throughout the whole adventure, and cursed myself for having blown $25 on someone I didn't even know. . . .

We are never quite sure, in reading this passage, whether the writer's main target is the artificiality of "James Bond" conventions or his own fantasy of being a "powerful person." But precisely because we are not being bludgeoned by obvious sarcasms, we are eager to keep reading.

If you plan to submit an essay of broad irony, check with your instructor first. Many writing assignments have important purposes that cannot be met once you have adopted the broad-ironical stance. Beware of reaching for irony simply because you would rather not fulfill the terms of the assignment.

3f   Aim for a measured tone.

The tone, or quality of feeling, conveyed by an essay can be somber or playful, formal or informal, earnest or droll, excited or deliberate, angry or appreciative. But whatever tone you are aiming for, you must check your draft to see that you have sustained it throughout.

Tone is not something to fuss about in the early stages of writing an essay. Once you have finished a draft, however, try to reread it as if you didn't know the writer, and ask yourself, "What is this person's mood?" Frequent underlinings, dashes, and exclamation points, for example, are signs of excitement. Is that the effect you want to create in the final version? In revising, you may decide you would rather show composure and control. On the other hand, if your draft sounds like the work of a bored and listless writer, you can look for ways of showing more engagement.

aud
3f

Avoiding emotionalism

Strong emotions have their place in essay rhetoric. Sometimes, for example, righteous sarcasm works better than a studiously neutral weighing of pros and cons—provided the writer can count on the reader's sympathy. Hence the abrupt and cutting tone in much commentary found in magazines whose audience consists of a single political faction. But in college writing there is rarely a good reason for sounding as if you couldn't possibly be wrong.

The chief threat to an adequately controlled tone comes not from strong emotions but from **emotionalism,** the condition of someone who is too upset to think clearly. Compare, for instance, the following passages:

x A. The slaughter of whales is butchery pure and simple! Can you imagine anything more grotesque than the hideous, tortured death of a whale, shot with a grenade-tipped harpoon that *explodes* deep inside its body? *And for what?* Why the sadistic murder? Because certain profiteers want to turn the gentlest creature on this planet into *crayons, lipstick, shoe polish, fertilizer, margarine,* and *pet food,* for God's sake! If this doesn't make you sick—well, all I can say is that you must be ripping off some of those obscene profits yourself.

The second passage shows at least as much conviction—probably more—but the emotionalism of passage A is nowhere to be seen:

• B. The killing of a whale at sea isn't pleasant to witness or even to contemplate. Hunted down through sonar and other highly specialized equipment, the whale has no more chance of escape than a steer in a slaughterhouse. The manner of his death, however, is very different. A grenade-tipped harpoon explodes deep within his body, often causing prolonged suffering before the gentle giant, whose intelligence may be second only to our own, is reduced to a carcass ready for processing into crayons, lipstick, shoe polish, fertilizer, margarine, and pet food.

The inhumane manner of death, however, is the least part of the scandal known as the whaling industry. Much more important is the fact that the killing is quite unnecessary. Adequate substitutes exist for every single use to which whale carcasses are currently put, and although some 32,000 whales are killed every year, the sum of commodities they provide is insignificant in the world's economy. Indeed, two already wealthy nations, Russia and Japan, account for eighty percent of all the whales "harvested" annually. Though the Japanese claim that whale meat is a vital source of protein for them, less than one percent of the Japanese protein diet usually comes from that source. Yet the slaughter goes on unchecked. The alarming truth is that one of the noblest species on earth is being pressed toward extinction for no justifiable reason.

If you already agree with the author of passage A, you may find yourself aroused by his overemphatic prose. In that case nothing has been gained or lost. If you disagree, you find yourself insulted as a profiteer. And if you are neutral, wondering which side possesses the strongest argument, you may notice how little relevant information is being offered. Should whaling be stopped because of the mere fact that whales are slaughtered and turned into commodities? So are many other animals. In his outrage the writer has neglected to supply a reasoned analysis that would keep him from being regarded as a sentimentalist.

The measured language of passage B is much more effective than the exclamations and italics of passage A. Take the description of a whale's death: we see, not the writer emoting over the fact, but the fact itself, which becomes more impressive without the signs of agitation. Similarly, by not calling special attention to the list of commodities from *crayons* through *pet food,* passage B achieves a powerful quality of understatement, whereby the mere reality appears more expressive than any editorializing about it would be. And above all, note that writer B provides detailed evidence for the belief that whale slaughter, whether or not it revolts us, is economically unnecessary. In reading passage A, our only options are to share or reject a fit of temper. But even if we lean at first toward a pro-whaling stance, we find it hard to dismiss writer B's objectively reported facts. Here and elsewhere, reasons prove to be not just fairer but also more persuasive than sentiment.

The problem of maintaining a fair tone will probably be most acute when you are coping with objections to your thesis. See pp. 26–27, 2f.

4 Drafting and Revising

DRAFTING

4a Find the most effective organization for your ideas.

The key to arriving at a sound essay structure is to put yourself in your reader's place. Beginning in ignorance, your reader wants to know certain things that fall into a natural order:

1. what is being discussed;

2. what your point is;

3. why objections, if any, to that point are not decisive;

4. on what positive grounds the point should be believed.

As a diagram, then, the most reliable essay structure would look like this:

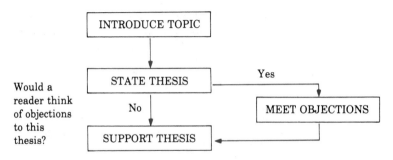

If you try to rearrange this common order, you will find it difficult. How, for example, could a reader want to know the writer's thesis before knowing the issue at stake? Why ask for supporting evidence before knowing what it is evidence *for?* Even the optional part of the sequence, the handling of objections, falls into a logical place. When (as in any argument) it does become important to address objections, the handiest place to do so is right after the thesis has been revealed— for that is where the objections are most likely to occur to your reader and hence to threaten your credibility.

Using the full thesis statement as a guide

By following the simplified model just discussed, you can derive the structure of a brief essay directly from your full thesis statement.

1. The *topic,* the first element of the model, is known from the thesis statement because it is the question answered by the thesis.

2. The *thesis* is directly named in the thesis statement.

3. If the thesis contains an *although* clause, at least one important *objection* has been isolated.

4. *Because* clauses in the thesis statement specify the final element of structure, the main points of *support* for the thesis.

Moving beyond a fixed pattern

The principles of organization mentioned above will serve you best if you take them as a starting point rather than an inflexible guide. There are things the model cannot do—choices you must settle either through a detailed outline (4b) or through problem solving as you work your way through a draft. Specifically, the model

—does not tell you how to catch a reader's interest;

—does not say how many objections, if any, you should deal with, or whether they should be met by concession or by refutation (pp. 26–27);

—does not say how much space you should devote to any single point; and

—does not indicate whether you will need a formal concluding paragraph.

Thus your developing sense of problems, opportunities, and paragraph-by-paragraph tactics should be your final guide.

Suppose, for instance, you notice that the best positive evidence for your thesis consists of points that also answer main objections. In that case it would be wasteful to treat objections and supporting evidence separately. Or, again, the decision to include or skip a summary paragraph at the end is a matter of weighing available alternatives. If your essay is long and complex, a conclusion is probably called for. But if you have saved a decisive point of evidence, a revealing incident, or a striking sentence, you may be well advised to end dramatically with that clincher and omit a concluding paragraph (p. 123, 9i).

4b   Suit an outline to your purpose.

An outline can be an important aid to your composing, but to make good use of it you must appreciate what it *cannot* do. Briefly, it cannot replace a sound thesis.

Some writers, equating an outline with "good organization," are tempted to go directly from a subject area or topic (p. 6, 1b) to an outline.

DON'T:

x Topic: Commercial Airlines
  I. Relation to Military
  II. The Jet Age
  III. Fare Wars in the 1990s
  IV. Future of the Industry

An analytic or argumentative essay, you recall, must pursue a point from beginning to end. In contrast, the outline above merely identifies assorted subtopics that the writer hopes to cover. It is actually doing

the writer a disservice by giving a false appearance of order and purpose. Be sure, then, that any outline of your own is preceded by and
derived from a thesis statement. Even if some parts of your outline
look like subtopics, you will know that they represent necessary steps
in the case you will be making for your thesis.

Competent writers differ greatly in their fondness for an outline.
If, like some of them, you find that you simply cannot work from an
outline in writing your first draft, you should nevertheless make an
outline of that draft when you have finished it. There is no better way
of spotting redundancies and inconsistencies that need fixing.

Scratch outline

If your essay is going to be brief and you simply need to decide on an
order for several paragraphs, you will be adequately served by a
scratch outline—that is, one showing no subordination of some points
to others.

Suppose, for instance, you had hit upon the following thesis statement for an analytic 600-word essay: *Although television and radio
both cover news developments and sports events, their styles are necessarily different, TV leaning toward "editorial" and radio toward "reportorial" coverage.* A serviceable scratch outline of your paragraphs
might look like this:

¶1
1. TV and radio cover many of the same happenings, e.g., news
developments and sports events.

2. Thesis: But the two styles differ. Because TV can show what
radio has to describe, TV has more air time to comment on
events.

¶2
3. News developments (film clips of speeches, interviews, battles,
election returns, etc.): only on TV are the events partly allowed
to speak for themselves, with occasional or follow-up commentary by news analysts.

¶3
4. Sports events: TV, relatively free from reporting what is happening, includes more commentary than radio does.

¶ 4   5. In summary: TV coverage doesn't abolish the spoken word, but because we can *see,* the balance tips toward "editorial" as opposed to radio's "reportorial" coverage.

Subordinated outline

For longer and more complex essays you may want to use a *subordinated outline*—one that shows, through indention and more than one set of numbers, that some points are more important than others

Suppose, for instance, you had decided to write a 1000-word argument opposing rent control of off-campus housing, and you were satisfied with the following thesis statement: *Although off-campus rent control is aimed at securing reasonable rents for students, it would actually produce four undesirable effects: establishment of an expensive, permanent rent-control bureaucracy; landlord neglect of rental property; a shortage of available units; and a freezing of currently excessive rents.* Knowing that your argument would be fairly complex, you might want to draw up a full outline:

  I. The Problem Is That Students Now Face Hardships in Securing Adequate Housing.
     A. Students are currently subject to rent gouging.
     B. High rents force many students to live far from campus.

 II. The Promise Is That Rent Control Will Guarantee Reasonable Rents near Campus.

III. Thesis: The Reality Is That the Actual Effects of Rent Control Would Be Undesirable.
     A. An expensive, permanent rent-control bureaucracy would be established.
     B. Landlords would neglect rent-controlled property.
     C. The shortage of units would *worsen,* because:
        1. Owners would have no incentive to increase the number of rental units.
        2. Competition for rent-frozen units would be more intense.
     D. Currently excessive rents would be frozen, thus ruling out any possible reduction.

Notice that this outline establishes three degrees of importance among your ideas. The Roman numerals running down the left margin point to the underlying structure of the essay, a movement from problem to promise to reality. These main categories come straight from the thesis statement. The *problem* is the topic itself; the *promise* is the "although" consideration, which is taken care of early; and the *reality,* the thesis itself, consists of the "four undesirable effects" of off-campus rent control.

At the next level of subordination, the indented capital letters introduce ideas that contribute to these larger units. The problem, says Part I of the outline, has two aspects: rent gouging and the forcing of students to seek lower rents far from campus. By listing those aspects as *A* and *B,* you assign them parallel or roughly equivalent status in your argument.

Points A through D in Part III are also parallel, but one of them, C, is supported in turn by two narrower points. By assigning those two points Arabic numerals and by a further indention from the left margin, you indicate to yourself that these considerations go to prove the larger idea just above them. Thus the three sets of numbering/lettering and the three degrees of indention display the whole logic of your essay.

Sentence versus topic outline

The example just given is a *sentence outline,* using complete sentences to state every planned idea. A sentence outline is the safest kind, because its complete statements ensure that you will be making assertions, not just touching on subjects, in every part of your essay.

But if you are confident of keeping your full points in mind, you can use the simpler *topic outline,* replacing sentences with concise phrases:

    I. The Problem
       A. Rent Gouging
       B. Students Forced to Live Far from Campus (etc.)

The form you choose for an outline is hardly an earthshaking matter; just be sure the outline gives you enough direction, and do not waste time elaborating an outline until it is more intricate and hair-splitting than your essay itself.

Keeping outline categories in logical relation

If you do use subordination in an outline, observe that one heading or subheading should always have at least one mate—no *I* without *II,* no *A* without *B.* The reason is that headings and subheadings represent divisions of a larger unit, either a more general point or the thesis of the whole essay. It is of course impossible to divide something into just one part. If you have a lonesome *A* in a draft outline, work it into the larger category:

ILLOGICAL:
- x I. Problems
     A. Excessive Noise
  II. Cost Factors
     A. Overruns

BETTER:
- • I. Problem of Excessive Noise
  II. Cost Overruns

In addition, you should always check a draft outline to make sure that all the subheadings under a given heading logically contribute to it. Do not try to tuck in irrelevant items just because you find no other place for them; that would defeat the whole purpose of outlining, which is to keep your essay coherent and logical in moving from one idea to the next.

4c Supply evidence for your ideas.

A college writer cannot afford to say in effect, *Believe my thesis because I am telling you to.* Readers expect to be shown that the thesis rests on sound reasoning about established facts. And evidence is essential to support not just the thesis (p. 24, 2f) but any important judgment that departs from what readers are already likely to accept.

"Facts and figures"

When most people think of evidence, they call to mind "facts and figures"—statements and numerical data that are regarded as well established. Though useful evidence goes well beyond such items, they can have a compelling effect on a reader. Suppose, for example, you were intuitively convinced that American blacks are economically much worse off than the usual income figures show. Personal testimony could be affecting, but what you would really need is statistics to support your point. You could discover them in a U.S. Census Bureau report of 1986 which calculated relative *wealth* rather than income. To be sure, the average income of blacks is more than half that of whites. But the *wealth* of blacks—measured as home equity, savings, and personal property—is ten times lower than the wealth of whites. Armed with that finding, you would be able to make your case with confidence.

To see how an array of facts and figures can add weight to a claim, study the following paragraph from an article advocating that warning labels be placed on alcoholic beverage containers:

> Alcoholism and alcohol abuse are recognized as two of our nation's most serious problems. According to estimates, 18.3 million American adults are "heavy drinkers," which is defined as consuming more than 14 drinks per week. In 1985, over 12 million American adults had one or more symptoms of alcoholism, an increase of 8.2 percent from 1980. In addition, an estimated 3.3 million teenagers show signs that they may develop serious alcohol-related problems. These statistics are all the more alarming when considered against the staggering human cost involved with drunken driving. In 1984 there were 44,241 traffic fatalities nationwide, 53 percent of which were deemed to be alcohol-related.
>
> —STROM THURMOND,
> "Should Congress Pass Legislation to Require
> Warning Labels on Alcoholic Beverages?"

Reasoning

When you put forward a challengeable claim, you naturally want to show that "logic is on your side." This does not mean that you have to move stiffly from premises to conclusions, as if you were conducting a formal proof. That way lies tedium for your reader. Simply, you should be ready to appeal to the reader's commonsense grasp of sound reasoning.

Study the following student paragraph, written before Congress repealed the federal 55-miles-per-hour speed limit:

> Most people believe that the lower speed limit has saved many thousands of lives—but can we be sure? Highway fatalities certainly dropped after the 55-mph limit was imposed in 1974. Yet they have continued to drop in subsequent years, as drivers' speeds have been creeping steadily *upward* toward the old 65-mph norm. This can only mean that other factors—safer cars and roads, less reckless driving habits, mandatory seat belt laws, harsher penalties for drunken driving—have been influencing the statistics. Thus, strictly speaking, we have no way of knowing how much the lower speed limit has actually contributed to safety.

We could restate this writer's reasoning more formally using **syllogisms,** or chains of deduction from premises to conclusions:

Opponents believe:

> Premise: If highway deaths decline, the lower speed limit deserves the credit.
>
> Premise: Highway deaths have declined.
>
> Conclusion: Therefore the lower speed limit deserves the credit.

But: The lower speed limit has been gradually disregarded by drivers, while deaths have continued to decline. So:

> Premise: If actual speeds have been increasing while deaths have been declining, we cannot say for sure that the lower speed limit is responsible for the savings in lives.
>
> Premise: Speeds *have* increased, and deaths *have* declined.
>
> Conclusion: We cannot say for sure that the lower speed limit is responsible for the savings in lives.

Principles of sound reasoning are violated by **fallacies,** or illegitimate shortcuts to a favored conclusion. For the most important fallacies, see pages 17–24, 2c–e. Learning to detect fallacious reasoning will help you not only to strengthen the evidence for your own conclusions but also to fend off fallaciously based objections.

Quotation

Whenever you make a claim about the language of a text—a claim, for instance, that Hemingway's sentences are more complex and varied than most people suppose, or that Robert Frost's pleasant nature imagery often carries sinister undertones—you ought to quote representative samples of that language. If the quotations alone do not make your point, follow them with passages of analysis. Note how a student writer mixes quotation with commentary in the following paragraph from a paper about Wallace Stevens's poem "The Death of a Soldier":

> But this is not to say that "The Death of a Soldier" lacks artfulness. On the contrary, the poem hinges on a brilliant surprise. The simile "As in a season of autumn" sets up a trite anticipation: the soldier falls, we assume, as do autumn leaves. In the third stanza, with the strange repetition of line 2, we begin to see that something more unusual is brewing: death is somehow like the stopping of autumn *wind.* Only in the final stanza do we grasp why. What matters about death, for Stevens, is not that a life ceases but that everything else proceeds as before: "The clouds go, nevertheless, / In their direction." Thus even the absoluteness of death is, we might say, nothing to write home about.

Quotation can serve as convincing evidence not just in literary analysis but in any essay that focuses on what someone said or meant. The important thing is not to quote vast chunks of material but, on the contrary, to use only the most telling passages and to make sure your reader sees their point. Observe, for example, how discreetly—but also how effectively—a skeptical observer of "New Age consciousness" handles a key statement and two revealing phrases:

> The bedrock of New Age thought now is the fulfillment of individual potential, with the implicit consequence of bringing the New Age closer.

How fulfillment is achieved—whether through meditation, pop psychology, physical fitness, est, whatever—and what form it takes (money, power, sex) doesn't matter. What counts is the awareness that one has such potential and can exploit it. Thus *Pathways,* a New Age newspaper in Washington, D.C., defines itself with this credo: "The world public has become disenchanted with both the political and financial leadership. . . . All the individuals of humanity are looking for the answers to what the little individual can do that can't be done by great nations and great enterprises." *Pathways* then encourages the " 'little individual' to join together in the dynamic process of personal and sociological transformation."

If all of this makes New Age sound like a religion, that's because for many adherents it is. Like most religions, it attempts to address believers' spiritual concerns with the promise of an afterlife (or rather, another life). And it demands that its believers have faith in things that cannot be scientifically proven—channeling, for instance. But there is no God in the New Age church. Rather, god is within everyone, a universal characteristic New Agers sometimes refer to as "god-force" or "pure-consciousness." Reaching the god-force within you is easy if you know how to do it, like knowing the combination to a bank vault. And if you don't know how to do it, there are plenty of New Age teachers to show you how—for a price.

—RICHARD BLOW, "Moronic Convergence"

In his first paragraph this writer, concerned to expose the New Age movement as pseudoreligious, quotes language that conveys religious overtones, and in his second paragraph he dwells on that connection, adding the corroborative terms *god-force* and *pure-consciousness.* The quotations make his reasoning more believable. But observe how that reasoning, not the borrowed material, dominates his presentation, and note how selective he is, omitting any language that would stray from the point.

Citation of authority

In theory, the least impressive evidence ought to be the citing of authority; after all, authorities are often proved to have been wrong. In practice, however, we all wisely respect the judgment of people who are better placed than we are for understanding a given issue or technical field. Thus, if a committee of distinguished scientists declares that a proposed weapons system lies beyond the reach of existing technology, we have to be impressed—even if we may harbor some doubts about their unstated political motives. Again, an opponent of placing warning labels on alcoholic beverages (p. 48) could score a telling point by mentioning that the prestigious American Council on Alcoholism *disapproves* of such labeling. Such citation of authority does not by itself win an argument, but it can leave your reader favorably disposed toward your more substantial evidence.

4d Mix improvising with planning in writing your first draft.

Even after much preparation, you may feel some resistance to committing your first draft to paper. If the opening paragraph (pp. 115–122, 9a–h) looms as an especially big obstacle, try skipping it and starting with a later one. If you seem to be losing momentum in the middle of a sentence, shift into a private shorthand that will keep you from worrying about the fine points of expression; you can return to them later. And instead of writing, you may find it easier to talk into a tape recorder and then transcribe the better parts. Whether you write or dictate, do not be afraid to include too much, to leave blank spaces, or to commit errors of usage and punctuation. What matters is that you move ahead, understanding that you will have a substantial job of revision to do (see below).

Do not be alarmed if you find new possibilities coming into view as you finish one sentence and struggle to begin the next one. Some of your best ideas—perhaps even a radically improved thesis—can be generated by that friction between the written sentence and the not-yet-written one. So long as you anticipate the need to reconsider and reorganize after your first draft is complete, the tug of war between plans and inspirations should result in a subtler, more engaging paper than you originally expected to submit.

REVISING

Many students are willing enough to revise their work but are held back by two misconceptions. First, they suppose that revision begins only when an essay is nearly ready to be turned in; and second, they think that revision involves only a tidying up of word choice, spelling, punctuation, and usage. But experienced writers revise their prose even while they are first producing it—adding, deleting, replacing, and rearranging material at every opportunity (see pp. 3–4, 1a). They never assume that any given draft will be the last one. And they stand ready to make *conceptual* and *organizational* changes as well as *editorial* ones.

If you have access to a word processor (Chapter 42), you will find revising a text much simplified. The word processor allows you to move, delete, or insert a passage without having to do substantial retyping.

4e Seek responses to your draft.

If you could put a draft aside for a week or two, you would see flaws in it that a quick reading cannot uncover. Unfortunately, student writers rarely have that luxury. But perhaps a classmate, a roommate, a writing lab tutor, or your instructor may be willing to advise you about needed revisions. You, of course, must be the final judge of which advice to take and which to disregard as unreliable. Yet by posing key questions, you can actually oblige people to give you their best judgment. Ask them:

1. Can you accurately state my thesis?

2. What is the main impression (positive or negative) my essay has made on you?

3. Have I left you with any unanswered questions? If so, what are they?

4. What points need further—or less—development?

5. Are my opening and closing paragraphs effective?

6. Which words strike you as "off" in meaning, tone, correctness of usage, or spelling?

These questions form only a fraction of the checklist you should apply to your own work (pp. 61–62, 4i), but anyone who addresses all of them will be doing you a considerable favor.

4f   Be open to conceptual and organizational revision.

Because sentence-by-sentence composing often leads to new ideas, you must read through your completed draft to be sure it makes a consistent impression. Do not hesitate to alter your thesis or even reverse it if you become more swayed by objections than by supporting points. Such a shift can be painful and time-consuming, but in the long run it will spare you many hours of trying to show interest in ideas that you now consider fatally weak.

You should be prepared to make less sweeping conceptual changes as well. Have you exaggerated your claims? Are your explanations clear? Do you need to supply more evidence? Give your conceptual revisions top priority; there is no reason to tinker with phraseology if the whole direction of your essay has to be changed.

After you have made necessary changes in your ideas, check your draft to see if your points appear in a logical and persuasive order. Have you placed your thesis prominently? Have you waited to unveil it until you have attracted the reader's interest and clearly identified the topic? Have you avoided digressions, or passages that stray from the issue at hand? Have you avoided redundancy, or needless repetition of assertions? Are all of your quotations succinct and necessary? And have you included all necessary information—for example, the setting for your discussion of an event, the rules of a little-known game, or the plot of an unassigned novel? Here as elsewhere the key to successful revision is to "play reader" and probe for sources of puzzlement or dissatisfaction.

4g   Attend to editorial revision.

Though editorial revision is rarely the most important kind, it does cover the greatest number of problems. They range from such finicky matters as citation form (Chapter 37) to such broad ones as the striking of an appropriate voice, stance, and tone (pp. 32–40, 3c–f). In every case, effective revision flows from putting the reader's convenience ahead of your own.

FEATURE	REVISE FOR	HELPS READER TO
voice, stance, tone	appropriateness to audience and purpose	appreciate writer's point of view and consistency
paragraphs	unity, continuity, development	see relations between major and minor points
sentences	distinctness, subordination, emphasis, variety	follow ideas, avoid tedium
words	appropriateness, liveliness	get clear information, avoid jarring effects
usage, punctuation, spelling, other conventions	conformity with standard written practice	concentrate on substance of essay
citation form	fullness, exactness, consistency	have access to secondary sources

For an idea of how instructors typically draw attention to editorial problems and how students then revise, consider the following made-up paragraph and the **symbols for comment and revision** (see the inside back cover) that have been added to it:

Once people have gone to the trouble of acquiring the capacity to treat everyone as equals, they can *wdy* work with others for the common good. A <u>great</u> ex- *exagg* *pred* ample is <u>how</u> the Los Angeles area handled <u>it's</u> pol- *sp* lution problem. Everyone was aware of the stifling *nop* smog. But the majority of <u>these people</u> were will- *ref* ing only to complain. One group of citizens, how- ever came up with a creative plan for carpooling. ✓

rev
4g

dm <u>Providing</u> an incentive, one lane of freeway was set

wdy aside for cars carrying three or more people. [But

after a short period of time] the <u>committment</u> was *Sp*

abandoned. [Because of the <u>godawful</u> traffic jams in *Colloq*

frag the other lanes] <u>It</u> was a promising idea, but most *ref*

pass people <u>are made</u>[less upset by smog so that] they *Comp*

actually prefer it to <u>traffic jams in freeway lanes</u> *red*

The most important of these markings is ¶ *un*, since it calls for a substantial rewriting that would automatically eliminate some of the smaller problems. But if the student were to address those problems as they stand, the diagnoses and the most likely remedies would be these.

SYMBOL	PROBLEM AND SOLUTION	UNREVISED VERSION	REVISION
wdy	the expression is wordy; make it more concise	x Once people have gone to the trouble of acquiring the capacity to treat everyone as equals	• Once people can recognize others as equals
		x after a short period of time	• soon
exagg	the expression is overstated; tone it down	x A great example	• One example
pred	faulty predication; do away with the mismatch between subject and predicate	x One example is how . . .	• One example is the handling . . . ; *or* Consider, for example, how Los Angeles handled . . .

rev
4g

SYMBOL	PROBLEM AND SOLUTION	UNREVISED VERSION	REVISION
sp	spelling error; look the word up and spell it correctly	x it's x committment	• its • commitment
chop	choppy sentences: several plain, brief sentences in a row; introduce variety of structure	x A great example is how Los Angeles . . . willing to complain.	• Consider, for example, how Los Angeles handled its pollution problem. Even though everyone was aware of the stifling smog, few people were willing at first to do anything more than complain.
ref	pronouns or demonstratives lack clear, explicitly stated antecedents; make the reference clear	x these people x It was a promising idea	• residents • The carpooling plan was a promising idea
p	punctuation error; correct it	x One group of citizens, however came up with	• One group of citizens, however, came up with
dm	dangling modifier; supply an agent to perform the action	x Providing an incentive, one lane of freeway was set aside	• Providing an incentive, county officials set aside

rev
4g

SYMBOL	PROBLEM AND SOLUTION	UNREVISED VERSION	REVISION
colloq	the expression falls beneath the level of diction appropriate to this paper; find a middle-level substitute	x godawful	● serious
frag	sentence fragment; rewrite or combine to form a grammatically complete sentence	x Because of serious traffic jams in the other lanes.	● But because of serious traffic jams in the other lanes, the commitment was soon abandoned.
pass	unnecessary use of passive voice; shift to active voice	x most people are made less upset	● most people would rather
comp	faulty comparison; match the compared terms or completely recast the expression	x most people are made less upset by smog so that	● most people prefer smog to traffic jams; *or* most people find smog less offensive than traffic jams
red	this expression repeats an earlier one; rephrase it	x traffic jams in the other lanes . . . traffic jams in freeway lanes	● . . . can't take lung congestion any more seriously than they do traffic congestion.

As for ⏀ ʋ𝘯, notice that the writer began by asserting that *people can work for the common good* but then went on to illustrate a nearly opposite point, that *most people cannot put the public interest before their immediate convenience.* Until that contradiction is resolved, no amount of tinkering can make the paragraph effective.

To weigh the writer's options, ask yourself which idea shows more regard for real experience, the initial one or the one that surfaced in the drafting process. It is really no contest. *Working with others for the common good* is a limp "motherhood" concept, wishful and unchallenging. The conflict between selfish private habits and the common good is a more balanced, less simplistic notion—one that indicates an ability to face facts. Thus the writer would do well to skip the moralizing and rethink the whole thesis. An eventual, radically improved version of the paragraph might look like this:

**rev
4h**

```
When selfish private habits and the common good come

into conflict, the outcome is likely to be all too

predictable. Take a recent example from Los Angeles,

where everyone's health would be safeguarded by a sig-

nificant reduction in automobile exhausts. Acting on

the suggestion of a citizens' group, county officials

tried to promote carpooling by setting aside one lane

of each freeway for cars carrying three or more peo-

ple. If it had worked, this plan would have enabled

everyone to breathe more easily. The plan had to be

dropped, however, when so few people cooperated that

motorists refusing to share rides were hopelessly

clogging the remaining lanes. Los Angelenos, it

seems, can't take lung congestion any more seriously

than they do traffic congestion.
```

4h Make your title definite

Do not bother thinking of a title until you have finished at least one draft, and be ready to change titles as your later drafts change emphasis. If you begin with a title, it will probably indicate little more than the subject matter treated in your essay. Replace it later with a title expressing your *view of* that subject matter, or at least posing the question answered by your thesis. Thus, asked to write about revision, do not remain satisfied with "Revision" or "Revising College Essays"; such toneless titles suggest that you have no thesis at all. Instead, try something like "The Agony of Revision," "Revision as Discovery," or "Is an Essay Ever Really Finished?" Each of those versions tells the reader that you have found something definite to say.

That impression will be especially strong if you can make your title surprising and vivid. Look for a striking figure of speech (see Chapter 15) that could suggest your thesis with pointed wit. One common device is to combine such a phrase with a more straightforwardly informative subtitle:

- Downhill All the Way: My Melting Career as a Ski Racer
- Going High for the Rebound: Drugs as a Menace to Athletes' Careers

If your essay contains especially significant phrases (original or quoted), see if any of them could be borrowed for your title. One freshman student, for example, began a prizewinning essay about *Hamlet* with the following paragraph:

```
While showing Guildenstern how to play the recorder,
Hamlet remarks that it is "as easy as lying"
(III.ii.343). In a sense, much of the play's meaning
is expressed in this line. Almost every character in
Hamlet is to some extent living a lie: hiding
thoughts, playing a role, trying to deceive another
character. Claudius conceals his crime; Hamlet feigns
madness; private schemes prevail. In the end, Hamlet
may even be deceiving himself, forcing himself into a
role of avenger when he may not actually fit.
```

For a title, the writer chose "As Easy As Lying"—a phrase that stirred curiosity and gave promise of a well-considered, original thesis.

4i Test your draft against a checklist for revision.

rev
4i

Since you cannot always count on having a friendly critic available, you will need to test your drafts yourself against standards that readers commonly hold. The following questions form a checklist that you can consult as soon as you have finished a draft or two. Running through the questions, you may be able to pinpoint any remaining problems and locate the relevant discussions of them in this book.

A CHECKLIST FOR REVISION

1. Do I have a clear, properly limited, and interesting thesis (pp. 16–27, Chapter 2)?

2. Have I provided adequate evidence for my thesis (pp. 45–52, 4c)?

3. Have I dealt with probable objections to my thesis (pp. 20–27, 2d–f)?

4. Is my thesis conspicuously stated (p. 54, 4f)?

5. Are my voice, stance, and tone appropriate to my audience and purpose (pp. 28–40, Chapter 3)?

6. Are my paragraphs unified and fully developed (pp. 81–103, Chapters 6–7)?

7. Does my first paragraph attract the reader's interest (pp. 114–123, 9a–h)?

8. Have I made clear and helpful transitions between paragraphs (pp. 91–93, 6h–i)?

9. Does my last paragraph give enough sense of completion (pp. 123–125, 9i–m)?

10. Does my title indicate that I have a definite point to make (pp. 59–60, 4h)?

11. Are my sentences distinct, with effective subordination of minor elements (pp. 129–146, Chapters 10–11)?

12. Do my sentences show enough emphasis and variety of structure (pp. 147–159, Chapter 12)?

13. Do all of my words mean what I think they mean (pp. 161–168, 13a–c)?

14. Is my language appropriate to the occasion (pp. 168–174, 13d–g)?

15. Is my language as lively and imaginative as the occasion allows (pp. 175–194, Chapters 14–15)?

16. Have I looked up the spelling of doubtful words (pp. 388–399, Chapter 32)?

17. Have I kept to standard written usage (pp. 197–308, Chapters 16–23)?

18. Does my punctuation bring out my meaning (pp. 311–351, Chapters 24–28)?

19. Have I followed correct form for quoting other people's words (pp. 338–351, 28d–r)?

20. Have I followed correct form for capitals, italics, abbreviations, and numbers (pp. 408–432, Chapters 34–35)?

21. Have I supplied all necessary documentation and followed a standard form for doing so (pp. 458–490, Chapter 37)?

4j Follow standard typescript form in your final copy.

No matter how many changes you make between drafts, the essay you eventually submit should look unscarred, or nearly so. It should also meet certain technical requirements of form. The following advice reflects general practice and should be followed whenever your instructor does not specify something different.

1. Type your essay if possible, using standard-sized (8½″ × 11″) unlined white paper of ordinary weight, not onionskin. If you

must write longhand, choose paper with widely spaced lines or write on every other line. Type with an unfaded black ribbon or write in dark ink. Use only one side of the paper.

2. Put your name, the course number, your instructor's name, and the date of submission on four double-spaced lines at the upper left corner of your first page, above your title. Do not put your title in quotation marks or underline it. Capitalize words within it according to the advice on pages 410–411, 34e–f. Skip four lines between the title and the beginning of your text. For an example, see page 73.

3. If you are asked to supply a thesis statement and/or an outline, put them on a separate page, after a title page like the one shown on page 492. Repeat the title on your first page of text, as on page 494.)

4. Allow at least one-inch margins on all four sides of each page of your main text. Your right margins need not be even. In a handwritten essay, be sure to leave as much space as in a typewritten one.

5. Leave the first page of text unnumbered, but put your last name and unpunctuated Arabic numerals (2, 3, 4) in the upper right corners of subsequent pages, including pages devoted to your endnotes and reference list, if any.

6. Double-space your whole paper, including any reference list, endnotes, or bibliography. Single-space any footnotes. Follow your instructor's specifications for the spacing of indented quotations.

7. Indent the first line of each paragraph by five type-spaces; that is, press the space bar five times and then begin typing. In a handwritten essay, indent by about an inch. Do not skip extra lines between paragraphs. When a quoted passage is long enough to require indention (see p. 343, 28h), generally indent it by ten spaces—fewer if a quoted poem uses very long lines.

8. Retype any pages on which you had to make more than a few last-minute changes. Otherwise, type those changes or write them clearly in ink, using the following conventions:

a. Remove unwanted letters with a diagonal slash:

```
indigestio/n
```

b. Remove unwanted words by running a line through them:

```
~~nasty~~ slur
```

c. Replace a letter by putting the new letter above your slash:

```
      s
compo/ition
```

d. Replace words by putting the new word above your canceled one:

```
                writer
please every ~~reader~~
```

e. Add words or letters by putting a caret (∧) at the point of insertion and placing the extra words or letters above it:

```
     notable
Another∧feature of this device
```

f. Separate words or letters by placing a vertical line between them:

```
steel and/iron
```

g. Close up separated letters with a curved line connecting them from above:

```
hic⌢cup
```

h. Transpose (reverse) letters or words with a curved enclosing line:

```
Al⁀ice, ⁀Carroll⁀Lewis⁀
```

i. Indicate a paragraph break by inserting the paragraph symbol before the first word of the new paragraph:

```
depends on development.¶Transitions, too, have a
certain importance.
```

j. Run two paragraphs together by connecting them with an arrow and writing *no ¶* in the margin:

```
She has found a way of turning "nothing" time into
pleasure or learning⌐
```

no ¶ ```
        ↳ Isn't that better than having some trivial
        chitchat on the sidewalk?
```
```

9. Carefully proofread your final copy, looking especially for typing errors. Check all quotations against your notes or, better, against the printed passages.

rev
4j

10. Make sure you have assembled your pages in order. Fasten them with a paper clip or, second best, with a staple.

11. Make a photocopy of your essay, and retain the copy until you get the original back. Keep the graded original at least until the course is over. These steps will protect you if your instructor should mislay an essay or misrecord a grade.

For the forming and spacing of punctuation marks, see pages 352–357, Chapter 29. For citation form, see pages 462–490, Chapter 37.

5 One Essay From Start To Finish

A freshman student, asked to save her notes and drafts, found herself with a week and a half in which to write a 1000-word essay on any topic within the subject area "Technology and the Quality of Life." She knew that her topic would have to be narrower than that. In her earliest notes she mulled over several possibilities:

Computers . . . too broad. Subject doesn't seem to fascinate me anyway.

Cordless phones: nothing here? So you can take the phone into the kitchen without tripping over the cord. That's nice, but so what?

VCR's: OK in theory—no real ideas yet.

Portable headsets—maybe something here? The world is getting divided into people who do and don't live inside those things.

Robots in factories?

Janet liked the idea of writing about radios and tape players that can be carried in a pocket and played through earphones, but she didn't yet know *why* she liked it or what she wanted to say. To explore her trial topic, she began with reporters' questions (p. 14, 1g), seeing if any of the answers would lead her further:

Who? Joggers, bicyclists, misc. pedestrians, students crossing campus. . . . Mostly middle-class.

What? Walkman, etc.

When? Any waking hours. . . . Addiction?

Where? Buses, streets, workplaces, running trails, elevators, lavatories—where *not?* Urban only?

How? Made possible by micro-miniaturization, I guess.

Why? Love of music? I wonder. Are they just counteracting boredom? Sound junkies? *Tune out the world!*

Already Janet was beginning to crystallize her attitude toward portable headsets. She felt it was time to draw out further thoughts through a session of freewriting (p. 11–12, 1f):

People looking like space creatures; bugs; glazed eyes. Turtles inside their shells? But be fair; they're getting technically great sound quality. Run longer without boredom, blot out ugly street sounds—well, why not? Sights too; life goes by like a movie. Except here the music *is* the movie, i.e., the main thing, instead of being background. Social danger here? Definitely a *physical* danger: get run over, mugged, etc. Maybe it's not so good in less obvious ways, too. Shrinking into yourself: trend of the era? These people look peaceful, but what have they got (besides some money for toys)? Another fix that they may not be able to do without. (But this is getting a bit too moralistic, maybe?) Anyway, general problem: technological marvels bring new fun but make us less able to be *really* calm when *really* alone. Also, no improvement in the stuff people want to hear.

Having gone this far, Janet was reasonably sure she would keep her tentative topic, but now she had to decide what *kind* of essay to write:

> Argument or analysis? What would an argument be—that headsets
> should be banned? I distrust them, but *that's* too strong. So—no policy
> issue here. OK, analysis, but what kind? Maybe cause & effect: show
> where the fad came from and what it may do to us.

Her next step was therefore to make lists of causes and effects:

> Causes:
>   technological advances
>   outgrowth of stereo boxes
>   general conditioning to an electronic environment
>   retreat from public world—cult of privacy?
> Effects:
>   physical danger? (maybe too trivial)
>   restlessness *without* sets—no real peace
>   more shrinking into oneself
>   less tolerance for disturbance, diversity—just play *your* already
>   known program
>   loss of sympathy with others? political indifference?

Looking over these lists, Janet realized two things: that she was
much more interested in the effects of portable stereo headsets than in
their causes and that all the effects she had named were negative. Her
essay, then, was beginning to take shape as *an analysis of the negative
social effects of the headsets*. But now she had to consider her reader,
who might regard her as a spoilsport and a fanatic if she took a dooms-
day approach to a harmless-looking appliance. Thus, as a last exercise
before attempting a thesis statement, Janet tried to moderate her
stance by listing as many "pluses" as she could find. She was determined to work at least some of those positive qualities into her essay,
preferably at a point early enough to stave off doubts about her open-
mindedness.

In her first stab at a thesis statement, Janet came up with this:

TRIAL THESIS STATEMENT:
Although we can at least be thankful that portable headphone sets are quiet, they are a perfect symbol of a society that has become dependent on artificial sources of calm, out of touch with reality, and indifferent to other people's problems.

That statement had the degree of complexity Janet needed for a 1000-word paper, but it left her uneasy. The "although" clause seemed like a throwaway remark rather than a real concession; the sweeping condemnation of all American society looked excessive; and there was something awkward about accusing a *society* of being indifferent to *other people's* problems. In a second version Janet scaled down her claims and tried to sound fairer:

REVISED THESIS STATEMENT:
Although portable headphone sets are undoubtedly convenient and pleasurable, they raise disturbing questions about many Americans' dependency on artificial sources of calm, decreased contact with reality, and shrinkage of concern for others.

Since the point about "shrinkage of concern" was the one that mattered most to Janet, she kept it in the last (most emphatic) position.

Because her essay was to be only a few pages long, Janet thought she could make do with a casual scratch outline (pp. 44–45, 4b):

1. Introduce headsets as topic.

2. Admit appeal.

3. No immediate threat to anybody.

4. But (thesis here) three disturbing implications (name them).

5. #1: Dependency for calm.

6. #2: Loss of reality.

7. #3: Shrinkage of concern for others.

8. Conclusion: Though more a symptom than a cause of isolation, sets fit all too well with trend of the times.

essay
5

As things turned out, Janet found no need to revise this plan. But because she was worried about making her case too one-sided, she devoted two paragraphs instead of one to the positive appeal of the headsets.

At last it was time to draft the essay itself. In its earliest version, this was her opening paragraph (already somewhat revised for conciseness):

```
When I stop to think about technology and the quality
of life, several interesting possibilities come to
mind. Personal computers, of course, are revolutioniz-
ing the world in many ways. Robots in industry are
giving us more reliable products at the same time that
they are throwing many potential consumers out of
work. In the field of entertainment, we are deluged
with video games and special-effects extravaganzas
from Hollywood. But if I had to choose one piece of
technology to sum up the quality of our times--a none
too flattering symbol--I think I would take those port-
able headsets that one sees everywhere in the street
today.
```

Shown this paragraph, Janet's roommate commented that it would do in a pinch but that she didn't feel particularly motivated to keep reading. Janet had created a classic "funnel opener" (p. 115), but she had also come close to a "deadly opener" (p. 121) as well—the kind that lamely calls an assignment "interesting" instead of showing interest in it. Her revised introduction, Janet decided, would be a "baited opener" (p. 116)—a vivid image of somebody cruising down the sidewalk under earphones (See page 73 for the final version.)

As for editorial revisions, Janet worked chiefly on problems her instructor had spotted in earlier papers. For example:

PROBLEM	ORIGINAL	REVISED
exaggerated language, sarcasm	x No doubt it is glorious to be surrounded by one's favorite music (however awful) all day. . . .	● No doubt it is pleasant to be surrounded by one's favorite music all day. . . .
comma faults	x The quality of sound, as I discovered when I once borrowed a set for thirty seconds is extra-ordinary. People who should know, claim that the reproduction	● [add comma after *seconds*; remove comma after *know*]
faulty parallelism	x is as faithful as an ex-pensive home stereo	● . . . as faithful as that of an expensive . . .

And since she knew that her main liability was wordiness, Janet worked to tighten her phrasing throughout the essay. For example:

FIRST DRAFT:

```
But what worries me the most about the people who wear
headphones is their indifference to other people--an
indifference that probably has some political effects,
too.  Even when he or she is doing something as active
as running or skiing, the person who is wearing the
speakers has retreated within a cozy space that is
shut off from the real-life situations and needs of
other people.  The same holds true if the headset is
being worn on a city street.  Perhaps the street is
full of old people, or sick people, or crazy people.
It wouldn't matter who they are--workers, people out
```

```
on strike, immigrants, or whoever. It would be as if
they weren't there at all. For all that the headset
wearer knows or cares, World War III could be start-
ing!
```

REVISED:

```
What worries me most about the headphone wearers is
their social--and therefore also political--indiffer-
ence. Even when running or skiing, the person sand-
wiched between the speakers has retreated within a
cozy space, insulated from the claims of other people
and their problems. That space remains just as pri-
vate on a city street, where no one--not the old or
the sick or the crazy, not workers or strikers or im-
migrants or beggars--can interrupt the programmed
mood. If the city is decaying, if depression or race
war is just around the corner, what does it matter?
One can always raise the volume if the world's trou-
bles approach too near.
```

For a title, Janet had expected to use either "Personal Convenience versus Social Concern" or "Stereo Headsets: Symbol of an
Indifferent Age." The second seemed better because it was more
definite, but neither of them sounded especially lively. Reading
through a draft, Janet ran across something more promising, the
phrase "head tripper." What about "The New Head Trippers" for a
title? It might whet the reader's interest, set an informal tone, hint at
Janet's disapproval of the stereo fad, and refer both to headgear and to
portability.

Here is Janet's essay as submitted.

Janet Stein

English 1A, sec. 2

Mr. Peterson

February 20, 1989

THE NEW HEAD TRIPPERS

Most of us by now have had the experience of
coming across a friend or acquaintance dreamily
tuned in to a stereo headset as she weaves through
a crowd of pedestrians. We are glad to recognize
Sally, as I will call her; we slow down, smile, and
prepare a greeting. But Sally, though she is looking our way, sees nothing at all. She is on automatic pilot, avoiding the other walkers by a kind
of radar that never requires her eyes to focus. And
suddenly we change our mind about saying hello to
her. To take Sally away from her tapes--assuming we
could get her attention at all--would be as intru-
sive as waking her with a midnight phone call or
dropping in to share her dinner. We pass by, disappointed and vaguely bothered.

And perhaps vaguely envious as well. For, unless we happen to have a headset of our own, we can
only imagine how agreeable it must be for Sally to
occupy a movable cocoon of rock music or Beethoven
or language lessons. Sally has missed out on a
small personal encounter, but so what? She has
found a way of turning "nothing" time into pleasure
or learning. Isn't that better than having some
trivial chitchat on the sidewalk?

Let us admit it: those little tape players are
a marvel. The quality of sound, as I discovered
when I once borrowed a set for thirty seconds, is
extraordinary. People who should know claim that
the reproduction is as faithful as that of an expensive home stereo. In fact, if you want sheer
music without distraction or irrelevant noise,
you might do better to play tapes on your headset
than to attend the finest live concert.

Though Sally may risk being run over in the
intersection, she is not threatening or endangering

Stein 3

anyone else. Indeed, she makes a favorable contrast
with the brash kid who climbs aboard a bus with his
giant hand-held stereo box turned all the way up.
He may be looking for trouble; at the very least he
is trying to impose his music on a captive audience. But Sally is the very picture of somebody
minding her own business. Why, then, is there something unsettling about watching her electronic
trance?

I can only answer for myself. For all I know,
I may be the only person in the world to find this
wonder of technology a little scary. But even very
enjoyable novelties can have negative consequences
for the society as a whole. Many informed experts
now consider television, for all its obvious benefits, to be such a mixed blessing, and video games
may offer a less debatable example. Surely there is
something a little flabby and weird about a mass
passion for shooting down little figures of space-
ships that appear on idiotically beeping screens.

To me, the tiny stereos look like a similar development. In particular, I am worried about three
implications of the headset vogue: a growing
dependency on artificial means of staying calm,
decreased contact with reality, and a corresponding
shrinkage of concern for other people.

First, the matter of dependency. No doubt it
is pleasant to be surrounded by one's favorite music all day, but I wonder if the experience isn't
addictive. To be constantly under the earphones in
the midst of other activities seems rather like
having to pop "happy pills" to keep one's sanity or
good temper. What becomes of the headset junkies
when they are stranded without their fix? I suspect
that they are left more fidgety than they were before Sony or Sanyo came to their aid. The possibility is worth looking into, anyway.

Second, as you could tell from seeing her
glazed expression, Sally is not exactly alert to
new experience. In a literal sense she has become a

head tripper, tuning out whatever may be fresh or
unpredictable in her environment while she strolls
to the beat of tapes that are totally, soothingly
familiar. She is turning life into a movie with
background music--but there is a revealing difference. In the movies, the music builds appropriate
excitement or emotion for a significant action. For
Sally, in contrast, the music <u>is</u> the action; reality will get through to her only when it is compatible with her mental Muzak.

But what worries me most about the headphone
wearers is their social--and therefore political--
indifference. Even when running or skiing, the person sandwiched between the speakers has retreated
within a cozy space, insulated from the claims of
other people and their problems. That space remains
just as private on a city street, where no one--not
the old or the sick or the crazy, not workers or
strikers or immigrants or beggars--can interrupt
the programmed mood. If the city is decaying, if

depression or race war is just around the corner,
what does it matter? One can always raise the
volume if the world's troubles approach too near.

Of course I am overdramatizing here; we are
not yet a nation of callous zombies. Furthermore,
for all I know, the movable cocoon may be more a
symptom than a cause of isolation. Let me admit the
point but still insist that even as symbolism, the
image of the musically tranquilized citizen, aloof
from everything except that steady tapping on the
cranium, tells us something unsettling about the
times we live in. Not long ago, the latest toy was
CB radio--a means of communicating, even when there
was nothing much to say. If we have been living in
the self-absorbed era of the head tripper, those
who wear the sets are not the only ones who will
want to put this period out of mind as soon as it
is over.

II
PARAGRAPHS

Paragraphs

Once you have mastered paragraph form, you have an invaluable means of keeping your reader's interest and approval. Although each sentence conveys meaning, an essay or paper or report is not a sequence of sentences but a development of one leading point through certain steps of presentation. Those steps are, or ought to be, paragraphs.

The sentences within an effective paragraph support and extend one another in the service of a single unfolding idea, just as the paragraphs themselves work together to make the thesis persuasive. In key respects, then, you can think of the paragraph as a mini-essay. Like the full essay, a typical paragraph

1. *presents one main idea;*

2. *conveys thoughts that are connected both by logical association and by word signals;*

3. *often reveals its main idea in a prominent statement, usually but not always toward the start;*

4. *usually supports or illustrates that idea;*

5. *may also deal with objections or limitations to that idea, but without allowing the objections to assume greater importance than the idea itself; and*

6. *may begin or end more generally, taking an expanded view of the addressed topic.*

In one sense, nothing could be easier than to form paragraphs; you simply indent the first word of a sentence by five spaces. But those indentions must match real divisions in your developing thought if you are to keep your reader's respectful attention. All readers sense that a new paragraph signals a shift: a new subject, a new idea, a change in emphasis, a new speaker, a different time or place, or a change in the level of generality. By observing such natural breaks and by signaling in one paragraph how it logically follows from the preceding one, you can turn the paragraph into a powerful means of communication.

6 Paragraph Unity and Continuity

6a Highlight your leading idea.

As a rule, every effective paragraph has a leading idea to which all other ideas in the paragraph are logically related. A reader of your essays or papers should be able to tell, in any paragraph, which is the **main sentence** (often called *topic sentence*)—the sentence containing that one central point to be supported or otherwise developed in the rest of the paragraph.

It is true that in some prose—for example, descriptions, narratives, and the parts of a report that present data or run through the steps of an experimental procedure—many paragraphs contain no single sentence that stands out as the main, controlling one. Such a paragraph can be said to have an implied main sentence: "This is the way it was," or "These are the procedures that were followed." But in college essays and term papers that call for analysis and argument (p. 30, 3b), you should try to see that each paragraph contains not only a leading idea but an easily identified main sentence as well.

We will see (Chapter 7) that a main sentence can occur anywhere in a paragraph if the other sentences are properly subordinate to it. More often than not, however, a main sentence comes at or near the beginning, as in this student example:

> Walt Whitman's "A Noiseless Patient Spider" is built on a comparison of the poet's soul to a spider. Both of them, he says, stand isolated, sending something from inside themselves into the surrounding empty space; in their obviously different ways they are both reaching for *connection*. Whitman does not say what the spiritual connection may be, except that

his soul hopes to find "the spheres to connect" the "measureless oceans of space" out there. He is vague—but so is the unknown realm toward which he yearns.

The heart of this paragraph is its opening sentence, which reveals the leading idea: Whitman's poem is built on a comparison of the poet's soul to a spider. Reread the other three sentences and you will see that each of them contributes to that leading idea, remaining within its organizing control.

¶ un
6b

6b Keep to your point.

A paragraph can include negative as well as positive considerations, but it should never "change its mind," canceling one point with a flatly contrary one.

DO:

- A. The seepage of dioxin into a community's water supply always terrifies everyone once it has been discovered. Citizens naturally expect the Environmental Protection Agency and the guilty industry to remove the source of risk as soon as possible. Unfortunately, however, this chemical is so incredibly toxic in small doses that decades may pass before the threat to public health is truly over.

DON'T:

x B. The seepage of dioxin into a community's water supply always terrifies everyone once it has been discovered. Citizens naturally expect the Environmental Protection Agency and the guilty industry to remove the source of risk as soon as possible. Yet many people react to the crisis quite calmly, refusing to worry about cancer, birth defects, and other proven results of contact with dioxin.

Each of these paragraphs ends with a sentence that "goes against" the preceding two sentences. In paragraph A, however, there is no contradiction; the writer simply turns from one aspect of the dioxin problem (citizens' demand for a speedy solution) to a more serious aspect (long-term toxicity). But in paragraph B the writer says two *incompatible* things: that everyone is alarmed and that some people are not alarmed. The writer of paragraph B could eliminate the contradiction by rewriting the opening sentence:

- The seepage of dioxin into a community's water supply provokes mixed reactions once it has been discovered. Citizens naturally expect the Environmental Protection Agency and the guilty industry to remove the source of risk as soon as possible. Yet many people react to the crisis quite calmly, refusing to worry about cancer, birth defects, and other proven results of contact with dioxin.

¶ un
6c

A paragraph that shows strong internal continuity (6d), hooking each new sentence into the one before it, can cover a good deal of ground without appearing disunified. Every sentence, however, should bear some relation to the leading idea—either introducing it, stating it, elaborating it, asking a question about it, supporting it, raising a doubt about it, or otherwise reflecting on it. A sentence that does none of those things is a **digression**—a deviation. Just one digression within a submitted paragraph may be enough to sabotage its effectiveness.

Suppose, for example, paragraph A on dioxin contained this sentence: *The Environmental Protection Agency, like the Federal Communications Commission, is an independent body.* Even though that statement deals with the EPA, which does figure in the paragraph, it has no bearing on the paragraph's leading idea: that dioxin can remain hazardous for decades. Thus the statement amounts to a digression. Unless the writer decided to shift to a different leading idea, the digression would have to be eliminated in a later draft.

6c Give your leading idea the last word.

If it is sometimes useful to include statements that limit the scope of a paragraph's leading idea or that raise objections to it (pp. 96–98, 7b), you should never *end* a paragraph with such a statement. Final positions are naturally emphatic. If your last sentence takes away from the main idea, you will sound indecisive or uncomfortable, and the paragraph will lack emphasis.

INDECISIVE:

x A. One reason for the recent popularity of Hollywood autobiographies must surely be the decline of serious fiction about important, glamorous people. We know that readers crave intimacy with the great, and we also know that modern novelists have ignored that craving. What people no longer get from fiction, they now seek in true confessions from Tinseltown. Of course, other factors must be at work as well; literary fads are never produced by single causes.

FIRM:

• B. One reason for the recent popularity of Hollywood autobiographies must surely be the decline of serious fiction about important, glamorous people. Of course, other factors must be at work as well; literary fads are never produced by single causes. But we do know that readers crave intimacy with the great, and we also know that modern novelists have ignored that craving. What people no longer get from fiction, they now seek in true confessions from Tinseltown.

Notice that these paragraphs say the same thing but leave the reader with different impressions. Paragraph A trails off, as if the writer were having second thoughts about the leading idea. Paragraph B gets its "negative" sentence about *other factors* into a safely unemphatic position and then ends strongly, reinforcing the idea that was stated in the opening sentence. The confident treatment of an objection makes the paragraph supple rather than self-defeating.

PARAGRAPH CONTINUITY

6d Use one sentence to respond to the previous one.

To maintain **continuity,** or linkage between sentences or whole paragraphs, you need to write each new sentence with the previous one in mind. You want your reader to feel that one statement has grown naturally out of its predecessor—an effect that comes from picking up some element in that earlier sentence and taking it further.

If, for example, the most recent sentence in your draft reads *The economic heart of America has been shifting toward the Sunbelt,* you could maintain continuity in any of the following ways, depending on the point you wish to make:

- The economic heart of America has been shifting toward the Sunbelt. But how much longer will this trend continue? [Ask a question.]

¶
cont
6d

- The economic heart of America has been shifting toward the Sunbelt. The recent history of Buffalo, New York, is a case in point. [Illustrate your point.]

- The economic heart of America has been shifting toward the Sunbelt. It may be, however, that the country also has a quite different kind of heart—one that is not so easily moved. [Limit your point.]

- The economic heart of America has been shifting toward the Sunbelt. Without forgetting that trend, let us turn now to less obvious but possibly more important developments. [Provide a transition to the next idea.]

- The economic heart of America has been shifting toward the Sunbelt. If so, it can only be a matter of time before the moral or spiritual heart of the country is similarly displaced. [Reflect on your point; speculate.]

In short, reread the sentence you have just written and ask yourself, "All right, what follows from this?" What follows may be

1. a question (or further question);

2. an answer (if the sentence above is a question);

3. support or illustration of the point just made;

4. a limitation or objection to the point just made;

5. further support or illustration of an earlier point, or further limitation or objection to an earlier point;

6. a transition; or

7. a conclusion or reflection appropriate either to the sentence above or to the whole idea of the paragraph.

6e   Include signal words and phrases.

Though you may sometimes want to delay stating your paragraph's leading idea (pp. 96–100, 7b–c), you should never put your reader to the trouble of puzzling out hidden connections. By using unmistakable **signals of relation** from sentence to sentence, you can let the reader see at a glance that a certain train of thought is being started, developed, challenged, or completed.

¶
cont
6e

Those signals are chiefly words or phrases indicating exactly how a statement in one sentence relates to the statement it follows. The possible types of relation, along with examples of each type, are these:

CONSEQUENCE:
* therefore, then, thus, hence, accordingly, as a result

LIKENESS:
* likewise, similarly

CONTRAST:
* but, however, nevertheless, on the contrary, on the other hand, yet

AMPLIFICATION:
* and, again, in addition, further, furthermore, moreover, also, too

EXAMPLE:
* for instance, for example

CONCESSION:
* to be sure, granted, of course, it is true

INSISTENCE:
* indeed, in fact, yes, no

SEQUENCE:
* first, second, finally

RESTATEMENT:
* that is, in other words, in simpler terms, to put it differently

RECAPITULATION:
- in conclusion, all in all, to summarize, altogether

TIME OR PLACE:
- afterward, later, earlier, formerly, elsewhere, here, there, hither-to, subsequently, at the same time, simultaneously, above, below, farther on, this time, so far, until now

¶
cont
6e

Notice how a careful use of relational signals brings out the logical connectedness of sentences in the following student paragraph:

In the winter of 1973–74 drivers lined up all over America to fill their gas tanks. *But* it was not merely a question of a fifteen-minute wait and back on the road again. *On the contrary,* cars often began to congregate at dawn. *Similarly,* walkers appeared early on frigid mornings with an empty five-gallon can in one hand and a pint of steaming coffee in the other, determined to wait out the chill and avoid disappointment. Everybody had to wait. *As a result,* high-school kids took Saturday morning jobs as gas line sitters; spouses drove their mates to work and spent the rest of the day in line; and libraries had a surge of activity as people decided to catch up on their reading while waiting. *All in all,* Americans were at their best during that bizarre season, abiding by the new rules as if a place in the gas line had been guaranteed to everyone by the Bill of Rights.

In addition to signal words that show logical connections, you can gain continuity through words indicating that something already treated is still under discussion. Such signal words make sense only in relation to the sentence before.

PRONOUNS:
- Ordinary people know little about the causes of inflation. What *they* do know is that *they* must earn more every year to buy the *they* do know is that *they* must earn more every year to buy the same goods and services.

DEMONSTRATIVE ADJECTIVES:
- Mark Twain died in 1910. Since *that* date American literature has never been so dominated by one writer's voice.

REPEATED WORDS AND PHRASES:
- We should conserve fossil fuels on behalf of our descendants as

well as ourselves. Those *descendants* will curse us if we leave them without abundant sources of light and heat.

IMPLIED REPETITIONS:

- Some fifty Americans were trapped in the embassy when the revolution broke out. *Six more* managed to scramble onto the last helicopter that was permitted to land on the roof.

¶
cont
6f

One key word, repeated several times, can do much to knit a paragraph together. Thus in the following paragraph the name *Ottawa* (italicized here for emphasis) is artfully plucked out from other names.

Perhaps a visitor cannot truly understand the country until he has traveled from the genteel poverty of the Atlantic coast with its picturesque fishing villages and stiff towns through the Frenchness of sophisticated Quebec cities and rural landscapes, past the vigorous bustling Ontario municipalities and industrial vistas, over mile after mile of wheat fields between prairie settlements into the lush and spacious beauty of British Columbia; but he must also visit *Ottawa* and the House of Commons. *Ottawa* the stuffy, with its dull-looking houses, its blistering summer heat, its gray rainy afternoons; *Ottawa* the beautiful, on a snowy day when the government buildings stand tall and protective, warmly solid above the white landscape; on a sunny spring afternoon with the cool river winding below, and people moving easily through the clean streets, purposeful but not pushed. Even during the morning and evening traffic rushes, *Ottawa* seems to remain sane.

—EDITH IGLAUER, "The Strangers Next Door"

In the first sentence *Ottawa* belatedly emerges as the key name among several; it gains importance by being weighted singly against all the "travelogue" references before the semicolon. In the second sentence (or intentional sentence fragment) the name is used insistently and fondly. And the author exploits this effect in her final sentence, using the name yet again to reinforce her idea that Ottawa stands apart from the rest of Canada.

6f   Keep related sentences together.

You can serve continuity by keeping together sentences that all bear the same general relation to the paragraph's leading idea. To simplify, let us reduce all such relations to *support* and *limitation* (qualification). Sentences that support the leading idea by restating it, illustrating it, offering evidence for its truth, or expanding upon it belong in an uninterrupted sequence. So do all sentences that limit the leading idea by showing what it does *not* cover or by casting doubt on it.

Continuity is especially threatened when a paragraph contains two isolated sets of limiting sentences. To see why, examine the following draft paragraph:

¶
cont
6f

limitation	x Not many people would want to endure the lonely hours, the aches and pains, and the probable injuries awaiting anyone who trains seriously for a mara-
main sentence	thon. The pride, however, that comes from finishing one's first marathon makes all the struggle seem
limitation	worthwhile. But is it really worthwhile? What does running twenty-six miles in glorified underwear have to do with real life? But for veteran marathoners,
support	long-distance racing *is* real life, while all other claims on their time are distractions or nuisances.

Here the main sentence establishes a pro-marathon direction. But that direction is opposed twice in the course of the paragraph; the main sentence is hemmed in by qualifications, and the reader is bounced back and forth between "pro" and "con" points. Compare:

limitation	Not many people would want to endure the lonely hours, the aches and pains, and the probable injuries awaiting anyone who trains seriously for a marathon. Is all the effort worthwhile? More than once, no doubt, exhausted beginners must ask themselves what running twenty-six miles in glorified underwear has to do with real life.
main sentence	Yet the pride that comes from finishing one's first marathon makes all the struggle seem worthwhile. And for
support	veteran marathoners, long-distance running *is* real life, while all other claims on their time are distractions or nuisances.

Now the paragraph's shuffling between pros and cons has been replaced by *one* definitive pivot on the signal word *Yet*. One such turn per paragraph is the maximum you should allow yourself. To observe that principle, make sure that your limiting and supporting sentences remain within their own portions of the paragraph—with the limiting sentences first to keep them from "having the last word."

For further discussion of the kind of paragraph that pivots to its leading idea, see pages 96–98, 7b.

¶
cont
6g

6g   Create linkage through varied and repeated sentence structure.

A further means of making the sentences of a paragraph flow together is to give them some variety of structure. In particular, avoid an unbroken string of choppy sentences, each consisting of one statement unmarked by pauses (see p. 154, 12f).

Within certain limits, however, you can show continuity by *repeating* a sentence pattern. Those limits are that (a) only parts of paragraphs, not whole paragraphs, lend themselves comfortably to such effects, and (b) the sentences so linked must be parallel in meaning. When you want to make their association emphatic, you can give them the same form.

The following paragraph relates American history textbooks to a transformed society. Notice, in the elements we italicize, how the writer makes use of identical structures in two sentences to underscore the changes in America that have made history books less predictable than they used to be:

> But now the texts have changed, and with them the country that American children are growing up into. *The society that was once uniform is now* a patchwork of rich and poor, old and young, men and women, blacks, whites, Hispanics, and Indians. *The system that ran so smoothly* by means of the Constitution under the guidance of benevolent conductor Presidents *is now* a rattletrap affair. The past is no highway to the present; it is a collection of issues and events that do not fit together and that lead in no single direction.
>
> —FRANCES FITZGERALD, *America Revised: History Schoolbooks in the Twentieth Century*

Again, note how a critic of urban planning gains emphatic continuity through two sets of identical structures:

But look what we have built with the first several billions: Low-income projects that become worse centers of delinquency, vandalism and general social hopelessness than the slums they were supposed to replace. Middle-income housing projects which are truly marvels of dullness and regimentation, sealed against any buoyancy or vitality of city life. Luxury housing projects that mitigate their inanity, or try to, with a vapid vulgarity. Cultural centers that are unable to support a good bookstore. Civic centers that are avoided by everyone but bums, who have fewer choices of loitering place than others. Commercial centers that are lackluster imitations of standardized suburban chain-store shopping. Promenades that go from no place to nowhere and have no promenaders. Expressways that eviscerate great cities. This is not the rebuilding of cities. This is the sacking of cities.

  —JANE JACOBS, *The Death and Life of Great American Cities*

¶
cont
6h

  The body of this paragraph consists of intentional sentence fragments (p. 207, 16e), each of which takes its sense from the writer's opening words. *But look what we have built. . . .* An entirely different parallelism of structure brings the paragraph to its emphatic end: *This is not the rebuilding of cities. This is the sacking of cities.* The writer has risked annoying us with relentless hammer blows, but her shifting to a second variety of patterning prevents monotony.

6h Link one paragraph to the previous one.

Just as linked sentences help to establish the internal continuity of a paragraph, so linked paragraphs help to establish the continuity of a whole essay or paper. Of course your paragraphs must actually *be* logically connected, not just appear so. But once again you can bring out the connections through conjunctions like *but* or *yet* and through sentence adverbs and transitional phrases like *thus, however, in fact,* and *on the contrary.* And the linkage is surest of all in a paragraph whose first sentence refers directly to a point made in the previous sentence: *These problems, however, . . . ; Nevertheless, that argument can be answered;* and so forth.

  Note, for instance, how the sample essay about headsets on pages 73–78 frequently "answers" the end of one paragraph with the beginning of the next one:

We pass by, disappointed and vaguely bothered.
And perhaps vaguely envious as well. . . .

Why, then, is there something unsettling about watching her electronic trance?
I can only answer for myself. . . .

In particular, I am worried about three implications of the headset vogue: a growing dependency on artificial means of staying calm, decreased contact with reality, and a corresponding shrinkage of concern for other people.
First, the matter of dependency. . . .

For Sally, in contrast, the music *is* the action; reality will get through to her only when it is compatible with her mental Muzak.
But what worries me most about the headphone wearers is their social—and therefore political—indifference. . . .

One can always raise the volume if the world's troubles approach too near.
Of course I am overdramatizing here; we are not yet a nation of callous zombies. . . .

Enumeration

One rather formal but occasionally helpful way of linking paragraphs is to enumerate points that have been forecast at the end of the earlier paragraph. If you assert, for example, that there are three reasons for favoring a certain proposal or four factors that must be borne in mind, you can begin the paragraphs that follow with *First, . . . , Second, . . . ,* and so on.

6i   Link several related paragraphs in a block.

A relatively long essay typically develops in groups of paragraphs that address major points. Within each of these **paragraph blocks,** one paragraph will usually state the dominant idea and the others will develop it. A writer working, for example, from the "rent control" outline on page 45 might decide to introduce Part III, the heart of the argument, with a "thesis" paragraph marking a major shift in emphasis:

> Such is the promise that advocates of rent control offer to students who are weary of expensive housing and long trips to campus. If the promise could be even partially realized, it might be worth giving rent control another try. Unfortunately, there is no reason to think that another experiment would work better than all previous ones. However bad the present housing crisis is, you can be sure that rent control would make it worse.

Then four paragraphs, covering points A through D in the outline, would follow, making a single paragraph block about the disappointing results of rent control.

7 Paragraph Development

Most of the advice you may have seen about constructing paragraphs deals with just one kind of development, which we will call *direct* (7a). Direct paragraphs are indeed the most common type. Capable writers, however, also feel at home with other ways of putting a paragraph together. For simplicity's sake we will recognize three patterns—the *direct,* the *pivoting,* and the *suspended* paragraph. They illustrate classic ways of combining the types of sentences most frequently found in paragraphs:

1. a **main sentence,** which carries the paragraph's leading idea;

2. a **limiting sentence,** which "goes against" the leading idea by raising a negative consideration either before or after that idea has been stated; and

3. a **supporting sentence,** which backs or illustrates the leading idea.

7a   Master the direct pattern.

In a **direct paragraph,** the most usual pattern, you place the main sentence at or near the beginning, before you have mentioned any limiting (negative or qualifying) considerations. The "Whitman" paragraph (pp. 81–82), the second "Hollywood" paragraph (p. 84), the "Ottawa" paragraph (p. 88), the "history textbooks" paragraph (p. 90), and this present paragraph all exhibit the direct pattern. The folllowing example is typical:

There is a paradox about the South Seas that every visitor immediately discovers. Tropical shores symbolize man's harmony with a kind and bountiful nature. Natives escape the common vexations of modern life by simply relaxing. They reach into palms for coconuts, into the sea for fish, and into calabashes for poi. But when the tranquilized tourist reaches Hawaii, the paradise of the Pacific, he finds the most expensive resort in the world and a tourist industry that will relieve him of his traveler's checks with a speed and ease that would bring a smile to the lips of King Kamehameha.

¶ dev
7a

> —TIMOTHY E. HEAD. *Going Native in Hawaii: A Poor Man's Guide to Paradise*

Here the main sentence announces a *paradox*—that is, a seeming contradiction—and the rest of the paragraph consists of supporting or explanatory sentences that develop the two halves of that paradox, harmonious nature and commercial exploitation. The result is extreme clarity: the structure of the paragraph fulfills the promise given in the main sentence, and the reader feels guided by that structure at each moment.

Note that a direct paragraph, just like an essay whose thesis is stated near the outset, can comfortably include *limiting* considerations—those that "go against" the leading idea. In the following student paragraph, for example, the writer can afford to offer a "con" remark, which is placed strategically between the main sentence and two final sentences of support for that statement:

main sentence { The "greenhouse effect," whereby the temperature of the atmosphere rises with the increased burning of hydrocarbons, may have devastating consequences for our planet within one or two decades. Similar scares, it

limiting sentence { is true, have come and gone without leaving any lasting mark. Yet there is an important difference this time. We

supporting sentences { know a good deal more about the greenhouse effect and its likely results than we knew, say, about invasions from outer space or mutations from atomic bomb tests. The greenhouse effect is already under way, and there are very slender grounds for thinking it will be reversed or even slowed without a more sudden cataclysm such as all-out nuclear war.

Direct paragraphs, then, can follow two models, one including and one omitting limiting sentences:

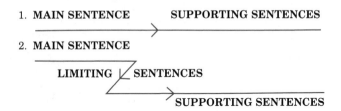

1. **MAIN SENTENCE**   **SUPPORTING SENTENCES**

2. **MAIN SENTENCE**

    LIMITING SENTENCES

        SUPPORTING SENTENCES

¶ dev
7b

Main sentence delayed

The main sentence in a direct paragraph need not be the first one; it must simply precede any limiting sentences. Note, for example, how the following student paragraph puts the main sentence second, after an introductory sentence that prepares for a shift of emphasis:

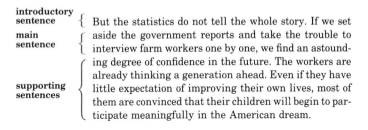

introductory sentence { But the statistics do not tell the whole story. If we set

main sentence { aside the government reports and take the trouble to interview farm workers one by one, we find an astound-

supporting sentences { ing degree of confidence in the future. The workers are already thinking a generation ahead. Even if they have little expectation of improving their own lives, most of them are convinced that their children will begin to participate meaningfully in the American dream.

7b   Master the pivoting pattern.

A **pivoting paragraph** not only delays the main sentence but begins by "going against it" with one or more limiting sentences. Characteristically, the pivoting paragraph then turns sharply ("pivots") toward the main sentence, usually announcing that shift of emphasis with a conspicuous signal word such as *but, yet,* or *however*. The leading idea, once announced, then dominates the rest of the paragraph. The opening paragraph of this chapter (p. 94) typifies the pattern. Its third sentence, containing the pivoting word *however,* reverses the paragraph's direction while stating the leading idea, which is then illustrated in the remaining sentences.

Notice how the following student paragraph pivots neatly on the word *But* and then develops its leading idea:

> **limiting sentence** { When we think of Gandhi fasting, plastering mud poultices on his belly, and testing his vow of continence by sharing a bed with his grand-niece, we can easily regard him as a fanatic who happened to be politically lucky.
>
> **pivot to the main sentence** { *But* the links between his private fads and his political methods turn out to be quite logical. Gandhi's pursuit of personal rigors helped him to achieve a rare degree of
>
> **supporting sentences** { discipline, and that discipline allowed him to approach political crises with extraordinary courage. The example of his self-control, furthermore, was contagious; it is doubtful that a more worldly man could have led millions of his countrymen to adopt the tactic of nonviolent resistance.

¶ dev
7b

Similarly, the classic pivoting signal *however* shows us that the third sentence of this next paragraph is making a reversal of emphasis:

> Health experts always seem to be telling Americans what *not* to eat. Cholesterol, salt and sugar are but a few of the dietary no-no's that threaten to make dinnertime about as pleasurable as an hour of push-ups. In a report last week on the role of nutrition in cancer, *however,* a blue-ribbon committee of the National Academy of Sciences offered a carrot—as well as oranges, tomatoes and cantaloupes—along with the usual admonitory stick. While some foods appear to promote cancer and should be avoided, said the panel, other comestibles may actually help ward off the disease.
>
> —MATT CLARK and MARY HAGER, "A Green Pepper a Day"

The further you venture from the direct pattern, the more important it is to guide your reader with signal words such as *but* or *however*. You can also make your pivot, if you prefer, by means of a whole sentence such as *That is no longer the case.* The next sentence can then state your leading idea. You can even pivot on something as small as a single italicized word, as in the following student paragraph:

**¶ dev
7c**

limiting
sentences

{ I don't usually like valet parking; in most cases, it is just
a pretentious attempt at fancifying a restaurant that
needs fancifying. In usual circumstances, people can

pivot to the
main
sentence

{ park on their own. Tesoro's Restaurant *needs* valet
parking. Cars are squeezed into its far from adequate

supporting
sentences

{ parking lot, leaving no space for opening a door wide
enough. Other cars make their own stalls and line the
residential streets. Neighborhood complaints about
blocked driveways are not uncommon, and it is not odd
at all to see ticketed cars cramped illegally close to
hydrants.

A scheme of the pivoting paragraph would look like this:

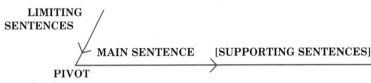

The brackets around "Supporting Sentences" indicate that a pivoting
paragraph can end with its main sentence. More commonly, though,
the main sentence is supported by one or more following sentences. In
pivoting paragraphs already used as sample passages, for instance,
the main sentence of the first "dioxin" paragraph (p. 82) comes at the
end, whereas the main sentence of the second "marathon training"
paragraph (p. 89) is followed by support. So are the main sentences of
the "Gandhi" and "nutrition" paragraphs just examined.

7c   Master the suspended pattern.

The final pattern that repays practice is the **suspended paragraph**—that is, a paragraph building to a climax or conclusion by
some means other than a sharp reversal of direction. In a suspended
paragraph the main sentence always comes at or near the end. Instead
of taking a sharp turn, like the pivoting paragraph, it moves from
discussion or exemplification to leading idea, maintaining the reader's

sentence-by-sentence interest until it arrives at a statement that brings things together at last:

DISCUSSION $\longrightarrow$ **MAIN SENTENCE**

Thus:

¶ dev
7c

discussion {
A man who once developed printed circuits for computers begs on street corners for enough coins to buy another bottle of cheap port. A woman whose husband walked out when she couldn't stop drinking at home sits stupefied on a park bench, nodding senselessly at passers-by. An anxious teenager raids her parents' liquor closet at every opportunity. These people, though they have never met, suffer from the same misfortune. If they were placed together in a room, each of them might recognize the others as alcoholics. Yet what they have most in common is their inability to see *themselves* as alcoholics—and this is the very worst

main sentence {
symptom of their disease. For until the alcoholic's self-deception can be broken down, not even the most drastic cure has a chance of success.

Or again:

discussion {
In the early fourteenth century, northern Europe was subjected to a terrible famine. Meanwhile, economic instability caused whole kingdoms to go bankrupt. Then in 1348–50 the worst plague in history ravaged the Continent, killing perhaps half the population. It is little wonder, therefore,

main sentence {
that this was a period of profound social and political unrest; the supposedly stable order of feudalism had proved helpless to cope with various forms of disaster.

Looking back on the "discussion" sentences in these paragraphs, we could regard them as providing support for the leading idea. But we cannot perceive a sentence as "supporting" if we have not yet been told what it supports. By withholding that information until the end, the suspended paragraph establishes itself as the most dramatic pattern as well as the hardest to manage.

Once you feel at ease with the suspended paragraph, you will find it especially useful as a means of introducing or concluding an essay

(Chapter 9). An opening paragraph that ends with its main sentence—a sentence revealing either your topic or your thesis—can gradually awaken the reader's interest and eagerness to move ahead. And a suspended final paragraph allows you to finish your essay with a "punch line"—an excellent tactic if you have saved a strong point for the end.

¶ dev
7d

7d Keep to a manageable paragraph length.

There is no single "right" size for all paragraphs. In newspaper reporting, where the purpose is to communicate information with a minimum of analysis, paragraphs consist of one, two, or three sentences at the most. Paragraphs of dialogue also tend to be short; most writers indent for every change of speaker. So, too, scientific and technical journals favor relatively brief paragraphs that present facts and figures with little rhetorical development. And essayists vary considerably among themselves, both in their preference for short or long typical paragraphs and in the paragraph sizes they use within a given essay.

Even so, it is possible to tell at a glance whether your essay paragraphs fall within an acceptable range. If you hardly ever write paragraphs of more than three brief sentences, you are erring on the side of choppiness. Readers will suspect that you have no great interest in exploring your ideas. And if your typical paragraph occupies nearly all of a typewritten, double-spaced page, you are being long-winded, making your reader work too hard to retain the connection between one leading idea and the next. The goal is to show careful sentence-by-sentence thought within a paragraph without allowing the main sentence to lose its prominence.

Avoiding the choppy paragraph

If you have a tendency to write brief, stark paragraphs in which the main sentence is accompanied by just one or two other short sentences, reread one of your main sentences and ask yourself what else a reader might want to know about its implications. Do any of its terms need explaining? Where does it lead? What questions or objections does it call to mind? The new statements thus generated can become supporting or limiting sentences (p. 94) that will flesh out the skeleton of your draft paragraph.

Suppose, for example, your draft paragraph looks like this.

¶ dev
7d

CHOPPY DRAFT PARAGRAPH:
Acid rain has been destroying the forests of Canada. Although it blows northward from the United States, no one is sure that American factories are the only guilty ones. The damage is extensive, and it may take a court case to find out who is liable.

To gather material for a more developed paragraph, ask yourself what else your reader might profit from knowing:

—*What questions might be asked about acid rain?* What is it? Is the damage irreversible? Can it be prevented?

—*What objections might be raised to the charge that American factories are responsible for destroying the forests of Canada*? Are there other causes? Are American factory emissions mixed with those from Canada itself?

—*Where does the issue of acid rain lead*? For example, to questions of legal liability for "pollution at a distance"?

Your revised, adequately developed paragraph might look like this:

ADEQUATELY DEVELOPED PARAGRAPH:
American factories, we are told, have been discharging atmospheric wastes that drift northward and fall on Canada as acid rain, destroying valuable forests. We cannot yet tell for certain how extensive the damage is, whether it is irreversible, and whether the pollution could be effectively stopped at its source. Indeed, we cannot be sure that American factories are the only guilty ones. Yet there is little reason to doubt that those factories are the primary source of acid rain and that the damage being caused is very considerable. If so, a landmark case of liability for "pollution at a distance" would seem to be in the offing.

Avoiding the bloated paragraph

If you see that your draft essay or paper contains a bloated paragraph—one that goes on and on without a strong sense of purpose—
seek out its main sentence. If you cannot find it, decide what you want
your leading idea to be. As soon as you are sure you have a leading
idea, check to see that every sentence has some bearing on it. In some
cases your long paragraph will split neatly into two new ones, but
you should never indent for a fresh paragraph without verifying that
both units are internally complete.

Many draft paragraphs begin purposefully but bloat as the writer
gets absorbed in details.

BLOATED DRAFT PARAGRAPH:

limiting sentence { 1. If a person feels guilty about something, the obvious thing to do is to get that guilt out in the open. 2. But many people take a different approach, one that only makes **main sentence** matters worse: they try to stifle their bad feelings by means of depressants or stimulants such as alcohol, Methedrine, or marijuana. 3. A friend of mine felt guilty about getting low grades. 4. Her solution was to stay high nearly all the time. 5. But of course that made her get even lower grades and it thus redoubled her guilt, so she had even more bad feelings to hide in smoke. 6. I tried to talk to her about her problems, but she was already too depressed **supporting sentences** to allow anyone to get through to her. 7. Finally, she left school. 8. I lost touch with her, and I never did learn whether she straightened herself out. 9. I think that people like her deserve a lot of pity, because if she hadn't been so sensitive in the first place, she wouldn't have had the guilt feelings that sent her into a tailspin. 10. People who just don't care are sometimes better off.

This begins as a competent pivoting paragraph, contrasting two
approaches to the problem of handling guilty feelings and providing
an example of the second, self-defeating, approach. The momentum,
however, begins to drag as the writer shifts attention to herself in
sentence 6, and the paragraph falls apart completely at sentence 9,
which escapes the control of the main sentence, number 2. Revising for

economy and relevance, the writer decided to do without the sentences about herself and her compassionate attitude.

ADEQUATELY FOCUSED PARAGRAPH:

limiting sentence { If a person feels guilty about something, the obvious thing to do is to get that guilt out in the open. But many people

main sentence { take a different approach—one that only makes matters worse. They try to stifle their bad feelings with stimulants

supporting sentences { or depressants such as alcohol, Methedrine, or marijuana. A friend of mine, for example, feeling guilty about her low grades, tried to stay high nearly all the time. The result was that she got even worse grades, felt guiltier still, smoked even more dope, and eventually dropped out of school. Her supposed remedy had become a major part of her problem.

¶ **dev 7d**

After establishing a middle-sized paragraph as your norm, you can depart from the norm with good effect. A reader who comes across a somewhat longer paragraph will know that a particularly complex point is being developed. Occasionally, you can insert a very short paragraph—a sentence or two, or even a purposeful sentence fragment—to make a major transition, a challenge, an emphatic statement, or a summary. A "punchy" one-sentence paragraph can create a particularly impressive turn or decisive assertion. The emphasis comes precisely from the contrast between the short paragraph and the more developed ones surrounding it. For examples, look at the "dinosaur" and "sanity" passages on pages 118 and 120.

8 Paragraph Functions

In Chapter 7 we considered the *direction* of paragraph development: forward from an opening main sentence in a **direct paragraph**, taking one tack and then an opposite one in a **pivoting paragraph**, and leading to a conclusion in a **suspended paragraph** (pp. 94–100, 7a–c). Gaining control of those three patterns can allow you to adapt your paragraph structure to the kind of emphasis you find desirable at any point in an essay.

Another, more traditional, way of mastering paragraphs is to familiarize yourself with typical functions that they serve, trying your hand at each type. With a minimum of general discussion, we here offer and comment on sample paragraphs illustrating eight common functions. With or without your instructor's guidance, you can sharpen your sense of paragraph structure by studying and emulating the following examples.

8a Create a vivid description.

It was an unattractive low-rent building in the Winter Hill section of Somerville. A strange exterior of deteriorating shingles, tarpaper, peeling clapboard, and weathered plywood gave the house a haunted look. When my young daughter and I moved in, the outer doors were never locked and the back hall was filled with old chairs and underbrush. In our apartment the ceilings were peeling, wallpaper buckled off the walls, and a mouse lived behind the stove. There were code violations too numerous to count. But light streamed in through the windows. It warmed the rooms, created brilliant patterns on the floor, made our

houseplants thrive. When the sun was out it was easy to understand why
this had once been the most beautiful house in the neighborhood.

—BEVERLY BELFER, "Stealing the Light"

Good descriptions are supposed to provide concrete details, and this
one comes up with them—*deteriorating shingles, tarpaper, peeling
clapboard,* and so on. But details alone cannot guarantee a strong
effect. You should also try to orchestrate your reader's responses in a
purposeful, coherent way. Note how Belfer's paragraph progresses
from the "bad news" to the "good news"—from unattractiveness to
beauty, from a depressing scene to an exhilarating one.

¶
func
8a

Imagine Banyan Street first, because Banyan is where it happened. The
way to Banyan is to drive west from San Bernardino out Foothill Bou-
levard, Route 66: past the Santa Fe switching yards, the Forty Winks
Motel. Past the motel that is nineteen stucco tepees: "SLEEP IN A WIG-
WAM—GET MORE FOR YOUR WAMPUM." Past Fontana Drag City and the
Fontana Church of the Nazarene and the Pit Stop A Go-Go; past Kaiser
Steel, through Cucamonga, out to the Kapu Kai Restaurant-Bar and
Coffee Shop, at the corner of Route 66 and Carnelian Avenue. Up Carnelian Avenue from the Kapu Kai, which means "Forbidden Seas," the
subdivision flags whip in the harsh wind. "HALF-ACRE RANCHES!
SNACK BARS! TRAVERTINE ENTRIES! $95 DOWN." It is the trail of an
intention gone haywire, the flotsam of the New California. But after a
while the signs thin out on Carnelian Avenue, and the houses are no
longer the bright pastels of the Springtime Home owners but the faded
bungalows of the people who grow a few grapes and keep a few chickens
out here, and then the hill gets steeper and the road climbs and even the
bungalows are few, and here—desolate, roughly surfaced, lined with
eucalyptus and lemon groves—is Banyan Street.

—JOAN DIDION, "Some Dreamers of the Golden Dream"

Accomplished descriptive writers can set a mood or make a social comment simply through their shrewd choice of details. In this instance
the comment appears in so many words—*it is the trail of an intention
gone haywire*—but the reader has already reached that same conclusion by the time it gets stated. Note as well that the passage
follows two unifying principles of organization: a *narrative progres-
sion,* as the reader is taken on a fantasy ride to a destination, and a
contrast, whereby the feverish, vulgar commercial development that

spewed forth the Pit Stop A Go-Go yields to the desolation of Banyan Street. Would it surprise you, by the way, to learn that Didion's essay is about a bizarre murder case?

¶
func
8b

8b Recount an event.

One of my earliest memories, from about four, is of my older brother and younger sister experimenting with matches. "They shouldn't be doing that," I thought. Sure enough, the kitchen curtain caught fire. There was smoke, flames; my mother came home in the nick of time and doused the fire with pots of water. When it was over she demanded, "What happened?" My brother and sister pointed fingers at each other. "I didn't do anything," I kept telling her. Finally she said, "I know, cookie, I know you didn't." The question years later is, *Why* didn't I do anything? Why was I such a goody-goody? Was I good because I chose to be or because I was too timid, too programmed, to do otherwise?

— PHILIP LOPATE, "Tests of Weakness: Samson and Delilah"

The story of the fire that he didn't cause has become important to this writer's sense of his early identity. Rather than head at once into a discussion of his "goody-goody" years, he engages us in an efficiently told narrative and *then,* when he knows he has caught our interest, raises the general question he has had in mind from the outset.

On the morning of August 7, 1987, a battery of emergency X-rays was run in the diagnostic unit of Executive Health Examiners in Manhattan. Five men nervously waited outside the twenty-first-floor radiology room while technicians inside went through their paces. When the film was processed, the pictures were snapped onto a light box for study. The X-rays were negative. Everyone breathed a collective sigh of relief. New York Mets third baseman Howard Johnson's bat was indeed a solid piece of wood.

— DAN GUTMAN, "The Physics of Foul Play"

Every good story has a point or a punch line. In this **baited opener** (p. 116, 9b), the writer is careful to save his secret for the end. It is, of course, a total surprise; up to the last sentence we have been expecting a medical diagnosis rather than one relating to "doctored" baseball bats.

8c   Illustrate a point with details.

Like all great work, *The Canterbury Tales* speaks differently to us at different ages. Rereading the tales after twenty years, I found some aspects less meaningful—for example, the hot astrology tips—and others much more so. This time, it occurred to me that the Merchant's diatribes against women from Eve on down might refer to me. This time, perhaps because I have children, the tale of patient Griselda—whose husband tests her by making her think that her children are dead and then threatens to divorce her and marry their daughter—revealed itself in all its true horror, and I was greatly relieved by Chaucer's caveat, at the end, warning husbands and wives against trying such ordeals by psychotorture on their own.

> —FRANCINE PROSE, "Naughty, Bawdy, and Wise—
> A Valentine for Chaucer"

¶
func
8c

Note how all the reflections in this paragraph give substance, and therefore interest, to the writer's opening statement that Chaucer's book "speaks differently to us at different ages."

The commonplace observation Europeans make about Americans is that we have not outgrown childhood. Crucial adult habits like discretion, and habits of mind like indirection, do not seem to take hold. These are less appealing to us than openness, directness, self-revelation—the way of kids. In middle age, on airplanes, in bars, along beaches, we introduce ourselves to a stranger, then provide an immediate autobiographical sketch; and, if he or she is still listening a half-hour later, we offer a complete tour of the psychic peaks and valleys of our lives. And we expect nothing less in return: Are you married? Divorced? What do you do for a living? Like it? Are you happy? Tell me, *honestly.*

> —RICHARD SENNETT, "A Republic of Souls:
> Puritanism and the American Presidency"

Here again an opening generalization sets the stage for a paragraph that is rich in pertinent detail. In this case, however, the writer concentrates those details within one imagined situation, the typical American's encounter with a stranger. Note how the paragraph, without ever saying so, manages to imply that our *psychic peaks and valleys* may not be as high or deep as we suppose.

8d Support a point with reasons.

Not only is putting the most difficult skill in the game, it's by far the most important. If par for a course is 72 strokes, 36 of those strokes are allotted for putts. Thus a round is evenly divided between putting and all the other skills combined that are needed to move a ball from tee to green. Further, from the standpoint of scoring, sinking a putt is always worth more than hitting a perfect drive or lofting a lovely iron. Every time you sink a putt you save a stroke; for all the brilliance of a drive or an approach, what you earn is a leg up on your next shot, which won't necessarily be worth a thing on the scorecard. Another way of saying this is that putting is important because it comes last. "You can recover from a bad shot," notes Chi Chi Rodriguez, the former P.G.A. player who dominated the senior tour last year. "But you can't recover from a bad putt."

—PETER DE JONGE, "When the Putting Goes Bad"

This paragraph begins with an assertion that could provoke disagreement. Consequently, the writer follows it with observations that all go to show the correctness of that first idea. Notice how, after presenting his reasons for regarding a putt as the most important golf stroke, he clinches the point with an apt quotation from someone whose authority cannot be doubted.

Not surprisingly, over the past thirty years the elderly's standard of living has improved faster than that of younger people. Quite apart from the significant increase in Social Security benefits and their protection from erosion by inflation, the Supplemental Security Income in effect guarantees them a minimum income; national health insurance is provided through Medicare; and special tax privileges protect their assets in retirement. They even receive discounts on movie and bus tickets, and much more. All of these entitlements are available to the elderly regardless of need. And while claiming that their own benefits are beyond challenge, locally the old organize to oppose tax hikes to pay for school bonds and other desirable social policies.

—HENRY FAIRLIE, "Talkin' 'bout My Generation"

Most of us have always assumed that the elderly are, in the aggregate, worse off financially than the young. Since this writer disagrees, he feels obliged to back up his opening claim with examples that justify it.

8e Draw a comparison or contrast.

> During the last half-century, we have been teaching the sciences as though they were the same collection of academic subjects as always, and—here is what has really gone wrong—as though they would always be the same. Students learn today's biology, for example, the same way we learned Latin when I was in high school long ago: first, the fundamentals; then, the underlying laws; next, the essential grammar and, finally, the reading of texts. Once mastered, that was that: Latin was Latin and forever after would always be Latin. History, once learned, was history. And biology was precisely biology, a vast array of hard facts to be learned as fundamentals, followed by a reading of the texts.
>
> —LEWIS THOMAS, "The Art of Teaching Science"

Here the writer *compares* the way science is now usually taught with the way all subjects used to be taught; nothing fundamental has changed, he says. Can you guess where his essay is headed from here? He has prepared us to be shown that the changing nature of science requires corresponding changes in the way it is taught.

> That Hawthorne and Melville couldn't be friends for long is hardly amazing. What is surprising is that they ever got along at all. Melville, if I can believe what I have read by and about him, was outgoing and expansive; Hawthorne was retiring and quiet. Hawthorne worked in an established, genteel mode of fiction, but Melville longed to create extravagant new forms. And Melville, unlike his companion, had daring ideas about the ultimate purpose of the universe and the nature of good and evil. If Hawthorne had anything of the religious seeker in him, he did a good job of keeping it to himself.

Since this student writer wants to draw a maximum *contrast* between two classic American authors, she organizes her paragraph as a "shuttle" between the two, bringing out a new difference with each new pairing. Note how the variety of her sentence structure prevents this technique from becoming monotonous.

8f Analyze causes or effects.

> In recent decades the reported death rate from cancer has been rising dramatically. How alarmed should we be by this statistical change? One

¶
func
8f

cause of the mounting curve is probably the simple fact that we are more conscious of cancer now than we used to be, and less ashamed to mention the feared disease. Another cause may be the fact that more and more people are dying in hospitals and undergoing autopsies: in earlier times the comparable deaths at home from cancer might have been attributed to "old age." But factors like these take us only so far. Eventually we have to admit that cancer has been gaining on us in an absolute sense. If so, the real causes must be environmental: the continued increase in smoking, the use of dangerous pesticides and food additives, and increased pollution from automobiles and industry. Some of those causes must be more responsible than others, but until we know more than we do, we had better give urgent attention to all of them.

This student writer, asking herself why the death statistics for cancer have kept going up, avoids the trap of simply offering a routine list of causes. Instead, she has sorted possible causes into insignificant and fundamental ones. Observe how she places the least important factors first, leaving the substantial ones for the naturally stronger late position.

In the next paragraph, a student writer attempts to correlate a popular dance style of the 1970s with other characteristics of that decade:

The clearest example of all is provided by disco dancing, which became a national craze in 1978. For several reasons disco was the perfect expression of the decade that produced it. For one thing, the seventies combined a rediscovery of "roots" with an easing of the racial tensions that were so explosive in the sixties. Disco was black and Latin in its origins, and it remained somewhat ethnic in flavor, yet it was accepted by the whole society. Second, disco was a high-technology form; its amplified sounds and its dazzling lights suggested the network of electronics that many people had come to think of as their real environment. Third, disco expressed "the me decade" because it demanded physical fitness and because it emphasized display. And finally, disco was more disciplined than the do-your-own-thing dances of the sixties. Disco swept the country at a time when nearly everyone who had once joined "the counterculture" was ready to give order a second chance.

Observe that in this passage, cause-and-effect reasoning merely *associates* a complex of factors with a certain result. The writer wisely refrains from risking everything on only one of four possible sources of the 1970s' disco craze—the emphases on race, technology, self, and discipline.

8g Clarify the meaning of a key term or concept.

We often hear today that police should be concentrating on violent offenses instead of wasting so much time, effort, and taxpayers' money on so-called victimless crime. This seems like a fine idea; nobody, after all, would want an officer to make a possession-of-marijuana arrest while a rape or murder was occurring across the street. But what exactly *is* a "victimless" crime? Are there no victims when pimps, prostitutes, and drug pushers take over the streets of a residential neighborhood, confining the fearful citizens to their homes at night? I too am against the prosecution of truly victimless "crimes"; I don't regard them as crimes at all. But let's be clear about our terms. For me, *victimless* means that the act in question produces *neither direct nor indirect* victims. If this meaning of the term is understood, the whole issue of victimless crime loses its air of simplicity and righteousness.

This student writer puts a definition to work in behalf of her argument for a crackdown on prostitution and drug dealing. Note how this tactic differs from the pathetic "dictionary opener" (p. 121, 9g)—the uncalled-for definition whose only function is to get the flow of words running. In the paragraph above, the writer prepares us with careful reasoning for her crucial definition of victimless crime, first showing us why a definition is necessary at all: without it, only a superficial and distorted view of the problem would be possible.

In order to have any hope of holding down the population in countries that already lack food, shelter, and employment for many of their present citizens, we must first recognize the components of the problem. To begin with, population growth is not simply a matter of more births; it is also a matter of fewer deaths, thanks largely to advances in health care and emergency relief. Needless to say, we can hardly propose to aid these countries by restoring the old death rate! But recognizing that birth control is only part of the dilemma can spare us from becoming too easily discouraged when a campaign of birth control fails to stabilize a certain population completely.

To make an important concept clear, you usually don't have to resort to a full, dictionary-style definition of it. In this student paragraph, an advocate of international birth control serves her purpose by emphasizing two key aspects of the population problem, the birth rate and the death rate. She is then well situated to maintain in subsequent paragraphs that, since we can hardly aim at increasing the number of deaths, our only hope is to place limits on the number of births.

For another use of definition to make a complex explanation easier to grasp, see the next sample paragraph.

¶
func
8h

8h   Show the steps or parts that make up a whole.

Making a sound with a computer requires generating a sequence of binary numbers, called samples, that describes the sound's waveform: the air-pressure fluctuations of the sound as a function of time. The samples can then be made audible by converting them into a sequence of proportional voltages, "smoothing" and amplifying the stream of discrete voltages and sending the electrical signal to a loudspeaker. The number of samples the computer must generate for each second of sound, called the sampling rate, depends on the highest component frequency of the sound's air-pressure fluctuations. In particular, the sampling rate must be twice the highest component frequency. This, for most purposes, means that if a computer is to synthesize or transform a sound, it must be capable of generating or manipulating in one second between 16,000 and 40,000 samples, each of which can require a number of calculations.

—PIERRE BOULEZ and ANDREW GERZSO, "Computers in Music"

In technical or scientific writing, complex matters must often be reduced to their component steps through **process analysis.** The paragraph above saves its most specific, numerical, point for last, using other sentences to build up to it in a logical sequence. Note how the paragraph tucks in three vital definitions—of *samples* and *waveform* and *sampling rate*—at appropriate moments without losing its focus on the developing point.

There are three ways in which I am able to navigate and know where I am. First is pilotage. This simply involves using a special aviation topographical map: I look out the airplane window and match the man-made and natural landmarks that I see with those on the map. Second is dead reckoning. If, for example, my airspeed is 100 mph and I fly north for two hours, I know how far I will have gone. And third is radio aids to navigation. Across the country, the government has set up a vast network of such aids, which trasmit on different frequencies. By tuning in to the proper channel and setting an instrument, I can home in on one of these stations and either fly directly to it or gauge where I am in relation to it. These stations are depicted on the previously mentioned topographical maps. With all this overlapping help, it is hard for me to get lost in the air. As a matter of fact, the hard part about flying, for me, is not *finding* an airport but following the sometimes confusing maze of taxiways to my destination on the field!

¶
func
8h

This student writer divides the ways in which he is able to navigate his plane into three categories, making a complex set of options clear for the inexperienced reader. Though the effect is dry and business-like, observe how the concluding remark gives the paragraph a more human, subjective touch.

9 Opening and Closing Paragraphs

OPENING PARAGRAPHS

A good introductory paragraph customarily accomplishes three things. It catches your reader's interest; it establishes the voice and stance of your essay or paper (pp. 32–38, 3c–3e); and—usually but not always—it reveals the one central matter you are going to address. Only rarely does a shrewd writer begin by blurting out the thesis and immediately defending it. The standard function of an introduction is to *move toward* disclosure of the thesis in a way that makes your reader want to come along. We begin with possible strategies for achieving that effect.

But if your mind goes blank when you try to write the opening paragraph, delay the opener until you have drafted subsequent paragraphs. Some writers routinely compose in that order, and nearly all writers return to adjust and polish their opening to suit the rest of the essay.

114

9a Try the funnel opener.

A **funnel opener** is a paragraph that begins with a wide view of a subject area, thus providing a general context for the specific topic of the essay, and then narrows its focus until the topic, or even the thesis, has been disclosed:

¶
open
9a

> Only a few politicians have taken a craftsman's pride in self-expression, and fewer still—Caesar, Lord Clarendon, Winston Churchill, De Gaulle—have been equally successful in politics and authorship. Of these, Churchill may be the most interesting, for he was not only among the most voluminous of writers, but also commented freely on the art of writing. He was, in fact, a writer before becoming a politician.
>
> —MANFRED WEIDHORN, "Blood, Toil, Tears, and 8,000,000 Words: Churchill Writing"

By the end of this paragraph we know that the topic will be Churchill's writing, but we arrive at that knowledge by sliding down the funnel:

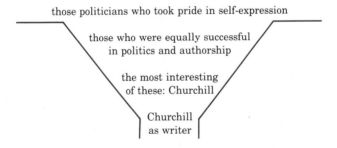

those politicians who took pride in self-expression

those who were equally successful in politics and authorship

the most interesting of these: Churchill

Churchill as writer

It is not necessary, however, to descend through several levels of generality before revealing your topic. You can get the funnel effect simply by starting with an appropriately broad perspective and then narrowing your focus just once. Notice, for example, how the following paragraph moves directly from a subject area—the function of the immune system—to the essay's real topic, autoimmune *disorders:*

**more
general level** {

It is generally assumed that the main job of the immune system is to distinguish between what is "self" and what is "not self." Once the distinction has been made, "self" is preserved and "not self" is destroyed. At the most general level, of course, this is true, and human beings remain alive and healthy only because it is so. Recently it has become clear, however, that at a finer level of detail the distinction between self and other is not absolute.

**level
of the
thesis** {

One of the paths to this insight has been provided by the autoimmune disorders, in which the immune system attacks normal, healthy tissue. Autoimmune disease, which may be crippling or fatal, can strike any tissue or organ. Its victims are often in the prime of life, and for unknown reasons they are more frequently women than men.

—IRUN R. COHEN,
"The Self, the World and Autoimmunity"

9b   Try the baited opener.

A **baited opener** is an introductory passage of one paragraph or more that not only saves its main idea for last (pp. 98–100, 7c) but also teases the reader by withholding a clear sense of the essay's topic. We are drawn ahead in the hope of getting our bearings.

At the funeral, the priest read from Ecclesiastes: "One generation cometh and another passeth away, but the land abideth forever." He stopped short of the words, "The sun also rises." Three men sat in the front pew, listening. Each had come into this old Idaho valley on a light plane, fixing on his own mortality. Afterward these three sons, who now had children of their own, received the news that their father had disinherited them.

The stone the family picked was flat to the ground and wide, as if to accommodate the special bulk beneath it. You can see this stone, between two 30-foot-high pines, in the town cemetery just north of Ketchum, and there is also a rough-made white wooden cross at the head of its smooth gray marble. There is only the name, "Ernest Miller Hemingway," and his dates, 1899–1961, cut carefully in.

Fathers and sons. It is a conflict that haunts literature—but life far more. And what is it like when your father is a kind of totem for the 20th century, an icon for maleness and grace under pressure, when he owns a terrifying unconscious and, not least, is gnawed on as you grow up, secretly and not so secretly, in ever larger bites, by fame and his own demons, until that Sunday morning in July when he blows away his entire cranial vault with a double-barreled 12-gauge Boss shotgun he had once shot pigeons with?

—PAUL HENDRICKSON, "Papa's Boys"

¶
open
9c

Readers who know their Hemingway can already guess whose funeral is being described in the first of these paragraphs. Only in the third paragraph, however, does the writer remove all doubt as to his topic: not Hemingway but his surviving, troubled sons.

Again, notice how firmly "hooked" we are by the following two-paragraph opening of a brief essay:

Natasha Crowe, a close acquaintance of mine, recently received an unsolicited invitation from Joanne Black, senior vice president of the American Express Co.'s Card Division. "Quite frankly," the letter began, "the American Express Card is not for everyone. And not everyone who applies for Card membership is approved." Tasha (as she is affectionately called) ignored the letter. A few weeks later she received a follow-up offer from a different vice president, Scott P. Marks Jr. "Quite frankly," Mr. Marks reminded her, "not everyone is invited to apply for the American Express Card. And rarer still are those who receive a personal invitation the second time."

Despite the honor, Tasha has continued to disregard this and similar invitations she has lately been receiving. For one thing, she has no job. Her savings are minimal. Her credit history is essentially a vacuum and therefore her credit rating, I'd imagine, is lousy. She doesn't even speak English. She's my cat, and I love her.

—STEVEN J. MARCUS, "How to Court a Cat"

For another example of a baited opener, look ahead to pages 119–120, 9e.

9c Speak directly to your reader.

Perhaps the hardest thing about composing an opening paragraph is the sense that you do not really know your reader. One simple, effective remedy is to pretend that the reader is standing right before you, awaiting your instruction to think of a scene or issue. In effect, you *command* your reader to share your responses—as, for example, in this beginning to an essay about motorcycle touring:

¶
open
9d

> The road glides beneath you. The sky flows over you. The wind rushes past, bringing new sounds and smells. Uninsulated, you touch the world as you press through it unencumbered by a cage. Beneath you, the machine hums and throbs, almost alive. It blends with you, telling you of the road surface and responding to your every movement.
>
> —ART FRIEDMAN, "Uninsulated, Unencumbered"

Again, study this opening to an essay about dinosaurs who, it has been found, were able to survive winters near the North and South Poles. Since the very existence of dinosaur fossils in those localities is just now coming to light, the writer begins by demanding that we get over a misconception:

> Picture a dinosaur in your mind. Then take a look at the surrounding landscape. What do you see?
>
> The images that come to mind are probably reminiscent of horror movies with either "lagoon" or "swamp" in the title. Clouds of fog blanket the still surface of some tropical waterway. Overhead, some mushy growth, the consistency of cooked spinach, hangs off lush, drooping leaves.
>
> Snow just doesn't seem to fit into the picture.
>
> —RICHARD MONASTERSKY, "Dinosaurs in the Dark"

Observe that one or two very brief, pointed paragraphs, like the first and third ones here, can sometimes make for an energetic beginning.

9d Begin on an opposite tack.

The "dinosaur" example just above illustrates a very common and useful way of getting started. Think about how your thesis significantly *differs from* some pattern, and begin with that pattern. Thus you are approaching your point by isolating its boundaries, showing its uniqueness:

Back in the 1970s I thought I could make my 14-month-old baby safe from drowning: I signed him up for swimming instruction. Virginia Hunt Newman's book *Teaching an Infant to Swim* had appeared not long before, and infant "waterproofing" programs were springing up at YMCAs and aquatic organizations everywhere. It was all the rage, with photos in national magazines of tiny "waterbabies" bubbling and bobbing in backyard pools. I was swept along in the movement: we were saving the nation's toddlers from the perils in their own backyards.

During that time, however, the statistics on childhood drowning accidents didn't decline; they went up. And now most swimming experts admit that this buoyant national experiment failed: swimming lessons in infancy do not make for waterproof toddlers. In fact, the popular waterproofing programs may actually have led to even more tragedies by giving youngsters and their parents a false sense of security.

—DIANE DIVOKY, "Waterproofing Your Baby:
Too Good to Be True"

This writer could have begun by declaring flatly that "waterproofing" doesn't work. Instead, she devotes her opening paragraph to the contrary possibility and then turns toward her thesis in the second paragraph. Her "opposite tack" opener provides historical background and a sense of dramatic reversal and control. Note that such a two-paragraph introduction serves the same purpose as a single **pivoting paragraph** (pp. 96–98, 7b).

9e   Begin with a story.

Look back to the "Hemingway" passage on pages 116–117. Would you find it possible to stop reading the writer's essay after those three paragraphs? Everyone loves a story, and one of the best ways to introduce an essay—even if your main purpose is not a narrative one—is to recount an intriguing incident. Here, for example, is the first paragraph of an essay-review about a seemingly undramatic topic, dictionaries and other books about language:

In 1897 James Murray, the first editor of *The Oxford English Dictionary*, paid a courtesy visit to one of the most prolific of his "voluntary readers"—the army of retired curates, amateur philologists, widows, and other people with time on their hands who supplied the dictionary with the hundreds of thousands of quotations needed to illustrate the history of words. The reader was a Dr. W. C. Minor, who gave his address as Crowthorne in Berkshire. When Murray arrived, he was driven from the station to an imposing brick building that seemed too large to be a house. In fact, he discovered, it was not a house; it was the Broadmoor Criminal Lunatic Asylum. Dr. Minor was an inmate.

—LOUIS MENAND, "Talk Talk"

¶
open
9f

The reader, needless to say, will eagerly plunge ahead to learn more. But like all storytellers, this writer is not simply "baiting" us; he has a larger point to make. As he says in his next sentence, "The story has piquancy not only because it suggests the ad hoc conditions in which the world's most famous dictionary was produced, but because the enterprise itself had something of a lunatic quality."

9f   Pose a question and address it.

If you find that your draft opener sounds vague, windy, and spiritless, try revising to begin with a blunt question—not any question, but one that leads directly or indirectly to your thesis. Jolted to attention, your reader will realize at once that you have been thinking analytically about the topic and have something definite to say:

If sanity and insanity exist, how shall we know them?
   The question is neither capricious nor itself insane. However much we may be personally convinced that we can tell the normal from the abnormal, the evidence is simply not compelling. It is commonplace, for example, to read about murder trials wherein eminent psychiatrists for the defense are contradicted by equally eminent psychiatrists for the prosecution on the matter of the defendant's sanity. More generally, there are a great deal of conflicting data on the reliability, utility, and meaning of such terms as "sanity," "insanity," "mental illness," and "schizophrenia." Finally, as early as 1934, Ruth Benedict suggested that normality and abnormality are not universal. What is viewed as normal in one culture may be seen as quite aberrant in another. Thus, notions of normality and abnormality may not be quite as accurate as people believe they are.

—D. L. ROSENHAN, "On Being Sane in Insane Places"

Observe how this writer has added emphasis to his initial question by devoting an entire paragraph to it.

9g Avoid the deadly opener.

¶
open
9g

An experienced reader can usually tell after two or three sentences whether the writer commands the topic and will be able to make it engaging. Never reach for one of the following classic sleeping pills:

1. The solemn platitude:

   x Conservation is a very important topic now that everyone is so interested in ecology.

   > Ask yourself if *you* would continue reading an essay that began with such a colorless sentence.

2. The unneeded dictionary definition:

   x The poem I have been asked to analyze is about lying. What is lying? According to *Webster's Eighth New College Dictionary,* to lie is "1: to make an untrue statement with intent to deceive; 2: to create a false or misleading impression."

   > Ask yourself if your reader is actually in the dark about the meaning of the word you are tempted to define. *Lie* obviously fails that test.

3. Restatement of the assignment, usually with an unenthusiastic declaration of enthusiasm:

   x It is interesting to study editorials in order to see whether they contain "loaded" language.

   > If you are actually interested, you would do well to *show* interest by beginning with a thoughtful observation.

4. The bald statement of the thesis:

x In this essay I will prove that fast food restaurants are taking the pleasure out of eating.

¶ open 9h

But you are also taking the pleasure out of reading. You want to *approach* your thesis, not to drop it on the reader's foot like a bowling ball that has slipped out of your grasp.

5. The "little me" apology:

x After just eighteen years on this earth, I doubt that I have acquired enough experience to say very much about the purpose of a college education.

Is this going to whet your reader's appetite for the points that follow?

9h   Sharpen your opening sentence.

If your first paragraph is the most important one, its first sentence is your most important sentence as well. When that sentence betrays boredom or confusion, you reduce your chances of gaining the reader's sympathy. If your first sentence is crisp and tight and energetic, its momentum can carry you through the next few sentences at least. This is why some people take pains to make that first sentence *epigrammatic*—pointed and memorable. Thus one writer begins a review of a book about Jewish immigrants by declaring:

> The first generation tries to retain as much as possible, the second to forget, the third to remember.
>
> —THEODORE SOLOTAROFF,
> review of *World of Our Fathers,* by Irving Howe

Another wittily begins an essay on divorce:

> There was a time when a woman customarily had a baby after one year of marriage; now she has a book after one year of divorce.
>
> —SONYA O'SULLIVAN, "Single Life in a Double Bed"

And a student writer advocating gun control begins:

> Thousands of people in this country could make an overwhelming case for the banning of handguns, except for one inconvenient fact: they aren't so much *in* the country as *under* it, abruptly sent to their graves with no chance to protest or dissuade. Arguing with a gun nut may be futile, but have you ever tried arguing with a gun?

¶
close
9j

CLOSING PARAGRAPHS

9i Save a clinching statement for your closing paragraph.

Remember that the final position within any structure—sentence, paragraph, or whole essay—is naturally emphatic. To take advantage of that fact, delay writing your conclusion until you have found material that bears reemphasizing or expanding. Look especially for a striking quotation or story that might drive your point home. You can either end with that passage or, as in this example, add a final comment of your own:

> Robert M. Hutchins has described the editors of *Britannica 3* as pioneers. After they had established their design "the question became one of execution . . . there were no models to imitate and no horrible examples to shun." One of those deficiencies has been made good by *Britannica 3* itself: they have their horrible example now.
> —SAMUEL MCCRACKEN, "The Scandal of Britannica 3"

9j Try recalling your opening paragraph in your closing one.

Look for ways of making your concluding paragraph show some evident, preferably dramatic, relation to your introductory one. If you already have a sound first paragraph and are groping for a last one, reread that opener and see if it contains some hint that you can now develop more amply. Here, for instance, is the concluding paragraph of the essay (quoted on p. 97) that began by asking whether Mahatma Gandhi was nothing more than a fanatic:

Gandhi's arguments reveal an underlying shrewdness. Far from betraying the dogmas of a fanatic, they are at once moral and cunningly practical. His genius, it seems, consisted in an unparalleled knack for doing right—and, what isn't quite the same, for doing the right thing. It is hard to come up with another figure in history who so brilliantly combined an instinct for politics with the marks of what we call, for lack of a better name, holiness.

¶
close
9l

Note how the writer has put his opening question into storage until it can be answered decisively, with a pleasing finality, in his closing lines.

9k   Look beyond your thesis in a closing paragraph.

Just as you can lead to your thesis by beginning on a more general plane (pp. 115–116, 9a), so you can end by looking beyond that thesis, which has now been firmly established. Thus, in a paper defending the thesis that unilateral disarmament is a dangerous and unwise policy, a student writer concluded as follows:

> There is no reason to expect, then, that the world would be safer if we laid down our arms. On the contrary, we could do nothing more foolhardy. *We must look to other means of ensuring our security and that of the nations we have agreed to protect.*

The sentence we have emphasized "escapes" the thesis, posing a relevant goal for future investigation. But note that it does so without embarking on a new topic; it provokes thought by looking further in the direction already taken.

9l   Avoid the deadly conclusion.

Readers want to feel, at the end of a piece of writing, that it has truly finished and not just stopped like some toy soldier that needs rewinding. Further, they like to anticipate the end through a revealing change in tone or intensity or generality of reference.

Though you may not always come up with a punchy conclusion, you can avoid certain lame devices that would threaten your good relations with your reader. Check your draft endings against the following cautions:

1. Do not merely repeat your thesis.

2. Though you can look beyond your thesis (9k), do not embark on a completely new topic.

3. Do not pretend to have proven more than you have.

4. Do not apologize or bring your thesis into doubt. If you find anything that requires an apology, fix it!

¶
close
9m

Remember that readers come away from an essay with the last paragraph ringing in their ears. If you end by sounding bored or distracted or untrustworthy or hesitant, you are encouraging your readers to discount everything you have worked so hard to establish.

9m If your essay is brief, feel free to omit a formal conclusion.

A short essay may make its point thoroughly within five hundred words; your readers will be insulted or bored by a heavy-handed reminder of the points they have just finished reading. Sometimes a brief concluding paragraph—consisting of no more than one or two sentences—can effectively end a short essay. But you can also save one of your strong supporting points for the last paragraph, counting on an emphatic final sentence to give a feeling of completion.

III
SENTENCES

Sentences

Strong sentences have much in common with strong paragraphs and whole essays, including a clear idea, emphatic placement of that idea, and subordination of other elements. You can think of the fully developed sentence as a skeletal paragraph containing major and minor components that ought to be easy for a reader to spot:

	ESSAY		**PARAGRAPH**		**SENTENCE**
MAJOR	Thesis	=	Leading Idea	=	Independent Clause
MINOR	Supporting Paragraphs		Supporting Sentences		Free Elements

On each level—essay, paragraph, sentence—your chief purpose in redrafting should be to highlight the major element and to see that it is adequately backed by minor elements that are clearly subordinate to it.

The chapters in Part III assume that you can already recognize the parts of sentences—subjects and verbs, for example, or independent and subordinate clauses—and put together grammatically coherent statements of your own. If you feel uncertain about fundamentals of usage, you may want to begin by reviewing several chapters in Part V. But since you have already succeeded in getting countless sentences onto paper, we start our discussion not with the blank page but with draft sentences that a student writer might want to improve. Our keynote will be revising to make your meaning easier to grasp and your sentences more fluent and varied.

10 Distinct Expression

10a Put your meaning into grammatically important words.

Writing proceeds not word by word but sentence by sentence—an obvious point, but one with crucial implications for your relation to your reader. That reader wants above all to grasp the point of each sentence, to take in your idea without difficulty. Even if the idea is a clear one, you must be sure to make it *distinct*—that is, readily comprehended on a first reading. While such a task sounds easy enough, in practice most draft sentences, even those written by very accomplished writers, are to some extent indistinct. Left unrevised, they would put their reader to extra trouble, thus sapping precious energy and attention.

When you think of revising a draft sentence, start by looking for its main idea—the point that *ought* to be conveyed by a clear, concise **independent clause** (p. 201, 16c). If, instead, you see that the point goes on and on or is trapped in a subordinate part of the sentence, you are ready to make your most essential improvement. Move your idea into an independent clause, making sure that the grammatically strongest parts of that clause convey important information.

The strongest parts of a clause are generally a *subject* and a *verb,* possibly linked to either a *direct object* or a *complement* (p. 198, 16a):

- The *committee exists.*

    S   V

- The *committee meets* on Tuesdays.

    S   V

- The *committee* S *is drafting* V a *report.* D OBJ

- The *committee* S *is* V an official *body.* C

- The *committee seems prepared.* S V C

Consider the "correct" but unimpressive sentence that follows.

DON'T

**vague
10a**

x The *departure* S of the fleet *is thought* V to be necessarily conditional on the weather.

Here the essential grammatical elements are a subject and verb, *The departure . . . is thought.* This is scanty information; we must root around elsewhere in the sentence to learn what is being said *about* the departure. The idea is that bad weather—here tucked into a prepositional phrase, *on the weather*—may delay the fleet's departure. Once we recognize that point, we can get *weather* into the subject position and replace the wishy-washy construction *is thought to be conditional on* with a verb that transmits action to an object.

DO:

- *Bad weather may keep* S V the *fleet* D OBJ at anchor.

    Notice that we now have three grammatically strong elements—a subject, a verb, and a direct object—that do carry significant meaning.

DON'T:

x The *thing* S the novelist seems to say *is* V that the human race is lacking what is needed to keep from being deceived.

    Notice how little information is conveyed by this subject and verb: *The thing is.* To find the writer's meaning, we must disentangle various embedded infinitives, subordinate clauses, and a prepositional phrase, each of which adds a little more strain to our memory.

DO:

- $\overset{\text{S}}{\text{Human beings}}$, the novelist seems to say, necessarily $\overset{\text{V}}{deceive}$

  $\overset{\text{D OBJ}}{themselves}$.

  Now the subject and verb do convey information. The key grammatical elements, subject–verb–direct object, bear the chief burden of meaning: *Human beings deceive themselves.* And as a result of this realignment, the sentence core now takes up just a few words instead of twenty-two. Notice, too, how the commas make it easy for a reader to tell where the central statement is being interrupted.

10b Avoid an overstuffed sentence.

Check your drafts for formless sentences that do not distinguish primary from subordinate elements.

DON'T:

x $\overset{\text{S V}}{It\ is}$ what she recalled from childhood about the begonia gardens that were cultivated in Capitola that drew her to return to that part of the coastline one summer after another.

Since such a sentence demands that all of its elements be kept in mind until the point eventually becomes clear, the sentence often will require two readings. The solution, as we will see more fully in the next chapter, lies in shortening the independent clause and clearly setting the minor elements apart.

DO:

- Summer after summer, drawn by her childhood recollections of

  the Capitola begonia gardens, $\overset{\text{S}}{she}$ $\overset{\text{V}}{returned}$ to that portion of the coastline.

  Note how, through a separating out of significant elements, the sentence becomes more dramatic and easier to grasp. Its core, instead of being thirty-one words jostling together in a mass, is a readily understood eight-word statement: *she returned to that portion of the coastline.*

10c   Do not overuse the verb *to be.*

You can make your prose more expressive by cutting down on the colorless, actionless verb *to be* (*is, are, were, had been,* etc.) and substituting action verbs.

"CORRECT" BUT ACTIONLESS:

x It *was* clear that the soprano *was* no longer in control of the high notes that *had been* a source of worry to her for years.

STRONGER:

• Clearly, the soprano *had lost* control of the high notes that *had been worrying* her for years.

> The action-bearing verbs in the revised version trim away needless words—notably the plodding prepositional phrases *in control, of worry,* and *to her*—and convey the key activities of losing and worrying.

"CORRECT" BUT ACTIONLESS:

x One source of tension in Dickinson's poetry *is* the fact that her shyness *is* in conflict with a tendency *to be* stagey.

STRONGER:

• In Dickinson's poetry, tension *arises* when shyness *conflicts* with staginess.

10d   Convey action through a verb, not a noun.

As the first example in 10c illustrates, a sentence whose core is indistinct typically uses nouns instead of verbs to express the action. In such **nominalization,** the action becomes an abstract state such as *in* *control of the high notes* and *a source of worry.* By moving the action into verbs *(had lost, had been worrying),* you allow your reader to feel the energy of your statement. Notice the relative vitality of the "do" examples below.

DON'T:

ˣ Many young single people are in a financial arrangement that enables them to have joint ownership of a house.

DO:

• Many young single people *arrange* their finances so that they can own a house jointly.

vague
10e

DON'T:

ˣ A single parent stands in need of occasional relief from the endless responsibilities of workplace and household.

DO:

• Sometimes a single parent *must get away* from the endless responsibilities of workplace and household.

The "don't" examples above are not "wrong"; they just place a little more strain on the reader's patience than is necessary.

10e In most contexts, prefer the active voice.

In addition to choosing verbs that show action (10d), you can make your sentences more distinct by generally putting your verbs into the active rather than the passive voice: not *was done* but *did,* not *is carried* but *carries.* (For further illustration of the active and passive voices, see p. 362, 30b, and p. 369, 30d.)

Passive verbs typically saddle you with three problems. First, they make the sentence a little longer, risking an effect of wordiness. Second, since they can never take direct objects, their energy isn't conveyed to another element in the sentence. And third, they oblige the performer of the deed to go unnamed or to be named only in a postponed and grammatically minor element. All three features go to make up a wan and evasive effect.

DON'T:

x *It is believed* by the candidate that a ceiling *must be placed* on the budget by Congress.

DO:

- The candidate *believes* that Congress *must place* a ceiling on the budget.

**vague
10e**

DON'T:

x Their motives *were applauded* by us, but their wisdom *was doubted.*

DO:

- We *applauded* their motives but *doubted* their wisdom.

In scientific writing, which often stresses impersonal, repeatable procedures rather than the individuals who carried them out, passive verbs are common. You can also use them in essay prose whenever you want your emphasis to remain on the person or thing acted upon. Suppose, for example, you are narrating the aftermath of an accident. Both of the following sentences would be correct, but you might have good reason to prefer the second, passive one.

ACTIVE VERB:

- Then three hospital attendants and the ambulance driver *rushed* Leonard into the operating room.

PASSIVE VERB:

- Then Leonard *was rushed* into the operating room.

Although the second sentence is less vivid, it keeps the focus where you may want it to be, on the injured man.

Passive verbs, then, are not automatically "wrong." As you revise your prose, look at each passive form and ask yourself whether you have a good justification for keeping it.

10f Use formulas like *it is* and *there are* only for special emphasis.

If one of your sentences begins with a subject-deferring expression such as *it is* or *there are,* take a close look at the subject (*it is the weather*; *there was a princess*). That "announced" word stands out emphatically in its unusual position. If you have a special reason for highlighting it, your delaying formula may be justified:

vague
10f

- It is the weather that causes her arthritis to act up.
- There was a princess whose hair reached the ground.

> In the first of these sentences, *weather* is isolated as the cause of the arthritis; in the second, the writer succeeds in getting an intended "fairy tale" effect.

More often than not, however, delaying formulas show up in first-draft prose simply because the writer is postponing commitment to a clearly stated idea. The price of delay is that, without any gain in emphasis, essential information is pushed further back into subordinate parts of the sentence (see 10a, p. 129). Frequently the result is an awkward and indistinct statement.

DON'T:
x *There is* no reason to suspect that *there is* much difference between what she wrote in her last years and what she felt when *it was* not so easy for her to be candid in her thirties.

DO:
- Her statements in her last years probably express ideas she already held, but had to censor, in her thirties.

> Note how much more easily you can take in the revised sentence; you do not have to hold your breath until you can dis-

cover what the statement is about. The complete grammatical
subject, *Her statements in her last years,* immediately gives us
our bearings.

10g   Avoid an unnecessary *that* or *what* clause.

Look at the last "don't" example above in 10f *(There is no reason to
suspect that . . .).* Part of the indistinctness of that sentence comes
from its *that* and *what* clauses, which further tax the reader's patience. Such clauses can, it is true, serve a good purpose—for example, arousing a curiosity that can then be emphatically answered:

- *What he needed* above all, after eight hours of steady questioning,
  was simply a chance to close his eyes.

In much first-draft prose, however, *that* and *what* clauses serve only
to nudge the intended statement along in little jerks.

DON'T:

x At the present time, the realities of nuclear terror are such *that*
   countries *that* possess equal power find, when they oppose each
   other, *that* the weapons *that* carry the most force are precisely
   the weapons *that* they cannot use.

DO:

- In this age of nuclear terror, equal adversaries are equally powerless to use their strongest weapons.

  Here thirty-nine words have been compressed into sixteen,
  and a slack, cud-chewing sentence has become tight and balanced *(equal adversaries are equally powerless).* And notice
  how the grammatical core of the sentence has been given
  something definite to convey: not *realities are such* but *adversaries are powerless.* Strong, message-bearing elements of
  thought have been moved into subject-verb-complement positions, where they normally belong.

11 Subordination

The first thing to do with any draft sentence—even an adequate-looking one—is to see if you can make its idea more distinct (Chapter 10). In doing so, you will often find yourself using **subordination**—that is, giving secondary grammatical emphasis to certain parts of the sentence. As a rule, the act of subordinating brings out the primary importance of the elements that remain unsubordinated. We will see some interesting exceptions, however; on occasion a subordinated element, shrewdly placed, can pack a curious wallop (pp. 145–146).

Our discussion emphasizes the usefulness of *free subordination* (11c–d), which typically gets set off by commas. Once you can manage free subordination effectively, you have in hand one of the most fruitful of all revision strategies.

11a Subordinate to highlight the key idea of your sentence.

When one of your thoughts in a sentence is less important than another, you should put it into a subordinate structure. Thus, if your draft sentence says *The government collects billions of dollars in taxes, and it must meet many obligations,* you should recognize that by using *and* you have given equal weight to two independent remarks. Are they of equal importance in your own mind? If you decided that you really meant to stress the collecting of money, you would want to turn the statement about meeting obligations into a subordinate element:

SUB EL
- *Because it has many obligations to meet,* the government collects billions of dollars in taxes.

But if you wanted to stress the meeting of obligations, you would subordinate the remark about collecting money:

SUB EL
- The government is able to meet its obligations *by collecting billions of dollars in taxes.*

When you make an element subordinate, it will usually fit into one of the following (left-column) categories. Note how subordinating words like *because, where,* and *although* (p. 202, 16c) not only spare us the trouble of locating the main idea but specify the relation between that idea and the subordinate element.

sub 11a

	WITHOUT SUBORDINATION	WITH SUBORDINATION
Time	The earthquake struck, and then everyone panicked	Everyone panicked *when* the earthquake struck.
Place	William Penn founded a city of brotherly love. He chose the juncture of the Delaware and Schuylkill rivers.	*Where* the Schuylkill River joins the Delaware, William Penn founded a city of brotherly love
Cause	She was terrified of large groups, and debating was not for her.	*Because* she was terrified of large groups, she decided against being a debater.
Concession	He claimed to despise Vermont. He went there every summer.	*Although* he claimed to despise Vermont, he went there every summer.
Condition	She probably won't be able to afford a waterbed. The marked retail prices are just too high.	*Unless* she can get a discount, she probably won't be able to afford a waterbed.
Exception	The grass is dangerously dry this year. Of course I am not referring to watered lawns.	*Except for* watered lawns, the grass is dangerously dry this year.

	WITHOUT SUBORDINATION	WITH SUBORDINATION
Purpose	The Raiders moved to Los Angeles. They hoped to find bigger profits there.	The Raiders moved to Los Angeles *in search of* bigger profits.
Description	The late Edward Steichen showed his reverence for life in arranging the famous exhibit "The Family of Man," and he was a pioneer photographer himself.	The late Edward Steichen, *himself a pioneer photographer,* showed his reverence for life in arranging the famous exhibit "The Family of Man."

sub
11b

11b Avoid such vague subordinators as *in terms of* and *being as*.

Sometimes you can make a sentence more distinct not by adding subordination but by sharpening a vague subordinate element or eliminating it altogether. In rereading your drafts, watch especially for formulas like *in terms of, with regard to,* and *being as*. Such expressions are inherently woolly; they fail to specify exactly *how* the subordinated element relates to the primary one.

DON'T:

x *In terms of swimming,* she was unbeatable.

> Here a rather pompous subordinate element hints at a cloudy connection between swimming and being unbeatable. The connection can be stated more straightforwardly.

DO:

- *As a swimmer* she was unbeatable.

or

- She was an unbeatable swimmer.

DON'T:

x He felt sympathetic *with regard to their position.*

DO:

● He sympathized with their position.

DON'T:

x *Being as it was noon,* everyone took a lunch break.

DO:

● Everyone took a lunch break at noon.

**sub
11c**

Other potentially vague subordinators include *with, as, as to, in the area of, in connection with, in the framework of, along the lines of, pertaining to,* and *as far as.*

DON'T:

x *With all that he says about the English,* I believe he has misrepresented them.

DO:

● I believe he has altogether misrepresented the English.

DON'T:

x *As far as finals,* I hope to take all of them in the first two days of exam week.

> To be correct in usage the writer would have to say *As far as finals are concerned,* . . . But unless there is some special reason for singling out *finals,* a more concise statement would be preferable.

DO:

● I hope to take all of my finals in the first two days of exam week.

11c Gain clarity through free subordination.

In the right-hand column of the chart on pages 138–139, note that all but two of the italicized elements are set apart from the main statements by commas. They are **free elements** in the sense of standing alone. By contrast, the sentences *Everyone panicked when the earthquake struck* and *The Raiders moved to Los Angeles in search of bigger profits* contain **bound elements**—that is, they are tied together with the main statements. Here are some further contrasts:

BOUND:	FREE:
The Germany *that he remembered with horror* had greatly changed.	Germany, *which he remembered with horror,* had greatly changed.
Germany was now inclined toward neutralism *instead of being fiercely militaristic.*	*Instead of being fiercely militaristic,* Germany was now inclined toward neutralism.
Hitler had vanished from the scene *along with everything he stood for.*	*Along with everything he stood for,* Hitler had vanished from the scene.

**sub
11c**

In general, bound elements are **restrictive,** or defining, and thus they should not be set off by commas (see p. 254, 19m). Free elements, being **nonrestrictive,** or nondefining, should be set apart. But since any phrase or subordinate clause at the beginning of a sentence can be followed by a comma (p. 251, 19i–j), a restrictive element that comes first can be free—that is, followed by a comma:

RESTR AND FREE
* *In September or October,* heating bills begin to rise.

The distinction between free and bound elements is a valuable one for mastering an efficient style. When one of your draft sentences is clumsily phrased, you can often attack the problem by looking for bound elements and then setting them free.

WITH BOUND SUBORDINATION:
x The censorship *that is not directly exercised by a sponsor when a program is being produced* may be exercised in many instances by the producers themselves.

WITH FREE SUBORDINATION:

• *Even when a sponsor does not directly censor a program,* the producers often censor it themselves.

> Note the importance of the comma after *program,* leaving the
> reader in no doubt about where the main statement begins.
> Observe, too, that the revised sentence shifts from passive to
> active verbs (pp. 133–134, 10e). Use of the passive voice al-
> most always results in the addition of bound prepositional
> phrases (*by a sponsor, by the producers*).

**sub
11c**

WITH BOUND SUBORDINATION:

x Nuclear power is an energy source *whose enormous risks to
health and safety are out of scale in importance with the fact that it
accounts for less than five percent of energy production in the
United States.*

> Here a main statement has been glued tight to eight subordi-
> nate elements: two subordinate clauses *(whose enormous risks
> . . . , that it accounts for . . .)* and six prepositional phrases *(to
> health and safety, of scale, in importance, with the fact, of
> energy production, in the United States).* The result is an
> unnecessarily heavy demand on the reader's patience; the sen-
> tence offers no resting place and no clear sign of its logical
> structure.

WITH FREE SUBORDINATION:

• *Although nuclear power accounts for less than five percent of
our energy production,* it poses enormous risks to health and
safety.

> Subordination does lead to clarity in this revision, for the com-
> ma sets the subordinate element apart from the main state-
> ment. We thus get two crucial advantages: the main statement
> now takes up only eight words, and the *Although* construction
> immediately tells us what the sentence's logic will be *(al-
> though x, nevertheless y).*

WITH BOUND SUBORDINATION:

x One need only look *to the unnecessarily complex and finally
implausible psychological apparatus constructed by scholars to*

explain this curious fascination with money on Dreiser's part to perceive the pitfalls that threaten the unwary commentator.

Notice how one embedded infinitive phrase (*to explain this curious fascination . . .*) makes it hard for us to decipher the function of the next one (*to perceive the pitfalls. . .*).

WITH FREE SUBORDINATION:

- *To perceive the pitfalls that threaten the unwary commentator,* one need only study the example of Dreiser scholars. *In their eagerness to explain Dreiser's curious fascination with money,* they have constructed an unnecessarily complex—and finally implausible—psychological apparatus.

> **sub**
> **11d**

As this revision suggests, when your draft sentence contains too many boxes-within-boxes to be easily unpacked, you probably have the makings of *two* revised sentences. Using free subordinate elements in both of them, you can convey your original meaning without short-circuiting the reader's brain.

11d Follow sentence logic in placing a subordinate element.

One important feature of free subordinate elements is that they can be moved without a radical loss of meaning. How can you tell where a free element would be most effective? If you do not trust your ear, you can apply one of the following three principles:

1. *Explain or place conditions on an assertion.* If your free element explains your main statement or puts a condition on it, you should consider placing the free element *first.* In that position it will allow your reader to follow your logic from the start:

- *Unless scientists come up with a better explanation,* we will have to lend our belief to this one.
- *Although he finished the test in time,* he missed many of the answers.

- *Because he becomes nervous whenever he isn't listening to music,* he wears earphones while he works.

In first-draft prose, main statements tend to come first, with limiting or explanatory elements dragging behind. Get those elements into early positions; they will show that you have the entire logic of the sentence under control. And since last positions tend to be naturally emphatic, you can generally make a stronger effect by putting your main statement after your free subordinate element.

sub
11d

2. *Add to an assertion.* If your free element, instead of explaining the main statement or placing a condition on it, merely adds a further thought about it, you should place that free element *after* the main statement:

- Her smile disguised her fierce competitiveness, *a trait revealed to very few of her early teammates.*
- His life revolved around his older brother, *who never ceased making unreasonable demands.*

3. *Modify one part of an assertion.* If your free element modifies a particular word or phrase, consider placing it *right after* that element:

- Cézanne's colors, *earthy as his native Provence,* are not adequately conveyed by reproductions.
- They gave me, *a complete newcomer,* more attention than I deserved.

A less usual but sometimes effective position is *right before* the modified element:

- *Earthy as his native Provence,* Cézanne's colors are not adequately conveyed by reproductions.

Placing sentence adverbs and transitional phrases

A **sentence adverb** (p. 214, 17c) such as *however, nevertheless,* or *furthermore* constitutes a movable subordinate element in its own right. The placement of a sentence adverb is highly flexible, but different positions suggest different emphases. In general, a sentence adverb puts stress on the word that precedes it:

- I, *however,* refuse to comply. [I contrast myself with others.]
- I refuse, *however,* to comply. [My refusal is absolute.]

In the first and last positions of a sentence, where a sentence adverb cannot be set off on both sides by commas, it makes a less pointed effect:

- *However,* I refuse to comply. ⎫ No single element within the
- I refuse to comply, *however.* ⎭ main statement is highlighted.

**sub
11d**

The final position is the weakest—the one that gets least stress from the logical force of the sentence adverb. In some sentences, however, this may be just the effect you are seeking.

The same principles of emphatic placement apply to **transitional phrases** like *in fact, on the contrary,* and *as a result,* which are really multiword sentence adverbs. Note how meaning as well as emphasis can sometimes be affected by different placement of the same transitional phrase:

- *In fact,* Marie was overjoyed. [Marie was not unhappy. No, indeed. . . .]
- Marie, *in fact,* was overjoyed. [Others were happy, but one person—singled out here—was more so.]

For fuller lists of sentence adverbs and transitional phrases, see page 215, 17c.

Emphatic subordination

Once you are sure of your control over subordination, you can occasionally surprise your reader by saving a "bombshell" for a late, subordinate element:

There was nothing unusual in the visit *except that Thoreau fell utterly in love with her as soon as she arrived.*
—ROBERT D. RICHARDSON, JR., *Henry Thoreau: A Life of the Mind*

In one sense, this statement means what it starts out to say; nothing outwardly noteworthy happened during Ellen Sewell's visit to Concord, Massachusetts, in July 1839. But something privately momentous did happen: Henry Thoreau fell in love. The writer gains an effect of **irony** (p. 35, 3e), or incongruity between what is said and meant, by tucking that important news into an "afterthought" subordinate clause.

Free subordinate elements, "casually" appended to straightforward-looking sentences, are especially suited to ironic effects:

**sub
11d**

> Perhaps the Las Vegas wedding industry achieved its peak operational efficiency between 9:00 P.M. and midnight of August 26, 1965, *an otherwise unremarkable Thursday which happened to be, by Presidential order, the last day on which anyone could improve his draft status merely by getting married.*
>
> —JOAN DIDION, "Marrying Absurd"

This writer mocks the "peak operational efficiency" of the Las Vegas wedding industry by explaining it away in an "unremarkable" sequence of subordinate clauses and phrases. Her sentence is an exploding cigar, with the explosion timed to occur when we could least expect it.

We have previously advised you to "subordinate to highlight the key idea of your sentence" (11a). Here you see, however, that the rule can be twisted for purposes of irony or humor; you can put your key idea into the subordinate structure if you know exactly why you are doing so.

12 Emphasis and Variety

12a Use parallelism to show that elements belong together.

You can write more forceful sentences by making your statements more distinct (Chapter 10) and by highlighting them through subordination (Chapter 11). In addition, you can revise to give the same grammatical structure to elements that are closely related in meaning. Such use of **parallelism** (Chapter 22) is emphatic because it makes logical relations immediately apparent to your reader. The idea is to have your grammar reinforce your meaning, not only through the choice of a main subject and verb but also through the aligning of key words, phrases, and clauses.

To appreciate the advantage that parallelism brings, compare two passages that convey the same information:

A. Animals think *of* things. They also think *at* things. Men think primarily *about* things. Words are symbols that may be combined in a thousand ways. They can also be varied in the same number of ways. This can be said of pictures as well. The same holds true for memory images.

B. Animals think, but they think *of* and *at* things; men think primarily *about* things. Words, pictures, and memory images are symbols that may be combined and varied in a thousand ways.

—SUSANNE K. LANGER, "The Lord of Creation"

147

Passage A, a classically choppy paragraph, takes seven sentences and fifty-one words to say what passage B says in two sentences and thirty-one words. In passage B, seven statements are condensed to four, with a corresponding gain in understanding. And the key to this concentration is parallelism—of paired clauses (*Animals think, but they think . . .*), of conspicuously equal halves of a sentence marked by a semicolon, of nouns in a series (*Words, pictures, and memory images*), and of verb forms (*combined and varied*). Passage B inspires confidence in the writer's control; we feel that she could not have packed her sentences with so much parallel structure if she had not known exactly what she wanted to say.

emph 12a

Most instances of parallelism involve two items that are conspicuously equivalent in emphasis. The following table shows how such items can be made parallel, with or without conjunctions (joining words such as *and* and *or*).

PATTERN	EXAMPLE
x and *y*	She was tired of *waiting* and *worrying*.
x or *y*	If he had continued that life, he would have faced death *in the electric chair* or *at the hands of the mob*.
x, y	He strode away, *the money in his hand, a grin on his face*.
x: y	He had *what he wanted: enough cash to buy a new life*.
x; y	*He wanted security; she wanted good times*.

As you can see from these few examples, parallelism can involve units as small as single words (*waiting* and *worrying*) or as large as whole statements (*he wanted security* and *she wanted good times*).

For problems of usage and punctuation arising with parallelism, see pages 284–297, Chapter 22.

12b   Use anticipatory patterns.

In the boxed sentences on page 148, each *y* element comes as a mild surprise; we discover that a parallel structure is in process only when we reach the second item. Other parallel formulas, however, anticipate the pairing of items by beginning with a "tip-off" word.

PATTERN	EXAMPLE
both *x* and *y*	*Both* guerrillas *and* loyalists pose a threat to the safety of reporters covering foreign revolutions.
either *x* or *y*	*Either* reporters should be recognized as neutrals *or* they should not be sent into combat zones.
neither *x* nor *y*	*Neither* the competition of networks *nor* the ambition of reporters justifies this recklessness.
whether *x* or *y*	Reporters must wonder, when they wake up each morning in a foreign city, *whether* they will be gunned down by the loyalists *or* kidnapped by the guerrillas.
more (less) *x* than *y*	It is *more* important, after all, to spare the lives of journalists *than* to get one more interview with the typical freedom fighter.
not *x* but *y*	It is *not* the greed of the networks, however, *but* the changed nature of warfare that most endangers the lives of reporters.

emph 12b

PATTERN	EXAMPLE
not only *x* but also *y*	Now reporters covering a guerrilla war find it hard *not* x *only* to distinguish "friendly" from "unfriendly" elements y *but also* to convince each side that they are not working for the other one.
so *x* that *y*	Such reporting has become *so* risky *that* few knowledge- y able jornalists volunteer to undertake it.

emph
12b

Note how the first word of the anticipatory formula prepares us for the rest. As soon as we read *both* or *either* or *so,* we know what kind of logical pattern has begun; we are ready to grasp complex paired elements without losing our way. Anticipatory parallelism always means improved readability—provided, of course, that the grammar and punctuation of your sentence make the intended structure clear.

To see how anticipatory patterns can aid a reader, compare an imagined first-draft passage with the actual finished version:

A. He swore a lot. He would swear at absolutely anybody. For him it was just the natural thing to do. The people who worked for him probably thought he was angry at them all the time, but it wasn't necessarily true. A man like that could have been just making conversation without being angry at all, for all they knew.

B. He swore so often and so indiscriminately that his employees were sometimes not sure whether he was angry at them or merely making conversation.

—NORA EPHRON, "Seagram's with Moxie"

Passage A uses more words to make more assertions, yet it never lets us see where it is headed. Nora Ephron's more economical passage B uses two anticipatory structures—*so x and so y that z* and *whether he was x or y*—to pull elements of thought into alignment without squandering whole sentences on them.

12c Make your series consistent and climactic.

One indispensable form of parallelism (12a) is the **series** of coordinated items, three or more elements in parallel sequence. A series tells your reader that the items it contains each bear the same logical relation to some other part of the sentence:

emph 12c

- *Declining enrollments*, *obsolete audio equipment*, and *hostility from the administration* have hurt the language departments.

This says that *x, y,* and *z* are comparable factors, each making its contribution to the effect named. Such a condensed, immediately clear statement could replace as many as three rambling sentences in a draft paragraph.

  Although the parts of a series must be alike in form, they may have different degrees of importance or impact. Since the final position is by far the most emphatic one, that is where the climactic item should go:

- He was prepared to risk everything—*his comfort, his livelihood, even his life*.

  If you try to put *his life* into either of the other positions in the series, you will see how vital a climactic order is.

  As the example above shows, you do not always have to put *and* or *or* before the last member of a series. Omitting the conjunction can give the series an air of urgency or importance:

- A moment's *distraction, hesitation, impatience* can spell doom for an aerialist.

Again, if you want to make a crowded or overwhelmed effect, you can omit the commas and put coordinating conjunctions between all members of the series:

- No sooner does one international crisis fade from the headlines than a new one arrives, *an Iran or Nicaragua or Lebanon or South Africa.*

For problems of usage and punctuation arising with series, see pages 296–297, 22k–l.

**emph
12d**

12d   Use balance for special emphasis.

When a sentence uses emphatic repetition to achieve parallelism (12a), it shows **balance.** A balanced sentence usually does two things: (1) it repeats a grammatical pattern, and (2) it repeats certain words so as to highlight key differences. Thus the two halves of *He wanted security; she wanted good times* use the same subject-verb-object pattern and the same verb, *wanted,* in order to contrast *he* with *she* and *security* with *good times.*

You can see the ingredients of balance in the following **aphorisms,** or memorable sentences expressing very general assertions:

- What is *written without effort* is in general *read without pleasure.* (Samuel Johnson)
- We must indeed *all hang together,* or, most assuredly, we will *all hang separately.* (Benjamin Franklin)
- Democracy substitutes *election by the incompetent many* for *appointment by the corrupt few.* (George Bernard Shaw)

Notice in each instance how the writer has used identical sentence functions to make us confront essential differences: *written/read, effort/pleasure, together/separately, election/appointment, incompetent/corrupt, many/few.*

The art of creating balance consists in noticing elements of sameness and contrast in a draft sentence and then rearranging your grammar so that those elements play identical grammatical roles.

DRAFT SENTENCE:

- Love of country is a virtue, but I think that it is more important today to love the human species as a whole.

BALANCED VERSION:

- Love of country is a virtue, but love of the human species is a necessity.

  The first sentence is adequately formed, but it still reads like an idea-in-the-making, the transcript of a thought process. The second, radically concise, sentence uses balance to convey authority and finality.

**emph
12e**

12e Take advantage of the emphatic final position in a sentence.

If you want to make an expression dramatic and memorable, try putting it at the end of its sentence. With a proper buildup, the final position is naturally punchy. Notice, for example, how every sentence in the following paragraph about "snap books"—that is, books by "name" authors who write about countries they have scarcely visited—saves its most biting expressions (italicized here) for the end:

> What really distinguishes snap books from other genres is not so much their length as *their self-consciousness.* They are the creation of individuals who, thrust into a wrenching world of death squads and land mines, *profess to know terror through having been forced to eat dinner in the dark.* In snap books, war and revolution serve primarily as backdrops *against which star writers can shine.*
>
> —MICHAEL MASSING, "Snap Books"

The same effect is even more apparent in the following passage, with its one-word punch line:

> No wonder the TV industry is finally wooing black audiences. They've come to embody its favorite color, which is, of course, *green.*
>
> —HARRY F. WATERS, "TV's New Racial Hue"

For the emphatic use of subordination, see also page 145, 11d.

VARIETY

12f Combine choppy sentences to set off related elements.

Bear in mind that your prose will be read not in isolated sentences but in whole paragraphs. You, too, should read your drafts that way, checking to see that the sentences within each paragraph sound comfortable in one another's company. If they seem abrupt and awkward, the problem may be a discontinuity of thought. Yet your sentences can be related in thought and still feel unrelated because they are too alike in structure. Watch especially for **choppy sentences**—a monotonous string of brief, plain statements containing few if any internal pauses. What you want instead is movement between relatively plain sentences and sentences that do contain pauses.

You can break up monotony just by adding one punctuated modifier—a *however* or a *furthermore*—to a sentence in a choppy sequence: *The storm, however, was not expected to end the drought.* But you can also look for ways to combine two or more choppy sentences into one. Ask yourself what the logical relation between those sentences is, and then turn one statement into a punctuated modifier of the other.

CHOPPY:

x The president serves a four-year term. He must seek reelection when it is over.

COMBINED:

• After serving a four-year term, the president must seek reelection.

   The first sentence in the choppy sequence has been turned into a **free element** (pp. 140–141, 11c), duly set off by punctuation.

CHOPPY:

x Some experts favor a six-year term of office. They say that reelection causes too many pressures. Long-term problems get neglected. These problems are both domestic and foreign.

var
12f

COMBINED:

- Some experts, maintaining that both domestic and foreign problems get neglected in the rush for reelection, favor a six-year term of office.

    Here four abrupt, disjointed sentences, each as unemphatic as the next, have been transformed into one sentence that sorts out major and minor elements and gets its key point into the emphatic final position (see 12e).

CHOPPY:

x Some knowledgeable observers do think that the present arrangement is superior. One of them is the noted historian Arthur Schlesinger, Jr. He argues that a president must be accountable to the people. It is the core of our democracy. Schlesinger says that a four-year term answers this need.

var
12g

COMBINED:

- Some knowledgeable observers, among them the noted historian Arthur Schlesinger, Jr., believe that the present arrangement is superior. In Schlesinger's opinion, a four-year term answers our fundamental democratic need to keep the president accountable to the people.

12g Practice the emphatic interruption.

To give special emphasis to one statement or piece of information, try turning it into an interruption of your sentence:

- The street Jerry lived on—*it was more like an alley than a street*—was so neighborly that he scarcely ever felt alone.
- The hot, moist summer air of Florida—*people call it an instant steambath*—makes an air conditioner a necessity in every home and office.
- A woman of strong opinions—*her last movie grossed $50 million, and she calls it a turkey*—she is not exactly a press agent's dream come true.

As you can gather, dashes are the normal means of punctuating an emphatic interruption.

The "false start"

In a variation on the interruptive pattern, you can begin your sentence with a lengthy element—for example, a series (p. 151, 12c)—and follow it with a dash announcing that the grammatical core of the sentence is about to begin:

- *Going to hairdresser school, marrying the steady boyfriend, having the baby, getting the divorce*—everything in her life seemed to follow some dreary script.

var
12h

Such a sentence takes the reader off guard by making a **"false start."** We assume at first that the opening element will be the grammatical subject, but we readjust our focus when we see that the true subject will come after the dash. (The first element is actually in apposition to the subject; see page 257, 19n.)

12h Practice the cumulative sentence.

A **cumulative sentence** is one whose main statement is followed by one or more free subordinate elements (pp. 140–141, 11c). It is called *cumulative* because it "accumulates," or collects, modifying words, phrases, or clauses at the end. The following sentences, encountered earlier, are typical:

- Her smile disguised her fierce competitiveness, *a trait revealed to very few of her early teammates.*
- He was prepared to risk everything—*his comfort, his livelihood, even his life.*
- No sooner does one international crisis fade from the headlines than a new one arrives, *an Iran or Nicaragua or Lebanon or South Africa.*

The beauty of the cumulative pattern is that it offers refinement without much risk of confusing the reader. Since the basic structure of the sentence is complete before the end-modifiers (italicized above) begin, your reader has a secure grasp of your idea, which you can then elaborate, illustrate, explain, or reflect on. And since much of our speech follows the cumulative model of statement-plus-adjustment, a cumulative sentence on the page can make a pleasantly conversational effect, as if one afterthought had brought the next one into mind.

12i Try an occasional question or exclamation.

Usually a paragraph develops as a succession of statements, or **declarative sentences.** But to show strong feeling, to pinpoint an issue, to challenge your reader, or simply to enliven a string of sentences, you can make use of a strategically placed question or exclamation:

var
12j

- *What are we to make of such turmoil over the narrow, arid Gaza Strip?* A full answer would take us back to the era of the Roman emperors.
- And this is all the information released so far. *Does anyone doubt that the Congressman has something to hide?*
- *A million tons of TNT!* The power of this bomb was beyond anyone's imagination.
- Once the grizzlies were deprived of garbage, their population declined steeply. *So much for the "back to nature" school of bear management!*

Note, in the second of these examples, that the writer asks the question without expecting an answer, for the question "answers itself." Such a **rhetorical question** can work well for you in driving home an emphatic point. Since rhetorical questions have a coercive air, however, you should use them sparingly.

12j Practice inverted syntax.

Readers normally expect subjects to come before verbs, but for that very reason you can gain emphasis by occasionally reversing that order. As a result of such **inverted syntax,** the subject becomes more prominent:

- In the beginning was the *Word.*

- Most important of all, for the would-be-tourist, is a *passport* that has not expired.

Similarly, any sentence element that has been wrenched out of its normal position and placed first gets extra attention.

- *Never again* will she overlook the threat of an avalanche.
- *Not until then* had he understood how miserable he was.

Again:

var
12k

- *About such a glaring scandal* nothing need be said.

    The subject and verb, *nothing* and *need,* are in the usual sequence, but the writer begins with a prepositional phrase that would normally come last.

12k   Practice the suspended sentence.

If you substantially delay completing your main statement, forcing your reader to wait for the other shoe to drop, you have written a **suspended sentence** (often called a *periodic sentence.*) Through its use of delaying elements (italicized in the following examples), a suspended sentence can be an effective means of leading to a climax:

- It appears that their success was due more to the influence of their father, *so dominant in the worlds of business and politics that every door would open at his bidding,* than to any merits of their own.
- The states argued that they had indeed complied, *if compliance can mean making a good-faith effort and collecting all the required data,* with the federal guidelines.
- If you are still unused to the idea of gasohol, you will certainly not be ready to hear that some diesel engines will soon be running on *that most humble and ordinary of products, taken for granted by homemakers and never noticed by auto buffs,* vegetable oil.

IV
WORDS

Words

To convey your ideas successfully, you need to know words well and to respect their often subtle differences from one another. Specifically, when revising your drafts you should make sure that your words

1. *mean what you think they mean;*

2. *are appropriate to the occasion;*

3. *are concise;*

4. *are neither stale, roundabout, nor needlessly abstract; and*

5. *show control over figurative, or nonliteral, implications.*

Chapters 13–15 discuss these requirements of **diction,** *or word choice. For an alphabetically arranged treatment of problem expressions, see the Index of Usage beginning on page 540.*

13 Appropriate Meaning

13a Know how to use your college dictionary.

To make progress in your control of **denotation,** or the dictionary meaning of words, it is essential that you own a college dictionary such as *The Random House College Dictionary, Funk and Wagnalls Standard College Dictionary, Webster's New World Dictionary of the American Language, Webster's New Collegiate Dictionary,* or *The American Heritage Dictionary of the English Language.* These volumes are large enough to meet your daily needs without being too cumbersome to carry around. Once you learn from the prefatory guide to your dictionary how to interpret its abbreviations, symbols, and order of placing entries, you can find in it most—perhaps all—of the following kinds of information:

spelling	usage levels
parts of speech	syllable division
definitions	principles of usage
synonyms	abbreviations
antonyms	symbols
alternate forms	biographical and given names
pronunciation	places and population figures
capitalization	weights and measures
derivations	names and locations of colleges

To see what a college dictionary can and cannot do, look at *Random House*'s entry under *fabulous:*

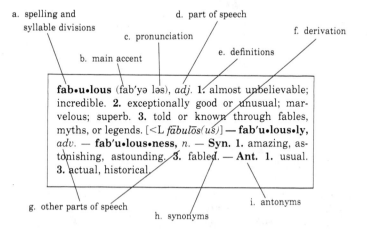

a. spelling and syllable divisions
d. part of speech
c. pronunciation
f. derivation
b. main accent
e. definitions

fab•u•lous (fab′yə ləs), *adj.* **1.** almost unbelievable; incredible. **2.** exceptionally good or unusual; marvelous; superb. **3.** told or known through fables, myths, or legends. [<L *fābulōs(us)*] — **fab′u•lous•ly,** *adv.* — **fab′u•lous•ness,** *n.* — **Syn. 1.** amazing, astonishing, astounding. **3.** fabled. — **Ant. 1.** usual. **3.** actual, historical.

g. other parts of speech
h. synonyms
i. antonyms

mean 13a

The entry shows, in the following order:

a. how the word is spelled and the points where syllable divisions occur *(fab•u•lous);*

Comment: The lowercase *f* shows that *fabulous* is not normally capitalized.

If this word could be spelled correctly in different ways, the less common form would appear in a separate entry with a cross reference to the more common form; thus the entry for *reenforce* merely sends you to *reinforce.* In your writing, use the spelling under which a full definition has been given.

Syllable division is not completely uniform from one dictionary to another, but you cannot go wrong by following your dictionary's practice in every case. (You can also spare yourself trouble by not breaking up words at all; a little unevenness in right-hand margins is normal.)

b. where the main accent falls *(fab′);*

Comment: If the word had another strongly stressed syllable, like *hand* in *beforehand,* you would find it marked with a secondary accent: *bi•for' hand'.*

c. how the word is pronounced;

Comment: The pronunciation key at the bottom of every pair of pages reveals, among other things, that ə = *a* as in *alone.* (One dictionary's key will differ from another's.) College dictionaries make no attempt to capture regional or nonstandard pronunciations, like x *nōo'kul ər* for *nōo'klē ər (nuclear).*

d. the part of speech *(adj.* for *adjective);*

Comment: Some words, like *can* and *wait,* occupy more than one part of speech, depending on the context. Definitions are grouped according to those parts of speech. Transitive verbs (those that take an object—p. 197, 16a) are usually listed separately from intransitive verbs (those that take no object). Thus *Random House* gives all the intransitive senses of *wait (v.i.),* as in *Wait for me,* before the transitive senses *(v.t.),* as in *Wait your turn!*

mean 13a

e. three definitions of *fabulous;*

Comment: No dictionary lists definitions in the order of their acceptability. The dictionary illustrated here begins with the most common part of speech occupied by a given word and, within each part of speech, offers the most frequently encountered meaning first. Some other dictionaries begin with the earliest meaning and proceed toward the present. The system used in your dictionary is clearly set forth in the prefatory material, which you should read through at least once.

f. the word's derivation from the first three syllables of the Latin word *fabulosus;*

Comment: The derivation, or *etymology,* of a word is given only if its component parts are not obviously familiar—as they are, for example, in *freeze-dry* and *nearsighted.* Many symbols are used in stating etymologies; look for their explanation in the prefatory material of your dictionary.

g. an adverb and a noun stemming from the main word;

Comment: Fabulously and *fabulousness* are "run-on entries," words formed by adding a suffix (p. 395, 32e) to the main entry.

h. synonyms of definitions 1 and 3;

Comment: In most dictionaries a word with many apparent synonyms—words having the same or nearly the same meaning—is accompanied by a "synonym study" explaining fine differences. Thus, this dictionary's entry for *strength* concludes:

—**Syn. 4.** STRENGTH, POWER, FORCE, MIGHT suggest capacity to do something. STRENGTH is inherent capacity to manifest energy, to endure, and to resist. POWER is capacity to do work and to act. FORCE is the exercise of power: *One has the power to do something. He exerts force when he does it. He has sufficient strength to complete it.* MIGHT is power or strength in a great degree: *the might of an army.*

This would be useful information if you were wondering which of the four similar words to use in a sentence. If you looked up *power, force,* or *might,* you would find a cross reference to the synonym study under *strength.*

i. antonyms (words with the opposite meaning) of definitions 1 and 3.

Comment: If you are searching for a word to convey the opposite of a certain term, check its listed antonyms. But if you still are not satisfied, look up the entries for the most promising antonyms and check their synonyms. This will greatly expand your range of choice.

So much for *fabulous.* But other sample entries would reveal still further kinds of information:

1. *inflected forms.* Some entries show unusual inflected forms—that is, changes in spelling expressing different syntactic functions. You will find unusual plurals *(louse, lice);* unusual principal parts of verbs *(run, ran, run*—see p. 364, 30b); pronoun forms *(I, my, mine,* etc.); comparative and superlative degrees of adjectives *(good, better, best*—see p. 241, 19a).

2. *restrictive labels.* The entry will show how a word's use may be limited to a region *(Southern U.S., Austral., Chiefly Brit.);* to an earlier time or a kind of occasion *(Archaic, Obs., Poetic);* to a subject *(Bot., Anat., Law);* and, most important for the writer, to a level of usage for words not clearly within standard American English *(Nonstandard, Informal, Slang).*

3. *usage study.* Beyond its usage levels, your dictionary may offer especially valuable discussions of usage problems surrounding certain controversial words or meanings, such as *ain't, different from/than,* or *hardly* with negative forms:

> —**Usage.** HARDLY, BARELY, and SCARCELY all have a negative connotation, and the use of any of them with a supplementary negative is considered nonstandard, as in *I can't hardly wait* for *I can hardly wait.*

13b Keep a vocabulary list.

The only way to be certain that you have broadened your written vocabulary is to try out new words in your papers, risking an occasional inaccuracy while gradually building your store of useful words. But how are you to acquire those words in the first place?

Many student writers rely on a *thesaurus,* or dictionary of synonyms and antonyms, to learn new words and to jog their memory of words already known. A thesaurus can be especially handy if it is included in the word processing program you happen to be using with a computer. You should realize, however, that the synonyms found in a thesaurus are only approximate. To use the thesaurus shrewdly in composing a given sentence, you must already be familiar with the term you select.

The best way to build vocabulary, with or without a thesaurus, is to notice how words are being used by published authors and to keep a record of your growing knowledge. Specifically:

1. Keep a section of your notebook for listing and defining words that you didn't previously know, words whose meanings you misunderstood, and words you understand and admire but haven't yet had occasion to use in your writing.

2. Begin your list by going over the Index of Usage on pages 540–566, making an entry for each expression whose indicated meaning is new to you. Note especially those terms that get easily confused (*affect* versus *effect, imply* versus *infer,* etc.)

3. Add to your notebook continually as you keep reading and receiving comments on your written work.

4. Every time you make an entry, quickly scan the previous entries to see if you have mastered them yet. Cross out or asterisk terms that you now consider to be part of your normal working vocabulary.

**mean
13c**

13c Use words in established senses.

English is probably the fastest-changing of all languages, and yesterday's error often becomes today's standard usage. As a writer, however, you should be concerned not with anticipating shifts in taste but with communicating your ideas effectively. Many readers are upset by diction that is being used in some capricious or momentarily popular way. By being conservative in your choice of words, you can avoid arousing automatically negative responses to the content of your work.

Many fad words have a common feature: they usually belong to one part of speech but are being used as another. Sometimes a suffix

(p. 395, 32e) such as *-wise* or *-type* has been added to turn a noun into an adjective or adverb.

DON'T:

x *Gaswise,* the car is economical.

DO:

• The car gets good mileage.

DON'T:

x *Preferencewise,* she is looking for a *commuter-type* car.

DO:

• She wants a car suitable for commuting.

More often, one part of speech simply takes over another.

DON'T:

x It was a *fun* party.
x She *authored* the book in 1989.
x We *gifted* the newlyweds with a toaster.
x Mark is a *together* person.
x I would give anything for an *invite* to the party.

DO:

• The party was *fun.*
• She *wrote* the book in 1989.
• We *gave* the newlyweds a toaster.
• Mark is a *confident, competent* person.
• I would give anything for an *invitation* to the party.

The use of nouns as adjectives deserves special mention in an age of spreading bureaucracy. Standard English allows many such **attributive nouns,** as they are called, as in *mountain time, night vision, cheese omelet,* and *recreation director.* But officials have a way of jamming them together in a confusing heap. A frugal governor, for example, once proposed what he called a *community work experience program demonstration project.* This row of nouns was meant to describe,

**mean
13c**

or perhaps to conceal, a policy of getting welfare mothers to pick up highway litter without receiving any wages. As a student writer, you would be wise to avoid changing the customary part of speech of a word or piling up attributive nouns.

13d   Control connotations.

The prime requirement for controlling meaning is to know the *denotations,* or dictionary definitions, of the words you use. (See 13a–b.) But words also have important **connotations**—further suggestions or associations derived from the contexts in which the words have been habitually used. By and large, you will not find connotations in your dictionary; you have to pick them up from meeting the same words repeatedly in reading and conversation. Of course you cannot expect to learn all the overtones of every English word. But as a writer you can ask yourself whether the words you have allowed into your first drafts are suited to the occasion. When you are unsure, think of related words until you find one that conveys appropriate associations.

mean
13d

Take, for example, the words *store, shop,* and *boutique.* Because of the contexts in which the words most often appear, they *connote* different things. When we think of a *store,* we picture an establishment where merchandise is sold. A *shop* suggests a smaller establishment selling a specific type of goods, or a department in a larger store, such as the *card shop* at Field's. A *boutique* is a small shop that specializes in fashionable items, often clothing or accessories. If you were writing about the corner grocery that keeps your neighborhood in bread, milk, and other staples seven days a week, you would want to call it a *store.* To call it a *shop* or a *boutique* would undercut your purpose in pointing out the establishment's diverse and ordinary stock.

Consider two further examples, *complex* versus *complicated* and *workers* versus *employees.* Although the members of each pair are close in denotation, their connotations differ. Suppose you wanted to characterize an overelaborate instruction manual. Would you call it *complex* or *complicated?* We hope you would choose *complicated,* which can imply not just intricacy but more intricacy than is called for. And if you were criticizing harsh factory conditions, you would want to write about mistreated *workers,* not mistreated *employees.* These words denote the same people, yet *employees* characterizes them from a corporate point of view, whereas *workers* calls to mind laborers whose interests and loyalties may be quite different from those of the company.

Note that there is such a thing as getting connotations too lopsidedly in favor of your own position on an issue. Suppose, for example, you were writing an essay about discourtesy among adolescents. If you chose the term *young thugs* to characterize teenagers, you would certainly be making your feelings clear, but you would also be *prejudging* your thesis (p. 20, 2d), forcing your reader to respond emotionally with you or against you. In revising your essays, tone down any inflammatory language that seems to convey ready-made conclusions.

mean
13e

13e   Avoid racist and sexist language.

Since you are writing to convince, not to insult, nothing can be gained from using offensive terms. Racial slurs like *nigger, honky,* and *wop,* demeaning stereotypes like *pushy Jew* and *dumb Swede,* and sexually biased phrases such as *lady driver, female logic,* and *typical male brutality* make any fair-minded reader turn against the writer.

The problem of sexism in language deserves special discussion because it goes beyond any conscious wish to show prejudice. In recent decades people have been increasingly realizing that long-accepted conventions of word choice imply that women are inferior or are destined for restricted roles. To keep sexist language out of your prose, then, it is not enough to avoid grossly insulting terms; you must be watchful for subtler signs of condescension as well.

If, for example, you call William Shakespeare *Shakespeare,* why should you call Emily Dickinson *Miss Dickinson* or, worse, *Emily?* Such names imply that a woman who writes poems is not really a poet but a "poetess," a "lady poet," or even a "spinster poet." Write about *Dickinson's poetry,* thus giving it the same standing you would the work of any other author. Similarly, use *sculptor* and *lawyer* for both sexes, avoiding such designations as *sculptress* and *lady lawyer.* And do without *coed,* which suggests that the higher education of women is an afterthought to the real (male) thing. Make your language reflect the fact that, in North America at any rate, men and women are now considered equally eligible for nearly every role.

Tact is necessary, however, in deciding how far to go in changing traditional expressions. The ideal is to avoid sexism without sacrificing clarity and ease of expression. If you wrote *actor* for *actress* and *waiter* for *waitress,* for example, your readers would be confused; rightly or wrongly, common usage still recognizes separate terms for male and female performers of those functions. But when in doubt, choose a sex-neutral term: not *mankind* but *humanity,* not *man-made* but *artificial.*

-Person

mean 13e

Try to find nonsexist alternatives to awkward *-person* suffixes, which sound ugly to many readers of both sexes.

SEXIST	NONSEXIST BUT AWKWARD	PREFERABLE
chairman	chairperson	chair, head
Congressman	Congressperson	Representative
mailman	mailperson	letter carrier
policeman	policeperson	police officer
weatherman	weatherperson	meteorologist

The pronoun dilemma

Perhaps the sorest of all issues in contemporary usage is that of the so-called **common gender.** Which pronouns should you use when discussing an indefinite person, a "one"? Traditionally, that indefinite person has been "male": *he, his, him,* as in *A taxpayer must check his return carefully.* For the centuries in which this practice went unchallenged, the masculine pronouns in such sentences were understood to designate not actual men but people of either sex. Today, however, many readers find these words an offensive reminder of second-class citizenship for women. Remedies that have been proposed include using the phrase *he or she* (or *she or he*) for the common gender, treating singular common words as plural *(A taxpayer must check their return)*, combining masculine and feminine pronouns in forms like *s/he,* and using *she* in one sentence and *he* in the next.

Unfortunately, all of these solutions carry serious drawbacks. Continual repetition of *he or she* is cumbersome and monotonous; many readers would regard *A taxpayer must check their return* as a blunder, not a blow for liberation; pronunciation of *s/he* is uncertain; and the use of *she* and *he* in alternation, though increasingly common, risks confusing the reader by implying that two indefinite persons, a female and a male, are involved.

To avoid such awkwardness, follow these five guidelines:

1. Use *she* whenever you are sure the indefinite person would be female (a student in a women's college, for example):

   **mean
   13e**

   - Someone who enters a nunnery must sacrifice everything from *her* former life.

2. Do not use *she* for roles that have been "traditionally female" but are actually mixed: secretary, school teacher, laundry worker, and so forth. Female pronouns in such contexts imply an offensive prejudgment about "women's place." Use plural forms to show a sex-neutral attitude.

   DON'T:
   x A kindergarten teacher has *her* hands full every day.

   DO:
   - Kindergarten teachers have *their* hands full every day.

3. Use an occasional *he or she* or *she or he* to indicate an indefinite person:

   - When a driver is stopped for a traffic violation, *he or she* would do well to remain polite.

     But be sparing with this formula; it can quickly become annoying.

4. Avoid the singular whenever your meaning is not affected.

DON'T:

x A taxpayer must check *his* return.

DO:

• Taxpayers must check *their* returns.

5. Omit the pronoun altogether whenever you can do so without awkwardness.

ACCEPTABLE:

• Everyone needs *his or her* vacation.

mean
13f

BETTER:

• Everyone needs *a* vacation.

13f   Avoid jargon.

Jargon is specialized language that appears in a nonspecialized con-text, thus giving a technical flavor to statements that would be better expressed in everyday words. When you are writing a paper in, say, economics, anthropology, or psychology, you can and should use terms that are meaningful within the field: *liquidity, kinship structure, paranoid,* and so forth. But those same terms become jargon when used out of context.

DON'T:

x My liquidity profile has been weak lately.

DO:

• I have been short of cash lately.

DON'T:

x Her kinship structure extends from coast to coast.

DO:

• Her family is scattered from coast to coast.

DON'T:

x Roland was really paranoid about the boss's intentions.

DO:

• Roland was suspicious of the boss's intentions.

Most jargon today comes from popular academic disciplines such as sociology and psychology, from government bureaucracy, and from the world of computers. Here is some of the more commonly seen jargon, accompanied by everyday equivalents that would usually be preferable.

JARGON	ORDINARY TERM
access (v.)	enter, make use of
behaviors	acts, deeds, conduct
correlation	resemblance, association
cost-effective	economical
counterproductive	harmful, obstructive
ego	vanity, pride
facilitate	help, make possible
feedback	response
finalize	complete
input	response, contribution
interface (v.)	meet, share information with
maximize	make the most of
obsession	strong interest
parameters	borders
prioritize	prefer, rank
reinforcement schedule	inducements
sociological	social
syndrome	pattern
trauma	shock
user-friendly	uncomplicated

**mean
13f**

You can put jargon to good comic or ironic use, but when you find it appearing uninvited in your drafts, revise.

13g   Aim for middle diction in most contexts.

SLANG	MIDDLE DICTION	FORMAL DICTION
mug	face	visage
kicks	pleasure	gratification
threads	clothes	attire
specs	glasses	spectacles
rip off	steal	expropriate
big-mouthed	talkative	voluble

**mean
13g**

Different situations call for different levels of diction (word choice), from the slang that may be appropriate in a letter to a friend, to the formal language expected in a legal document, to the technical terms demanded by a scientific report. But whenever you are writing outside such special contexts, you should aim for *middle diction*—language that is neither too casual to convey serious concern nor too stiff to express feeling.

The best way to recognize levels of diction is to be an observant reader of different kinds of prose and a close listener to conversations. But if you have studied Latin or a "Latinate" modern language such as Spanish, French, or Italian, you have a head start toward spotting formal English diction. All the words in the right column above are both formal and Latinate.

14 Liveliness

14a Be concrete.

Concrete words name observable things or properties like *classroom* and *smoky;* **abstract** words convey ideas like *education* and *pollution*—nonphysical things that we can grasp only with our minds, not with our senses. Of course there are gradations between the extremes: a *university* is more concrete than *education* but less so than a *classroom,* a distinct physical place. The more concrete the term, the more vivid it will be to a reader.

Whenever you are describing something or telling a story, you can hardly go wrong by making your successive drafts more concrete. Suppose you are trying to characterize your new typewriter, which you have praised in your first draft as *extremely modern.* That is an abstract judgment that could mean anything to anyone. What precisely is modern about the machine? In revising, think about *the daisy wheel printing unit, the automatic return, the automatic correction, the sixteen-character memory, the programmable margin settings,* and so forth. Get the concrete details into your essay, convincing your reader that your general statements rest on observations.

Even in papers of analysis and argument (p. 30, 3b), where the thesis is necessarily an abstract idea, concrete language will help you provide supporting details and retain your reader's interest. Here, for example, are two versions of a student paragraph. In drafting the first one, the writer was evidently thinking of himself as a social-science major. When asked to revise for an essay audience, he looked for ways of turning abstract statements into concrete ones:

A. Lasting trauma from early stress is probably causally related to two factors: heritability of susceptibility and the age at which the stress occurs. In infant rhesus monkeys, certain members of the experimental population prove more susceptible to permanent disturbance than others; heritability is thus an indicated factor. Furthermore, the entire population yields a finding of greater vulnerability when administration of stress occurs between the precise ages of two and seven months. Such a finding suggests that among humans, too, a period of maximum vulnerability may obtain.

B. A recent study of rhesus monkeys may offer us some clues to the way people react—and sometimes don't react—to early stress. Baby monkeys who have been put into solitary cages tend to become feisty and to stay that way. We might have expected as much. But some monkeys, oddly, act normal again almost as soon as they have rejoined their fellows; it seems that they have inherited a resistance to trauma. Furthermore, the most aggressive monkeys turn out to be those who were isolated within a precise period, between the ages of two and seven months. If these findings carry over to humans, we can see why it is risky to generalize about the effects of *all* early stress. What matters may not be whether you suffered in infancy, but who your parents were and exactly when your ordeal occurred.

livel 14b

Neither of these paragraphs abounds in concrete language, but the relative concreteness of passage B helps to explain why it is easier to grasp and more pleasurable to read. Note that weighty, awkward abstractions like *heritability of susceptibility* have disappeared and that we now see *Baby monkeys . . . in solitary cages,* not a *population* that has undergone *administration of stress.*

14b Be concise.

Your reader's attention will depend in large part on the ratio between information and language in your prose. *Wordiness,* or the use of more words than are necessary to convey a point, is one of the most common and easily corrected flaws of style. The fewer words you can use without harm to your meaning, the better.

WORDY	CONCISE
among all the problems that exist today	among all current problems
an investment in the form of stocks and bonds	an investment in stocks and bonds
at this point in time	now
due to the fact that	because
during the course of	during
for the purpose of getting rich	to get rich
for the simple reason that	because
in a very real sense	truly
in spite of the fact that	although
in the not too distant future	soon
in view of the fact that	since
it serves no particular purpose	it serves no purpose
majoring in the field of astronomy	majoring in astronomy
my personal preference	my preference
on the part of	by
owing to the fact that	because
proceeded to walk	walked
rarely ever	rarely
seldom ever	seldom
the present incumbent	the incumbent
to the effect that	that

livel 14b

Avoiding redundancy

A **redundancy** is an expression that conveys the same meaning more than once—for example, *circle around*, which says "go around around." The difference between writing *She circled the globe* and x *She circled around the globe* is that in the second version the word *around* delivers no new information and thus strains the reader's patience.

Examine your drafts to see if they contain redundancies, and be uncompromising in pruning them. The following examples are typical.

REDUNDANT	CONCISE
adequate enough	adequate
advance planning	planning
both together	both
but yet	but
contributing factor	factor
deliberate lie	lie
equally as far	as far
exact same symptoms	same symptoms
few in number	few
final outcome	outcome
free gift	gift
join together	join
large in size	large
past experience	experience
past history	history
refer back	refer
set of twins	twins
share in common	share
shuttle back and forth	shuttle
two different reasons	two reasons

livel 14b

Avoiding circumlocution

All redundancies fall into the broader category of **circumlocutions**—
that is, roundabout forms of expression. But some circumlocutions,
instead of saying the same thing twice, take several words to say
almost nothing. Formulas like *in a manner of speaking* or *to make a
long story short,* for example, are simply ways of making a short story
long. Watch especially for cumbersome verb phrases like *give rise to,
make contact with,* and *render inoperative;* prefer *arouse, meet, destroy.*
And if you mean *because,* do not reach for *due to the fact that.* When
five words do the work of one, all five are anemic.

CIRCUMLOCUTION	CONCISE EXPRESSION
He was of a kindly nature.	He was kind.
It was of an unusual character.	It was unusual.
My father and I have differences about dating.	My father and I differ about dating.
I finally made contact with my supervisor.	I finally met my supervisor.
The copy that is pink in color is for yourself.	Keep the pink copy.
She suspected she would be in an unemployment-type kind of situation when the overflow of customers due to the Christmas shopping circumstances was no longer in effect.	She suspected she would be laid off after the Christmas rush.

livel
14c

14c Prune intensifiers.

In conversation most of us use **intensifiers**—"fortifying" words like *absolutely, basically, certainly, definitely, incredibly, intensely, just, of course, perfectly, positively, quite, really, simply, so, too,* and *very*—without pausing to worry about their meaning. And in telling stories or expressing opinions we veer toward the extremes of *fantastic, terrific, sensational, fabulous,* and *awful, horrible, terrible, dreadful.* Our listeners know how to allow for such exaggeration. Most written prose, however, aims at a more measured tone. Look through your drafts for intensifiers, and see how many of them you can eliminate without subtracting from your meaning. Your revised work will not only be more concise and therefore less taxing to read, it will also sound more assured. Readers sense that intensifiers are morale-building words meaning *maybe* or *I hope;* doing without such terms is a sign of your confidence that you are making a sound case for your ideas.

WITH INTENSIFIERS:

x It was another *very* routine start to a two-week vacation. I *definitely* had no fixed plans other than *simply* flying to Denver. I knew Colorado was a *fantastic* state, and *basically* that is all I thought about as I settled into my assigned seat. As the aircraft door was about to be closed, a man walked in and occupied the vacant seat next to me. He mumbled something to me in an *absolutely* foreign accent. The departure was *very* uneventful. All we *really* did was try to kill time, but the book he was reading *just* attracted my interest: *Cave Exploring in the USA.* I was *so* curious and asked him if cave exploring interested him. That was when he explained—*incredibly*—that in France he was a professional cave explorer. After the dinner service ended, we talked, and his stories of days underground were *too* fascinating. Finally, he invited me to join him, and I *quite* happily accepted.

livel 14d

WITHOUT INTENSIFIERS:

• It was another routine start to a two-week vacation. I had no fixed plans other than flying to Denver. I knew Colorado was an exceptional state, and that is all I thought about as I settled into my assigned seat. As the aircraft door was about to be closed, a man walked in and occupied the vacant seat next to me. He mumbled something in a foreign accent. The departure was uneventful. All we did was try to kill time, but the book he was reading attracted my interest: *Cave Exploring in the USA.* I was curious and asked him if cave exploring interested him. That was when he explained that in France he was a professional cave explorer. After the dinner service ended, we talked; his stories of days underground were fascinating. Finally, he invited me to join him, and I happily accepted.

14d Put your statements in positive form.

Negative ideas are just as legitimate as positive ones; you may have to point out that something did not happen or that an argument leaves you unconvinced. But the negative modifiers *no* and *not* sometimes make for wordiness and a slight loss of readability. If you write *We are not in agreement,* you are asking your reader to go through two steps, first to conceive of agreement and then to negate it. But if you simply write *We disagree,* you have saved three words and simplified the mental operation. The gain is small, but good writing results from a sum of small gains.

Of course you need not develop a phobia against every use of *no* or *not*. Observe, however, that negatively worded sentences tend to be slightly less emphatic than positive ones. Compare:

NEGATIVE	POSITIVE
She did not do well on the test.	She did poorly on the test.
He was not convicted.	He was acquitted.
They have no respect for rationing.	They despise rationing.
It was not an insignificant amount.	It was a significant amount.

livel 14e

14e Avoid euphemisms.

A **euphemism** is a squeamishly "nice" expression standing in the place of a more direct one. Some words that began as euphemisms, such as *senior citizen* and *funeral director,* have passed into common usage, but you should try to avoid terms that still sound like ways of covering up a meaning instead of conveying it. Euphemisms often conceal a devious political or commercial motive. If you want to be regarded as candid and trustworthy, do not write *discomfort* for *pain, memory garden* for *cemetery, pass away* for *die, relocation center* for *concentration camp, revenue enhancement* for *tax raise,* and so forth.

DON'T:

x The governor is extremely concerned about *human resources development.*

DO:

• The governor is extremely concerned about *unemployment.*

DON'T:

x The candidate issued a press release *declaring* that her earlier remarks about her opponent were now to be considered *inoperative.*

DO:

- The candidate issued a press release *admitting* that her earlier remarks about her opponent were *untrue.*

DON'T:

x We are recalling all late models because the bearings *at variance with production code specifications* may *adversely affect vehicle control.*

DO:

- We are recalling all late models because the *defective* bearings may cause drivers to *lose control of the steering.*

14f   Avoid clichés.

livel 14f

A **cliché** is a trite, stereotyped, overused expression such as *throw money around* or *bring the house down.* Clichés are **dead metaphors**—that is, they are figures of speech that no longer sound figurative. When someone writes *off the wall* or *the bottom line,* no reader sees a wall or a line. On the other hand, a writer could blunder into causing people to see real bricks by saying *On the first day that June worked in the construction crew, Steve fell for her like a ton of bricks.* (For such accidentally revived clichés, see page 189, 15b.) But the usual effect of clichés is not unintended comedy but simple boredom. The reader feels that the writer is settling for prepackaged language instead of finding the exact words to convey a particular thought. And matters are not improved by the apologetic addition of *so to speak* or *as the saying goes.* When you need to apologize for any expression, change it.

The worst thing about cliché-ridden prose is its predictability. As soon as we register one element of the cliché, the rest of it leaps to mind like an advertising jingle:

pleasingly . . . plump

lines of . . . communication

the foreseeable . . . future

the pieces . . . of the puzzle . . . fall into place

The resultant prose—*to be brutally frank*—is a *far cry* from being a *sure winner* in the *hearts and minds* of readers *from every walk of life.*

Three lists of clichés follow. List A includes examples of gross clichés, which you can spot fairly easily and eradicate as you revise. List B includes less obvious clichés, pairs of seemingly inseparable adjectives and nouns, clusters that choke out your originality as a writer. List C consists of pat expressions that say too little in a wordy and predictable manner.

LIST A: GROSS CLICHÉS

a needle in a haystack	one in a million
blind as a bat	quiet as a mouse
carve a niche for oneself	rule with an iron fist
drive one to distraction	sly as a fox
happy as a lark	smart as a whip
live like a king	sow one's wild oats
make a beeline for	the top of the heap
old as the hills	tough as nails

LIST B: "INSEPARABLE" PAIRS

bounce back	supreme moment
flawless complexion	tempestuous affair
grave danger	tender mercies
high spirits	unforeseen obstacles
integral part	vicious circle
nuclear holocaust	vital role

LIST C: PAT EXPRESSIONS

after all is said and done	in this day and age
at this point in time	it goes without saying
far be it from me	it stands to reason
in a very real sense	once and for all
in the final [last] analysis	when push comes to shove

level 14f

14g   Watch for sound patterns.

Knowing that repeated sounds draw attention, you can sometimes use them deliberately, as Mark Twain did in referring to

- the *calm confidence* of a *Christian* with four aces,

or as Thomas Paine did in writing

- These are the *times* that *try* men's souls.

In these examples the "poetic" quality goes along with the effort to make a concisely emphatic statement.

livel 14g

Unless you are after some such effect, however, beware of making your reader conscious of rhymes *(the side of the hide)* or alliteration *(pursuing particular purposes)* or repeated syllables *(apart from the apartment).* These snatches of "poetry" usually result from an unconscious attraction that words already chosen exert on subsequent choices. Having written *the degradation,* you write *of the nation* because the *-ation* sound is in your head. You may have to read your first draft aloud, attending to its sound and not its sense, in order to find where you have lapsed into jingling.

Abstract Latinate words—the ones that usually end in *-al, -ity, -ation,* or *-otion*—are especially apt to make a repetitive sound pattern. It is worth the pains to rewrite, for example, if you find bunched words like *functional, essential, occupational,* and *institutional or equality, opportunity, parity,* and *mobility.*

Finally, watch for clusters of prepositions that can be annoying:

DON'T:
x A lot *of* journalists *of* different points *of* view were there.

DO:
- Many journalists holding different points of view were there.

DON'T:
x She was altogether charmed *by* her weekend *by* the lake.

DO:
- She found her weekend by the lake altogether charming.

15 Figurative Language

15a Highlight your meaning with vivid figures of speech.

Consider the following two sentences:

LITERAL:
- I ate until I wasn't hungry any longer.

FIGURATIVE:
- I ate until I was as stuffed as a taxidermist's owl.

The first statement is **literal** because it makes its point without requiring us to call up any picture, or **image,** of something other than the matter at hand. The second statement is **figurative** (also called *metaphorical*); it asks for an effort of imagination on our part. The writer wants us to see the point in different terms—specifically, to compare a person to a stuffed owl. The comparison is appropriate because, though exaggerated, it is relevant to the intended effect: a person's full stomach is likened to the mounted owl's entire body, as if the person's insides consisted altogether of packing. Whenever your language makes such a nonliteral appeal, you are using what is known as a *figure of speech.*

The more closely we examine common terms, the more figurative they come to appear. Take, for example, a phrase used in the previous paragraph: *the matter at hand.* In that expression, both *matter* and *at hand* could be called metaphorical, since the sentence that contained them wasn't literally about either matter (physical material) or anybody's actual hand. But you almost certainly didn't notice this figurative quality at the time. Practically speaking, then, *the matter at hand* doesn't call on our imagination; it is not experienced as figurative language. In this chapter, we will call an expression figurative or metaphorical only if it makes its reader conscious of a departure from the literal plane.

Why should you bother incorporating figures of speech into your prose? The answer is that such language, when thoughtfully managed, achieves an impressive effect of vividness, condensation, and wit. Note the striking differences of appeal between the following literal and figurative passages.

**fig
15a**

LITERAL:

The primary Whitman, psychologically speaking, is the Whitman who, at some point in his thirties, made a new connection between two kinds of energy, that of his sensuality and that of language. Thenceforth, his identity was defined by his ability to reconcile those opposite forces.

FIGURATIVE:

The primary Whitman, psychologically speaking, is the Whitman who, at some point in his thirties, opened a new circuit between the energies of sensuality and the energies of language, making them the electric poles of his identity.

— HELEN VENDLER, "Body Language: *Leaves of Grass*
and the Articulation of Sexual Awareness"

LITERAL:

Chicago used to have a great vitality in its downtown area, but by now the city has deteriorated. Much of its life has been transferred to the suburbs, occupying a larger area but lacking that optimism and concentration for which the original Chicago was known.

FIGURATIVE:

Chicago's rising star is now a worn-out supernova, which has exploded all over suburbia.

— THOMAS GEOGHEGAN, "Chicago, Pride of the Rustbelt"

LITERAL:

In New England in autumn, the leaves on the trees are dying. Another common feature of that season is that the Red Sox have typically failed to fulfill people's expectation that they would win their league championship.

FIGURATIVE:
Dying leaves and dead Red Sox—that's the New England autumn.
                                    —RUSSELL BAKER, "New England Gray"

In each figurative expression above, we feel ourselves to be as far from the groping of first-draft prose as we can get. The writer has reduced a complex thought not only to relatively few words but also to a mental picture that lingers in our minds, giving pleasure and information at the same time.

Again, note how the italicized figurative expressions in the following passages bring our imagination into play:

fig
15a

Seeing Tina Turner onstage is *like watching a demented child who stamps her feet, twirls in circles, and bops around bow-legged as though she's wearing a diaper.*
                                    —MICK LASALLE, "She's Her Own Best Imitator"

One of the world's favorite views of Orson Welles in later life . . . shows him inside a limousine, sucking imperiously on *a torpedo-sized cigar.* The venomous intentness of his profile is explained by what we can see in the background: a giggling, gawping multitude pressing against the side windows of the vehicle. Being inside it with Welles, we can participate a little in his visible scorn. . . . *It is like sharing an aquarium with a very large ocean-going predator of uncertain appetite.*
                                    —RUSSELL DAVIES, "A Prodigious One-Man Show"

This generation thinks—and this is its thought of thoughts—that nothing faithful, vulnerable, fragile can be durable or have any true power. *Death waits for these things as a cement floor waits for a dropping light bulb. The brittle shell of glass loses its tiny vacuum with a burst, and that is that.*
                                    —SAUL BELLOW, *Herzog*

Simile and metaphor

Two closely related figures of speech allow you to draw imaginative likenesses. A **simile,** by including the word *like* or *as,* explicitly acknowledges that a comparison is being made.

SIMILE:

- *Like* a patio rotisserie, George's mind always keeps turning at the same slow rate, no matter what is impaled on it.

George's mind is explicitly compared to a rotisserie.

A **metaphor** omits *like* or *as*.

METAPHOR:

- George's hedgeclipper mind gives a suburban sameness to everything it touches.

George's mind is compared to hedgeclippers, but without either of the explicit terms of comparison, *like* or *as*.

**fig
15a**

In theory a metaphor is a more radical figure of speech than a simile, for it asserts an identity, not just a likeness, between two things (George's mind "is" a gardening tool). But in practice one kind of figure can be as striking as the other. What counts is not the choice between simile and metaphor but the suitability of the **image** to your intended meaning. The two images about George, for example, call to mind not only his conformism but also his specifically suburban background (the carefully tended hedge, the patio rotisserie).

Simile and metaphor predominate among the figures of speech you have already studied in this chapter:

SIMILE	METAPHOR
• I ate until I was *as* stuffed *as* a taxidermist's owl.	• The primary Whitman . . . opened a new circuit between the energies of sensuality and the energies of language, making them the electric poles of his identity.
• Seeing Tina Turner onstage is *like* watching a demented child who stamps her feet, twirls in circles, and bops around bow-legged *as though* she's wearing a diaper.	• Chicago's rising star is now a worn-out supernova, which has exploded all over suburbia.
• It is *like* sharing an aquarium with a very large ocean-going predator of uncertain appetite.	• Dying leaves and dead Red Sox—that's the New England autumn.

Understatement and hyperbole

Language that conspicuously minimizes an extreme state of affairs can also be regarded as figurative, even if it doesn't draw a comparison. Thus imaginative effects are at work in the following examples of **understatement:**

- You get *a little sweaty* out there fighting a forest fire.
- To be born with a cocaine addiction is *not necessarily the most advantageous way to enter the world.*
- She worked at the office from nine until five, endured a second rush-hour traffic jam, cooked the dinner, and rushed off to the emergency room with her suddenly feverish child—*just a routine day in the life of a single mother.*

Similarly, you can get a figurative effect through **hyperbole,** or overstatement:

**fig
15b**

- . . . sucking imperiously on *a torpedo-sized cigar.*
    (See the Orson Welles passage, p. 187.)
- They won't do a thing about smokestack pollution *until the view from their penthouses is a solid wall of soot.*
- The moths on the Puerto Vallarta coast *were as big as B-52s, and the cockroaches looked like Winnebagos.*

As you can see, understatement and hyperbole produce an effect of **irony** (p. 35, 3e), or the conveying of something quite different from what one's words seem to say. Like other successfully handled figures of speech, these devices tell the reader that the writer has been confident enough to play with language while still maintaining rhetorical control. The effect would be ruined, of course, if it were carried through an entire serious essay.

15b Aim for unstrained similes and metaphors.

If you know when you are using figurative language, you can check your drafts to see that each image is carried through in a consistent way. Thus you will avoid the embarrassment of **mixed metaphor**—the clashing of one image with a neighboring one.

MIXED METAPHOR:

x A tiger in the jungle of politics, he was a cream puff around the house.

The reader's mind strains unsuccessfully to grasp how a *tiger* is meaningfully related to a *cream puff*—that is, how a wild animal can be changed into a dessert.

EFFECTIVE METAPHOR:

● A tiger in the jungle of politics, he was a pussycat around the house.

—CLIFTON DANIEL, "Presidents I Have Known"

The images of *tiger* and *pussycat* are closely related, and the writer (characterizing his father-in-law, Harry Truman) fully controls the different implications of the two terms.

fig 15b

Again, note how the following paragraph jumbles several figures of speech.

MIXED METAPHOR:

x Although some analysts feel that the presidential primary system is the wrong game plan for choosing the best nominee, they forget that primaries are an important mirror and proving ground of our democracy. To be sure, candidates can get burned out on the hustings. But by diving into the very heart of state and county politics, the survivors of this pressure cooker can acquire a hands-on feeling for the people they hope to govern.

This passage begins with a sports metaphor, *game plan,* but before the first sentence is over we have been taken through two more incompatible images, a *mirror* and a *proving ground.* The next sentence tells us that candidates can get *burned out on the hustings* (literally, speaking platforms)—a mixed metaphor that unintentionally suggests a public execution. And finally, those candidates who survive the *pressure cooker* are said to be *diving into a heart* where they can get a *hands-on feeling.* Emergency surgery in the kitchen? Clearly, this writer likes to reach for the handiest figurative language without taking responsibility for its implications.

Perhaps you feel that you can avoid mixed metaphors by shunning figurative language altogether. But insofar as you do, your prose will be flat and colorless. Besides, it is not really possible to be completely unfigurative. Many ordinary terms and nearly all clichés (p. 184, 14f) are **dead metaphors**—that is, they contain the faint implication of an image which we are not supposed to notice as such (the *leg* of a table, a *blade* of grass). When clichés are used in close succession, they mischievously come back to life as mixed metaphors:

x *Climbing to the heights* of oratory, the candidate *tackled* the issue.

x Either we *get a handle* on these problems or we are all *going down the drain.*

x You can't *sit on your hands* if a recession is developing, because *you don't know where the bottom is.*

Figurative language, then, can be tricky. When you intend an abstract meaning, you have to make sure that your dead metaphors stay good and dead. But when you do wish to be figurative, see whether your image is vivid, fresh, and consistent. Literal statement may be safe, but a striking figure carried through consistently can unify and intensify your sentences.

fig 15c

15c Practice the extended figure of speech.

If you have hit upon a suitable image to convey your meaning, you can sometimes add a sentence or two, or even a whole paragraph, that will draw further implications from it. One such *extended figure of speech* is Saul Bellow's "light bulb" passage on page 189. Here, from a student writer, is another:

> For me, the idea of going on for an advanced degree is like that of rowing across the ocean. Perhaps I could do it and perhaps I couldn't. But what, I wonder, is waiting for me on the other side, and isn't there some faster and safer way of getting there? Until I know the answers to these questions, I intend to keep my feet planted on familiar soil.

This writer begins with a simile *(the idea of going on for an advanced degree is <u>like</u> that of rowing across the ocean)* and then extends it through three more sentences, making sure that the rest of her language remains compatible with that initial image.

To be effective, an extended figure must above all be apt. That is, the chosen image ought to convey natural-looking resemblances to the situation it is meant to express, so that the writer can draw out those resemblances without seeming to labor over them:

EFFECTIVE:

I am a kind of human snail, locked in and condemned by my own nature. The ancients believed that the moist track left by the snail as it crept was the snail's own essence, depleting its body little by little; the farther the snail toiled, the smaller it became, until it finally rubbed itself out. That is how perfectionists are. Say to us Excellence, and we will show you how we use up our substance and wear ourselves away, while making scarcely any progress at all. The fact that I am an exacting perfectionist in a narrow strait only, and nowhere else, is hardly to the point, since nothing matters to me so much as a comely and muscular sentence. It is my narrow strait, this snail's road: the track of the sentence I am writing now; and when I have eked out the wet substance, ink or blood, that is its mark, I will begin the next sentence.

—CYNTHIA OZICK, "On Excellence"

The key question about an extended figure of speech, beyond its aptness, is when to abandon it. As soon as your reader becomes conscious of the pains you are taking to keep the image self-consistent, the extended figure starts to become a liability. Consider the following passage, which stretches a rather unpromising image through a fully developed paragraph:

OVEREXTENDED:

The ivory tower, as college students—and psychiatrists—across the country will testify, is not nearly so pleasant an abode as it appears from the outside. It shelters its inhabitants from some of life's pedestrian difficulties, but at the same time creates new traumas and problems, which take on, in such closed quarters, an importance of which the real world cannot conceive. The legendary tower of learning is not a stable structure: it is buffeted by the high winds of exam periods, by the gales of preprofessional competition; it shakes with the constant underground rumblings of adolescent crises. What shall I be? What shall I do? Will I

fig 15c

succeed? At times it sways so forebodingly that the unfortunate standing on top sees his future in a heap of broken bones and ivory rubble.
                    —ABIGAIL ZUGER, "Acrophobia in the Ivory Tower"

This is accomplished prose, but the writer's *ivory tower,* unlike Cynthia Ozick's *snail,* threatens at every moment to revert to its original
status as a cliché. By the final sentence we may feel that the writer has
become a prisoner of her own image. Wisely, she drops the ivory tower
figure altogether in the next paragraph of her essay.

15d   Use an analogy to reason from one situation to another.

Think for a moment about the nuclear arms race—already in itself a
metaphor (15a), since countries that stockpile weapons are not literally involved in a *race.* If you were to write *This is a race in which all
the runners and spectators dread the finish line,* you would be engaging in another metaphor. But suppose you wrote instead, *In their
nuclear arms race, the United States and the USSR are like two people
sitting in a pool of gasoline. One of them has seven matches and the
other has only five.* That would be an **analogy**—an elaborated likeness purporting to show that the rule or principle behind one thing
also holds for the quite different thing being discussed. If an extended
figure of speech (15c) draws out the implications of an image that
remains metaphorical, an analogy asks us to *reason from one situation
to another.*

fig
15d

   Why bother with analogies when more direct forms of explanation
are available? The arms race example—actually used by Representative Barbara Boxer—shows why. A good analogy makes a point vivid,
memorable, and easy to comprehend. We immediately see what is fool-
ish about stockpiling matches while sitting in a pool of gasoline, and
our minds readily apply that lesson to the arms race. If a nuclear war
will engulf both nations in destruction, both should stop "playing with
matches."
   But this same example also shows the limited force of even the
best analogies. An analogy can be persuasive on an emotional or imaginative plane, but it can never prove the intended point. An opponent

is always free to brush the analogy aside and talk about factors that the analogizer has left out of account. An advocate of nuclear "parity," for example, could maintain that the theory of deterrence has prevented another world war for over forty years now, whereas the theory of nuclear disarmament faces many untested difficulties. For every analogy urging one side of the case, a contrary analogy could be devised: *The United States and the USSR are like two people who hate each other but have to act cautiously because they live together in a room full of TNT. The advocates of nuclear disarmament would take away the explosive and leave the adversaries alone with their guns and knives.* Which of the two analogies is "right"? Neither. Both of them are simply means of dramatizing beliefs that rest on other grounds.

fig 15d

Analogies can be used not only to argue but also to make an explanation clearer by putting it in simpler and more pictorial terms. Wherever you are worried that things may be getting too complicated for your reader to follow, you can consider resorting to this device. Here, for example, a writer who is seeking to explain a disastrous conjunction of weather fronts asks his readers to see the more readily apprehended image of an automobile crashing into a wall:

> The real problem with forecasting the generation of a storm such as this is gauging its severity. It is not like following a fully developed storm for several days as it moves across the ocean, watching it weaken or strengthen with some sort of regularity. It is more like watching a car about to crash into a brick wall; you know there is going to be a crash, there is an 80 percent chance the gas tank will explode, but you don't know how much gas is in the tank! Just as with the car, the measure of a storm's severity is gauged by its ingredients; the existence of a front (the brick wall), the amount of cold air coming down behind the front (speed of the car), and the degree of circulation in the upper air approaching the front (amount of gas in the tank).
>
> —ROB MAIRS, "How the Storm Developed"

Note how carefully this writer has developed the elements of his analogy, drawing out its lesson without pursuing it to the point of tedium.

V
USAGE

Usage

Whatever you have to say in your writing, you will want to say it within the rules of standard written English—*the "good English" that readers generally expect to find in papers, reports, articles, and books. Fortunately, you already follow most of those rules without having to think about them. In fact, if you did think about them while composing, you would have trouble concentrating on your ideas. The time to worry about correctness is after you have finished at least one draft. Then you can begin making certain that your points will come across without such distractions as incomplete sentences, spelling errors, and subjects and verbs that are incorrectly related.*

Problems with standard written English are usually divided into those of usage *and those of* punctuation—*that is, between rules for the choice and order of words (usage) and rules for the insertion of marks to bring out a sentence's meaning (punctuation). But usage and punctuation work together toward the same end of making sentences coherent, or fitting together in an easily understood way. Certain classic "usage" problems, such as the sentence fragment and the run-on sentence, are punctuation problems as well. Therefore, though we review the punctuation marks and their functions separately (Chapters 24–29), we also deal with punctuation in the present set of chapters. For example, if you are having trouble with modifiers or parallel constructions, you will find those topics treated as whole units, without artificial postponement of the relevant comma rules.*

16 Complete Sentences

COMPLETE SENTENCE	SENTENCE FRAGMENT
● One-lane country roads un-nerve the best drivers.	x Which unnerve the best drivers.

Since a sentence is the basic unit of written discourse, you must be able to recognize complete and incomplete sentences in your drafts. A sentence begins with a capital letter and ends with a period, question mark, or exclamation point. Unfortunately, **sentence fragments** show those very features. You need to know, then, that a grammatically complete sentence normally requires a **verb** and its **subject** within an **independent clause**.

16a Recognize a verb.

A **verb** is a word that tells the state of its subject or an action that the subject performs. (If the verb consists of more than one word, as in *was starting* or *would have been accomplished*, it is called a *verb phrase*.) Every verb functions in one of three ways:

1. A **transitive verb** transmits the action of the subject to a **direct object:**

   - The *doctor solved* the *problem.*
     (S   V   D OBJ)

   - The *technician took* an *x-ray.*
     (S   V   D OBJ)

2. An **intransitive verb** in itself expresses the whole action:

   - The *patient recovered.*
     (S   V)

   - *Dr. McGill lectures* often.
     (S   V)

or

3. A **linking verb** connects the subject to a **complement,** an element that helps to identify or describe the subject:

   - Her *training has been scientific.*
     (S   V   C)

   - *She is* a recognized *professional.*
     (S V   C)

**frag
16a**

The verb plus all the words belonging with it make up the **predicate.**

Verb position

In normal word order for statements, the subject comes before its verb:

   - The *highway committee is meeting.*
     (S   V)

   - The *law will remain* on the books.
     (S   V)

But in some questions the verb comes before the subject:

   - *Are you* sure?
     (V S)

And in most questions the verb has two parts that surround the subject:

- *Is he driving* the Honda tonight?
  $\overset{\frown}{\underset{S}{}}$ V

- *Do you know* where she left the car?
  V
  S

Change of verb form

Verbs show **inflection,** or changes of form, to indicate **tense,** or time.

PRESENT TENSE	PAST TENSE	FUTURE TENSE
They *iron* their jeans.	They *ironed* their jeans.	They *will iron* their jeans.
He fights *hard.*	He *fought* hard.	He *will fight* hard.

frag
16a

Verb versus verbal

VERB (In complete sentence)	VERBAL (In fragment)
• We *will break* our record.	VERBAL x *To break* our record.
• Eve *was laughing* out loud.	VERBAL x *Laughing* out loud.
• *Are* they *winning* the championship?	VERBAL x *Winning* the championship.

Certain words resemble verbs and can even change their form to show different times. Yet these **verbals**—namely, **infinitives, participles,** and **gerunds**—function like nouns or modifiers instead of like verbs. Thus they do *not* supply a key element for sentence completeness.

Compare the complete sentences with the fragments in the box above. Note how you can tell that the three verbals in the right column are not functioning as verbs:

1. One kind of verbal, an infinitive, often follows *to (to break).* A true verb in a sentence stands without *to.*

2. A verbal ending in *-ing* is one word. When a true verb ends in *-ing,* it always follows a word or words that count as part of the verb *(was laughing, have been winning).*

You can write complete sentences that include verbals, but only by supplying true subject-verb combinations:

- *To break our record will be* difficult.

- *Laughing out loud, Eve ran* a victory lap.

- *Winning the championship is* not easy.

**frag
16b**

16b Recognize a subject.

- My *uncle* prefers a big car.

A **subject** is the person, thing, or idea about which something is said or asked. Locating a subject therefore involves locating its accompanying verb.

Most subjects are nouns—words like *uncle, philosophy,* and *Eve.* Some subjects are pronouns, such as *she* or *they* or *someone.* Others are noun phrases like *a very fine day.* And still others, which we will call **nounlike elements,** are groups of words that function together as single nouns: *to run fast, winning the championship,* and so forth. Thus you cannot spot a subject simply by its form. Find the verb and then ask who or what performs the action of that verb or is in the state expressed by it:

- That law *affects* all drivers.

What affects all drivers? *That law* is the subject.

- *Does* anyone *speak* Japanese?

  Does who speak Japanese? The subject is *anyone.*

- Whatever you see *is* for sale.

  What is for sale? *Whatever you see.* That whole clause is the subject.

Implied subject

- [You] Watch out!

You cannot write a grammatically complete sentence without a verb, but in commands, the subject *you* typically disappears. Since that subject is implied, however, the sentence is not regarded as a fragment.

16c   Distinguish an independent clause from a subordinate one.

frag
16c

INDEPENDENT CLAUSE	SUBORDINATE CLAUSE
Mike sells chickens.	Although *Mike sells chickens*, . . .
The *poster was badly printed.*	When the *poster was badly printed*, . . .
Dogs were running wild.	Because *dogs were running wild*, . . .

A **clause** is a cluster of words containing a subject-predicate combination (pp. 197-200, 16a). To avoid sentence fragments, you must be able to tell the difference between two fundamental kinds of clauses. An *independent clause* is a grammatically complete statement, question, or exclamation. It is capable of standing alone as a sentence. A *subordinate clause* (sometimes called a *dependent clause*) cannot stand alone, because it is typically introduced by a word that relates it to another part of the same sentence. Subordinate clauses serve important functions, but by themselves they are sentence fragments.

A subordinate clause is usually introduced by either

1. a *subordinating conjunction,* a word like *although, as, because,* or *when,* which subordinates (makes dependent) the following subject and predicate,

or

2. a *relative pronoun,* a word like *who, which,* or *that,* which begins a relative clause.

A **relative clause** is a subordinate clause that functions like an adjective by relating its statement to an earlier, or *antecedent,* part of the sentence.

ANT   REL CLAUSE

• She is the *one who ran the race.*

Sometimes you will find that an independent clause, like many subordinate ones, follows a conjunction. But that word will always be one of the seven *coordinating conjunctions.* If you keep those seven words distinct in your mind from subordinating conjunctions and relative pronouns, you will have a head start toward distinguishing between independent and subordinate clauses.

**frag
16c**

COORDINATING CONJUNCTIONS (May precede independent clauses)			
and	for	or	yet
but	nor	so	

SUBORDINATING CONJUNCTIONS (Begin some subordinate clauses)			
after	because	than	whenever
although	before	that	where
as	if	though	wherever
as if	in order that	till	while
as long as	provided (that)	unless	why
as soon as	since	until	
as though	so (that)	when	

RELATIVE PRONOUNS (Begin relative subordinate clauses)			
who	whom	which	that

Remember, then, that each of your sentences will normally contain at least one independent clause—a construction which, like *Mike sells chickens,* contains a subject and predicate but is not introduced by a subordinating conjunction or relative pronoun:

IND CLAUSE

- Acting on a hunch, *I removed the book from the shelf.*

IND CLAUSE

- As I opened the book, *twenty-dollar bills fluttered to the carpet.*

IND CLAUSE   IND CLAUSE
- *I stared intently,*and *my palms began to sweat.*

IND CLAUSE

- Although I am tempted to keep it, *this money will have to be turned over to the police.*

frag
16d

16d   Eliminate an unacceptable sentence fragment.

A **sentence fragment** is a word or set of words beginning with a capital letter and punctuated as a sentence but lacking an independent clause (16c). Typically, a fragment is either a subordinate clause (16c) or a **phrase**—a cluster of words lacking a subject-predicate combination:

SUBORDINATE CLAUSE AS FRAGMENT:
x Because milk and eggs are still a bargain.
x Unless winning at chess is important to you.
x Which makes my uncle nervous.

PHRASE AS FRAGMENT:
x Such as milk and eggs.
x Winning at chess.
x My uncle being nervous.

Most unacceptable fragments are really detached parts of the preceding sentence that the writer has mistakenly set off with a period. The handiest way to correct most fragments is to rejoin them to that earlier sentence:

UNACCEPTABLE FRAGMENTS (Italicized)	COMPLETE SENTENCES
Local agencies will become overcrowded and ineffective. x *Unless the number of mental health services is increased.*	● Unless the number of mental health services is increased, local agencies will become overcrowded and ineffective.
Alex and Dolores played tennis in the park. x *Instead of at school.*	● Alex and Dolores played tennis in the park instead of at school.
They stood back and watched the crows. x *Wheeling and cawing over the splattered melon.*	● They stood back and watched the crows wheeling and cawing over the splattered melon.
When they had rested, they continued up a path. x *A winding path that led to the top.*	● When they had rested, they continued up a path—a winding path that led to the top.

**frag
16d**

Again, the italicized parts of the following passage are unacceptable fragments.

CONTAINING FRAGMENTS:

On Thursday we reported the numbers of our missing traveler's checks. *Which were lost during our arrival in New Orleans that morning.* We sat down outside the American Express office and watched other tourists. *Who were sunning themselves on the levee.* We were feeling low because we thought we had missed our chance to hear some Dixieland jazz. We were overjoyed, though, when a group of musicians ambled by and set up their instruments. *Right there on the levee.* We spent the rest of the afternoon listening to their music. *The best open-air jazz concert in town.*

REVISED:

On Thursday we reported the numbers of our missing traveler's checks, which we had lost during our arrival in New Orleans that morning. We sat down outside the American Express office and watched other tourists sunning themselves on the levee. We were feeling low because we thought we had missed our chance to hear some Dixieland jazz. We were overjoyed, though, when a group of musicians ambled by and set up their instruments right there on the levee. We spent the rest of the afternoon listening to their music—the best open-air jazz concert in town.

How to spot a fragment

You can recognize many fragments by the words that introduce them—subordinating terms such as *although, because, especially, even, except, for example, including, instead of, so that, such as, that, which, who,* and *when.* Of course, many acceptable sentences also start with such words but are complete because they include a full independent clause (p. 201, 16c). When you see a draft "sentence" beginning with one of those words, just check to be sure that an independent clause is also present.

DRAFT (Fragments italicized):

I always helped my brother. *Especially with his car.* I assisted him in many chores. *Such as washing the car and vacuuming the interior.* He let me do whatever I wanted. *Except start the engine.* Now I drive my own car. *Which is a 1983 Chevy.* I am thinking of possible jobs to help pay the cost of upkeep. *Including driving a cab. Because maintaining a car these days can be expensive.*

frag
16d

REVISED:

I always helped my brother, especially with his car. I assisted him in many chores, such as washing the car and vacuuming the interior. He let me do whatever I wanted except start the engine. Now I drive my own car, a 1983 Chevy. I am thinking of possible jobs, including driving a cab, to help pay the cost of upkeep. Maintaining a car these days can be expensive.

Learn to recognize the following five types of fragments.

1. A subordinate clause posing as a whole sentence.

DRAFT:

Living in the city is more dangerous than ever. *Especially if you are wearing a gold chain.* During the past several weeks gold snatchers have been on a crime spree. *Although the police have tried to track down the thieves.* Nobody with a chain is safe. *Because the victims range from drivers stalled in traffic jams to students in gym classes.*

REVISED:
Living in the city is more dangerous than ever, especially if you are wearing a gold chain. Although the police have tried to track down the thieves, during the past several weeks gold snatchers have been on a crime spree. Nobody with a chain is safe; the victims range from drivers stalled in traffic jams to students in gym classes.

2. A verbal (p. 199, 16a) or a phrase (p. 203, 16d) unaccompanied by an independent clause.

DRAFT:
Before the start of the race, the drivers sat in their cars. *Revving up their engines.* They all had the same dream. *To see that checkered flag waving when they crossed the finish line.*

REVISED:
Before the start of the race, the drivers sat in their cars, revving up their engines. They all had the same dream: to see that checkered flag waving when they crossed the finish line.

frag
16d

3. An appositive (p. 257, 19n) standing alone.

DRAFT:
I love to read about the Roaring Twenties. *A decade that had its own personality.* People did their best to blot out the horrors of the recent past. *The Great War, the worldwide flu epidemic, the ominous revolution in Russia.*

REVISED:
I love to read about the Roaring Twenties, a decade that had its own personality. People did their best to blot out the horrors of the recent past—the Great War, the worldwide flu epidemic, the ominous revolution in Russia.

4. A disconnected second verb governed by a subject in the sentence before.

DRAFT:

The speech for my film course took a long time to prepare. *And then turned out poorly.* I needed a live audience. *But didn't have one for the test.*

REVISED:

The speech for my film course took a long time to prepare and then turned out poorly. I needed a live audience but didn't have one for the test.

5. A "sentence" lacking a verb in an independent clause.

DRAFT:

If there are no more malpractice suits, the hospital to win its license renewal. But no one can be sure. *Because patients these days are very quick to go to court.*

REVISED:

If there are no more malpractice suits, the hospital will win its license renewal. But no one can be sure, because patients these days are very quick to go to court.

frag
16e

Sentence beginning with a coordinating conjunction

Note that there is nothing wrong with beginning a sentence with a coordinating conjunction (p. 202, 16c) such as *and* or *but*, provided you want the effect to be informal or conversational.

ACCEPTABLE:

COORD
CONJ
- I said farewell to my friends in high school. *And in September I began a completely new life.*

16e   Note the uses of the intentional sentence fragment.

Some composition instructors advise against any use of fragments in submitted work. They feel, understandably, that students should eliminate habitual mistakes before trying flourishes of style. But you should know that practiced writers do resort to an occasional **intentional fragment** when they want to reply to a question in the previous sentence or make a point concisely and emphatically.

ACCEPTABLE:

- He sets him up with jabs, he works to the body, he corners him on

  INTENTIONAL FRAG

  the ropes. *Then the finish, a left hook to the jaw that brings him down.*

- Many secretaries were outraged by the shift to a later working

  INTENTIONAL FRAG

  day. *But not quite all of them.*

  INTENTIONAL FRAG
- And now for dessert. *Pecan pie and ice cream!*

You will see from your reading of published authors that intentional fragments usually possess a certain "shock value." Whereas an unacceptable fragment looks like a missing part of a neighboring sentence, an intentional fragment is a condensed means of lending punch to a new statement.

**frag
16e**

17 Joining Independent Clauses

17a Note the two common ways of joining independent clauses.

An **independent clause** is a grammatically complete statement, question, or exclamation—one that could stand alone as a full sentence, whether or not it actually does stand alone (p. 201, 16c).

INDEPENDENT CLAUSES:
- I need a rest. [statement]
- Have I ever been this tired before? [question]
- Leave me alone! [exclamation]

Comma and coordinating conjunction

There are two usual ways of joining independent clauses within a single sentence. The first way is to put a comma after the first independent clause and to follow the comma with a coordinating conjunction—that is, one of the following seven connectives: *and, but, for, or, nor, so, yet.*

IND CLAUSE	COORD CONJ	IND CLAUSE

- I am not prepared **,** *and* I dread seeing the questions.

IND CLAUSE   COORD   IND CLAUSE
                          CONJ

- Many students took this course, *but* few have kept up with the
  work.
                    COORD
  IND CLAUSE   CONJ   IND CLAUSE

- Am I going crazy, *or* do I just need a good night's sleep?

Semicolon

Alternatively, you can join independent clauses with a semicolon
alone if they are closely related in meaning and spirit or show a striking, pointed contrast:

IND CLAUSE   IND CLAUSE

- I am not prepared; I dread seeing the questions.

      IND CLAUSE   IND CLAUSE

- Many students took this course; few have kept up with the
  work.

**un-on
17a**

     When using a semicolon, test to see if what comes before it could
make a complete sentence and if what comes after it could also make a
complete sentence. If either test fails, your draft sentence is faulty.

DON'T:

x She said she was sorry I was leaving; especially because it would
   not be easy to find a replacement.

   Especially because it would not be easy to find a replacement
   could not stand as a complete sentence.

DO:

- She said she was sorry I was leaving; it would not be easy, she
  said, to find a replacement.

DON'T:

x My wife thought I should have apologized; since I was the one
   who had left the directions at home.

   The *since . . .* clause could not stand as a complete sentence.

DO:

• My wife thought I should have apologized; after all, I was the one who had left the directions at home.

In some cases you will find it easier simply to eliminate the semicolon or replace it with a comma.

DON'T:

x He strode into the room; while flicking the light switch on.

DO:

• He strode into the room while flicking the light switch on.

DON'T:

x My grandparents said that they were too tired to see me; but that they would phone me later.

DO:

• My grandparents said that they were too tired to see me, but that they would phone me later.

run-on
17b

17b Avoid a run-on sentence.

RUN-ON SENTENCES	**PROPERLY PUNCTUATED SENTENCES**
x I need a rest, I must keep studying for the exam.	• I need a rest, but I must keep studying for the exam.
x I am not prepared I dread seeing the questions.	• I am not prepared; I dread seeing the questions.

If you remember how to join independent clauses, you will be able to spot and correct a **run-on sentence**—that is, a sentence in which two or more independent clauses are joined with only a comma between them or with no punctuation at all.

There are other ways to correct a run-on sentence besides inserting a semicolon or a comma and a coordinating conjunction—for example, by changing one of the independent clauses to a subordinate clause or a phrase (p. 203, 16d). But if you decide to keep your two independent clauses, remember the rules for joining them correctly (17a).

COMMA AND COORDINATING CONJUNCTION:
- I need a rest, *but* I must keep studying for the exam.

SEMICOLON:
- I am not prepared; I dread seeing the questions.

Comma splice

A run-on sentence in which a comma alone joins two independent clauses is known as a **comma splice.** Such a construction does not seriously garble the statement being made, but it fails to indicate how its two clauses are related in meaning.

**run-on
17b**

DONT:

FIRST IND CLAUSE	SECOND IND CLAUSE

x Faulkner's novel is psychologically deep, they wanted to explore it further.

FIRST IND CLAUSE	SECOND IND CLAUSE

x They discussed Faulkner's novel, the class hour ended all too soon.

How to revise a comma splice

If you find a comma splice in one of your drafts, you can revise it in a number of ways, including the subordinating of one element to another.

COMMA AND COORDINATING CONJUNCTION (p. 209, 17a):
- Faulkner's novel is psychologically deep, *and* they wanted to explore it further.

SEMICOLON (p. 210, 17a):
- Faulkner's novel is psychologically deep; they wanted to explore it further.

SUBORDINATE CLAUSE (p. 201, 16c):
- *Although they did make some progress in discussing Faulkner's novel,* the class hour ended all too soon.

PHRASE (p. 203, 16d):
- The class hour came to an end, *leaving them unable to finish their discussion of Faulkner's novel.*

Exception: Note that a tag such as *she thought* or *he said* can be joined to a quotation by a comma alone, even if the quotation is another independent clause.

IND CLAUSE   IND CLAUSE
- "That is a matter of opinion," Emily replied.

For further ways of joining independent clauses, including another exception to the rule against committing comma splices, see pages 218–220, 17d–e.

run-on 17b

Fused sentence

A run-on sentence in which independent clauses are merged with no sign of their separateness—neither a comma nor a coordinating conjunction—is called a **fused sentence.**

DON'T:

IND CLAUSE   IND CLAUSE
x Some people can hide their nervous habits I envy them.

IND CLAUSE   IND
x Sometimes I have to stand up in front of other students it makes

CLAUSE
me sick.

How to revise a fused sentence

Revise by choosing from the same options given above for correcting a comma splice.

COMMA AND COORDINATING CONJUNCTION:
- Some people can hide their nervous habits, *and* I envy them.

SEMICOLON:
- Some people can hide their nervous habits; I envy them.

SUBORDINATE CLAUSE:
- I feel sick *whenever I have to stand up in front of other students.*

PHRASE:
- I feel sick *standing up in front of other students.*

run-on
17c

17c   Watch especially for run-on sentences using connectors like *however, also,* and *then.*

RUN-ON SENTENCES	PROPERLY PUNCTUATED SENTENCES
x We planted a garden, *however* nothing grew.	• We planted a garden; however, nothing grew.
x We used a plastic mulch, *also* we watered vigorously.	• We used a plastic mulch, and we also watered vigorously.
x We scanned the gardening encyclopedia for help, *then* we phoned Ms. Green Thumb on WKGB.	• After scanning the gardening encyclopedia for help, we phoned Ms. Green Thumb on WKGB.

Look through the following terms, which often lead a writer to commit a comma splice (p. 212, 17b):

SENTENCE ADVERBS

again	hence	nonetheless
also	however	otherwise
besides	indeed	similarly
consequently	likewise	then
further	moreover	therefore
furthermore	nevertheless	thus *(etc.)*

TRANSITIONAL PHRASES

after all	for example	in reality
as a result	in addition	in truth
at the same time	in fact	on the contrary
even so	in other words	on the other hand *(etc.)*

**run-on
17c**

A **sentence adverb** (also called a *conjunctive adverb*) is a word that modifies a whole previous statement. Note how such a term differs from an ordinary adverb.

ORDINARY ADVERB:
- She applied for the job *again* in March.
- *Then* she made arrangements to have her furniture stored.

SENTENCE ADVERB:
- *Again,* there is still another reason to delay a decision.
- We see, *then,* that precautions are in order.

An ordinary adverb modifies part of the statement in which it appears: she applied *again;* she stored her furniture *then.* But a sentence adverb modifies the whole statement by showing its logical relation to the preceding statement: after the already stated reason to delay, here *(again)* is another one; because of the preceding statement, we therefore *(then)* see that precautions are in order. A **transitional phrase** is a multiword expression that functions like a sentence adverb.

What makes these modifiers tricky is that they "feel like" conjunctions such as *and, but, although, so,* and *yet.* If you treat a sentence adverb or transitional phrase as if it were a conjunction, the result will be a comma splice. You can revise such sentences in any of the ways previously discussed, either by properly joining the independent clauses (p. 209, 17a) or by changing the whole construction.

DON'T:

SENT ADV

x Severe rains washed away our seeds, *furthermore,* a late freeze occurred in April.

DO:

SENT ADV

• Severe rains washed away our seeds, and *furthermore,* a late freeze occurred in April.

**run-on
17c**

DON'T:

TRANS
PHRASE

x Our garden was a disappointment, *in fact* it was a disaster.

DO:

TRANS
PHRASE

• Our garden was a disappointment; *in fact,* it was a disaster.

If you are not sure whether a certain word is a sentence adverb, test to see whether it could be moved without loss of meaning. A conjunction must stay put, but a sentence adverb can always be moved to at least one other position:

• We planted a garden; *however*, nothing grew.
• We planted a garden; nothing, *however,* grew.
• We planted a garden; nothing grew, *however*.

When you are sure of the difference between conjunctions and sentence adverbs, you will be able to avoid putting an unneeded comma after a conjunction.

DON'T:

CONJ

x He swam for the island, *but,* the current exhausted him.

DO:

CONJ

• He swam for the island, *but* the current exhausted him.

DON'T:

CONJ

x The threat is serious, *yet,* I think we have grounds for hope.

DO:

CONJ

• The threat is serious, *yet* I think we have grounds for hope.

Setting off sentence adverbs and transitional phrases

Since these expressions modify a whole previous statement, they are usually set apart by punctuation on both sides. Do not allow a sentence adverb or transitional phrase to "leak" at one end or the other.

run-on 17c

DON'T:

SENT ADV

x John, *however* was nowhere to be seen.

DO:

SENT ADV

• John, *however,* was nowhere to be seen.

DON'T:

TRANS
PHRASE

x Guatemala *in contrast,* has a troubled history.

DO:

TRANS
PHRASE

• Guatemala, *in contrast,* has a troubled history.

In some cases you can omit commas or other punctuation around a sentence adverb *(And thus it is clear that . . .)*. But if you supply punctuation at one end, be sure to supply it at the other end as well.

17d Correct a run-on sentence by bringing out logical relations.

If you habitually write run-on sentences, you may think you can solve your problem by keeping to safe, short sentences that scarcely combine clauses at all. But that can only be a stopgap measure; before long you will want to aim for more variety and logical development. Begin thinking, then, not of stripping down your sentences but of developing them by showing just how one element relates to another. Note the following options.

run-on
17d

1. **semicolon** (p. 210, 17a). Use a semicolon to show that two independent clauses are closely related in meaning:

   • The seed company recently went bankrupt; apparently the other customers were as unhappy as we had been.

2. **comma and coordinating conjunction** (p. 209, 17a). Show the roughly equal importance of two independent clauses by means of a comma and a coordinating conjunction:

   • The garden was a failure, *but* at least we got some fresh air and exercise.

3. **subordinate clause** (p. 201, 16c). Use a subordinate clause— one that cannot stand alone—to show that one element is logically dependent on the other one:

   • *Although the garden was a failure,* at least we got some fresh air and exercise.

4. **phrase** (p. 203, 16d). Use a phrase—a cluster of words lacking a subject-predicate combination—to reduce your sentence to one statement accompanied by a modifier.

   • *After bruising our hands in the garden,* we were ready for a new form of recreation.

For further options in sentence variety see Chapter 12, especially pages 154–158.

17e Recognize exceptional ways of joining independent clauses.

Optional comma after brief independent clause

If your first independent clause is brief, consider the comma optional:

- *I was late* and it was already growing dark.

   But a comma after *late* would also be correct. When in doubt, retain the comma.

Optional conjunctions in series of independent clauses

When you are presenting several brief, tightly related independent clauses in a series (p. 296, 22k), you can gain a dramatic effect by doing without a coordinating conjunction:

- He saw the train, he fell to the tracks, he covered his head with his arms.

   By omitting *and* before the last clause, the writer brings out the rapidity and urgency of the three actions. This is a rare case of an acceptable comma splice.

Reversal of negative emphasis

If a second independent clause reverses the negative emphasis of the first, consider joining them only with a comma:

- That summer Thoreau did not read books, he hoed beans.

   The *not* clause leaves us anticipating a second clause that will say what Thoreau did do. The absence of a conjunction brings out the tight, necessary relation between the two statements.

run-on
17e

Compare:

x Thoreau hoed beans all summer, he did not read books.

Lacking a "reversal of negative emphasis," this sentence shows a classic *unacceptable* comma splice.

18 Joining Subjects and Verbs

SUBJECT-VERB COHERENCE

18a Avoid a mixed construction.

DON'T:

x A hobby that gets out of hand, it becomes an obsession.

DO:

• A hobby that gets out of hand becomes an obsession.

If your subjects and verbs (pp. 197–201, 16a–b) are to work efficiently together, you cannot leave your reader wondering which part of a sentence is the subject. Do not start a sentence with one subject and then change your mind. In the "don't" example above, the reader begins by expecting that *hobby* will be the subject. After the comma, however, the writer serves up a new subject, *it,* leaving *hobby* grammatically stranded. The result is a **mixed construction,** whereby two elements in a sentence are competing to serve the same function.

DON'T:

x In doing the workbook problems was extremely useful.

The sentence begins with a prepositional phrase (p. 587) that can only serve as a modifier (p. 240)—as it would, for example, in this sentence: *In doing the workbook problems I had trouble with quadratic equations.* But the writer has tried unsuccessfully to turn *In doing the workbook problems* into a subject.

When you suspect that a draft sentence suffers from mixed construction, first isolate the predicate (p. 198, 16a); then ask yourself what *one* thing makes that predicate meaningful. Thus, *what* was extremely useful? *Doing the workbook problems.* That phrase should become the subject.

DO:

• Doing the workbook problems was extremely useful.

The problem of mixed construction actually extends beyond subjects and verbs. Consider the following sentence.

DON'T:

      D OBJ?   D OBJ?

x They gave *it* to her for Christmas *what* she had been asking for.

Here *it* and *what* are competing to be the direct object (p. 198, 16a) of the verb *gave*. The solution is to choose one or the other and make a consistent pattern.

s–v
agr
18b

DO:

• For Christmas they gave her what she had been asking for.

If your prose contains mixed constructions, review the essential sentence elements: subject, verb, direct object, complement (pp. 197-198, 16a). And be aware that in written prose you cannot make your meaning clear by changing your voice or by abandoning a sentence in the middle and starting over. The first element in a written sentence usually commits it to a certain structure that you must then follow. If you run into trouble, recast the sentence from the beginning.

18b Watch for faulty predication.

Predication—saying something about a grammatical subject—is the essence of all statement. In first-draft prose, however, writers sometimes yoke subjects and predicates that fail to make sense together. A mixed construction (18a), which typically prevents the reader from knowing which word is the intended subject, shows faulty predication in an extreme form. But predication can also go awry if the writer asks a subject to perform something it could not possibly do.

DON'T:

S   V

x The *capabilities* of freshmen in high school *function* on an adult level.
                PRED

> Can capabilities function? No; they are abstractions (p. 175, 14a), not agents. People or things function, and they do so because they possess certain capabilities. Thus the revised sentence must reflect that fact.

DO:

S   V

- *Freshmen* in high school *are* capable of functioning like adults.
         PRED

s–v agr 18b

or

S   V

- *Freshmen* in high school *have* the capabilities of adults.
        PRED

or

S   V

- The *capabilities* of freshmen in high school *match* those of adults.
      PRED

You can see that the problem in faulty predication often lies in treating an abstraction as if it were a performer of action. Once you have hit upon a subject like *capabilities* (or *inventiveness, symmetry, rationality, reluctance,* etc.), your predicate must reflect the fact that you are not writing about an agent.

SUBJECT-VERB AGREEMENT

18c Make a verb agree with its subject in person and number.

In grammar we refer to three **persons:**

	EXAMPLE	IDENTITY
First Person	I pull	the speaker or writer
	we pull	the speakers or writers
Second Person	you pull	the person or persons addressed
Third Person	he, she, it pulls the mother speaks the signal changes	the person or thing spoken or written about
	they pull the mothers speak the signals change	the persons or things spoken or written about

s–v
agr
18c

We also refer to the *time* of a verb as its **tense**—present, past, future, and so forth.

In standard written English, the ending of a verb often shows the **number** of the subject—that is, whether the subject is *singular* (one item) or *plural* (more than one item). A singular subject requires a singular verb; a plural subject requires a plural verb.

       S   V
- The *river flows* south.

> Here the *-s* ending on the verb *flows* indicates that the verb is in the third person, is singular, and is in the present tense.

The grammatical correspondence of subjects and verbs is called **agreement.** In *The river flows south* the verb *flows* is said to agree with its singular, third-person subject *river.* Note that the singular subject usually has no *-s* ending but that a singular, third-person verb in the present tense does have an *-s* ending: *flows.* Compare:

S   V
- The *rivers flow* south.

> The lack of an -*s* ending on the verb *flow* indicates that the verb is plural, in agreement with its plural subject *rivers*. Notice that the -*s* on *rivers* marks it as a plural noun.

SINGULAR:
- The river flows.

PLURAL:
- The rivers flow.

Many native speakers of English use the same forms for both the singular and plural of certain verbs in the present tense: *she don't, they don't; he is, we is.* In standard written English, however, it is important to observe the difference: *she does not, she doesn't, they do not, they don't; he is, we are.*

DON'T:
x They *is* having a party.

DO:
- They *are* having a party.

DON'T:
x He *don't* expect to rent a car.

DO:
- He *doesn't* expect to rent a car.

For further verb forms in various tenses, see pages 362–371, 30b–d.

s–v
agr
18d

18d Be sure you have found the true subject.

Sometimes you will have a good stylistic reason for putting your subject after its verb *(Chief among her virtues was her honesty)* or for separating the subject and verb with other language *(Her honesty,* *acquired from her strictly religious parents, <u>was</u> her chief virtue).* Be careful, though, that you don't lose track of the subject and mistakenly allow the verb to be governed by another word. Here are the constructions—allowable but potentially tricky—that call for particular attention.

Intervening clause or phrase

DON'T:

$$\underset{\text{S}}{\qquad} \overbrace{\text{INTERVENING CLAUSE}}$$

x The *highway* that runs through these isolated mountain

$$\underline{\qquad}\ \text{V}$$

towns *are* steep and narrow.

> The subject, *highway,* is so far from its verb that the writer has absent-mindedly allowed that verb to be governed by the nearest preceding noun, *towns.*

s–v
agr
18d

DO:

$$\underset{\text{S}}{\qquad}\ \underset{\text{V}}{\qquad}$$

• The *highway . . . is* steep and narrow.

Again:

DON'T:

$$\underset{\text{S}}{\qquad} \overbrace{\text{INTERVENING PHRASE}}\ \text{V}$$

x The *pleasures* of a motorcyclist *includes* repairing the bike.

DO:

$$\underset{\text{S}}{\qquad}\ \underset{\text{V}}{\qquad}$$

• The *pleasures . . . include* repairing the bike.

Learn to locate the true subject by asking who or what performs the action of the verb or is in the state indicated by the verb. Test for singular or plural by these steps:

1. Locate the verb and its subject.

2. Put the phrase between them into imaginary parentheses:

The pleasures {of a motorcyclist} $\dfrac{\text{include}}{\text{includes}}$. . . .

3. Then say aloud:

"The pleasures include"

and

"The pleasures includes."

The form of the verb that is correct without the element "in parentheses" is also correct with it. *The pleasures of a motorcyclist include. . . .*

A phrase like <u>along with</u> or <u>in addition to</u>

DON'T:

```
            S   ┌─────── ADDITIVE PHRASE ───────┐   V
```
x *Jill,* along with her two karate instructors, *are* highly disciplined.

DO:

- Jill, along with her two karate instructors, *is* highly disciplined.

s–v
agr
18d

An expression that begins with a term like *accompanied by, along with, as well as, in addition to, including,* or *together with* is called an **additive phrase.** Though it is typically set off by commas (p. 253, 19l), it can "feel like" part of the subject. If you write *Jill, along with her two karate instructors,* you certainly have more than one person in mind. But grammatically, additive phrases do *not* add anything to the subject. Disregard the additive phrase, just as you would any other intervening element. If the subject apart from the additive phrase is singular, make the verb singular as well.

DON'T:

```
           S              ┌────── ADDITIVE PHRASE ──────┐
```
x *Practical knowledge*, in addition to statistics and market theory,
```
   V
```
enter into the training of an economist.

DO:

- Practical knowledge, in addition to statistics and market theory, *enters* into the training of an economist.

Subject following verb

DON'T:

                V   S

x Beside the blue waters *lie Claire,* waiting for Henry to bring the
towels.

> To find the true subject, mentally rearrange the sentence into
> normal subject-verb word order: *Claire lies beside. . . .*

DO:

• Beside the blue waters *lies* Claire, waiting for Henry to bring the
towels.

Watch especially for agreement problems when the subject is delayed
by an expression like *There is* or *Here comes*. By the time such a sentence is finished, its subject may be plural.

DON'T:

           V   S

**s–v
agr
18e**

x Here *comes a clown and three elephants.*

IMPROVED:

• Here *come* a clown and three elephants.

Or, since this example sounds strained:

PREFERABLE:

• Here *comes* a clown leading three elephants.

18e When the subject is a phrase or clause, make the verb singular.

         PHRASE AS S

                            V

• *Having a robot with eight arms is* quite a convenience.

           CLAUSE AS S

                                         V

• *Whenever you have time to test these skates is* a good time for
me.

A phrase or clause acting as a subject takes a singular verb, even if it
contains plural items. Do not be misled by a plural word at the end of
the phrase or clause. The two examples above are correct.

18f Usually treat a noun like *crowd* or *audience* as singular.

- The faculty *has* voted against allowing musicians to perform outside classroom windows.
- The audience *is* on its feet and applauding wildly.
- The orchestra *returns* and *takes* another bow.

A **collective noun** is one having a singular form but referring to a group of members: *administration, army, audience, class, crowd, orchestra, team,* and so forth. This conflict between form and meaning can lead to agreement problems. But in general you should think of a collective noun as singular and thus make the verb singular, too.

Once in a while, however, you may want to emphasize the individual members of the group. Then you should make the verb plural:

- The faculty *have* come to their assignments from all over the world.

s–v
agr
18g

Plural of construction

A plural verb is especially common when a collective noun is followed by a plural *of* construction:

$$\overbrace{\text{A team of experts}}^{\text{s}} \overset{\text{v}}{are} \text{ arriving by plane tomorrow.}$$

- In this sentence *is* would also be correct, but it would put emphasis on the collective *team* instead of on the individual *experts.*

18g If a subject contains two parts, usually treat it as plural.

$$\overbrace{\text{A teller and a guard}}^{\text{s}} \overset{\text{v}}{operate} \text{ the drive-in window at the bank.}$$

$$\overbrace{\text{A bouquet and a box of candy}}^{\text{s}} \overset{\text{v}}{are} \text{ no substitute for a fair wage.}$$

A **compound** subject, such as *a clown and three elephants,* is made up of more than one unit. In most instances, such a subject calls for a plural verb.

Note, in the second example above, that *substitute* is singular even though the subject and verb are plural. Agreement does not extend to complements (p. 198, 16a)—words in the predicate that identify or modify the subject.

Exception: both parts refer to the same thing or person

Even when the parts of a compound subject are joined by *and,* common sense will sometimes tell you that only one thing or person is being discussed. Make the verb singular in such a case:

* My best friend and severest critic has moved to Atlanta.

> One person is both friend and critic. By changing the verb to *have* the writer would be saying that two people, not one, have moved to Atlanta. Both sentences could be correct but their meanings would differ.

18h Avoid a clash of singular and plural subjects linked by *or* or *nor.*

Compound subjects (18g) joined by *or, either . . . or,* or *neither . . . nor* are called **disjunctive.** They ask the reader to choose between two or more parts. Consequently, the verb should agree with only one of those parts—the one nearest the verb.

DON'T:

                DISJUNCTIVE S
     ┌─────────────────────────────┐   V
X *Either his children or his cat are* responsible for the dead gold-fish.

BETTER: NEAREST PART OF
                           DISJUNCTIVE S
                              ┌─────┐
* Either his children or *his cat is* responsible for the dead gold-fish.
                                      V

But such conflicts of number are awkward. Rewrite to avoid the problem.

PREFERABLE:

- Either *his children are* responsible for the dead goldfish or *his cat is.*

or

- *No one* but his children or his cat *could have killed* the gold-fish.

Some disjunctive subjects "feel plural" even though each item within them is singular, for the writer is thinking about two or more things. But so long as the individual disjunctive items are singular, the verb must be singular, too.

DON'T:

s–v
agr
18i

          DISJUNCTIVE S   V

x *Neither WNCN nor WQXR carry* the country-western sing-off.

DO:

- Neither WNCN nor WQXR *carries* the country-western sing-off.

18i If you have placed *each* or *every* before a compound subject, treat the subject as singular.

- *Every linebacker and tackle in the league was pleased* with the settlement.

- Before being put away for the summer, *each coat and sweater is* to be mothproofed.

Each or *every,* if it comes before the subject, guarantees that the subject will be singular even if it contains multiple parts.

Note, however, that when *each* comes *after* a subject, it has no effect on the number of the verb:

     S   V

* *They* each *have* their own reasons for protesting.

18j Observe the agreement rules for terms of quantity.

Numerical words (*majority, minority, number, plurality,* etc.) and plural terms of quantity (*three dollars, fifty years,* etc.) can take either a singular or a plural verb. If you have in mind the *totality* of items, make the verb singular:

                  S   V

* The Democratic *majority favors* the bill.

But if you mean the separate items that make up that totality, make the verb plural:

          S   V

s–v agr 18j

* *The majority of Democrats* on the North Shore *are* opposed to building a bridge.

The word number

When the word *number* is preceded by *the,* it is always singular:

     S   V

* The *number* of unhappy voters *is growing.*

But when *number* is preceded by *a,* you must look to see whether it refers to the total unit (singular) or to individual parts (plural).

TOTAL UNIT (SINGULAR):

     S   V

* A *number* like ten billion *is* hard to comprehend.

INDIVIDUAL PARTS (PLURAL):

            S   V

* *A number of voters have arrived* at their choice.

    Note that although *of voters* looks like a modifier of the subject *number,* we read *a number of* as if it said *many.*

When your subject contains an actual number, decide once again whether you mean the total unit or the individual parts.

TOTAL UNIT (SINGULAR):

$$\overbrace{\text{S}}$$

- *Twenty-six miles is* the length of the race.

INDIVIDUAL PARTS (PLURAL):

$$\overbrace{\text{S}}$$

- *Twenty-six difficult miles lie* ahead of her.

Mathematical operations

When adding or multiplying, you can choose either a singular or a plural verb:

- One and one *is* two.
- One and one *are* two.

When subtracting or dividing, keep to the singular:

- Sixty minus forty *leaves* twenty.
- Eight divided by two *is* four.

s–v
agr
18k

18k   As a rule, use a singular verb with a subject like *everyone* or *nobody*.

An *indefinite pronoun* leaves unspecified the person or thing it refers to.

INDEFINITE PRONOUNS					
all	anything	everybody	most	no one	some
another	both	everyone	much	nothing	somebody
any	each	everything	neither	one	someone
anybody	each one	few	nobody	others	something
anyone	either	many	none	several	such

Some of these words serve other functions, too; they are indefinite pronouns only when they stand alone without modifying another term.

ADJECTIVE:
● *All* leopards are fast.

INDEFINITE PRONOUN:
● *All* have spots.

Some indefinite pronouns, such as *another,* are obviously singular, and some others, such as *several,* are obviously plural. But there is also a borderline class: *each, each one, either, everybody, everyone, everything, neither, nobody, none, no one.* These terms have a singular form, yet they call to mind plural things or persons. According to convention, you should generally treat them as singular:

s–v
agr
18k

         s   v
● *Everyone seems* to be late tonight.
        s   v
● *Neither has brought* the music for the duet.

Keep to a singular verb even when the indefinite pronoun is followed by a plural construction such as *of them:*

     s   v
● *Neither* of them *has* the music for the duet.
    s   v
● *Each* of those cordless phones *has* a touch-tone dial.

None

None is usually treated as singular:

     s   v
● *None* of us *is* ready yet.

> But some writers recognize an option here. If you mean *all of us are not ready* rather than *not one of us is ready,* you can make the verb plural:

$$\overset{\text{S}}{}\quad\overset{\text{V}}{}$$
- *None of us are* ready yet.

> Since some writers would consider this sentence mistaken, keep to the singular wherever it does not sound forced.

18l Watch for a subject with plural form but singular meaning.

Some nouns have an -*s* ending but take a singular verb: *economics, mathematics, mumps, news, physics,* and so forth:

- *Physics* has made enormous strides in this century.

Some other nouns ending in -*s* can be singular in one meaning and plural in another. When they refer to a body of knowledge, they are singular.

AS BODY OF KNOWLEDGE:

S   V
- *Politics is* an important study for many historians.

S   V
- *Acoustics requires* an understanding of mathematics.

But when the same words are used in a more particular sense—not politics as a field but somebody's politics—they are considered plural.

IN PARTICULAR SENSE:

S   V
- Gloria's *politics are* left of center.

V   S
- How *are* the *acoustics* in the new auditorium?

18m In a *that* or *which* clause, make the verb agree with the antecedent.

Consider the following correctly formed sentence:

s–v agr 18m

REL CLAUSE
- The telephone bill *that is overdue* includes a charge for a twenty-minute call to Paris.

Here *that is overdue* is a **relative clause**—a subordinate clause (p. 201, 16c) that functions like an adjective. A relative clause usually begins with a word like *who, whom, whose, that,* or *which.* The relative clause modifies an **antecedent,** a noun or nounlike element in the previous clause. In this case the antecedent is *telephone bill.*

Relative clauses can make for tricky agreement problems. You will avoid trouble, however, if you remember that the verb in a relative clause agrees in number with its antecedent. Thus, in the example above, *is* agrees with the singular antecedent *telephone bill.* Again:

ANT   V
- There have been complaints about *service* that *is* painfully slow.

Note that you cannot automatically assume that the antecedent is the last term before the relative clause.

s–v
agr
18m

ANT   V
- There have been *complaints* about service that *were* entirely justified.

ANT   V
- The *oceans* of the world, which *have become* a dumping ground, may never be completely unpolluted again.

Ask yourself what the verb in the relative clause refers to:

What is painfully slow? Service.
What was entirely justified? Complaints.
What has become a dumping ground? Oceans.

Once you have an answer, a singular or plural term, you also have the right number for the verb in your relative clause.

Singular complement in relative clause

Look at the following mistaken but typical sentence.

DON'T:

PLURAL ANT   V   SING C
x *Math problems,* which *is* her *specialty,* cause her no concern.

A singular complement (p. 198, 16a) in a *who, which,* or *that* clause can trick you into making the verb in that clause singular when the antecedent is actually plural. Here the complement *specialty* has wrongly influenced the number of the verb *is*. That verb, like any other verb in a relative clause, must agree with its antecedent.

DO:

    PLURAL ANT   V
* *Math problems*, which *are* her specialty, cause her no concern.

One of those who

Consider the following sentences, both of which are correct:

                ANT   V
* Joe is one of those *chemists* who *believe* that science is an art.

                ANT   V
* Joe is the only *one* of those chemists who *believes* that science is an art.

The expression *one of those who* contains both a singular and a plural term—*one* and *those*. To avoid confusion, be careful to decide which of the two is the antecedent. In most cases it will be the plural *those* (or *those chemists,* etc.), but to be sure you must isolate the relative clause and ask yourself what it modifies.

s–v
agr
18n

18n   Prefer a singular verb with the title of a work.

Titles of works are generally treated as singular even when they have a plural form, because only one work is being discussed:

       S   V
* Joyce's *Dubliners has justified* the author's faith in its importance.

             S   V
* Camus's *Lyrical and Critical Essays was* required reading in Comparative Literature 102 last term.

    The plural verb *were* would misleadingly refer to the individual essays rather than the whole book.

PUNCTUATION BETWEEN A SUBJECT AND VERB

18o Omit an unnecessary comma between a subject and its verb.

DON'T:

    S   V
x *Ishi* alone, *remained* to tell the story of his tribe.

DO:

• Ishi alone remained to tell the story of his tribe.

An element that comes between a subject and its verb may need to be set off by commas, as in the sentence *Teenage suicide, which has become common in recent years, is a matter of urgent public concern* (p. 253, 19l). But beware of inserting commas simply to draw a breath, for the demands of grammar and of easy breathing do not always match up. You want to show your reader that a subject is connected to its verb.

DON'T:

                               S   V
x *A pair of scissors, a pot of glue, and a stapler, are* still essential to a writer who does not use a word processor.

DO:

• A pair of scissors, a pot of glue, and a stapler are still essential to a writer who does not use a word processor.

18p Note where it is appropriate to insert punctuation between a subject and its verb.

Whenever you place an **interrupting element** (p. 253, 19l) between a subject and verb, you need to set that element apart by a pair of punctuation marks—usually commas:

s–v agr 18p

-      ^S   INT EL   V
The pilot, *having failed to secure clearance to land,* circled the field as she pleaded desperately with the chief traffic controller.

-              S   INT EL
Tax simplification—*a major goal of this administration*—re-
    V
mains a distant promise.

S—V
agr
18p

19 Modifiers

A **modifier** is an expression that limits or describes another element:

- *tall* messenger
- *the tall* messenger *with blond hair*
- *the tall* messenger *with blond hair who is locking his bicycle*
- *The tall* messenger *who is locking his bicycle* is *from Finland.*

A modifier can consist of a single word, a phrase, or a subordinate clause.

1. a single word:

   - The *tall* boy is from Finland.
   - A *new* star appeared in the *darkening* sky.
   - They did it *gladly.*
   - *That* proposal, *however,* was *soundly* defeated.

2. a **phrase,** or cluster of words lacking a subject-verb combination (p. 203, 16d):

   - The boy *with blond hair* is *from Finland.*
   - *At ten o'clock* she gave up hope.
   - *In view of the foul weather,* they remained *at home.*

3. a **subordinate clause,** or cluster of words that does contain a subject-verb combination but does not form an independent statement (p. 201, 16c):

- The tall messenger *who is locking his bicycle* is from Finland.
- The largest telephone company, *which once enjoyed a near monopoly on phone appliances,* is now being challenged in the open marketplace.

A single-word modifier is usually either an adjective or an adverb. An **adjective** modifies a noun, pronoun, or other element that functions as a noun. An **adverb** can modify not only a verb but also an adjective, another adverb, a preposition, an infinitive, a participle, a phrase, a clause, or a whole sentence.

All modifiers are subordinate, or grammatically dependent on another element. But there is nothing minor about the benefit that a careful and imaginative use of modifiers can bring to your style. Some modifiers lend vividness and precision to descriptions, stories, and ideas, while others establish logical relationships, allowing a sentence to convey more shadings of thought and complexity of structure.

DEGREES OF ADJECTIVES AND ADVERBS

**mod
19a**

19a Learn how adjectives and adverbs are compared.

Comparing adjectives

Most adjectives can be *compared,* or changed to show three **degrees** of coverage.

POSITIVE DEGREE	COMPARATIVE DEGREE	SUPERLATIVE DEGREE
wide	wider	widest
dry	drier	driest
lazy	lazier	laziest
relaxed	more relaxed	most relaxed
agreeable	more agreeable	most agreeable

POSITIVE DEGREE	COMPARATIVE DEGREE	SUPERLATIVE DEGREE
wide	less wide	least wide
dry	less dry	least dry
lazy	less lazy	least lazy
relaxed	less relaxed	least relaxed
agreeable	less agreeable	least agreeable

The base form of an adjective is in the *positive* degree: *thin*. The *comparative* degree puts the modified word beyond one or more items: *thinner* (than he is; than everybody). And the *superlative* degree unmistakably puts the modified word beyond all rivals within its group: *thinnest* (of all).

The comparative and superlative degrees of adjectives are formed in several ways.

**mod
19a**

1. For one-syllable adjectives: *wide, wider, widest* (but *less wide, least wide).*

2. For one- or two-syllable adjectives ending in -*y,* change the -*y* to -*i* and add -*er* and -*est: dry, drier, driest; lazy, lazier, laziest* (but *less lazy, least lazy).*

3. For all other adjectives of two or more syllables, put *more* or *most* (or *less* or *least*) before the positive form: *relaxed, more relaxed, most relaxed (less relaxed, least relaxed).*

4. For certain "irregular" adjectives, supply the forms shown in your dictionary. Here are some common examples.

POSITIVE DEGREE	COMPARATIVE DEGREE	SUPERLATIVE DEGREE
bad	worse	worst
good	better	best
far	farther, further	farthest, furthest
little	littler, less, lesser	littlest, least
many, some, much	more	most

Comparing adverbs

Like adjectives, adverbs can be compared: *quickly, more quickly, most quickly; less quickly, least quickly.* Note that *-ly* adverbs—that is, nearly all adverbs—can be compared only by being preceded by words like *more* and *least.* But some one-syllable adverbs do change their form: *hard/harder/hardest, fast/faster/fastest,* and so forth.

19b Avoid constructions like *more funnier.*

DON'T	DO
x more funnier	● funnier
x least brightest	● least bright
x more quicklier	● more quickly

Be careful not to "double" the comparison of an adjective or adverb. A term like *funnier* already contains the meaning that is wrongly added by *more.*

**mod
19c**

CHOOSING AND PLACING MODIFIERS

19c Avoid a dangling modifier.

DON'T:
     DANGL MOD

x *Pinning one mugger to the ground,* the other escaped.

DO:
     MOD   MODIFIED
               TERM
● *Pinning one mugger to the ground,* the *victim* helplessly watched the other escape.

When you use a modifier, it is not enough for you to know what thing or idea you are modifying; you must openly supply that modified term within your sentence. Otherwise, you have written a **dangling modifier**—one modifying nothing that the reader can point to. In the "don't" example above, the person doing the *pinning* is left out, and *the other* looks at first like the modified term. In the revised sentence, with its explicit mention of the *victim,* the uncertainty is resolved.

DON'T:

DANGL MOD

x *Once considered a culturally backward country,* Australian film-makers have surprised the world's most demanding audiences.

The writer, criticized for a dangling modifier, might protest, "Can't you see I was referring to Australia in the first phrase?" But where is *Australia* in the sentence? Since *Australian film-makers* can hardly be called a *country,* the modifier does dangle.

DO:

| MOD | MODIFIED TERM |

• *Once considered a culturally backward country, Australia* has surprised the world's most demanding audiences with its excellent filmmakers.

mod 19d

DON'T:

DANGL MOD

x *To win in court,* an attorney's witnesses must convince the jury.

Readers must do a double take to realize that it is the attorney, not the witnesses, who wants to win in court.

DO:

| MOD | MODIFIED TERM |

• *To win in court, an attorney* must choose witnesses who can convince a jury.

19d Avoid a misplaced modifier.

MISPLACED MODIFIER	REVISED
x *Driving to the basket unopposed,* it was an easy layup for Jordan.	• Driving to the basket unopposed, *Jordan* dropped in an easy layup.

MISPLACED MODIFIER	REVISED
x *Marinated in white wine and sprinkled with parsley,* Linda slid the halibut into the casserole.	• Linda slid the *halibut,* marinated in white wine and sprinkled with parsley, into the casserole.

Merely including a modifier and a modified term (pp. 240–241) is not enough; you need to get them close together so that the reader will immediately grasp their connection. Otherwise, a nearby noun or nounlike element may be mistaken for the modified term. Thus, in the left column above, a mysterious *it* appears to be driving to the basket, and poor Linda gets *marinated* before the party has even begun. In the right-hand examples, note how the true modified terms, *Jordan* and *halibut,* are properly placed.

DON'T:

MISPLACED MOD   MODIFIED TERM?

x *Stolen out of the garage the night before, my grandmother* spot-
                       MODIFIED TERM?

ted *my station wagon* on Jefferson Street.

**mod
19d**

   The reader must reassess the sentence to get over the impression that it was the grandmother who was stolen from the garage.

DO:

MOD   MODIFIED TERM

• *Stolen out of the garage the night before, my station wagon* was on Jefferson Street when my grandmother spotted it.

DON'T:
                                MODIFIED
         MISPLACED MOD   TERM?

x *Towering across the African plain, it* seemed impossible to pho-
            MODIFIED TERM?

tograph *the giraffes.*

   Here *it* is merely an anticipatory word, not a thing that could be towering across the plain. Unfortunately, readers are put to the trouble of reaching that conclusion for themselves after momentary confusion.

Squinting modifier

You may find that in a draft sentence you have surrounded a modifier with two elements, either of which might be the modified term. Such a misplaced modifier is called **squinting** because it does not "look directly at" the real modified term.

DON'T:

SQ MOD
x How the mechanic silenced the transmission *completely* amazed me.

Did the mechanic do a complete job of silencing, or was the writer completely amazed? Readers should never be left with such puzzles to solve.

**mod
19d**

DO:

MODIFIED
MOD   TERM
● How the mechanic *completely silenced* the transmission amazed me.

or

MODIFIED
MOD   TERM
● I was *completely amazed* by the way the mechanic silenced the transmission.

DON'T:

SQ MOD
x They were sure *by August* they would be freed.

Were they sure by August, or would they be freed by August?

DO:

MODIFIED
TERM   MOD
● They were *sure by August* that they would be freed.

or

MOD   MODIFIED
                          TERM

- They were sure that *by August* they *would be freed.*

Notice how the insertion of *that* either before or after the modifier clarifies the writer's meaning.

19e   Avoid a split infinitive if you can do so without awkwardness.

DON'T:

SPLIT INF

x It is important *to clearly see* the problem.

DO:

INF   ADV

- It is important *to see* the problem *clearly.*

Some readers object to every **split infinitive,** a modifier placed between *to* and the base verb form: *to clearly see.* To avoid offending such readers, you would do well to eliminate split infinitives from your draft prose.

But when you correct a split infinitive, beware of creating an awkward construction that announces in effect, "Here is the result of my struggle not to split an infinitive."

**mod
19e**

DON'T:

x It is important *clearly to see* the problem.

The writer has avoided a split infinitive but has created a pretzel. The "split" version, *It is important to clearly see the problem,* would be preferable. But *It is important to see the problem clearly* would satisfy everyone.

Even readers who do not mind an inconspicuous, natural-sounding split infinitive are bothered by *lengthy* modifiers in the split-infinitive position.

DON'T:

SPLIT INF
x We are going *to soberly and patiently analyze* the problem.

DO:

• We are going to analyze the problem soberly and patiently.

or

• We are going to make a sober and patient analysis of the problem.

19f Place a modifier where it will bring out your meaning.

More often than not, adjectives and adverbs come just before the modified term *(a beautiful moon; We hastily adjusted the telescope).* In contrast, a *predicate adjective* always follows the verb: *The moon was beautiful.* There is nothing problematic about such placement.

**mod
19f**

In contrast, adverbs like *only, just,* and *merely* can be moved about rather freely without sounding nonsensical. The sense that they make, however, changes drastically from one position to another. Consider:

• *Only* I can understand your argument. [No one else can.]

• I can *only* understand your argument. [I cannot agree with it.]

• I can understand *only* your argument. [But not your motives; *or* The arguments of others mystify me.]

• She had *just* eaten the sandwich. [A moment ago.]

• She had eaten *just* the sandwich. [Not the rest of the food.]

You can see that it requires some thought to put "movable" adverbs exactly where they belong—namely, just before the terms they are meant to emphasize.

For the effective placement of whole modifying elements—that is, subordinate clauses and phrases—see p. 143, 11d.

19g Do not hesitate to make use of an absolute phrase.

ABS PHRASE

- He rose from the negotiating table, *his stooped shoulders a sign of discouragement.*

Fear of dangling and misplaced modifiers (19c–d) leads some readers to shun the **absolute phrase,** a group of words that acts as a modifier to a whole statement. But a well-managed absolute phrase can be an effective resource. It allows you, for example, to craft a graceful **cumulative sentence** (p. 156, 12h)—one that sharpens or elaborates an initial main statement.

A classic absolute phrase differs from a dangling modifier by containing its own "subject," such as *his stooped shoulders* in the example above. Again:

"SUBJECT"
- *All struggle over,* the troops lay down their arms.

ABS PHRASE

- The quarterback called three plays in one huddle, *the clock*

"SUBJECT"

having stopped after the incomplete pass.

ABS PHRASE

Some other absolute phrases do look exactly like dangling modifiers, but they are accepted as **idioms**—that is, as fixed expressions that everyone considers normal:

ABS PHRASE
- *Generally speaking,* the economy is sluggish.

ABS PHRASE
- *To summarize,* most of your energy is still untapped.

mod
19h

19h Avoid a double negative.

DON'T:

x She *didn't* say *nothing.*

DO:

- She *didn't* say *anything.*

or

- She said *nothing.*

In written English the modifier *not* does all the work of denial that a negative statement needs. A **double negative,** though common in some people's speech, is considered a mistake rather than an especially strong negation.

Cumbersome negative formulas

Avoid certain negative constructions which are roundabout or confusing:

1. negatives following *shouldn't wonder, wouldn't be surprised,* etc.

   mod 19h

   DON'T:

   x I shouldn't wonder if it *didn't* rain.

   DO:

   - I shouldn't wonder if it *rained.*

2. *cannot help but*

   DON'T:

   x They *cannot help but* think sadly about the Challenger Seven.

   DO:

   - They *cannot help thinking* sadly about the Challenger Seven.

3. *can't hardly, can't scarcely,* etc.

   DON'T:

   x We *can't hardly* wait to visit Mexico City.

   DO:

   - We *can hardly* wait to visit Mexico City.

4. *no doubt but what, no doubt but that*

DON'T:

x She does not *doubt but what* dreams foretell the future.

DO:

• She *does not doubt that* dreams foretell the future.

PUNCTUATING MODIFIERS

19i Include a comma after an initial modifying element that is more than a few words long.

SUB CLAUSE
• *When they learned that the Metroliner had been derailed,* they spent the night at the Y.

PHRASE
• *Instead of having the chocolate mousse,* Walter ordered an apple for dessert.

mod
19j

If a modifying element preceding your main clause is itself a clause, as in the first example above, you should automatically follow it with a comma. A comma is also appropriate after an opening phrase (p. 203, 16d), as in the second example.

19j If your sentence begins with a brief phrase, consider a following comma optional.

If a modifying phrase (p. 203, 16d) preceding your main clause is no more than a few words long, you can choose whether to close it off with a comma. A comma indicates a pause, and it marks a more formal separation between the modifier and the main clause. Follow your sense of what the occasion calls for.

WITH COMMA: MORE FORMAL	WITHOUT COMMA: LESS FORMAL
Until this week, I had kept up with my assignments.	*Until this week* I had kept up with my assignments.
For a beginner, she did remarkably well.	*For a beginner* she did remarkably well.

When in doubt, just include the comma; it is always an available option.

19k Use commas to set off a term like *however* or *on the contrary.*

SENT ADV
* Lori, *however,* finds the microwave oven too complicated to use.

TRANS PHRASE
* *On the contrary,* nothing could be simpler.

Look back to page 215, 17c, for lists of *sentence adverbs* and *transitional phrases.* Such modifiers, instead of narrowing the meaning of one element in a statement, show a relationship between the whole statement and the one before it. To bring out this function, be sure your sentence adverbs and transitional phrases are "stopped" at both ends, either by two commas, by a semicolon and a comma, or by a comma and the beginning or end of the sentence:

SENT ADV
* A circus, *furthermore,* lifts the spirits of young and old alike.

SENT ADV
* Laughter is good for the soul; *moreover,* it reduces bodily tension.

TRANS PHRASE
* *In reality,* she intends to stay where she is.

TRANS PHRASE
* The deficit has continued to grow, *as a matter of fact.*

mod
19k

Exception: some brief sentence adverbs

Certain brief sentence adverbs such as *thus* and *hence* are often seen without commas:

- We can *thus* discount the immediate threat of war.
- *Hence* there is no need to call up the reserves.

19I   Set off an interrupting element at both ends.

- Our leading advocate of clean streets, *you understand,* is the mayor.

- The city council, *however,* has no funds for a clean-up squad.

- You, *Frank,* will sweep the sidewalk at 7 A.M.

- The mayor's televised plea, *which is rebroadcast every evening on the 6 o'clock news,* reaches everyone in town.

mod
19I

In each instance above, the italicized words constitute an **interrupting element** (also known as a *parenthetical element*). An interrupting element can be a phrase, a clause, a sentence adverb like *however,* a transitional phrase like *in fact,* an appositive (19n), a name in direct address (*you, Frank*), or an inserted question or exclamation. Since an interrupting element comes between parts of the sentence that belong together in meaning, you must set it off by punctuation at both ends. Note the commas in all four examples above.

The main risk in punctuating an interrupting element is that you may forget to close it off before resuming the main sentence. The risk increases if the last words of the interrupting element happen to fit grammatically with the words that follow.

DON'T:

x The mayor's televised plea, which is rebroadcast every evening on the 6 o'clock news reaches everyone in town.

You can expect to come across such "unstopped" interrupting elements in your first drafts. When in doubt as to whether the element is truly an interruption, reread the sentence without it: *The mayor's televised plea reaches everyone in town.* Since that statement makes complete sense, you know that the omitted part *is* interruptive and must be set off at both ends.

Other punctuation

Commas are the most usual but not the only means of setting off an interrupting element. Extreme breaks such as whole statements, questions, or exclamations are often better served by parentheses or dashes:

INT EL
- The sky in New Mexico (*have you ever been there?*) is the most dramatic I have seen.

INT EL
- Our recent weather—*what snow storms we have had!*—makes me long to be back in California.

When you need to interrupt quoted material to insert words of your own, enclose your insertion in brackets (p. 350, 28r).

mod
19m

19m Learn how to punctuate restrictive and nonrestrictive modifying elements.

RESTRICTIVE	**NONRESTRICTIVE**
This is the lamp *we bought yesterday.*	This lamp, *which we bought yesterday,* is defective.
Suzanne is a woman *who started her own business.*	*Suzanne, who started her own business,* is an enterprising woman.
The coffee *that comes from Brazilian mountainsides* is the best.	The best coffee, *which comes from Brazilian mountainsides,* is also the most expensive.

To punctuate modifying elements in every position except the opening one (19j), you must recognize a sometimes tricky distinction between two kinds of modifiers—restrictive and nonrestrictive.

RESTRICTIVE	NONRESTRICTIVE
defining	nondefining
identifying	nonidentifying
essential to establishing meaning	meaning already established
no commas	**commas required**

Restrictive element

A **restrictive element** is essential to the identification of the term it modifies. It restricts or narrows down the scope of that term, identifying precisely *which* lamp, woman, or coffee the writer has in mind. Study the two columns in the first box above and you will see that only the left-hand sentences contain modifiers of this kind. In the right-hand sentences the lamp, woman, and coffee under discussion do not need to be identified by restrictive modifiers; presumably the reader already knows which person or thing the writer intends.

mod
19m

Note also how the absence or use of commas marks the difference of function. A restrictive element can do its job of narrowing only if it is *not* isolated by commas.

DON'T:

x Women, *who are over thirty-five,* tend to show reduced fertility.

> The commas absurdly suggest that all women are over thirty-five.

DO:

RESTR EL
● Women *who are over thirty-five* tend to show reduced fertility.

> With the commas gone, the restrictive element narrows the subject to what the writer had in mind all along, women over thirty-five.

DON'T:

x I admire bus drivers, *who announce the streets as they come up.*

    The comma suggests that all bus drivers announce the streets as they come up and that the writer therefore admires all of them. This is not what was meant.

DO:

                      RESTR EL

• I admire bus drivers *who announce the streets as they come up.*

    Without a comma, the modifier restricts those bus drivers who are admired to just one kind, those who announce the streets.

DON'T:

x Many junk-food addicts change their diet, *when they develop a vitamin deficiency.*

    The comma after *diet* tells us that the main statement ends there. But the writer is trying to say that junk food addicts change their diet only at a certain point. The intended meaning becomes clear when the comma is removed.

DO:

                      RESTR EL

• Many junk food addicts change their diet *when they develop a vitamin deficiency.*

Nonrestrictive element

A **nonrestrictive element** is not essential to the identification of the term it modifies. Instead of narrowing that term, it adds some further information about it. To perform this task the nonrestrictive element must be set off by punctuation, usually commas.

DON'T:

x The reference librarian *who is a writer's best resource* is often acknowledged in the preface to a book.

The absence of commas after *librarian* and *resource* implies that the italicized element is restrictive, telling us which reference librarian is meant. Notice that when the modifier is left out altogether, there is nothing misleading about the statement: *The reference librarian is often acknowledged in the preface to a book.* That is a sure sign that the modifier is nonrestrictive and that it therefore deserves to be set off.

DO:

NONR EL
● The reference librarian , *who is a writer's best resource* , is often acknowledged in the preface to a book.

DON'T:

x They snack on trail mix *which is a wholesome blend of nuts, seeds, raisins, and other dried fruit.*

The absence of a comma after *mix* implies that one particular kind of trail mix is being identified. By adding a comma the writer can make it clear that trail mix in general is intended.

**mod
19n**

DO:

NONR EL
● They snack on trail mix , *which is a wholesome blend of nuts, seeds, raisins, and other dried fruit.*

19n **In punctuating an expression like *Teresa, an old friend*, observe the restrictive/nonrestrictive rule.**

APP
● Teresa , *an old friend of mine* , has scarcely changed through the years.

APP
● What they saw , *a black bear approaching the baby's cradle* , riveted them with fear.

APP
● *A musical genius* , he began playing Mozart at five.

An **appositive** is a word or group of words that identifies or restates a neighboring noun, pronoun, or nounlike element. Most appositives, like those above, are set off by commas. Nevertheless, you should not automatically make that choice. Instead, ask whether the appositive narrows down ("restricts") the term it follows or merely restates that term. To see why some appositives should appear without commas, compare these sentences.

- My sister, *Diane,* studied Portuguese in the Navy. <small>NONR APP</small>

- My brother *Bert* played baseball in college, but my brother *Jack* was not athletic at all. <small>RESTR APP / RESTR APP</small>

The commas in the first sentence tell us that the writer has only one sister—namely, Diane. The appositive does not restrict our understanding of *sister;* it merely supplies the sister's name. In contrast, the absence of commas in the second example reflects the fact that the writer has at least two brothers. *Bert* and *Jack* are restrictive appositives, since each name tells us *which* brother is meant.

The distinction here is a fine one, and few readers would object if the commas were dropped from the "Diane" example. But whenever you use an appositive to narrow the meaning of a term (which brother, which friend, etc.), you should omit the commas.

mod 19o

19o Use commas in constructions like *a sunlit, windy day* but not in constructions like *a popular rock group.*

If a draft sentence contains two or more modifiers in a row, should you put commas between them? The answer depends on whether the modifiers all modify the same term. Usually they do; such modifiers are *coordinate,* or serving the same grammatical function. You should separate coordinate modifiers from each other by commas:

                                      MODIFIED
                          MOD   **MOD TERM**

• I arrived at my new school on a *sunlit, windy day.*

> Since *sunlit* and *windy* both modify the same term, *day,* they
> are separated from each other by a comma.

    But sometimes you will find that an apparent modifier is actually
part of the term being modified. In that case, omit a comma after the
modifier that comes before the whole modified term.

DON'T:

x She never forgave them for the way they insulted her on that

           MODIFIED
    MOD   **TERM**
infamous, first day of school.

> Does *infamous* modify *day?* No, it modifies *first day.* The com-
> ma is mistaken.

DO:

• She never forgave them for the way they insulted her on that
infamous first day of school.

> The absence of commas shows that there are no coordinate
> modifiers in the sentence. Note, in the following example, how
> the punctuation changes when genuine coordinate modifiers
> are added.

DO:

• She never forgave them for the way they insulted her on

                               MODIFIED
    MOD   **MOD**   **MOD**   **TERM**
that *infamous, outrageous, unforgettable first day* of school.

> Now the sentence contains three coordinate modifiers, proper-
> ly separated by commas. A comma after *unforgettable* would
> still be wrong, for *first day* continues to be the whole modified
> term.

**mod
19o**

DO:

                                          MODIFIED
                              MOD   TERM
- For three years he played drums in a *popular rock group.*

    Since *popular* modifies the whole term *rock group,* a comma
    after *popular* would be wrong.

    To test whether you are dealing with coordinate modifiers, try
shifting the order of the words. Truly coordinate terms can be reversed
without a change of meaning: *a sunlit, windy day; a windy, sunlit day.*
Noncoordinate terms change their meaning *(a blue racing car; a racing blue car)* or become nonsensical *(a popular rock group; a rock popular group).*

19p Omit a comma between the final modifier and the modified term.

When a modifier comes just before the modified term, no punctuation
should separate them. Thus, however many coordinate modifiers you
supply, be sure to omit a comma after the final one:

                                                    FINAL MOD
- O'Keeffe produced an intense, starkly simple, *radiantly glow-*
    MODIFIED
    TERM
  ing painting of a flower.

    A comma after *glowing* would be mistaken. The whole set of
    coordinate modifiers—*intense, starkly simple, radiantly glow-
    ing*—already stands in proper relation to the modified term,
    painting.

For an exception to this rule, keep reading.

19q Consider enclosing a modifier in commas if it qualifies the modifier just before it.

              PRECEDING   MOD
              MOD
- It was an *inaccurate , perhaps even deceitful ,* account of the
  meeting.

mod
19q

If one modifier serves in part to qualify or comment on the modifier preceding it, you can bring out that function by enclosing it in commas. The sentence above would still be considered acceptable if the commas were omitted, but those commas show that *perhaps even deceitful* is a "second thought" about the first modifier, *inaccurate.*

If you set off a "backward-looking" modifier at one end, be sure to supply a second comma at the other end.

DON'T:

x She told a fascinating, but not altogether believable story.

DO:

• She told a fascinating, but not altogether believable, story.

or

• She told a fascinating but not altogether believable story.

mod
19q

20 Noun and Pronoun Case

CASES:	SUBJECTIVE	OBJECTIVE	POSSESSIVE
Personal Pronouns	I you he she it we they	me you him her it us them	my, mine your, yours his her, hers its our, ours their, theirs
Who	**who**	**whom**	**whose**
Nouns	car cars Janice Soviet Union	car cars Janice Soviet Union	car's cars' Janice's Soviet Union's

Nouns and pronouns change their form to show certain grammatical relations to other words within a sentence. These forms are called

cases. They show whether a term is a subject of discussion or performer of action *(subjective case)*, a receiver of action or an object of a preposition *(objective case)*, or a "possessor" of another term *(possessive case)*:

1. subjective case: *I, we they, who, Bill, cars*, etc.

2. objective case: *me, us, them, whom*, etc.

3. possessive case: *my, mine; our, ours; their, theirs; whose, Bill's, cars'*, etc.

Most personal pronouns (*I, she*, etc.) show changes of form for all three cases, and so does the relative pronoun *who*. Nouns, however, do not change for the objective case.

A change in form helps to show which sentence function a word is performing. For example:

SUBJECTIVE CASE
1. Subject of verb (p. 200, 16b):
   - *He* went home.
   - *They* went home.
   - The one *who* went home was disappointed.

2. Complement (p. 198, 16a):
   - It was *she* who was guilty.
   - The victims are *we* ourselves.

OBJECTIVE CASE
1. Direct object of verb (p. 198, 16a):
   - They praised *him*.
   - We fed the child *whom* the agency had entrusted to us.

2. Indirect object of verb (p. 580):
   - They taught *him* a lesson.
   - The fine cost *them* a pretty penny.

3. Object of preposition (p. 587):
   - She explained the software to *us*.
   - For *whom* did you work last year?

case 20a

4. Subject of infinitive (p. 595):
   - They wanted *her* to stay.
   - She expected *them* to give her a raise.

POSSESSIVE CASE

1. With nouns:
   - *Our* hats were all squashed.
   - *James's* case was the worst of all.
   - The *Beatles'* music still keeps its freshness.
   - *Whose* pen is this?

2. With gerunds (p. 199, 16a):
   - *His* departing left us sad.
   - *Their* training every day made them too tired for fun.
   - *Jane's* humming all day drove everyone wild.

In general, case forms must match sentence functions: subjective case for subjects of clauses, objective case for objects of several kinds, and possessive case for a possessing relation to the governed term.

We will see that in practice the choice of case can become tricky. Note at the outset that the "subject" of an infinitive takes the objective case and that the "subject" of a gerund usually takes the possessive case. The names are unfortunate, but most writers intuitively choose case by function, not by name.

**case
20b**

20b Keep the subject of a clause in the subjective case.

DO:

- *He* and *I* were good friends.
$\qquad$ S

DON'T:

x *Him* and *me* were good friends.
$\qquad$ S

Standard usage requires that you avoid using objective-case pronouns for subjects of clauses.

See page 268, 20h, for a pronoun subject in a subordinate clause.

20c Avoid awkwardly "correct" constructions like *I am she.*

WRONG	AWKWARD	PREFERABLE
I am *her.*	I am *she.*	I am the one you mean.
The person I miss is *her.*	The person I miss is *she.*	She is the person I miss.

The left-column examples above are wrong because pronoun complements (p. 198, 16a) should not appear in the objective case. Yet the "corrections" in the middle column sound pompous and prissy. Try, as in the right-column sentences, to find a natural-sounding way of conveying the same point.

20d Watch out for constructions like *for you and I.*

case
20d

The rule for pronoun objects of all kinds is simple: put them in the objective case.

DIRECT OBJECT OF VERB:
• Many differences separate *us.*

INDIRECT OBJECT OF VERB:
• She gave *me* cause for worry.

OBJECT OF PREPOSITION:
• Toward *whom* is your anger directed?

SUBJECT OF INFINITIVE:
• They asked *her* to serve a second term.

> Note that the "subject" of the infinitive appears in the objective case because it is at the same time the indirect object of the verb.

Choice of a correct objective form becomes harder when the object is **compound,** or made up of more than one term. Knowing that it is wrong to write *Him and me were good freinds,* some writers "overcorrect" and put the subjective forms where they do not belong.

DON'T:

OBJS OF
PREP╱PREP╲
x That will be a dilemma for *you* and *I.*

DO:
• That will be a dilemma for you and *me.*

When in doubt, test for case by disregarding one of the two objects. Since you would never write x *That will be a dilemma for I,* you know that both of the objects must be objective in case.

The danger of choosing the wrong case seems to increase still further when a noun and a pronoun are paired as objects.

**case
20e**

DON'T:

OBJS OF
PREP ╱PREP╲
x As for *Jack* and *I,* we will take the bus.

Would you write *As for I?* No; therefore, keep to the objective case.

DO:
• As for Jack and *me,* we will take the bus.

20e Observe the grammatical distinction between *who* and *whom.*

In informal speech and writing, *whom* has become a rare form even where grammar strictly requires it. When the pronoun appears first in a clause, the subjective *who* automatically comes to mind.

COLLOQUIAL:
• *Who* did he marry?
• *Who* will you play against?

In standard written English, however, the question of *who* versus *whom* is still determined by grammatical function, not by speech habits. Note the reason for choosing *whom* in each of the following revisions:

D OBJ ⌒V⌒
* *Whom* did he marry?

    Whom is the direct object of the verb *did marry.*

OBJ OF
PREP   PREP
* *Whom* will you play against?

or
        OBJ OF
    PREP   PREP
* Against *whom* will you play?

    Whom is the object of the preposition *against.*

For more on *who* versus *whom,* see p. 268, 20h.

case
20f

20f   Avoid an awkward choice of pronoun case after *than* or *as.*

Many writers agonize over the case of a pronoun following *than* or *as.* Should one write *Alex is taller than I* or *Alex is taller than me*? Technically, the answer is that both versions are correct. In the first instance *than* serves as a subordinating conjunction: *Alex is taller than I [am].* In the second, *than* has become a preposition with the object *me.*

In other sentences, however, one choice is clearly incorrect. Consider:

* The cows chased Margaret farther than $\begin{Bmatrix} I \\ me \end{Bmatrix}$.

Here *I* would indicate that Margaret was chased by both the cows and the writer: *The cows chased Margaret farther than I did.* Since that is surely not the intended meaning, the right choice is *me.*

When in doubt, consider your intended meaning and mentally supply any missing part of the clause:

• The cows chased Margaret farther than ⟨they chased⟩ me.

The added words will tell you which case to use for the pronoun.

Wherever both choices sound awkward, as in the "Alex" example above, look for an alternative construction:

SUB CLAUSE
• Alex is taller *than I am.*

By supplying the whole subordinate clause, you can avoid any hesitation between *I* and *me.*

20g   Avoid constructions like *for we students.*

DON'T:

PRO   APP
x Inflation is a problem for *we* students.

DO:

• Inflation is a problem for *us* students.

When an appositive (p. 257, 19n) follows a pronoun, some writers automatically put the pronoun in the subjective case *(we)*. As often as not, the result is a usage error. A wiser course is to test for the right pronoun case by leaving the appositive out of account. In the example above, *for we* is obviously wrong; so, then, is *for we students.* The rule is that a following appositive should have no influence on the case of a pronoun.

20h   Choose a pronoun's case by its function within its own clause.

One of the hardest choices of case involves a pronoun that seems to have rival functions in two clauses.

DON'T:

x He will read his poems to *whomever* will listen.

The writer has made *whomever* objective because it looks like the object of the preposition *to: to whomever.* But the real object of *to* is the whole subordinate clause that follows it.

DO:

$$\overset{\text{S}\qquad\text{V}}{}$$
• He will read his poems to <u>*whoever will listen.*</u>
                                SUB CLAUSE

The subject of the subordinate clause *whoever will listen* belongs in the subjective case.

Whenever a subordinate clause is embedded within a larger structure, you can settle problems of case by mentally eliminating everything but the subordinate clause.

DON'T:

x Josh had no doubt about *whom* would plan the geriatric meeting.

The test for case shows that *whom would plan the geriatric meeting* is ungrammatical. The object of *about* is the whole subordinate clause, which requires a subject in the subjective case.

case
20h

DO:

$$\overset{\text{S}\qquad\text{V}}{}$$
• Josh had no doubt about <u>who would plan the geriatric meeting.</u>
                                  SUB CLAUSE

When a choice of pronoun case is difficult, the air of difficulty may remain even after you have chosen correctly. Your reader may be distracted by the same doubt that you have just resolved. It is therefore a good idea to dodge the whole problem.

DO:

• He will read his poems to *anyone* who will listen.
• Josh was sure that *he* would be the planner of the geriatric meeting.

20i Use the possessive case in most constructions like *Marie's coming to Boston is a rare event.*

In the phrase *Marie's coming to Boston,* the word *coming* is a **gerund**—that is, a verbal (p. 199, 16a) that functions as a noun. Most gerunds, like this one, end in *-ing,* but there is also a two-word past form.

PRESENT GER
- There is less *swooning* in Hollywood movies than there used to be.

PAST GER
- *Having swum* across the lake made him generally less fearful.

A gerund can be preceded not only by a word like *a, the,* or *this,* but also by a governing noun or pronoun known as the subject of the gerund: <u>Wilson's</u> *achieving unity,* <u>his</u> *having achieved unity.* (A gerund can also take an object; see page 585.) The name *subject* is misleading, for most subjects of gerunds, just like words that "possess" nouns, belong in the possessive case.

case 20i

POSSESSION OF NOUN	POSSESSION OF GERUND
our departure	our departing
Marian's reliance	Marian's relying
Jules's loss	Jules's having lost

In general, then, put subjects of gerunds into the possessive case:

- *Esther's* commuting ended with her graduation.

Even if the subject of a gerund feels like an object, you should keep to the possessive form.

DON'T:

OBJ OF
PREP PREP?
x Harold wondered why people laughed at *him* wearing that hat.

Here the writer has made *him* objective because it "feels like" the object of the preposition *at.* In fact, the object of that preposition is the whole gerund phrase *his wearing that hat.*

DO:

S   OBJ
OF GER GER   OF GER

● Harold wondered why people laughed at <u>*his* wearing that hat.</u>

OBJ OF PREP

Note how the possessive *his* directs a reader's attention to the next word, *wearing.* The activity, not the person, inspired laughter.

Exceptions

When the subject of a gerund is an abstract or inanimate noun—one like *physics* or *chaos*—it can appear in a nonpossessive form.

ACCEPTABLE:

S OF GER   GER

● We cannot ignore the danger of *catastrophe striking* again.

> case
> 20i

But the possessive *catastrophe's* would also be acceptable here. Rather than choose, however, why not recast the sentence?

PREFERABLE:

● We cannot ignore the danger that catastrophe will strike again.

When a gerund's subject is separated from the gerund by other words, the gerund tends to change into a modifier (a participle). In such a sentence the possessive form is not used:

D OBJ   PART

● They admired *him,* a Canadian, *enduring* the heat of Kenya.

Without the intervening appositive (p. 257, 19n), *a Canadian,* we would recognize *enduring* as a gerund: *They admired his enduring. . . .* But in the sentence as it stands, *him* is a direct object modified by the whole phrase *enduring the heat of Kenya.*

20j Feel free to make use of constructions like *a picture of Barbara's*.

Compare these two sentences:

- He sighed over a picture of Barbara.
- He sighed over a picture of Barbara's.

Both sentences are handled correctly, but their meanings are quite different. The first deals with a picture—no doubt a photograph—*of* Barbara, while the second involves a picture created or owned *by* Barbara.

Some writers worry that a **double possessive** such as *a picture of Barbara's* may be a usage error, just as a double negative (p. 249, 19h) is. But everyone freely uses the double possessive with pronouns: *a peculiarity of hers, that nasty habit of his,* and so forth. Feel free to use nouns in exactly the same way: *a peculiarity of Nancy's, that nasty habit of Ralph's*.

case
20j

21 Pronoun Agreement and Reference

PRONOUN AGREEMENT	PRONOUN REFERENCE
Does the pronoun have the same gender, number, and person as its antecedent?	Can the reader see without difficulty which term is the pronoun's antecedent?
DON'T:	DON'T:
x Although the union struck the *plant, they* remained open. The antecedent *plant* and the pronoun referring to it must be made to agree in number.	x The strikers used violence against the management, *which* made a final reconciliation difficult. Does *which* refer to *violence* or to *management?*
DO:	DO:
• Although the union struck the plant, *it* remained open.	• It was the strikers' *violence that* made a final reconciliation with management so difficult.

Pronouns—words used in place of nouns—offer you relief from the monotony of needlessly repeating a term or name when your reader already knows what or whom you mean. But precisely because many pronouns are substitutes for other words, they raise a variety of usage problems, including subject-verb agreement (Chapter 18) and choice of the correct case (Chapter 20). Here we consider the two main kinds of relation between a pronoun and its **antecedent,** the term it refers to. First, a pronoun should show **agreement** with its antecedent in gender, number, and person. And second, the identification of the antecedent—that is, the pronoun's **reference** to it—should never be in doubt.

PRONOUN AGREEMENT

21a Make a pronoun agree with its antecedent in gender, number, and person.

pr
agr
21a

GENDER	NUMBER	PERSON
masculine *(he)*	singular *(her, it,* etc.)	first *(I, we, our,* etc.)
feminine *(she)*	plural *(they, theirs,* etc.)	second *(you, your, yours)*
		third *(he, she, it, they, their,* etc.)

If the antecedent of a pronoun is explicitly female, make the pronoun feminine: *Ellen . . . she; her; hers.* If the antecedent is plural, make the pronoun plural: *cats . . . they; them; their; theirs.* And if the antecedent is first person, the pronoun should be first person as well: *I . . . me; my; mine.* The following examples show standard practice:

ANT   PRO
- *Philip* still has not tried *his* sailboard in rough weather.

 The antecedent and pronoun are both masculine, singular, and third person.

        ANT   PRO
- Sooner or later, all *dancers* suffer injuries to *their* feet.

 The antecedent and pronoun are both plural and third person.

```
   ┌─────────────┐      ┌──────────────┐
   ANT         PRO    ANT          PRO
```
- *We* should allow *our daughter* to decide on *her* own career.

   The first antecedent-pronoun pair are plural and first person; the second pair are singular, feminine, and third person.

All this looks straightforward enough, but points 21b–g below take up some potentially tricky applications of the rule.

21b Usually refer to a noun like *mob* or *jury* with a singular pronoun.

```
       ANT                          PRO
```
- The *mob* of angry demonstrators pushed *its* way into the mayor's office.

```
          ANT              PRO
```
- At last the *jury* came forward with *its* verdict.

A term like *mob* or *jury* is called a **collective noun** (p. 229, 18f) because, though singular in form, it designates a group of members. In most instances, like those above, a collective noun as antecedent calls for a singular pronoun.

   When you wish to emphasize the separate members of the group, however, make the pronoun plural:

```
                                 ANT    PRO
```
- The television camera followed the *jury* as *they* scattered

```
                    PRO
```
   through the courtyard to *their* waiting cars.

pr agr 21c

21c If the antecedent contains parts linked by *and,* usually refer to it with a plural pronoun.

```
        ─────ANT──────              PRO
```
- The *architect* and the *contractor* worked out *their* differences.

Two or more items in the antecedent generally call for a plural pronoun, as in the sentence above. But when both parts refer to the same thing or person, make the pronoun singular:

- My $\overset{\overbrace{\text{ANT}}}{son}$ and $chief\ antagonist$ tries out $\overset{\text{PRO}}{his}$ debating speeches on me.

  One person is both son and chief antagonist; hence the singular pronoun *his*.

21d Avoid a clash of singular and plural antecedents linked by *or* or *nor*.

The schoolbook rule is that if two parts of an antecedent differ in number, the pronoun must agree with the *nearest* part.

"CORRECT":

- Neither the coach nor the $\overset{\substack{\text{NEAREST PART} \\ \text{OF ANT}}}{players}$ will tell $\overset{\text{PRO}}{their}$ story to the press.

- Neither the players nor the $\overset{\substack{\text{NEAREST PART} \\ \text{OF ANT}}}{coach}$ will tell $\overset{\text{PRO}}{his}$ story to the press.

But this "rule" often produces a strained effect, as in the second example above. You would do better to recast any sentence containing a conflict of number in the antecedent. Either eliminate that conflict *(Neither the coaches nor the players will tell their story . . .)* or do without the pronoun:

PREFERABLE:

- Neither the coach nor the players will tell the story to the press.

21e If you have placed *each* or *every* before a noun, refer to it with a singular pronoun.

- $\overset{\text{ANT}}{Each\ lion}$ that was tranquilized has had a tag attached to $\overset{\text{PRO}}{its}$ ear.

- $\overset{\text{ANT}}{Every\ pregnant\ woman}$ in this exercise class is in $\overset{\text{PRO}}{her}$ third trimester.

pr
agr
21e

Use a singular pronoun even if the term is compound (21c):

┌───────────────── ANT ─────────────────┐   /PRO\
• *Every financial vice president and accountant* gave *his* or *her*
  budgetary projections for the coming year.

21f When in doubt, treat a pronoun like *everyone* or *nobody* as singular.

Review pages 233–235, 18k, which treat verb agreement with such
indefinite pronouns as *each, everybody, neither,* and *none.* Those pronouns are singular in form but not necessarily in meaning. As antecedents, however, they generally require singular pronouns:

  ANT   PRO
• *Everyone* on the swimming team had remembered to bring *her*
  goggles and nose clip.

                                 ANT   PRO
• Tests on the two viruses show that *neither* has had *its* life span
  shortened by the new drug.

Keep to a singular pronoun even when the indefinite pronoun is
followed by *of them:*

• *Each of them* has brought *her* accessories.
• *Neither of them* has had its life span shortened.

None, however, forms a partial exception to the rule. Although
some writers insist that *none* is always singular *(None of them has
surrendered his gun),* others construe *none* as plural when the intended meaning is *all:*

• *None* of them have memorized *their* automatic teller numbers.

21g Watch for an antecedent with plural form but singular meaning.

  ANT   PRO   PRO
• *Statistics* is a fine discipline, but *it* has *its* pitfalls.

  ANT   PRO
• His *statistics* were at *their* most impressive in the middle of the
  season.

pr
agr
21g

Both of these sentences are correctly handled. In the first, *statistics* carries a plural *-s* ending but is rightly construed as a singular thing, the discipline of statistics. In the second example, the writer has in mind a collection of many numbers; hence the plural pronoun. Review page 235, 18l, for discussion of antecedents that take this form.

21h Avoid an abrupt pronoun shift.

Your choice of a noun or pronoun in one sentence or part of a sentence establishes a certain person and number; see page 274, 21a. When you refer again to the same individual(s) or thing(s), do not shift unexpectedly between persons and numbers—for example, from the singular *someone* to the plural *they,* from the third-person *students* or *they* to the second-person *you,* or from the third-person plural *people* to the second-person singular *you.* Keep to one person and number.

pr
ref
21i

DON'T:

	THIRD PERSON	SECOND PERSON

x A good song stays with *someone,* making *you* feel less alone.

> Having committed the sentence to a third-person pronoun, the writer jars us by switching to the second-person *you.*

DO:

	PLURAL ANT	PLURAL PRO

● A good song stays with *people,* making *them* feel less alone.

Or, more informally:

SAME PRO

● A good song stays with *you,* making *you* feel less alone.

PRONOUN REFERENCE

21i Make sure you have included a pronoun's antecedent.

In informal conversation, pronouns often go without antecedents, since both parties know who or what is being discussed: *He wants me to phone home at least once a week*. In writing, however, you want your antecedents to be explicitly (openly) stated.

DON'T:

x *They* say we are in for another cold winter.

Who is *They?*

DO:

              ANT   PRO
- *The weather forecasters* have more bad news for us. *They* say we are in for another cold winter.

DON'T:

x *It* explains here that the access road will be closed for repairs.

If the previous sentence has no antecedent for *It,* revision is called for.

DO:

    ANT
- *This bulletin* tells us why the backpacking trip was postponed.

PRO
It explains that the access road will be closed for repairs.

pr
ref
21j

21j Eliminate competition for the role of antecedent.

If you allow a pronoun and its antecedent to stand too far apart, another element in your sentence may look like the real antecedent. This confusion is usually temporary, but you should avoid putting your reader to any unnecessary work.

DON'T:

                      ANT?   ANT? PRO
x Keats sat under a huge *tree* to write his *ode. It* was dense and kept him from the Hampstead mist.

The nearness of *ode* to *It* makes *ode* a likely candidate for antecedent, especially since an ode might be described as dense. With a little extra thought the reader can identify *tree* as the real antecedent—but a good revision can make that fact immediately clear.

DO:

ANT PRO
- Keats wrote his ode while sitting under a huge *tree, which* was dense and kept him from the Hampstead mist.

or

ANT PRO
- Keats wrote his ode while sitting under a huge *tree, whose* dense foliage kept him from the Hampstead mist.

DON'T:

ANT?   ANT?
x Before I sold *cosmetics,* I used to walk by all the *clerks* in the
PRO
cosmetics department, amazed by *their* variety.

What was various, the cosmetics or the clerks?

DO:

- Before I sold cosmetics, I used to walk by all the clerks in the cosmetics department, amazed by the variety of makeup on display.

pr
ref
21k

21k Watch especially for a *which* with more than one possible antecedent.

When you find a clause beginning with the relative pronoun *which,* check to see whether that word refers to a single preceding term or to a whole statement. If the antecedent is a whole statement, you risk unclarity.

DON'T:

x In the subfreezing weather we could not start the car, *which* interfered with our plans.

Although a reader can see on a "double take" that the antecedent of *which* is not *car* but the whole preceding statement, writers should not put readers to such pains.

DO:

• The subfreezing weather interfered with our plans, especially when the car would not start.

or

• Since the car would not start in the subfreezing weather, we had to change our plans.

DON'T:

      ANT?   ANT?   PRO
x We *skate* on the frozen *pond, which* I enjoy.

    What is enjoyed, the activity or the pond?

DO:

• I enjoy skating on the frozen pond.

21l Guard against vagueness in using *this, that,* or *it.*

pr
ref
21l

Vague <u>this</u> or <u>that</u>

Study the following unclear passage.

DON'T:

x The town board voted to eliminate school crossing guards, even though a serious accident had recently occurred at the corner of Jefferson and Truman. *This* brought the parents out in protest.

    Does *This* refer to the elimination of the crossing guards, to the accident, or to the whole preceding statement?

When the word *this, that, these,* or *those* is used alone, without modifying another word, it is known as a *demonstrative pronoun.* Inexperienced writers sometimes use the singular forms *this* and *that* imprecisely, hoping to refer to a whole previous idea rather than to a specific antecedent. The problem is that nearby terms may also look like antecedents. While all writers use an occasional demonstrative pronoun, you should check each *this* or *that* to make sure its antecedent is clear. The remedy for vagueness is to make *this* or *that* modify another term or to rephrase the statement.

DO:

* The town board voted to eliminate school crossing guards, even though a serious accident had recently occurred at the corner of

  MOD   MODIFIED TERM
  Jefferson and Truman. *This dangerous economy* brought the parents out in protest.

  The writer has gone from *This* to *This dangerous economy,* turning a vague **demonstrative pronoun** *(this)* into a precise modifier—a **demonstrative adjective.**

DON'T:

x The cat shed great quantities of fur on the chair. *That* made Mary Ann extremely anxious.

  Though the antecedent of *that* (the whole previous sentence) is reasonably clear, the second sentence is not very informative. What was Mary Ann anxious about, the cat's health or the condition of the chair?

**pr
ref
21I**

DO:

* The cat shed great quantities of fur on the chair. Mary Ann worried that when her mother saw the chair, the cat would be banished from the house.

or

* The cat shed great quantities of fur on the chair. The possibility that he was ill made Mary Ann extremely anxious.

Vague *it*

DON'T:

INDEFINITE   PERSONAL
INDICATOR   PRO

x Although *it* is a ten-minute walk to the bus, *it* comes frequently.

It can serve as both a personal pronoun *(It is mine)* and an indefinite indicator *(It is raining),* but your reader will be momentarily baffled if you combine those two uses within a sentence.

DO:

● Although it is a ten-minute walk to the bus stop, *buses* come frequently.

21m Make sure the antecedent is a whole term, not part of one.

The antecedent of a pronoun should not be a modifier or a fragment of a larger term.

DON'T:

ANT?   PRO
x Alexander waited at the *train station* until *it* came.

> Here the word *train* is part of a larger noun, *train station*. The sentence contains no reference to a train, and thus *it* has no distinct antecedent. The pronoun "dangles" like a dangling modifier (p. 243, 19c).

pr
ref
21m

DO:

ANT   PRO
● Alexander waited at the station for the *train* until *it* came.

DON'T:

ANT?
x He was opposed to *gun control* because he thought the Constitu-

PRO
tion guaranteed every citizen the right to own *one.*

DO:

ANT
● He was opposed to the control of *guns* because he thought the

PRO
Constitution guaranteed all citizens the right to own *them.*

or

● He was opposed to gun control because he thought the Constitution guaranteed every citizen's right to own a gun.

22 Parallelism

FAULTY PARALLELISM	ADEQUATE PARALLELISM
x The studio was large, square, and had a sunny aspect.	● The studio was *large, square, and sunny.*
x Not only did the painter splash her canvases, but also the floor.	● The painter splashed *not only her canvases but also the floor.*
x She wanted to express not so much the form of her subjects, but rather the nature of paint itself.	● She wanted to express *not so much the form of her subjects as the nature of paint itself.*
x She was not an easy person to understand, and neither was her work.	● *Neither she nor her work* was easy to understand.
x She loved obscurity as much as, if not more, than publicity.	● She loved *obscurity as much as publicity.*
x She was neither a fraud nor was she a major pioneer.	● She was *neither a fraud nor a major pioneer.*

When two or more parts of a sentence are governed by a single grammatical device, they are said to be structurally **parallel.** As Chapter 12 makes clear, parallelism is a key instrument for achieving sentence emphasis (see especially pp. 147–152, 12a–d). At the same time, it is all too easy to allow would-be parallel constructions to fall out of proper alignment. The box above illustrates some of the problems and solutions that will be explained in this chapter.

JOINING PARALLEL ELEMENTS

22a Use like elements within a parallel construction.

However many terms you are making parallel, the first of them establishes what kind of element the others must be. If the first term is a verb, the others must be verbs as well. Align a noun with other nouns or nounlike elements, a participle (p. 199, 16a) with other participles, a whole clause (p. 201, 16c) with other clauses, and so forth. (In the following examples, parallel elements are marked by *x*'s and *y*'s.)

DON'T:

                                  x   y

x His black leather jacket was both *snug* and *looked wet.*

> Since the parallel formula here is *both x and y,* the first term within it is the adjective *snug.* Thus the *y* term should also be an adjective. Instead, we find the unwelcome verb *looked.* Revise to get the two adjectives *snug* and *wet* into parallelism.

DO:

                                  x   y

• His black leather jacket looked both *snug* and *wet.*

DON'T:

                         x   y

x He enjoyed *rocking his torso* and *to flail his arms.*

> The *x* element is a gerund phrase (p. 588), requiring the *y* element to be a gerund or gerund phrase as well. The infinitive phrase (p. 587) *to flail his arms* breaks the parallelism.

/ /
22a

DO:

$$\overbrace{}^{x} \qquad \overbrace{}^{y}$$

• He enjoyed *rocking his torso* and *flailing his arms.*

DON'T:

$$\overbrace{}^{x} \quad \overbrace{}^{y}$$

x She likes to *wear designer clothes, listen to classical music,* and

$$\overbrace{}^{z}$$

gourmet food is essential.

> The series begins with the completion of an infinitive: *to wear.*
> At this point the writer can either keep repeating the *to* or
> supply further verb forms to be governed by the original *to.*

DO:

$$\overbrace{}^{x} \qquad \overbrace{}^{y}$$

• She likes *to wear designer clothes, to listen to classical music,*

$$\overbrace{}^{z}$$

and *to eat gourmet food.*

or

$$\overbrace{}^{x} \qquad \overbrace{}^{y}$$

• She likes to *wear designer clothes, listen to classical music,*

$$\overbrace{}^{z}$$

and *eat gourmet food.*

> Either version adequately corrects the earlier one, in which a
> whole clause, *gourmet food is essential,* was forced into paral-
> lelism with two infinitive constructions. A further option, one
> that keeps the emphasis of the original statement, is to end the
> parallelism early.

DO:

$$\overbrace{}^{x} \qquad \overbrace{}^{y}$$

• She likes to *wear designer clothes* and *listen to classical music,*
  and she finds gourmet food essential.

Comparing comparable things

The problem of mismatched parallel elements arises most frequently
in comparisons. The writer knows what is being compared with what,
but the words on the page say something else.

DON'T:

x *The office in Boston* was better equipped than *New York.*

> The sentence appears to compare an office to a city. The writer must add *the one in* to show that one office is being compared to another.

DO:

• *The office in Boston* was better equipped than *the one in New York.*

DON'T:

x *Solar heating for a large office building* is technically different from *a single-family home.*

> The writer is trying to compare one kind of solar heating to another, but the sentence actually compares one kind of solar heating to a single-family home.

DO:

• *Solar heating for a large office building* is technically different from *that for a single-family home.*

22b   Make the second half of a parallel construction as grammatically complete as the first.

When you are aligning two elements *x* and *y*, be careful not to omit parts of your *y* element that are necessary to make it match the parts of the *x* element. The problem tends to arise when the parallelism comes at the beginning of the sentence, especially if the formula being used is *not only x but also y.*

DON'T:

$$\overset{\text{x}}{\overbrace{\text{x Not only } \textit{did Gregor Mendel study the color of the peas}}}, \text{ but also}$$

$$\underbrace{\textit{the shapes of the seeds}}_{\text{y}}.$$

> Some good writers would find this sentence adequate; after all, its meaning is clear. But other writers would want to make a better match between *x* and *y*. Since the *x* element contains a subject *(Gregor Mendel)* and a verb *(did study),* the *y* element should follow suit.

IMPROVED:

- Not only $\overbrace{\textit{did Gregor Mendel study}}^{\text{v}}$ the color of the peas, but

  S   V   S

  he also *studied* the shapes of the seeds.

> But this revision is wordy. Such a construction can be made more concise by shifting the *not only* to a later position.

// 22c

PREFERABLE:

- Gregor Mendel studied not only $\overbrace{\textit{the color of the peas}}^{\text{x}}$ but also $\textit{the}$

  $\underbrace{\textit{shapes of the seeds}}_{\text{y}}.$

22c Be sure to complete the expected parts of an anticipatory pattern.

Many parallel constructions are governed by **anticipatory patterns** (p. 149, 12b)—formulas that demand to be completed in a certain predictable way. If you begin the formula but then change or abandon it, your sentence falls out of parallelism.

Neither . . . nor

A *neither* demands a *nor,* not an *or.*

DON'T:

x Banging his fist on the table, he insisted that he had *neither* a drinking problem *or* a problem with his temper.

> Change *or* to *nor*.

More like x than y

Do not sabotage this formula by adding the word *rather*.

DON'T:

x He seemed *more like* a Marine sergeant *rather than* a social worker.

> Delete *rather*.

No sooner x than y

Here the common error is to change *than* to *when*.

DON'T:

x *No sooner* had I left *when* my typewriter was stolen.

/ /
22c

> *When* must be changed to *than* if the anticipatory formula is to complete its work.

Not so much x as y

Be sure that the necessary *as* is not replaced by an unwelcome *but rather*.

DON'T:

x She was *not so much* selfish, *but rather* impulsive.

DO:

• She was *not so much* selfish *as* impulsive.

or

• She was *not so much* selfish *as she was* impulsive.

Note the absence of a comma in the two satisfactory versions.

22d Watch for faulty parallelism with *not . . . neither.*

DON'T:

ₓ The Marquis de Sade was $\overbrace{not\ an\ agreeable\ man,}^{\text{x}}$ and $\overbrace{neither}$
$\overbrace{are\ his\ novels.}^{\text{y}}$

> The complement *man* in the x element makes the sentence appear to say that the novels were not an agreeable man.

DO:

● The Marquis de Sade was $\overbrace{not\ agreeable,}^{\text{x}}$ and $\overbrace{neither\ are\ his\ nov-}^{\text{y}}$ els.

// 22e Beware of a suspended verb or a suspended comparison.

Suspended verb

Be alert to likely difficulties with a **suspended verb**—the use of two forms of the same delayed verb, governed by the same subject: *The project can, and in all likelihood will, succeed.* That sentence, though cumbersome, is grammatically correct. But quite often the delayed verb turns out to fit with only one of the two expressions preceding it.

DON'T:

ₓ They can, and indeed have been, making progress on the case.

The way to check such sentences is to read them without the interruption: *They can making . . . ?* Once you spot a problem, decide whether you want to repair the construction or get rid of it. As a rule you will want to do without the double statement.

DO:

- They can make, and indeed have been making, progress on the case.

or, better:

- They have been making progress on the case.

Suspended comparison

Like those with a suspended verb, parallel constructions involving a **suspended** (delayed) **comparison** sometimes end in a tangle.

DON'T:

x Wendy likes jazz *as much,* if not *more than, folk music.*

Check the sentence by reading it without the interruption. *Wendy likes jazz as much folk music?* Recognizing that this is ungrammatical, you can either repair or discard the suspended comparison.

DO:

- Wendy likes jazz as much as, if not more than, folk music.

or, better:

- Wendy likes jazz at least as much as she does folk music.

22f Repeat *that* to show that two clauses are parallel.

When you are trying to make whole clauses parallel, watch out for allowing the parallel effect to lapse after the first clause. The danger is greatest when the *x* element is a *that* clause.

DON'T:

x Sue wrote *that she hated her job,* but *she was glad to be working.*

As worded, this sentence allows the *y* element to become a direct statement about how Sue felt. But the writer's intention was to reveal two things that Sue *wrote*. A second *that* brings out that meaning.

DO:

- Sue wrote *that* she hated her job but *that* she was glad to be working.

22g Include *who* or *which* before using *and who* or *and which*.

DON'T:

x She is a woman of action, *and who* cares about the public good.

DO:

- She is a woman *who* takes strong action *and who* cares about the public good.

   Alternatively, you can rewrite the sentence: *She is a woman of action, and one who cares about the public good.*

DON'T:

x That is a questionable idea, *and which* has been opposed for many years.

DO:

- That is a questionable idea, *and one which* has been opposed for many years.

or

- That is a questionable idea which has been opposed for many years.

22h Do not let an earlier term invade a parallel construction.

Remember that elements already in place before a parallelism begins should not be repeated *inside* it.

Either . . . or, neither . . . nor

A parallelism involving one of these formulas may be grammatically dependent on an immediately preceding word or sentence element *(he wants either sausage or bacon).* Be sure to keep the preceding expression from reappearing inside the parallel construction itself.

DON'T:

x They serve *as* either guidance counselors or *as* soccer coaches.

The way to check such sentences is to take note of where the parallelism is introduced—in this case, at the word *either.* Next, isolate the whole parallelism—*either guidance counselors or as soccer coaches*—and see if it repeats the word that came just before it. Yes, the second *as* must go.

DO:

• They serve as either guidance counselors or soccer coaches.

or

• They serve either as guidance counselors or as soccer coaches. **/ /**
22h

Here *as* is repeated *within* the parallelism in order to make the *x* and *y* elements, *guidance counselors* and *soccer coaches,* fully parallel. Note how the two allowable versions differ from the faulty one:

as either *x* or as *y*	wrongly repeats an earlier element, *as*
either *x* or *y*	fully parallel
either as *x* or as *y*	fully parallel

Not only x but also y

This formula, useful when it works, can be easily misaligned. Once again, you must see where the parallelism begins and avoid repeating an earlier element.

DON'T:

x She remembered not only *her maps* but *she also remembered her tire repair kit.*

The first *remembered* comes just before the parallel construction and governs both of its parts. The second *remembered* thus
breaks the parallel effect.

DO:

* She remembered not only *her maps* but also *her tire repair kit.*

               x   y

Now x and y are parallel; they are the two things that were
remembered. The sentence lines up like this:

She remembered   { *not only* her maps
                    but also her tire repair kit.
                    (not only x but also y)

22i   Carry through with any repeated modifier in a series.

// 22i

If you begin repeating any modifier within a series, be sure to keep
doing so for all the remaining items.

DON'T:

x He can never find *his textbooks, his tapes, calculator,* and
homework.

The modifier *his* in the x element commits the writer to using
the word again in y and z. Note the options for revision.

DO:

* He can never find *his textbooks, his tapes, his calculator,* and
his homework.

or

* He can never find his *textbooks, tapes, calculator,* and *homework.*

PUNCTUATING PARALLEL ELEMENTS

22j Join most paired elements without an intervening comma.

To show that two elements are meant to be parallel, omit a comma after the first one.

DON'T:

x Last night's storm blew out *my electric blanket,* and *my clock radio.*

> The comma implies that the only direct object of *blew out* has already been given and that the main statement is over. By removing the comma the writer can show that the *x* and *y* elements are parallel objects.

DON'T:

x Aspirin has been called *a blessing by some,* and *a dangerous drug by others.*

> Aspirin has been called *x* and *y;* remove the comma to show that *x* and *y* are tightly related.

**//
22j**

Pairing independent clauses

The no-comma rule above need not apply when the *x* element is an independent clause (p. 201, 16c), as in *Not only did they adjust the fan belt, but they also adjusted the brakes.* But in *either . . . or* constructions you should omit the comma to keep the *y* statement from escaping the controlling effect of the parallelism.

DON'T:

x Either *you are wrong about the guitar strings,* or *I have forgotten everything I knew.*

> Remove the comma and notice how the two statements then fit more tightly together.

22k As a rule, use commas and a word like *and* to separate items in a series.

- I used to sprinkle my writing with $\overset{x}{commas,}$ $\overset{y}{semicolons,}$ and

  $\overset{z}{dashes}$ as though they were salt and pepper.

The normal way to present a **series** (three or more parallel items) is to separate the items with commas, adding a coordinating conjunction such as *and* or *or* before the last one.

Optional final comma

Many writers, especially journalists, omit the final comma in a series. So can you if you are consistent about it throughout a given piece of writing.

ACCEPTABLE:

- $\overset{x}{Football,}$ $\overset{y}{baseball}$ and $\overset{z}{basketball}$ were his only concerns.

Note, however, that the *x, y and z* formula may not always allow your meaning to come through clearly. Consider the following sentences, which are identical except for the comma or its absence after *friends*.

ACCEPTABLE:

- When Alex joins the Air Force, he will leave behind $\overset{x}{\overline{a\ loving}}$

  $\overset{y}{\overline{family,}}\ friends$ and $\overset{x}{\overline{a\ room\ that\ he\ has\ had\ all\ to\ himself.}}$

  Has Alex had the friends to himself as well as the room? This is not the writer's intention, but the reader may wonder about it for a moment.

PREFERABLE:

- When Alex joins the Air Force, he will leave behind a loving family, friends, and a room that he has had all to himself.

Now there is no chance of misunderstanding. You can see why many good writers always use a final comma in a series.

22l   If an item within a series contains a comma, use semicolons to show where each of the items ends.

Once you have begun a series, you may find yourself using commas for two quite different purposes: to separate the $x, y,$ and z items and to punctuate *within* one or more of those items. If so, your reader may have trouble seeing where each item ends. To show the important breaks between the main parallel items, separate $x, y,$ and z with semicolons:

- The Director of Food Services said that during the renovation the students would have priority in the dining halls; that faculty members should plan to cook at home, eat elsewhere, or bring bag lunches to their offices; and that the college's neighbors, including several retired professors living nearby, would be barred from the student halls until the work had been completed.

/ /
22l

For other options in the ordering and punctuation of series, see page 151, 12c.

23 Relations between Tenses

Every time you write a sentence, you are expressing a *tense,* or time of action, through your verb. For a review of verb forms showing not only their tenses but also their **voices** and **moods**, see Chapter 30.

Some tenses are obviously appropriate to certain functions—the present for statements of opinion, the past for storytelling, the future for prediction. But choice of tense becomes trickier when you need to combine two or more time frames within a sentence *(He said he would have been ready if the plane had not been late; She will have finished by the day we get home;* etc.). When revising your work, check to see that your combinations of tenses follow the advice given below.

23a   Choose one governing tense for a piece of writing.

Stating facts and ideas

The normal way to state facts or offer your ideas about any general or current topic is to use the present tense:

- Water boils at 100° Celsius.
- Does the new divorce law protect the rights of children?

Note how the following passage establishes a present time frame, departing from it only to narrate events that occurred previously:

PRES
- The great debate *continues* between heredity and environment.
                                                              PRES
    Both sides have strong arguments, but I *am convinced* that
            PRES   PAST
    technology *adjusts* our fate. My grandfather, for example, *was*

                                                    PRES PERF
dead at forty from diabetes, a disease that my father *has lived*
with for sixty years, thanks to this century's advances in medical
research.

If you are stating ideas about the past, many of your verbs will be in
the past tense. Even so, the present is appropriate for conveying your
current reflections about past events:

    PRES   PRES   PAST
- I *believe* we *can prove* that the Etruscans *had* much more influ-
                                            PRES
  ence on Roman civilization than most people *realize*.

Narrating events

The usual tense for narrating events is the past:

    PAST   PAST
- She *arrived* home in a fury, and she *was* still upset when the
    PAST
  phone *rang*.
                PAST
- The solution *was allowed* to stand for three minutes, after
                            PAST
  which 200 cc of nitrogen *were added*.

In this second example the past verbs are in the passive voice (p. 369,
30d).

   Sometimes, to get a special effect of immediacy, you may even
want to use the present for narration:

            PRES   PRES
- When he *phones* her, she *tells* him to leave her alone.

But note that once you adopt this present-tense convention for storytelling, you have committed yourself to it throughout the piece of writing. Do not try to switch back to the more usual past.

DON'T:

            PRES   PRES
x When he *phones* her, she *tells* him to leave her alone. But he
  PAST   PAST PERF
  acted as if he *hadn't understood* her point.

**tense
23a**

For consistency, the second sentence should read: *But he <u>acts</u> as if he <u>hasn't</u> understood.* . . .

23b   Relate your other tenses to the governing tense.

Once you have established a controlling time frame, or **governing tense,** shift into other tenses as logic requires.

Present time frame

A present time frame, established by a present governing tense, allows you to use a variety of other tenses to indicate the times of actions or states. The following are ways of combining other tenses with the present:

* He *meditates* every day, and . . .

tense
23b

REST OF SENTENCE	TENSE
he *is meditating* right now.	present progressive (action ongoing in the present)
he *has meditated* five thousand times.	present perfect (past action completed thus far)
he *has been meditating* since dawn.	present perfect progressive (action begun in the past and continuing in the present)
he *meditated* for ten hours yesterday.	past (completed action)
he *was meditating* before I was born.	past progressive (action that was ongoing in a previous time)
he *had meditated* for years before hearing about the popularity of meditation.	past perfect (action completed before another past time)

REST OF SENTENCE	TENSE
he *had been meditating* for three hours before the interview.	past perfect progressive (ongoing action completed before another past time)
he *will meditate* tomorrow.	future (action to occur later)
he *will be meditating* for the rest of his life.	future progressive (ongoing action to occur later)
by next year he *will have meditated* for more hours than anyone ever has.	future perfect (action regarded as completed at a later time)
he *will have been meditating* for ten years by the time he is thirty.	future perfect progressive (ongoing action regarded as having begun before a later time)

tense
23b

Past time frame

When your time frame is in the past, choose other tenses according to the following patterns:

- There *were* rumors around school . . .

REST OF SENTENCE	TENSE
that the Dean *had been* a sergeant in Vietnam.	past perfect (action completed in an earlier past time)
that the Dean *had been lifting* weights all these years.	past perfect progressive (ongoing action that began earlier)
that the Dean *would take* disciplinary matters into his own hands.	conditional (later action)

Hypothetical condition

Certain sentences containing *if* clauses set forth **hypothetical conditions.** That is, they tell what would be true or would have been true in certain imagined circumstances. Note that such sentences differ in both form and meaning from sentences proposing likely conditions.

LIKELY CONDITION	HYPOTHETICAL CONDITION
I *will dance* if you *clear* a space on the floor.	I *would dance* if you *cleared* a space on the floor.
If she *studies* now, she *will pass*.	If she *studied* now, she *would pass*.
If I *marry* your sister, we *will be* brothers.	If I *married* your sister, we *would be* brothers.

tense 23b

The "likely condition" sentences anticipate that the condition may be met, but the "hypothetical condition" sentences are sheer speculation: what would happen if . . . ? These require use of the *subjunctive mood* (p. 371, 30e) in the *if* clause. And in the "consequence" clause they require a *conditional* form, either present or past:

CONDITIONAL FORMS		
Present	$\left.\begin{array}{l}would\\ could\end{array}\right\}$ + base verb	would go could go
Past	$\left.\begin{array}{l}would\\ could\end{array}\right\}$ + *have* + past participle	would have gone could have gone

Thus:

IF CLAUSE	CONSEQUENCE CLAUSE
PRES SUBJN If you *worked* overtime,	PRES CONDL you *would have* more spending money.

IF CLAUSE	**CONSEQUENCE CLAUSE**
PRES SUBJN If they *won* a million dollars,	**PRES CONDL** what *would* they *do* with the money?
PAST SUBJN If she *had concentrated,*	**PAST CONDL** she *could have written* a perfect translation.
PAST SUBJN If you *had been* old enough,	PAST CONDL *would* you *have married* Barbara?

The most common mistake in combining tenses is to use *would* in both parts of a conditional statement. Remember that *would* goes only in the consequence clause, not in the *if* clause.

DON'T:

x If they *would* try harder, they would succeed.

DO:

• If they *tried* harder, they would succeed.

DON'T:

x If they *would have* tried harder, they would have succeeded.

DO:

• If they *had tried* harder, they would have succeeded.

tense
23c

23c Learn how tenses differ between quotation and indirect discourse.

In the following chart, notice what happens to tenses when you shift from what was actually said (quotation or **direct discourse**) to a report of what was said (**indirect discourse**).

	QUOTATION	INDIRECT DISCOURSE
Present verb in quotation	"I *want* to join the Navy after graduation," he said.	He said that he *wanted* to join the Navy after graduation.
Past verb in quotation	"I *wanted* to join the Navy after my graduation," he revealed.	He revealed that he *had wanted* to join the Navy after his graduation.
Present perfect verb in quotation	He protested, "I *have* never *wanted* to join the Air Force."	He protested that he *had* never *wanted* to join the Air Force.
Past perfect verb in quotation	"Until then," he reminded us, "I *had* always *planned* to study photography."	He reminded us that until then he *had* always *planned* to study photography.
Future verb in quotation	"I *will want* to look into photographic training in the military," he said.	He said that he *would want* to look into photographic training in the military.

tense
23c

To summarize these changes of tense, indirect discourse:

	QUOTATION	INDIRECT DISCOURSE
Makes a present verb past	want ⟶	wanted
Makes a past or present perfect verb past perfect	wanted / have wanted ⟶	had wanted
Leaves a past perfect verb past perfect	had wanted ⟶	had wanted
Turns a future verb into *would* + a base (infinitive) form	will want ⟶	would want

You can deduce other tense changes in indirect discourse from these basic ones: *will have wanted* becomes *would have wanted, has been wanting* becomes *had been wanting,* and so forth.

23d Do not shift between quotation and indirect discourse within a sentence.

Once you have begun to quote someone's speech or writing, do not suddenly move into indirect discourse (23c). Similarly, do not leap from indirect discourse to quotation.

DON'T:

QUOTATION

x She said, *"I love science fiction movies,"* and *had I seen the one*
INDIRECT DISCOURSE

about the teenage Martians on a rampage?

tense
23d

DO:

QUOTATION

• She said, *"I love science fiction movies,"* and asked me, *"Have*
QUOTATION

you seen the one about the teenage Martians on a rampage?"

DON'T:

INDIRECT
DISCOURSE   QUOTATION

x My boss said *the key was gone* and *are you the one who took it?*

DO:

INDIRECT
DISCOURSE   INDIRECT DISCOURSE

• My boss said *the key was gone* and asked *if I was the one who had taken it.*

23e Use the present tense to write about action within a plot or about an author's ideas within a work.

Discussing actions within a plot

Unlike a real event, a scene within a work of art does not happen once and for all. It is always ready to be experienced afresh by a new reader, viewer, or listener. Consequently, the time frame for discussing such a scene is the present. Though you should use the past tense to write about the historical creating of the artwork, you should use the present tense to convey what the work "says to us." This function is called the **"literary" present tense.**

HISTORICAL PAST:
- Shakespeare *was* probably familiar with the plays of Kyd and Marlowe when he *wrote* his great tragedies. He *expressed* his deepest feelings in those plays.

**tense
23e**

LITERARY PRESENT:
- Shakespeare *reveals* Hamlet's mind through soliloquy.

- Hamlet's unrelenting psychological dilemma *drives* him toward catastrophe.

- The Misfit, in Flannery O'Connor's story "A Good Man Is Hard to Find," *murders* an entire family.

- In the 1949 film version of *Oliver Twist,* Alec Guinness *plays* Fagin.

  If the verb in this last example were *played,* the sentence would be making a statement not about the movie but about an event in Alec Guinness's acting career.

Discussing ideas within a work

No matter how long ago a book or other publication was written, use the "literary" present tense to characterize the idea it expresses:

- In *The Republic* Plato *maintains* that artists *are* a menace to the ideal state.

- Thoreau *says* in *Walden* that we *can* find peace by staying exactly where we *are*.

> The present-tense verbs are appropriate because any book "speaks to" its readers in a continuing present time.

If, on the other hand, you want to refer to a noncontemporary author's ideas without reference to a particular work, use the past:

- Plato *believed* that artists were a menace to the ideal state.

- Thoreau *was convinced* that people could find peace by staying exactly where they *were*.

23f   In discussing a plot, relate other tenses to the "literary" present.

Once you have established the "literary" present for action in a plot that is "happening right now" (23e), refer to earlier or later actions in that plot by using the past, future, and related tenses.

PAST
- When Hamlet's suspicion's *were* confirmed by the ghost, he
  PAST   PRES
  vowed revenge. But by Act Two he *fears* that his self-doubts
  PRES PERF   PRES
  have dulled his purpose. He *engages* a troupe of players to reen-
                    PRES   FUTURE
  act the murder and *swears* that the play *will* "catch the conscience of the King. . . ."

> Notice how the writer has chosen a point of focus in Act Two of *Hamlet*. The use of the "literary" present for that time determines which tenses are appropriate for the other described actions.

23g Do not allow the past form of a quoted verb to influence your own choice of tense.

It is hard to keep to the "literary" present (23e) when you have just quoted a passage containing verbs in the past tense. The tendency is to allow your own verbs to slip into the past. Keep to the rule, however, and use the present tense for actions or states under immediate discussion:

- D. H. Lawrence *describes* [PRES] Cecilia as "a big dark-complexioned, pug-faced young woman who very rarely *spoke*. . . ." [PAST] When she *does speak*, [PRES] however, her words *are* [PRES] sharp enough to kill her aunt Pauline.

tense 23g

VI
PUNCTUATION

Punctuation

Marks of punctuation are essential for clear meaning in written prose. Beyond showing where pauses or stops would occur in speech, they indicate logical relations that would otherwise be hard for a reader to make out. For example, parentheses, brackets, dashes, and commas all signal a pause, but they suggest different relations between main and subordinate material. The only way to be sure that your punctuation marks are working with your meaning, not against it, is to master the rules.

Part V above, "Usage," covers a good many punctuation rules for handling such grammatical features as independent clauses, modifying elements, and parallel constructions. This part repeats those rules (giving cross references to the fuller discussions), adds other rules, and shows how you can choose between punctuation marks that are closely related in function.

Note that the conventions of quoting are handled in Chapter 28. Apostrophes and hyphens are treated, respectively, in Chapters 31 and 33. To see how you should form and space the various punctuation marks, see Chapter 29.

24 Periods, Question Marks, Exclamation Points

PERIODS

24a **Place a period at the end of a sentence making a statement, a polite command, or a mild exclamation.**

STATEMENT:
- I think the Olympic Games have become too politicized.
- Art historians are showing new respect for nineteenth-century narrative painting.

POLITE COMMAND:
- Tell me why you think the Olympic Games have become too politicized.
- Consider the new respect that art historians are showing toward nineteenth-century narrative painting.

MILD EXCLAMATION:
- What a pity that the Olympic Games have become so politicized.
- How remarkable it is to see the art historians reversing their former scorn for nineteenth-century narrative painting.

    Exclamation points at the end of these two sentences would have made them more emphatic; see p. 315, 24j.

24b End an indirect question with a period.

- Ted asked me whether I was good at boardsailing**.**

An **indirect question,** instead of taking a question form, reports that a question is or was asked. Thus an indirect question is a **declarative sentence**—one that makes a statement. As such, it should be completed by a period, not a question mark.

24c Consider a period optional after a courtesy question.

- Would you be kind enough to reply within thirty days**.**

or

- Would you be kind enough to reply within thirty days**?**

Some questions in business letters (Chapter 40) are really requests or mild commands. You can end such a sentence with either a period or a question mark. The period makes a more impersonal and routine effect. If you want to express actual courtesy toward a reader you know, keep to the question mark.

24d 24d Eliminate an unacceptable sentence fragment [see discussion on p. 203, 16d].

DON'T:

x Most Americans should study recent changes in the tax laws.
FRAG

Especially those affecting deductions for medical expenses, child care, and IRAs.

DO:

- Most Americans should study recent changes in the tax laws, *especially* those affecting deductions for medical expenses, child care, and IRAs.

DON'T:

x They stood back and watched the crows. *Wheeling and cawing*
FRAG
over the splattered melon.

DO:

• They stood back and watched the crows wheeling and cawing over the splattered melon.

For discussion of the intentional sentence fragment, see p. 207, 16e.

24e If a sentence ends with an abbreviation, use only one period.

• She made many sacrifices to complete her Ph.D.

QUESTION MARKS

24f Place a question mark after a direct question.

Most questions are complete sentences, but now and then you may want to add a question to a statement or insert a question within a statement. In every instance, put a question mark immediately after the question:

• Do you like to write?
• Many people are proud of their written work, but *does anyone really like to write?*
• *"Can you imagine someone finding it easier to write,"* I asked, *"than to call?"*
• You and I—*is it possible?*—may yet learn to enjoy writing.

But if your sentence poses a question that is then modified by other language, place the question mark at the end:

• How could he treat me like that, after all the consideration I showed him?

24g To express doubt, use a question mark within parentheses.

- Saint Thomas Aquinas, 1225(?)–1274, considered faith more important than reason.

    If the dates here were in parentheses, the question mark would go inside brackets: *(1225[?]–1274)*.

Sarcastic question mark

No grammatical rule prevents you from getting a sarcastic effect from the "doubting" question mark. But if you are determined to be sarcastic, quotation marks will do a better job of conveying your attitude.

AVOID:
x The president expects to make four nonpolitical (?) speeches in the month before the election.

PREFER:
- The president expects to make four "nonpolitical" speeches in the month before the election.

24h If a sentence asking a question contains a question at the end, use only one question mark.

- Are you the skeptic who asked, "Why write?"

24i After a question mark, omit a comma or a period.

- Now I know the answer to the question, "Why study?"
- "Where is my journal?" she asked.

EXCLAMATION POINTS

24j Use exclamation points sparingly to express intense feeling or a strong command.

- My wallet, my glasses, my notes—all gone!
- So this is the result of their so-called peace offensive!
- Call a doctor!

Note that frequent use of exclamation points dulls their effect while making the writer appear too excitable. And though an exclamation point, like a question mark, can be inserted parenthetically to convey sarcasm (24g), the effect is usually weak.

AVOID:

x Warren thought that a black-and-white photocopy (!) of the Rembrandt painting would give him everything he needed to write his art history paper.

!
24j

25 Commas

Primary discussions of most comma rules appear in other chapters; see the cross references below. Here we bring all the rules together in an overview that shows (a) where you should use a comma or pair of commas, (b) where you should omit a comma, and (c) where you can include or omit a comma as you see fit. Wherever you need more examples or background, go to the cross-referenced discussions.

25a Learn where you should include a comma or pair of commas.

> **INCLUDE A COMMA OR PAIR OF COMMAS WHEN YOU . . .**
>
> **Join independent clauses** (see p. 209, 17a):
> • *Every blink is like fire,* and *tears well up constantly.*
>
> [The two clauses *Every blink is like fire* and *tears well up constantly* are **independent** because each of them could stand as a complete sentence. To avoid a **comma splice** or a **fused sentence,** you should join them either with a comma and a coordinating conjunction, as here, or with a semicolon: *Every blink is like fire; tears well up constantly.*]
>
> **Begin with a subordinate clause** (see p. 251, 19i):
> SUB CLAUSE
> • *Since you asked,* I will admit that I am exhausted.
>
> [*Since you asked* is a **clause** because it contains both a **subject** *(you)* and a **verb** *(asked).* It is a **subordinate clause** because it cannot stand alone as a complete sentence. Whenever you begin a sentence with such a clause, add a comma.]

INCLUDE A COMMA OR PAIR OF COMMAS WHEN YOU . . .

MOD PHRASE

Begin with a modifying • *In a spontaneous wave of enthu-*
phrase that is more than a few *siasm,* the audience rose to its
words long (see p. 251, 19i): feet.

[*In a spontaneous wave of enthusiasm* is a **phrase** because it forms a
multi-word unit without a subject-verb combination. Unless an
opening phrase is very brief, follow it with a comma.]

INT EL

Use an interrupting element • The deficit, *as a matter of fact,*
(see p. 253, 19l): has continued to grow.

[An **interrupting element** forces a break in the main flow of a
sentence. Set it off on both sides.]

NONR EL

Include a nonrestrictive • Women, *who have rarely been*
(nondefining) modifying *treated equally in the job mar-*
element (see p. 254, 19m): *ket,* still tend to be relatively
underpaid.

[The sentence refers to all women. Thus the subordinate clause *who
have rarely been treated equally in the job market* does not serve to
define or restrict the class of women who are meant. Such a
nonrestrictive element should always be set off from the rest of the
sentence.]

,
25a

Include items in a series (see p. • *Modems, plotters, baud rates,*
296, 22k): and *programming languages*
danced continually in Wilbur's
busy mind.

[A **series,** or set of three or more parallel items, requires commas
after each item but the last.]

Present certain quotations (see • *She said,* "I intend to be there
pp. 346–347, 28l–m): early."

[When you introduce a complete quoted sentence with a tag like *she
said* or *he exclaimed,* follow it with a comma. If the tag appears later,
surround it with commas: *"I intend," she said, "to be there early."*]

INCLUDE A COMMA OR PAIR OF COMMAS WHEN YOU . . .

Present a place name with a more inclusive location:
- *Laramie, Wyoming,* celebrates its Jubilee Days every July.

[When you add the name of a state, province, or country after a place name, set off the second name with commas on both sides.]

Present an address or a month-first date:
- 3945 Bushnell Road, University Heights, OH 44118
- March 17, 1964, was the date of his birth.

[Note the commas both before and after *1964*.]

Include a title or degree:
- Monica Wu, *Ph.D.,* is holding office hours today.

[Note the commas both before and after *Ph.D.*]

Include a number of more than four digits:
- 29, 368, 452

[Set off every three digits, working from right to left.]

25b Learn where you should omit a comma.

,
25b

OMIT A COMMA WHEN YOU . . .

Join a subject and verb (see p. 238, 18o):
- A *bird* in the hand *is* worth two in the bush.

(S, V, no comma)

[Note that *in the hand* does not interrupt the main statement; it is a **restrictive element** (see below), showing which bird is meant. Thus a comma after *hand* would wrongly separate the subject and verb.]

Join a verb and direct object (see p. 198, 16a):
- She *recognized* in a flash the *meaning* of her dream.

(V, D OBJ, no comma)

OMIT A COMMA WHEN YOU . . .

[Since no comma sets off *in a flash* at the front end, a comma after *flash* would be inappropriate. The verb *recognized* must be allowed to hook up with its object *meaning* without a pause.]

Join a verb and its complement (see p. 198, 16a):

- The laws against drug use *were*
  V
  not always so *strict* as they are
  C
  today.
  \no comma

[A verb's **complement**, appearing in the **predicate**, identifies or modifies the subject—in this case, *laws.* Since there is no real interruption between *were* and *strict,* a comma after *always* would be wrong.]

Join a subordinating conjunction and the rest of its subordinate clause (see pp. 201-202, 16c):

- One further reason for using the
  shopping mall is *that parking is*
                      SUB CLAUSE
  ample there.
                SUB \no comma
                CONJ

[*That parking is ample there* forms a **subordinate clause**—a subject-predicate combination that cannot stand alone. Since *that* is an essential part of the clause, a comma following it would be inappropriate.]

25b

Join a preposition and its object (see p. 587):

- My worries keep returning *to*
                              PREP
  inflation, unemployment, and
  OBJ OF PREP   no comma
  natural disasters.

[Even when the object of a preposition is lengthy, making you want to "catch a breath" just before it, you should resist the temptation to insert a comma. By omitting the comma, you honor the unity of the complete prepositional phrase. Note that a colon would also be unacceptable here (p. 326, 26g).]

OMIT A COMMA WHEN YOU ...

RESTR EL

Include a restrictive (defining) modifying element (see p. 254, 19m):

• A child *who likes to play with electrical outlets* must be carefully watched. no commas

[The subordinate clause *who likes to play with electrical outlets* serves to identify which child is meant. Thus it is defining, or **restrictive.** If you wrongly added commas after *child* and *outlets,* making that element **nonrestrictive,** you would be drastically changing the meaning of the sentence: every single child, everywhere, likes to play with electrical outlets and therefore must be carefully watched.]

Join a final modifier and the modified term (see p. 260, 19p):

• It was an intensely vivid,

FINAL MOD

compelling, *anxiety-producing*

MODIFIED TERM   no comma

account of the disaster.

[No matter how many modifiers you string together, omit a comma between the final one and the modified term—in this case, *account.*]

' 25b

Join paired elements (see p. 295, 22j):

• The cause of the fire was either
x

a leak from the ancient gas heat-
y

er or *a short circuit.*

no comma

[The formula here is *either x* or *y.* To cement the connection between the *x* and *y* items, join them without a comma.]

Include a day-first date:

• They were married on *23 January 1989.*

[Note that a comma would be required if the month came first: *January 23, 1989.*]

Include a numeral after a name:

• Oswald Humbert *IV* lost all his money in the crash. no commas

25c Learn where a comma is optional.

CONSIDER A COMMA OPTIONAL WHEN YOU . . .

Begin with a brief phrase (see p. 251, 19j):

- *After the storm,* the ground was strewn with leaves.
- *After the storm* the ground was strewn with leaves.

[When in doubt, you cannot go wrong by supplying the comma.]

Use *thus* or *hence* (see p. 253, 19k):

- *Hence,* there is no need for alarm.
- *Hence* there is no need for alarm.

Invert the normal order of sentence elements:

- *What she calls happiness,* I call slavery.
- *What she calls happiness* I call slavery.

[*What she calls happiness* is an **objective complement**—a complement of the direct object *slavery*. It normally follows the direct object, as in *They appointed him secretary*.]

Use one modifier to qualify the preceding one (see p. 260, 19q):

- It was a difficult, *but by no means impossible,* assignment.
- It was a difficult *but by no means impossible* assignment.

[Note how the second modifier, beginning with *but,* answers the modifier before it. Commas are optional in such a case.]

Follow a month with a year:

- *May, 1968,* was the time of the famous uprising.
- *May 1968* was the time of the famous uprising.

[If you add the date, commas are required on both sides: *May 14, 1968, was the time. . . .* Note also that a comma before the year obliges you to add another comma after the year.]

Use a four-digit number:

- 8,354
- 8354

26 Semicolons and Colons

SEMICOLON	COLON
Relates two statements	**Equates two items**
• We did not bully or threaten; we knew that justice was on our side. [The two parts of the sentence are logically connected; the second statement explains why no bullying or threatening was considered necessary.]	• We asked for just one thing: the return of our stolen land. [Everything following the colon serves to specify the *thing* preceding it. The colon means *namely*.]

SEMICOLONS

26a To keep two closely related statements within the same sentence, join them with a semicolon.

- My oldest sister is the boss in our family; what she says goes.
- The university conducts art history classes in Europe; the accessibility of great museums and monuments gives students a first-hand sense of the subject.

- Some of those painters influenced Cézanne; others were influenced by him.

The punctuation mark that comes nearest in function to the semicolon is the period. But whereas a period keeps two statements apart as separate sentences, a semicolon shows that two statements within one sentence are intimately related. When one statement is a consequence of another or contrasts sharply with it, you can bring out that tight connection by joining them with a semicolon instead of with a comma and a coordinating conjunction (p. 210, 17a).

Note that when a semicolon is used, the second statement often contains a sentence adverb or transitional phrase (p. 252, 19k) pointing out the logical relation between the two clauses:

- Misunderstanding is often the root of injustice; perfect under-
  SENT ADV
  standing, *however,* is impossible to attain.
                                                        TRANS
                                                        PHRASE
- Some parents weigh every word they speak; others, *in contrast,* do not think twice about their harsh language.

26b Make sure that a semicolon is followed by a complete statement.

; 26b

DO:

- I used to be afraid to talk to people; even asking the time of day was an ordeal. I always let my brother speak for me; he was everyone's buddy.

DON'T:

FRAG

x I used to be afraid to talk to people; *even to ask the time of day.*

FRAG

I always let my brother speak for me; *because he was everyone's buddy.*

An unacceptable sentence fragment (p. 203, 16d) is just as faulty when it follows a semicolon as when it stands alone.

26c   Feel free to use a word like *and* or *but* after a semicolon.

There is nothing wrong with following a semicolon with a conjunction, so long as the second statement is an independent clause (16c). Do so if you want to make explicit the logical connection between the statements coming before and after the semicolon:

CONJ

- All day long we loaded the van with our worldy goods; *but* when we were ready to leave the next morning, full of eagerness for the trip, we saw that the van had a flat tire.

   A comma after *goods* would also be appropriate, but the semicolon recommends itself because the second statement already contains two commas. Thus the semicolon helps to show the main separation in the sentence.

26d   If an item within a series contains a comma, use semicolons to show where each of the items ends [see discussion on p. 297, 22l].

- The Director of Food Services said that during the renovation the students would have priority in the dining halls; that faculty members should plan to cook at home, eat elsewhere, or bring bag lunches to their offices; and that the college's neighbors, including several retired professors living nearby, would be barred from the student halls.
- Student dining halls include the Servery, which is located on the ground floor of the Student Union; the Cafeteria, temporarily relocated in Jim Thorpe Gymnasium; and the Rathskeller, now in the basement of Anne Bradstreet Hall.

:
26e

COLONS

26e   Use a colon to show an equivalence between items on either side.

A colon introduces a restatement, a formal list, or a quotation. Use a colon if you can plausibly insert *namely* after it:

- Dinner arrives: [*namely*] a tuna fish sandwich and a cup of tea.
- The bill is unbelievable: [*namely*] $8.50 for the sandwich and $1.95 for the tea.
- Samuel Johnson offered the following wise advice: [*namely*] "If you would have a faithful servant, and one that you like, serve yourself."

The *namely* test can help you avoid putting semicolons where colons belong and vice versa.

DON'T:

x The results of the poll were surprising; 7 percent in favor, 11 percent opposed, and 82 percent no opinion.

Namely would be appropriate here; therefore the semicolon should be a colon.

x We slaved for years: we remained as poor as ever.

Namely is inappropriate, since the second clause makes a new point. The colon should be a semicolon.

26f Make sure you have a complete statement before a colon.

:
26f

Like a semicolon, a colon must be preceded by a complete statement.

DO:

COMPLETE STATEMENT
- *Occupations involving animals interest me:* beekeeper, horse groomer, dog trainer, veterinarian.

DON'T:

FRAG
x *Occupations that interest me:* beekeeper, horse groomer, dog trainer, veterinarian.

But remember that, unlike a semicolon, a colon need not be *followed* by a whole statement (p. 323, 26b).

26g   Omit a colon if it would separate elements that belong together.

DON'T:

                                              V   ⎯⎯⎯⎯⎯⎯⎯⎯⎯⎯⎯ D OBJ
x Before buying my Cavalier, I *tested: a Toyota Corolla, a Ford Escort, and a Nissan Sentra.*

> The colon separates a verb from its three-part direct object. Note that this practice would still be wrong if the direct object had any number of parts and extended for many lines.

                                V   C
x Her favorite holidays *are: Christmas, Halloween, and the Fourth of July.*

> The colon separates a verb from its three-part complement (p. 198, 16a).

x The exhibit contained works by many famous photographers,

   PREP   ⎯⎯⎯⎯⎯⎯⎯ OBJ OF PREP ⎯⎯⎯⎯⎯⎯⎯
   such as: Avedon, Adams, Weston, and Lange.

> The colon separates a preposition from its four-part object.

x The Renaissance naval adventurers set out *to: sack enemy cities,*

   COMPLETION OF INF PHRASES

   find precious metals, and claim colonial territory.

> The colon separates the infinitive marker *to* from the completion of three infinitive phrases (p. 587). Even if you had a long series of such phrases, the colon would be wrong.

In each of the four examples above, you need only drop the colon to make the sentence acceptable.

26h **Use a colon to separate hours and minutes, to end the salutation of a business letter, and to introduce a subtitle.**

HOURS AND MINUTES:
• The train should arrive at 10:15 P.M.

SALUTATION:
• Dear Mr. Green:

SUBTITLE:
• *Virginia Woolf: A Biography*

26h

27 Dashes and Parentheses

Both dashes and parentheses, as well as commas, can be used to set off interrupting elements (p. 253, 191). The difference is that dashes call attention to the interrupting material, whereas parentheses suggest that it is truly subordinate in meaning.

Dashes	—	most emphatic	The monsoon season—with incessant driving rain and flooding—causes much hardship.
Commas	,	"neutral"	The monsoon season, with incessant driving rain and flooding, causes much hardship.
Parentheses	( )	least emphatic	The monsoon season (with incessant driving rain and flooding) causes much hardship.

DASHES

27a Use a dash or pair of dashes to set off and emphasize a striking insertion.

- Poets have been fascinated by Narcissus—the most modern of mythological lovers.

- Narcissus—the most modern of mythological lovers—fell in love with himself.

27b Note the other uses of the dash.

TO OFFER AN EMPHATIC EXPLANATION:
- Narcissus was the most modern of mythological lovers—he fell in love with himself.

TO INTRODUCE A LIST ABRUPTLY:
- The new house has marvelous devices to let in light—skylights in the dining room, living room walls that slide open, and a breakfast porch constructed like a greenhouse.

TO MARK AN INTERRUPTION OF DIALOGUE:
- The man behind menaced us with his umbrella. "If you don't step aside, I'll—"

  "This is a line for people with tickets," I said. "We're not—"

  But our dispute was cut short by the usher, who was urging the line forward.

If a character's speech "trails off" instead of being interrupted, an ellipsis (p. 348, 28o) is more suitable than a dash: *"We're not . . ."* Note that you should begin a new paragraph for each change of speaker.

TO ISOLATE AN INTRODUCTORY ELEMENT THAT IS NOT THE GRAMMATICAL SUBJECT:
APP
- *Depression, compulsion, phobia, hallucination*—these disorders often require quick and emphatic treatment.

In a sentence that makes a "false start" for rhetorical effect (p. 156, 12g), you want to give a signal that the opening element is an appositive (p. 257, 19n) rather than the subject of the verb. A dash serves the purpose.

27b

27c   If your sentence resumes after an interruption, use a second dash.

When you begin an interruption with one dash, you must end it with another.

DO:
- Narcissus looked into a lake—so the story goes—and fell in love with his own reflection.

DON'T:
- x Narcissus looked into a lake—so the story goes, and fell in love with his own reflection.

DO:
- Somehow my aunt sensed the danger—perhaps she realized that my uncle should have been home by then—and she phoned me to come at once.

DON'T:
- x Somehow my aunt sensed the danger—perhaps she realized that my uncle should have been home by then, and she phoned me to come at once.

27d

27d   Make sure your sentence would be coherent if the part within dashes were omitted.

The elements of your sentence before and after the dashes must fit together grammatically.

DON'T:
- x *Because* he paid no attention to her—he was riveted to his cable sports channel day and night—*so* she finally lost her temper.

  Ask yourself if the sentence makes sense without the material between dashes: x *Because he paid no attention to her so she finally lost her temper*. Recognizing that this shortened sentence is grammatically askew, you can then correct the original.

DO:

- Because he paid no attention to her—he was riveted to his cable sports channel day and night—she finally lost her temper.

27e Do not use more than one set of dashes in a sentence.

Dashes work best when used sparingly. Within a single sentence, one interruption marked by dashes should be the maximum.

DO:

- We cannot expect a tax reform bill, or indeed any major legislation, to be considered on its merits in an election year—a time when the voters' feelings, not the country's interests, are uppermost in the minds of lawmakers.

DON'T:

- x We cannot expect a tax reform bill—or indeed any major legislation—to be considered on its merits in an election year—a time when the voters' feelings—not the country's interests—are uppermost in the minds of lawmakers.

( )
27f

PARENTHESES

27f Use parentheses to enclose and subordinate an incidental insertion.

Parentheses are appropriate for showing the incidental, lesser status of an illustration, explanation, or passing comment.

ILLUSTRATION:

- Some tropical reptiles (the Galápagos tortoise, for example) sleep in puddles of water to cool themselves.

EXPLANATION:
* A modem (a device for connecting a computer terminal to a central source of data) could easily be mistaken for an ordinary telephone.

PASSING COMMENT:
* The Ouse (a rather pretty, harmless-looking river) is known to literary people as the body of water in which Virginia Woolf drowned herself.

27g Note the other uses of parentheses.

TO RESTATE A NUMBER:
* The furniture will be repossessed in thirty (30) days.

TO ENCLOSE A DATE:
* The article on race and gender in literary study appears in *Feminist Studies* 9, no. 3 (Fall 1983), pages 435–63.

TO ENCLOSE A CITATION:
* Guevara first began studying Marxism in Guatemala in 1954 (Liss 256–57).

( )
27h

27h Learn when to supply end punctuation for a parenthetic sentence within another sentence.

If your whole sentence-within-a-sentence is a statement, do not end it with a period:

* Shyness *(mine was extreme)* can be overcome with time.

But if you are asking a question or making an exclamation, do supply the end punctuation:

* Today I am outspoken *(who would have predicted it?)* and sometimes even eloquent.
* To be able to give a talk without panic *(what a relief at last!)* is a great advantage in the business world.

Notice that the parenthetic sentence-within-a-sentence does not begin with a capital letter.

27i When placing a parenthetic sentence between complete sentences, punctuate it as a complete sentence.

A whole sentence within parentheses, if it is not part of another sentence, must begin with a capital letter and contain end punctuation of its own, *within* the close-parenthesis mark:

- Shyness can be a crippling affliction. *(The clinical literature is full of tragic cases.)* Yet some victims suddenly reach a point where they decide they have been bullied long enough.

27j Do not allow parentheses to affect other punctuation.

Remember these two rules:

1. No mark of punctuation comes just before an open-parenthesis mark.

2. The rest of the sentence must keep to its own punctuation, as if the parenthetic portion were not there.

( )
27j

Thus, to decide whether a close-parenthesis mark should be followed by a comma, mentally disregard the interruption:

- Shyness *(mine was extreme)* can be overcome with time.

   A comma after the close-parenthesis mark would make the following stripped-down sentence: x *Shyness, can be overcome with time.* Since that sentence would wrongly separate a subject *(Shyness)* from its verb *(can be overcome),* the comma must be omitted. (See p. 238, 18o.)

- My father was not as shy as I was *(otherwise he could not have succeeded in his work),* but he was soft-spoken and reserved.

   The stripped-down sentence correctly links two independent clauses with a comma and a coordinating conjunction (p. 209,

17a). Since the comma is appropriate without the parenthetic interruption, it is also appropriate with it. Note, however, that the comma belongs after the parenthesis, not before it.

27k   Use brackets, not parentheses, to interrupt a quotation.

Brackets (p. 350, 28r), not parentheses, are required when you want to insert information or commentary into quoted material.

DO:

• "Joan [Benoit] has to be the favorite in this race," Nancy said.

DON'T:

x "Joan (Benoit) has to be the favorite in this race," Nancy said.

28 Quoting

28a Quote only when you need the quoted language to make your point.

Handling quoted material is more than a matter of being accurate, knowing where to put the punctuation marks, and giving proper acknowledgment of your sources (for the last of these, see p. 458, 37a). Above all, it involves sensing when a quotation is called for and when it is not.

Some students, desperate to reach a minimum word limit, look to quotation as a readily available form of stuffing. They typically begin a paragraph with an introductory sentence and complete it with a long indented passage that they leave unanalyzed. And then they do the same thing again, rapidly accumulating precious words—but not ideas. An instructor need only glance through such a paper in order to see that the truly important language, the writer's own consecutive discourse, is a bare, inadequate skeleton.

When you are telling a story, quoted dialogue is almost always effective. But especially in analytic and argumentative writing, you should ask what a proposed quotation will be doing *for your reader*. Does the quoted language convey something that wouldn't be apparent in a summary or paraphrase (p. 455, 36f)? Quote only where that language actually makes a difference—as it does, for example, in the two-paragraph passage about New Age consciousness on pages 50–51.

Study that whole segment on quotation as evidence (4c), and review Chapter 9 to grasp how a quoted passage can contribute to a colorful, pointed introduction or conclusion. Look through the first drafts of your own work for places where you may need to *add* quoted material—for example, to support a point about the kind of language found in a certain poem or story. And look as well for places where a quotation ought to be replaced by your own reasoning.

28b Recognize the punctuation marks used with quotations.

The marks used in handling quotations are double and single quotation marks, the slash, the ellipsis, and brackets.

MARK	FORM	FUNCTION
double quotation marks (28d)	" "	to mark the beginning and end of a quotation
single quotation marks (28e)	' '	to mark a quotation within a quotation
slash (28f)	/	to mark a line break in a brief quotation of poetry
ellipsis (28o)	. . .	to mark an omission from a quotation
brackets (28r)	[ ]	to mark an explanatory insertion within a quotation

Note that these marks have other functions as well.

MARK	OTHER FUNCTION	EXAMPLE
quotation marks	to show distance from a dubious or offensive expression	Hitler's "final solution" destroyed six million Jews.
slash	to indicate alternatives	Try writing an invoice and/or a purchase order.
	to mean "per" in measurements	ft./sec. (feet per second)
	to indicate overlapping times	the Winter/Spring issue of the journal

MARK	OTHER FUNCTION	EXAMPLE
ellipsis	to show that a statement contains further implications	And thus he came to feel that he had triumphed over the government. How little he understood about bureaucracy • • • •
	to show that dialogue "trails off"	"What I am trying to tell you is • • • is • • •"
brackets	to insert material into a passage that is already within parentheses	(See, however, D. L. Rosenhan in *Science* 179 [1973]:250–58.)

28c Avoid the unnecessary use of quotation marks.

Slang and clichés

DON'T:

x He may be a little bit "goofy," but I think his "elevator" does, as they say, "go to the top floor."

DO:

• He may be eccentric, but I doubt that he is crazy.

When you have to apologize for your language by quarantining it within quotation marks, choose other language.

Widely recognized nicknames

DON'T:

x "Magic" Johnson may just be the most gifted basketball player ever.

DO:

- Magic Johnson may just be the most gifted basketball player ever.

or

- Earvin "Magic" Johnson may just be the most gifted basketball player ever.

Only when you are adding the nickname to the rest of the name, as in the last example, should you put the nickname in quotation marks.

The title of your paper

DON'T:

x "Rebellion: Alternatives to Yuppiedom"

DO:

- Rebellion: Alternatives to Yuppiedom

DON'T:

x " 'Nothing to Fear but Fear Itself': The Worst Days of the Depression"

DO:

- "Nothing to Fear but Fear Itself": The Worst Days of the Depression

When your title contains a quotation, indicate that fact with quotation marks. But your title itself, as it stands at the head of your paper, is *not* a quotation.

For the difference between quotation and **indirect discourse,** see p. 303, 23c.

INCORPORATING A QUOTATION

28d Use double quotation marks to set off quoted material that you have incorporated into your own prose.

If you are representing someone's speech or quoting a fairly brief passage of written work—no more than five typed lines of prose or no more than two or three lines of poetry—you should **incorporate** the quotation. That is, you should make it continuous with your own text instead of **indenting** it (p. 343, 28h). Be sure to enclose an incorporated quotation in quotation marks. In North American (as opposed to British) English, those marks should be double (" "):

- "Computers," as Bertini points out, "are unforgiving toward even the tiniest mistake in the instructions you give them."

28e Use single quotation marks for a quotation within a quotation.

If the passage you are incorporating already contains quotation marks, change them to single marks (' '):

- E. F. Carpenter, writing in *Contemporary Dramatists,* says of Butterfield: "The playwright knows where his best work originated. 'Everything that touches an audience,' he told me, 'comes from memories of the period when I was down and out.' "

Similarly, if a title you are quoting already contains quotation marks, change them to single marks:

- I refer to Joyce Molnar's recent article, "Norma Jean: Comic Self-Discovery in Bobbie Ann Mason's 'Shiloh.' "

" "
28e

Double quotation within a quotation

Try to avoid quoting a passage that already contains single quotation marks; the effect will be confusing. But if you find no alternative, change those single marks to double ones. Then check carefully to see that your *three* sets of marks are kept straight (" ' " ' "):

- Orwell's friend Richard Rees informs us that "when Socialists told him that under Socialism there would be no such feeling of being at the mercy of unpredictable and irresponsible powers, he remarked: 'I notice people always say "*under* Socialism." They look forward to being on top—with all the others underneath, being told what is good for them.' "

Here the main quotation is from Rees. Since Rees quotes Orwell, Orwell's words appear within single marks. But when those words themselves contain a quotation, that phrase ("*under* Socialism") is set off with double marks.

Note that British practice is just the opposite of North American: single marks for the first quotation, double marks for a quotation appearing within it, and single marks again for the very rare third quotation.

28f When incorporating more than one line of poetry, use a slash to show where a line ends.

You can incorporate as many as three lines of poetry instead of indenting them (28h). But if your passage runs beyond a line ending, you should indicate that ending with a slash preceded and followed by a space:

- In a snowstorm, says the noted Japanese poet Bashō, "Even a horse / Is a spectacle."

" "
28g

28g Learn how to combine quotation marks with other marks of punctuation.

1. Always place commas and periods inside the close-quotation marks. You do not have to consider whether the comma or period is part of the quotation or whether the quotation is short or long. Just routinely put the comma or period first:

- Francis Bacon said, "To spend too much time in study is sloth**.**"
- "To spend too much time in study is sloth**,**" said Francis Bacon.

2. Always place colons and semicolons outside the close-quotation marks:

- "Sloth"; that was Bacon's term for too much study.
- Francis Bacon called excessive study "sloth"; I call it inefficiency.

3. Place question marks, exclamation points, and dashes either inside or outside the close-quotation marks, depending on their function. If they are punctuating the quoted material itself, place them inside:

- "Do you think it will snow?" she asked.
- "Of course it will!" he replied.

But put the same marks *outside* the close-quotation marks if they are not part of the question or exclamation:

- Was Stephanie a sophomore when she said, "I am going to have a job lined up long before I graduate"?
- I have told you for the last time to stop calling me your "little sweetie"!

4. When the quotation must end with a question mark or exclamation point and your own sentence calls for a closing period, drop the period:

- Grandpa listens to Dan Rather every evening and constantly screams, "Horsefeathers!"

5. Otherwise, the end punctuation of the quotation makes way for your own punctuation. For example, if the quoted passage ends with a period but your own sentence does not stop there, drop the period and substitute your own punctuation, if any:

- "I wonder why they don't impeach newscasters," said Grandpa.

    The quoted passage would normally end with a period, but the main sentence calls for a comma at that point.

66 99
28g

6. When a quotation is accompanied by a footnote number, that number comes after all other punctuation except a dash that resumes your own part of the sentence:

- Bloomingdale's advertises women's skirts as "pencil-thin, get the point?"**6**

- Bloomingdale's advertises women's skirts as "pencil-thin, get the point?"**6**—but in fact the skirts come in all sizes.

7. When a quotation is incorporated into your text (without indention) and is followed by a parenthetic citation (p. 478, 37d), the open-parenthesis comes after the final quotation marks but before a comma or period—even if the comma or period occurs in the quoted passage:

- John Keegan begins his book about famous battles by confessing, "I have not been in a battle; nor near one, nor heard one from afar, nor seen the aftermath" (*The Face of Battle,* p. 15).

" "
28g

8. But if the incorporated quotation ends with a question mark or exclamation point, include it before the close-quotation marks and add your own punctuation after the parenthesis:

- He raises the question, "How would *I* behave in a battle?" (Keegan, p. 18).

9. If you indent a quotation, setting it apart from your text, and if you then supply a parenthetic citation, place that citation after all punctuation on a separate line:

- Gladly will I sell
  For profit,
  Dear merchants of the town,
  My hat laden with snow.
                    (Bashō, p. 60)

INDENTING A QUOTATION ("BLOCK QUOTATION")

28h   Indent a longer quotation.

PROSE	POETRY
Indent by ten spaces a passage of more than four lines.	Indent by ten spaces a passage of more than two or three lines; indent by fewer spaces if the lines are very long.

In the examples below, the red numbers are keyed to rules given on page 344.

INDENTED PROSE:

Margot Slade points to the bond between siblings that

is like no other connection between human beings: ——1

——————2

5

     Welcome to the sibling bond, that twilight
     zone of relationships between brothers and
     sisters, and any combination thereof, where
     parents must walk but often fear to tread.
     With good reason. As one well-seasoned
     father put it: "Under most circumstances,
     it can be suicide to interfere."——————6

3,4

     7——Siblings generally constitute an
     exclusive state--exclusive, that is, of
     parents. They are the keepers of each
     other's secrets and the supporters of each
     other's goals. They can be friends in the
     morning and enemies at night.——————5
                              (Slade 80)
                              ——————2

Now let us see if this special relationship exists

between the famous pair of siblings under consider-

ation here.

" "
28h

The writer is quoting from Margot Slade's article, "Siblings: War and Peace." For proper citation form, see p. 465, 37c.

INDENTED POETRY:

```
In "Crossing Brooklyn Ferry" Whitman calls out to

his fellow citizens of the future as well as the

present:                                  ————————1
      5                                    ————————2
     ⌐  I am with you, you men and women of a generation,
     |    or ever so many generations hence.
     |  Just as you feel when you look on the river and
  3,4,8     sky, so I felt.
     |  Just as any of you is one of a living crowd,
     |    I was one of a crowd, . . .        ————————5
     ⌐                                        ————————2

By creating a bond with unborn Americans, Whitman pro-

phesies the coming greatness of his country.
```

1. In most cases, introduce the passage with a colon.

2. Separate the passage from your main text by skipping an extra line above and below.

3. Indent the whole passage ten spaces from your left margin, or somewhat less if the quoted lines of poetry are very long.

4. If you are submitting a paper for a course, use single or double spacing according to your instructor's advice. But if you are writing for publication, double-space the passage, treating it just like your main text.

5. Omit the quotation marks you would have used to surround an incorporated quotation.

6. Copy exactly any quotation marks you find in the quoted passage itself.

7. In indenting prose, indent all lines equally if the passage consists of one paragraph or less. When you are quoting more than one paragraph of prose, indent the first line of each full paragraph by an additional three spaces.

8. In indenting poetry, follow the spacing (beginnings and endings of lines) found in the original passage.

28i   When quoting dialogue, indent for a new paragraph with each change of speaker.

After you have completed a quotation of speech, you can comment on it without starting a new paragraph. You can also resume quoting the speaker's words after your own. But do indent for a new paragraph as soon as you get to someone else's speech.

> "I can't understand," I said, "how you can win world-class distance races without having been coached in high school or college."
>
> "Oh, but sir," he protested with a polite smile, "I have been running since I was a little child. In Kenya this is how we get from village to village."
>
> "Yes, yes, but where did you get your training?" This man seemed to defy everything I knew about the making of a great runner.
>
> "Oh, my *training*!" He threw his head back and laughed. "Mister reporter, *you* run every day, year after year, at 8,000 feet, carrying boxes and fuel and whatnot. Then please come back and tell me if you think you need some training!"

28j   Learn how to punctuate a quoted speech that continues into a new paragraph.

In general, quotation marks come in pairs; for every mark that opens a quotation there must be another to close it. But there is one exception. To show that someone's quoted speech continues in a new paragraph, put quotation marks at the beginning of that paragraph, and keep doing so until the quotation ends:

> "I have two things to bring up with you," she said. "In the first place, which of us is going to be keeping the stereo? I'd like to have it, but it's no big deal to me.
>
> "Second, what about the dog? I'm the one who brought her home as a puppy, and I intend to keep her."

Note that in such a passage, no close-quotation marks are used until the full quotation is completed.

INTRODUCING A QUOTATION

28k If a quotation fits into your preceding phrase or clause, introduce it without punctuation.

The way to decide which punctuation, if any, to use in introducing a quotation is to read the quoted matter as part of your own sentence. Use introductory punctuation only if it would have been called for anyway, with or without the quotation marks:

- Macbeth expresses the depth of his despair when he characterizes life as "a tale told by an idiot."

  Since the quotation serves as an object of the writer's preposition *as,* a preceding comma would be wrong here (see p. 319, 25b). Note how smoothly the quoted passage completes the writer's sentence.

28l If a quotation does not fit into your preceding phrase or clause, introduce it with a comma or a colon.

66 99
28l

- Reynolds comments, "A close look at Melville's fiction reveals that his literary development was even more closely tied to popular reform than was Hawthorne's."
- Baym's thesis rests on one central assumption: that "we never read American literature directly or freely, but always through the perspective allowed by theories."

In these examples, the quotations do not complete the writer's own statements—as would occur, for example, in *Baym's thesis rests on the assumption that "we never read. . . ."* You can choose between a comma and a colon to introduce a quotation that stands apart from your own prose. The comma is more appropriate for tags such as *She said* and *He remarked* (28m). When the quotation is long enough to be indented (28h), you should prefer the more formal colon (28n).

- Gandhi, when asked what he thought of Western civilization, smiled and replied, "I think it would be a very good idea."

A colon would be equally correct here, but it would mark a more formal pause.

- Surrounded by surging reporters and photographers, the accused chairman tried to hold them all at bay with one repeated sentence: "I will have no statement to make before tomorrow."

  The colon is especially appropriate here because it matches *one repeated sentence* with the actual words of that sentence.

28m   Follow an introductory tag like *He said* with a comma.

Even if you do not feel that a pause is called for, put a comma after an introductory clause such as *She said* or *He replied:*

- He said, "I'd like to comment on that."
- She replied, "Yes, you are always making comments, aren't you?"

If the tag follows or interrupts the quoted speech, it must still be set apart:

- "I'd like to comment on that," he said.
- "Yes," she replied, "you are always making comments, aren't you?"

28n   As a rule, use a colon before an indented quotation.

Since an indented passage (p. 343, 28h) appears on the page as an interruption of your prose, you should usually introduce it with a colon, implying a formal stop.

- Here is Macbeth's gloomiest pronouncement about life:

  > it is a tale
  > Told by an idiot, full of sound and fury,
  > Signifying nothing.

But if the passage begins with a fragment that completes your own sentence, omit the colon:

- Macbeth considers life to be

> a tale
> Told by an idiot, full of sound and fury,
> Signifying nothing.

A colon would be wrong here, since it would separate an infinitive *(to be)* from its complement *(a tale . . .)*. Note that a comma would be unacceptable for the same reason.

OMITTING OR INSERTING MATERIAL

28o Use an ellipsis mark to show that something has been omitted from a quotation.

If you want to omit unneeded words or sentences from a quoted passage, accuracy requires that you show where you are doing so.

WHOLE PASSAGE:
- As I have repeatedly stated, those claims, which irresponsible promoters of tax shelter schemes continue to represent as valid, have been disallowed every time they have come before the IRS.

PARTIAL QUOTATION:
- Gomez reports that "those claims . . . have been disallowed every time they have come before the IRS."

66 99
28p

28p Distinguish between three kinds of ellipses.

Three dots

If an omission is followed by material from the same sentence being quoted, type the ellipsis mark as three spaced periods preceded and followed by a space:

• She characterized her early years as "a bad joke • • • hardly a childhood at all."

Four dots

Use four dots—a normal period followed by three spaced dots—if you are omitting (1) the last part of the quoted sentence, (2) the beginning of the next sentence, (3) a complete sentence or more, or (4) one or two complete paragraphs:

• She wrote, "I am always bored• • • • There is nothing here to keep me occupied."

• She described the apartment tower as "ridiculous, improbable• • • • I feel like a fairy princess who has been tucked away in the wrong castle by mistake."

If the sentence preceding your ellipsis ends with a question mark or exclamation point, keep that mark and add just three spaced dots:

• "Is Shaw," he asked, "really the equal of Shakespeare? • • • That seems extremely dubious."

• The champion shouted, "I am the greatest! • • • Nobody can mess up my pretty face."

A four-dot ellipsis is appropriate whenever your quotation skips material and then goes on to a new sentence, whether or not you are omitting material *within* a sentence. But note that you should always have grammatically complete statements on both sides of a four-dot ellipsis.

DON'T:

x She wrote, "I am always bored. . . . nothing here to keep me occupied."

Here the four-dot ellipsis is wrongly followed by a fragment.

Row of dots

Mark the omission of a whole line or more of poetry by a complete line of spaced periods:

● Pope writes:

> First follow nature, and your judgment frame
> By her just standard, which is still the same;
>
> . . . .
> Life, force, and beauty must to all impart,
> At once the source, and end, and test of art.

Notice that the line of spaced periods is about the same length as the preceding line of poetry.

28q Avoid beginning a quotation with an ellipsis.

If you make a quoted clause or phrase fit in with your own sentence structure (p. 346, 28k), you should not use an ellipsis mark to show that you have left something out.

DON'T:
x The signers of the Declaration of Independence characterized George III as " . . . unfit to be the ruler of a free people."

DO:
● The signers of the Declaration of Independence characterized George III as "unfit to be the ruler of a free people."

66 99
28r

28r Use brackets to insert your own words into a quotation.

To show that you are interrupting a quotation rather than quoting a parenthetical remark, be sure to enclose your interruption in brackets, not parentheses (p. 334, 27k):

● "I hope to be buried in Kansas City [her birthplace]," she said.

> Parentheses here would indicate that the woman who wanted to be buried in Kansas City was referring to another woman's birthplace. The brackets show that it is the writer, not the woman being quoted, who is supplying the extra information.

[sic]

The bracketed and usually italicized Latin word *sic* (meaning "thus") signifies that a peculiarity—for example, a misspelling—occurs in the quoted material:

- He wrote, "I am teaching these kids how to live outdors [*sic*] without being afraid."

Do not abuse the legitimate function of *[sic]* by applying it sarcastically to claims that you find dubious.

DON'T:

x Are we supposed to believe the "humane" *[sic]* pretensions of the National Rifle Association?

The quotation marks are already sarcastic enough without *[sic]* to redouble the effect. But why not eliminate both devices and let the language of the sentence do its own work?

DO:

- Are we supposed to believe the humane pretensions of the National Rifle Association?

" "
28r

29 Forming and Spacing Punctuation Marks

To see how punctuation marks are normally handled by typewriter or word processor, examine the typescript essays beginning on pages 73 and 492. In addition, note the following advice about forming marks and leaving or omitting spaces around them.

29a Learn the three ways of forming a dash.

Dashes come in three lengths, depending on their function.

1. A dash separating numbers is typed as a hyphen:

- pages 32-39
- October 8-14
- Social Security Number 203-64-7853

2. As a sign of a break in thought—its most usual function—a dash is typed as two hyphens with no space between:

• Try it--if you dare.

• They promise--but do not always come through with--
  overnight delivery.

3. Use four unspaced hyphens for a dash that stands in the place of an omitted word:

• He refused to disclose the name of Ms. ----

    This is the only kind of dash that is preceded by a space; see 29g.

29b Learn how to form brackets.

If your typewriter lacks keys for brackets, you can improvise them by either

1. typing slashes (/) and completing the sides with underlinings:

    /⁻ ⁻/

2. typing slashes and adding the horizontal lines later in ink:

    [ ]

3. leaving blank spaces and later writing the brackets entirely in ink:

    [ ]

p/
form
29c

29c Learn how to form the three kinds of ellipses.

1. An ellipsis (p. 348, 28o) is formed with three spaced dots if it signifies the omission of material within a quoted sentence. Note that a space is left before and after the whole ellipsis as well as after each dot:

• "The government," she said, "appears to be abandoning
  its . . . efforts to prevent nuclear proliferation."

2. A four-dot ellipsis, signifying the omission of quoted material that covers at least one mark of end punctuation, begins with that *unspaced* mark:

- "The government," she said, "appears to be abandoning
  its formerly urgent efforts to prevent nuclear proliferation. . . . There may be a terrible price to
  pay for this negligence."

3. Leave spaces between all the dots of an ellipsis that covers a whole row, signifying the omission of one or more lines of poetry:

- The river glideth at its own sweet will:

  . . . .

  And all that mighty heart is lying still!

29d Learn the two ways of spacing a slash.

p/
form
29d

1. When a slash separates two quoted lines of poetry that you are incorporating into your text (p. 340, 28f), leave a space before and after the slash:

- Shakespeare writes, "Shall I compare thee to a summer's day? / Thou art more lovely and more temper-
  ate."

2. But if your slash indicates alternatives or a span of time, leave no space before or after the slanted line:

- We are not dealing with an either/or situation here.
- The article will appear in the Winter/Spring issue of
  the journal.

29e Leave two spaces after a period, a question mark, an exclamation point, or a four-dot ellipsis.

- The Chinese leaders appear to be ready for a new dialogue with the United States. Should we let this opportunity slip away? Certainly not! Remember the words of the Foreign Minister: "If we do not take steps to ensure peace, we may find ourselves drifting into war. . . . Our two nations can work together without agreeing about everything."

29f Leave one space after a comma, a colon, a semicolon, a closing quotation mark, a closing parenthesis, or a closing bracket.

- Here is the real story, we believe, of last week's disturbance: it was not a riot but a legitimate demonstration. The city police chief thinks otherwise; but his description of the "riot" is grossly inaccurate. The chief (a foe of all progressive causes) erred in more than his spelling when he wrote of a "Comunist [sic] uprising."

p/
form
29g

29g Leave no space before or after a dash, a hyphen, or an apostrophe within a word.

- Wilbur__a first_rate judge of toothpaste flavors__ prefers Carter's Sparklefoam for its gum_tickling goodness.

29h When an apostrophe ends a word, leave no space before any following punctuation of the word.

- This ranch, the Johnsons', has been in the family for generations.

29i When a word is immediately followed by two punctuation marks, put them together without a space.

- Here is the true story of the "riot."
- When I_heard the truth about the riot (as the police chief called it), I was outraged.
- The protest, which the police chief called the work of "Comunists" [sic], was actually organized by members of the business community.

p/ form 29j

29j Do not begin a line with any mark that belongs with the last word of the preceding line.

DON'T:
x Here is why Carol refuses to sign the petition
: she objects to the dangerously vague language
about waterfront development.

DO:
- Here is why Carol refuses to sign the petition:
she objects to the dangerously vague language about
waterfront development.

29k Do not divide an ellipsis between one line and the next.

DON'T:

```
x Carol objected to the petition because of "the . .

  . language about waterfront development."
```

DO:

```
• Carol objected to the petition because of "the . . .

  language about waterfront development."
```

For combining quotation marks with other punctuation marks, see p. 340, 28g. For the spacing of periods within an abbreviation, see p. 426, 35k.

p/
form
29k

VII
CONVENTIONS

Conventions

In this section we consider rules affecting the form a word can take. These are small matters—if you get them right. If you do not, you will be handicapped in communicating your ideas. It is essential, then, to spell and hyphenate correctly and to be accurate in showing different forms of verbs, nouns, and pronouns. And it is useful, if less urgent, to know where such conventions as italics, abbreviations, and written-out numbers are considered appropriate in a piece of writing. Once the conventions have become second nature, both you and your reader can put them out of mind and concentrate on larger issues.

30 Verb Forms

30a Note how verbs change their form to show person and number in the present tense.

Within most **tenses,** or times of action, English verbs show no differences of form for person and number. That is, the verb remains the same whether its subject is the speaker, someone spoken to, or someone (or something) spoken about, and whether that subject is one person or thing or more than one. The past-tense forms of *move,* for example, look like this:

	SINGULAR	PLURAL
First Person	I moved	we moved
Second Person	you moved	you moved
Third Person	he, she, it moved	they moved

But in the most common tense, the present, the third-person singular verb shows **inflection**—that is, it changes its form without becoming a different word.

	SINGULAR	PLURAL
First Person	I move	we move
Second Person	you move	you move
Third Person	he, she, it **moves**	they move

The third-person singular form of a present-tense verb ends in *-s.* If the base form of the verb ends in *-ch, -s, -sh, -x,* or *-z,* the addition is *-es.*

BASE FORM	THIRD-PERSON SINGULAR PRESENT
lurch	he lurches
pass	she passes
wash	Harry washes
fix	Betty fixes
buzz	it buzzes

In some spoken dialects of English, this third-person *-s* or *-es* does not occur. Standard written English, however, requires that you observe it. You may have to check your final drafts to be sure that your *-s* or *-es* endings are in place.

DON'T:

x When Meg *get* a new idea, she always *say* something worth hearing.

DO:

• When Meg *gets* a new idea, she always *says* something worth hearing.

**verb
30b**

30b Note how the verb tenses are formed in the active voice.

The various tenses are shown by changed forms of the base verb *(try— tried; go—went)* and through forms of *be* and *have* in combination with base *(try)* and participial *(trying)* forms *(will try, was trying, had tried, will have tried).* Here are all the active-voice forms—first, second, and third person, singular and plural—for a verb, *walk,* in eight commonly used tenses. (For passive forms, see 30d.)

ACTIVE VOICE		
Present:		
I	he, she, it	we, you (sing./pl.), they
walk	walks	walk
Present Progressive:		
I	he, she, it	we, you (sing./pl.), they
am walking	is walking	are walking
Present Perfect:		
I	he, she, it	we, you (sing./pl.), they
have walked	has walked	have walked
Past:		
I	he, she, it	we, you (sing./pl.), they
walked	walked	walked
Past Progressive:		
I	he, she, it	we, you (sing./pl.), they
was walking	was walking	were walking
Past Perfect:		
I	he, she, it	we, you (sing./pl.), they
had walked	had walked	had walked
Future:		
I	he, she, it	we, you (sing./pl.), they
will walk	will walk	will walk
Future Perfect:		
I	he, she, it	we, you (sing./pl.), they
will have walked	will have walked	will have walked

**verb
30b**

In the future tense, *I* and *we* can be accompanied by *shall* instead of *will*. *Shall* is normal in questions about plans:

- *Shall* we go to the movies?

In addition, some writers still keep to the once common use of *shall* for all first-person statements *(I shall go to the movies)* and for taking a commanding tone *(you <u>shall</u> go to the movies!)*. But *will* is now usual in these functions. Keep to *will* unless you want to make an unusually formal effect.

Principal parts

	BASE	PAST TENSE	PAST PARTICIPLE
Regular	bake	baked	baked
	adopt	adopted	adopted
	compute	computed	computed
Irregular	choose	chose	chosen
	eat	ate	eaten
	write	wrote	written

All verbs have three **principal parts** used in tense formation: the infinitive or base form *(bake, choose),* the past tense *(baked, chose),* and the past participle *(baked, chosen).* The past participle is used with forms of *have* and with auxiliaries *(could have, would have,* etc.) to form various other past tenses *(had baked, would have chosen,* etc.). **Regular verbs**—those that simply add *-d* or *-ed* to form both the past tense and the past participle—cause few problems of tense formation. But you must take greater care to see how the following **irregular verbs** are formed.

**verb
30b**

PRINCIPAL PARTS OF IRREGULAR VERBS		
BASE	PAST TENSE	PAST PARTICIPLE
awake	awaked, awoke	awaked, awoke, awoken
be	was, were	been
beat	beat	beaten, beat
become	became	become
begin	began	begun

PRINCIPAL PARTS OF IRREGULAR VERBS		
BASE	**PAST TENSE**	**PAST PARTICIPLE**
bend	bent	bent
bite	bit	bit, bitten
bleed	bled	bled
blow	blew	blown
break	broke	broken
bring	brought	brought
build	built	built
burst	burst	burst
buy	bought	bought
catch	caught	caught
choose	chose	chosen
come	came	come
cost	cost	cost
cut	cut	cut
deal	dealt	dealt
dig	dug	dug
dive	dived, dove	dived
do	did	done
draw	drew	drawn
dream	dreamed, dreamt	dreamed, dreamt
drink	drank	drunk
drive	drove	driven
eat	ate	eaten
fall	fell	fallen
feed	fed	fed
feel	felt	felt
fight	fought	fought
find	found	found
fit	fitted, fit	fitted, fit
fly	flew	flown
forget	forgot	forgotten, forgot

**verb
30b**

PRINCIPAL PARTS OF IRREGULAR VERBS		
BASE	**PAST TENSE**	**PAST PARTICIPLE**
freeze	froze	frozen
get	got	gotten, got
give	gave	given
go	went	gone
grow	grew	grown
hang (an object)	hung	hung
hang (a person)	hanged	hanged
hear	heard	heard
hide	hid	hidden, hid
hit	hit	hit
hold	held	held
hurt	hurt	hurt
keep	kept	kept
kneel	knelt, kneeled	knelt, kneeled
knit	knit, knitted	knit, knitted
know	knew	known
lay (put)	laid	laid
lead	led	led
lean	leaned, leant	leaned, leant
leave	left	left
lend	lent	lent
let	let	let
lie (recline)	lay	lain
light	lighted, lit	lighted, lit
lose	lost	lost
make	made	made
mean	meant	meant
meet	met	met
pay	paid	paid
prove	proved	proved, proven
put	put	put
quit	quit, quitted	quit, quitted

**verb
30b**

PRINCIPAL PARTS OF IRREGULAR VERBS		
BASE	**PAST TENSE**	**PAST PARTICIPLE**
read	read	read
rid	rid, ridded	rid, ridded
ride	rode	ridden
ring	rang	rung
run	ran	run
say	said	said
see	saw	seen
sell	sold	sold
send	sent	sent
set	set	set
shake	shook	shaken
shine	shone, shined	shone, shined (transitive)
shoot	shot	shot
show	showed	showed, shown
shrink	shrank	shrunk
shut	shut	shut
sing	sang, sung	sung
sink	sank	sunk
sit	sat	sat
sleep	slept	slept
slide	slid	slid
speak	spoke	spoken
speed	sped, speeded	sped, speeded
spend	spent	spent
spin	spun	spun
spring	sprang, sprung	sprung
stand	stood	stood
steal	stole	stolen
stick	stuck	stuck
sting	stung	stung
strike	struck	struck, stricken

**verb
30b**

PRINCIPAL PARTS OF IRREGULAR VERBS		
BASE	**PAST TENSE**	**PAST PARTICIPLE**
swear	swore	sworn
swim	swam	swum
swing	swung	swung
take	took	taken
teach	taught	taught
tear	tore	torn
tell	told	told
think	thought	thought
throw	threw	thrown
wake	waked, woke	waked, woke, woken
wear	wore	worn
win	won	won
wring	wrung	wrung
write	wrote	written

30c Do not confuse the past tense with the past participle.

It is not enough to know the correct forms for the past participles of irregular verbs. You must also remember that past participles can form tenses only when they are combined with other words *(have gone, would have paid)*. Do not use an irregular past participle where the past tense is called for.

verb
30c

DON'T:

x She *begun* her singing lessons last Tuesday.

DO:

• She *began* her singing lessons last Tuesday.

DON'T:

x They *seen* him put on the wrong jacket.

DO:

• They *saw* him put on the wrong jacket.

DON'T:

x We *swum* across the pool.

DO:

• We *swam* across the pool.

Similarly, do not use the past-tense form of an irregular verb with an auxiliary:

DON'T:

x We *have* already *swam* across the pool.

DO:

• We *have* already *swum* across the pool.

30d Learn the tense forms in the passive voice.

The **voice** of a verb shows whether its grammatical subject performs or receives the action it expresses. A verb is **active** when the subject performs the action *(Frankie shot Johnny)* but **passive** when the subject is acted upon by the verb *(Johnny was shot by Frankie.)*

ACTIVE VOICE:

• The paramedics *took* the old man to the hospital.

> Note that the performers of the action (the paramedics) are also the grammatical subject.

PASSIVE VOICE:

• The old man *was taken* to the hospital by the paramedics.

> Note that the performers of the action (the paramedics) are not the grammatical subject of the passive verb *was taken*.

One peculiarity of the passive voice is that you need not mention the performer of action at all: *Johnny was shot; The old man was taken to*

**verb
30d**

the hospital. This feature can help you to remember the difference between the passive voice and the past tense. In *The ambulance <u>went</u> to the hospital,* the verb is past but not passive.

Here are the passive-voice forms of one verb, *show,* in the same tenses we reviewed in the active voice (p. 363):

PASSIVE VOICE		
Present: I am shown	he, she, it is shown	we, you (sing./pl.), they are shown
Present Progressive: I am being shown	he, she, it is being shown	we, you (sing./pl.), they are being shown
Present Perfect: I have been shown	he, she, it has been shown	we, you (sing./pl.), they have been shown
Past: I was shown	he, she, it was shown	we, you (sing./pl.), they were shown
Past Progressive: I was being shown	he, she, it was being shown	we, you (sing./pl.), they were being shown
Past Perfect: I had been shown	he, she, it had been shown	we, you (sing./pl.), they had been shown
Future: I will be shown	he, she, it will be shown	we, you (sing./pl.), they will be shown
Future Perfect: I will have been shown	he, she, it will have been shown	we, you (sing./pl.), they will have been shown

verb 30d

For the use of *shall* as an alternative to *will,* see page 363, 30b.

For the stylistic uses and limitations of the passive voice, see page 133, 10e.

30e Learn the forms and uses of the indicative, imperative, and subjunctive moods.

Verbs show certain other changes of form to convey the **mood** or manner of their action.

Indicative

Use the **indicative** mood if your clause is a statement or a question:

- The secretary of state *advises* the president.
- *Does* the secretary of state *advise* the president?

The forms of the indicative mood are those already given for normal tense formation (pp. 363, 370).

Imperative

Use the **imperative** mood for giving commands or directions, with or without an explicit subject:

- *Call* the police at once.
- You *stay* out of this!

The imperative mood uses the second-person form of the present tense.

verb 30e

Subjunctive

For a variety of less common purposes, use the **subjunctive** mood.

1. Hypothetical conditions:

   - He is, as it *were,* a termite gnawing at the foundations of our business.

     As it were is a fixed expression indicating that the writer is using a figure of speech (pp. 185–194, chapter 15) instead of making a literal statement.

- If I *were* on the moon now, I would tidy up the junk that has been left there. [not *was*]
- I wish I *were* in Haiti now. [not *was*]

2. *That* clauses expressing requirements or recommendations:

- The IRS requires that everyone *submit* a return by April 15. [not *submits*]
- It is important that all new students *be* tested immediately. [not *are*]

3. Expressions of a wish in which *may* is understood:

- long *live* the Queen [not *lives*]
- *be* it known [not *is*]
- so *be* it [not *is*]
- *suffice* it to say [not *suffices*]

For nearly all verbs, the subjunctive differs from the indicative only in that the third-person singular verb loses its -*s* or -*es: come what may,* not *comes what may.* The verb *to be* uses *be* for "requirement" clauses *(I demand that she be here early)* and *were* for hypothetical conditions *(if he were an emperor).*

The chart on the facing page summarizes the contrast between the subjunctive and indicative moods. Subjunctive verbs are underscored. For further discussion of sentences proposing the imagined consequences of hypothetical conditions, see page 302, 23b.

verb 30e

	SUBJUNCTIVE	INDICATIVE
	Hypothetical conditions with imagined consequences:	**Possibilities or probabilities with real consequences:**
Verb *to be*	• If I <u>were</u> a parent, I *would carry* life insurance.	• When I *am* a parent, I *will carry* life insurance.
Other verbs	• If he <u>*married*</u> your sister, you *would be* brothers.	• If he *marries* your sister, you *will be* brothers.
	***That* clauses expressing requirement or recommendation:**	**Actions that occur, have occurred, or will occur:**
Verb *to be*	• The government requires that tax returns <u>be</u> strictly accurate.	• My tax return *was* as accurate as I could make it.
Other verbs	• The art department insists that a lecturer <u>*leave*</u> all lights on during a slide show.	• Because my art lecturer *leaves* the lights on during every slide show, the class *stays* awake.

**verb
30e**

31 Plurals and Possessives

31a Do not confuse the plural and possessive forms of nouns.

SINGULAR	PLURAL	SINGULAR POSSESSIVE	PLURAL POSSESSIVE
temple	temples	temple's	temples'
pass	passes	pass's	passes'
squash	squashes	squash's	squashes'
annex	annexes	annex's	annexes'
Ford	Fords	Ford's	Fords'

In making a noun plural *(two temples; three Fords), do not* use an apostrophe. (For the only exception, see 31h.) In making a noun possessive *(the temple's roof; the Fords' debt to their grandfather), always* use an apostrophe.

DON'T:

x The two *priest's* made many *contribution's* to the parish.

DO:

• The two *priests* made many *contributions* to the parish.

DON'T:

x The *Kennedy's* have been stalked by tragedy.

DO:

• The *Kennedys* have been stalked by tragedy.

DON'T:

x In many *place's* the *oceans* depth is unknown.

DO:

• In many *places* the *ocean's* depth is unknown.

DON'T:

x The *clocks* hands stopped all across the city.

DO:

• The *clocks'* hands stopped all across the city.

PLURALS

31b Form the plural of most nouns by adding -s or -es to the singular, as in *computers*.

plur
31b

bat	bats
class	classes
house	houses
song	songs
summons	summonses
waltz	waltzes

31c   To form the plural of a noun ending in a consonant plus *-y*, change the *-y* to *-i* and add *-es*, as in *securities*.

army	armies
candy	candies
duty	duties
penny	pennies
warranty	warranties

31d   Note the differences in plural form among nouns ending in *-o*.

Most nouns ending in a vowel plus *-o* become plural by adding *-s:*

patio	patios
studio	studios

Nouns ending in a consonant plus *-o* become plural by adding *-es:*

potato	potatoes
veto	vetoes

But some plurals disobey the rule:

piano	pianos
solo	solos
soprano	sopranos

plur 31d

And some words have alternative, equally correct forms:

zero	zeros/zeroes
cargo	cargos/cargoes

Where your dictionary lists two forms, always adopt the first, which is more commonly used.

31e   To make a name plural, add *-s* or *-es* without an apostrophe, as in *the Smiths.*

Add *-s* to most names:

Smith	the Smiths
Perry	the Perrys
Helen	both Helens
Goodman	the Goodmans
Carolina	two Carolinas

When a name ends in *-ch, -s, -sh, -x,* or *-z,* add *-es.* The extra syllable that results should be pronounced:

Burch	the Burches
Jones	the Joneses
Weiss	the Weisses
Cash	the Cashes
Fox	the Foxes
Perez	the Perezes

plur
31f

31f   Form the plural of a noun ending in *-ful* by adding *-s* to the end.

cupful	cupfuls
shovelful	shovelfuls
spoonful	spoonfuls

Beware of the "genteel" but incorrect *cupsful, shovelsful,* and so forth.

31g   Follow common practice in forming the plural of a noun derived from another language.

A number of words taken from foreign languages, especially Greek and Latin, keep their foreign plural forms. But some foreign-based words have also acquired English plural forms. The rule for deciding which plural to use is this: look it up!

Even so, the dictionary cannot settle your doubts in every instance. It may not tell you, for example, that the plural of *appendix* is *appendixes* if you are referring to the organ but either *appendixes* or *appendices* if you mean supplementary sections at the ends of books. Similarly, your dictionary may not reveal that while an insect has *antennae,* television sets have *antennas.* The way to get such information is to note the practice of other speakers and writers.

When in doubt, prefer the English plural.

SINGULAR	PREFER	NOT
cherub	cherubs	cherubim
crocus	crocuses	croci
curriculum	curriculums	curricula
sanatorium	sanatoriums	sanatoria
stadium	stadiums	stadia

plur
31g

But note that certain foreign plurals are still preferred:

alumna	alumnae
alumnus	alumni
criterion	criteria
datum	data
phenomenon	phenomena
vertebra	vertebrae

Confusions between the singular and plural forms of these terms are common. Indeed, *data* as a singular is often seen in scientific publications. Many careful writers, however, while avoiding the rare *datum,* use *data* only when its sense is clearly plural: *these data,* not *this data.*

Note that Greek derivatives ending in *-is* regularly change to *-es* in the plural:

analysis	analyses
crisis	crises
parenthesis	parentheses
thesis	theses

31h   To form the plural of a word presented *as* a word, add -'s.

Add an apostrophe and an *-s* to show the plural of a word you are discussing as a word, not as the thing it signifies:

- The editor changed all the *he*'s in Chapter 4 to *she*'s.

    Note how the writer's meaning is made clearer by the italicizing of each isolated word but not of the -'s that follows it.

31i   Add -*s*, without an apostrophe, to form the plural of most hyphenated nouns, capital letters, capitalized abbreviations without periods, written-out numbers, and figures.

plur
31i

- two stand-ins
- three Bs
- four VCRs
- counting by fives and tens
- counting by 5s and 10s
- the 1980s

Use -'s wherever it is needed to avoid confusion.

DON'T:

x Charlene Armstrong Zeno uses her maiden name because she likes being called with the As.

> Here the plural of *A* looks confusingly like the preposition *as*.

DO:

● Charlene Armstrong Zeno uses her maiden name because she likes being called with the *A*'s.

When the first part of a compound term is the key identifying noun, as in <u>sister-in-law</u> and <u>president-elect</u>, add the -s to that noun: <u>sisters</u>-in-law, <u>presidents</u>-elect.

31j Add -'s to form the plural of an uncapitalized letter, an abbreviation ending in a period, or a lowercase abbreviation.

● *a*'s, *b*'s, and *c*'s

● the two *i*'s in *iris*

● too many *etc.*'s in your paper

● a shortage of M.D.'s

● thousands of rpm's

**poss
31j**

POSSESSIVES

A possessive form implies either actual ownership *(my <u>neighbor</u>'s willow, <u>Alice</u>'s computer)* or some other close relation (a <u>stone</u>'s throw, the <u>Governor</u>'s enemies). Nouns and some pronouns form the possessive either by adding an apostrophe with or without an -s or by preceding the "possessed" element with *of: my <u>husband</u>'s first wife, her <u>parents</u>' car, the wings <u>of the canary</u>.*

31k Do not add an apostrophe to a pronoun that is already possessive in meaning.

DON'T	DO
x his'	● his
x her's, hers'	● hers
x our's, ours'	● ours
x your's, yours'	● yours
x their's, theirs'	● theirs
x who'se	● whose

Note also that the possessive pronoun *its* (like *his*) has no apostrophe. *It's* is the correct form for the contraction of *it is* but a blunder for the possessive *its*. Similarly, *who's* is the correct contraction for *who is* but a blunder for the possessive *whose*.

DON'T:
x This album is *her's*.

DO:
● This album is *hers*.

DON'T:
x Why don't you drive *our's* and we drive *your's*?

DO:
● Why don't you drive *ours* and we drive *yours*?

DON'T:
x The dog seems to have lost *it's* collar.

DO:
● The dog seems to have lost *its* collar.

**poss
31k**

DON'T:

x This is the man *who's* stereo broke down.

DO:

• This is the man *whose* stereo broke down.

Again:

DON'T:

x The college canceled *it's* Saturday night film series.
x *Its* a baby girl!
x *Its'* a baby girl!
x *Whose* going to make the announcement?

DO:

• The college canceled *its* Saturday night film series.
• *It's* a baby girl!
• *Who's* going to make the announcement?

31I Add -'s to form the possessive of a singular noun, as in *the computer's power.*

• farm's
• Bill's
• Hayakawa's

poss
31I

Follow the rule even if the singular noun ends with an *-s* sound:

• horse's
• bus's
• quiz's

• Les's
• Jones's
• Keats's

Exception for certain names

In names of more than one syllable, the *-s* after the apostrophe is optional when it might not be pronounced.

PRONOUNCED -S	UNPRONOUNCED -S
Dickens's	Dickens'
Berlioz's	Berlioz'
Demosthenes's	Demosthenes'

Whichever of these practices you follow, make sure you keep to it throughout a given piece of writing.

31m Watch for certain unusual singular possessives.

Where an added -*s* would make for three closely bunched -*s* sounds, use the apostrophe alone:

- Moses'
- Ulysses'
- Jesus'

Note also that in certain fixed expressions (*for ―― sake*) the possessive -*s* after a final -*s* sound is missing: *for goodness' sake, for conscience' sake, for righteousness' sake.* Some writers even drop the apostrophe from such phrases. But note the -*'s* in *for heaven's sake.*

31n Make most plural nouns possessive by adding an apostrophe alone, as in *the elephants' stampede.*

- several *days'* work
- the *Americans'* views
- the *dictionaries'* definitions
- the *Stuarts'* reigns
- the *Beatles'* influence

**poss
310**

31o If a plural noun does not end in -s, add -'s to form the possessive.

- the *children's* room
- those *deer's* habitat
- the *mice's* tracks
- the *alumni's* representative

31p In "joint ownership" possessives like *Simon and Garfunkel's music,* give the possessive form only to the final name.

When two or more words are "joint possessors," make only the last one possessive:

- Laurel and *Hardy's* comedies
- John, Paul, George, and *Ringo's* movie
- Sally and *Vic's* restaurant

But give the possessive form to each party if different things are "owned":

- *John's, Paul's, George's,* and *Ringo's* personal attorneys once met to see if the Beatles could be kept from splitting up.

31q In a phrase like *my father-in-law's car,* add *-'s* to the last of the hyphenated elements.

- the mayor-*elect's* assistant
- a Johnny-come-*lately's* arrogance.

31r To avoid an awkward possessive, make use of the *of* construction.

**poss
31r**

DON'T:
x the revised and expanded edition's index

DO:
- the index of the revised and expanded edition

Wherever an *-'s* possessive sounds awkward, consider shifting to the *of* form. Suppose, for example, your "possessing" term or your "possessed" one is preceded by several modifiers. You can get rid of the bunched effect by resorting to *of.*

A possessive form following a word in quotation marks may sound all right but look awkward on the page. Again, prefer the *of* construction.

DON'T:
x "La Bamba" 's insistent rhythm

DO:
● the insistent rhythm of "La Bamba"

Watch, too, for an unnatural separation of the *-'s* from the word it belongs with.

DON'T:
x the house on the corner's roof

DO:
● the roof of the house on the corner

Finally, nouns for inanimate (nonliving) things often make awkward possessives.

DON'T:
x the page's bottom
x social chaos's outcome

DO:
● the bottom of the page
● the outcome of social chaos

**poss
31s**

31s Notice which indefinite pronouns form the possessive with *of*.

Some indefinite pronouns (p. 233, 18k) form the possessive in the same manner as nouns: *another's, nobody's, one's.* But others can be made possessive only with *of:*

of
{
all	each	most	some
any	few	much	such
both	many	several	
}

DO:

- I have two friends in Seattle, and I can give you the address of each.

DON'T:

x I have two friends in Seattle, and I can give you *each's* address.

31t   Learn the other uses of the apostrophe.

Contractions

Use an apostrophe to join two words in a contraction:

did not	didn't
have not	haven't
can not, cannot	can't
she will	she'll
we will	we'll
they are	they're
he is	he's
he has	he's
you have	you've

Beware of placing the apostrophe at the end of the first word instead of at the point where the omission occurs.

**poss
31t**

DON'T:

x He *did'nt* have a chance.
x They *have'nt* done a thing to deserve such punishment.

DO:

- He *didn't* have a chance.
- They *haven't* done a thing to deserve such punishment.

Omission of digits

Use an apostrophe to mark the omission of one or more digits of a number, particularly of a year: *the summer of '88*. In dates expressing a span of time, however, drop the apostrophe: *1847-63*. And omit the apostrophe when you are shortening page numbers: *pp. 267-91*.

Certain past-tense forms and past participles

Use an apostrophe to form the past tense or past participle of a verb derived from an abbreviation or a name:

- Martinez was *KO'd* in the twelfth round.
- They *Disney'd* the old amusement park beyond recognition.

"Possessives" indicating duration

- an *hour's* wait
- five *years'* worth of wasted effort

poss
31t

32 Spelling

If spelling causes you trouble, do not label yourself a poor speller and leave it at that; work to eliminate the wrong choices. You can attack the problem on two fronts, memorizing the right spellings of single words and learning rules that apply to whole classes of words. We will cover both of these strategies below.

If there is one key to better spelling, it is the habit of consulting your college dictionary whenever you are in doubt (p. 161, 13a). You need not pick up the dictionary until you have completed a draft, but you should check your final copy carefully for both habitual misspellings and typing errors.

For the role of hyphenation in spelling, see the following chapter. For the use of a spelling checker with a word processor, see Chapter 42.

TROUBLESOME WORDS

32a Keep a spelling list.

Keep an ongoing spelling list, including not only the words you have already misspelled in your essays but also words whose spelling in published sources looks odd to you. To begin that list, review the "commonly misspelled words" on pages 391–395 below and the Index of Usage that begins on page 540. You will find that many problems of inappropriate meaning really stem from confusion over spelling.

The most serious misspellings are not those that would eliminate you from the finals of a spelling contest but slips with ordinary words. If you regularly make such slips, you may not be able to cure them simply by noting the correct versions. You will need to jog your memory with a special reminder. Try a three-column spelling list, using the middle column to show how the real word differs from the misspelling.

MISSPELLING	REMEMBER	CORRECT SPELLING
x (seperate)	not like *desperate*	● sep*a*rate
x (alot)	one word is not *a lot*	● a lot
x (hypocracy)	not like *democracy*	● hypoc*ri*sy
x (heighth)	get the *h* out of here!	● height
x (concieve)	*i* before *e* except after *c*	● conce*i*ve
x (wierd)	a *weird* exception to *i* before *e*	● w*ei*rd
x (mispell)	don't *miss* this one!	● mis*s*pell
x (fiting)	doesn't sound like *fighting*	● fit*t*ing
x (beautyful)	*y* misspell it?	● beaut*i*ful
x (goverment)	*govern + ment*	● gover*n*ment
x (complection)	*x* marks the spots	● comple*x*ion

32b Note how spelling differs among English-speaking countries.

Many words that are correctly spelled in British English are considered wrong in American English. Canadian English resembles British in most but not all features. Study the following differences, which are typical.

AMERICAN	CANADIAN	BRITISH
center	cen*tre*	cen*tre*
flav*or*	flav*our*	flav*our*
preten*se*	preten*ce*	preten*ce*
real*ize*	real*ize*	real*ise*
trave*l*er	trave*ll*er	trave*ll*er

32c Check the spelling of words with unusual pronunciation.

Words having silent letters

- colum<u>n</u>
- mor<u>t</u>gage
- s<u>w</u>ord
- <u>W</u>e<u>d</u>nesday

Words having letters unpronounced by some speakers

- enviro<u>n</u>ment
- gover<u>n</u>ment
- pum<u>p</u>kin
- reco<u>g</u>nize
- stren<u>g</u>th
- withdraw<u>a</u>l

Words frequently mispronounced

1. Added or erroneous sound:

- athlete   x (not ath<u>a</u>lete)
- escape   x (not e<u>x</u>cape)
- height   x (not heigh<u>th</u>)
- memento   x (not m<u>o</u>mento)
- pejorative   x (not pe<u>j</u>orative)
- realtor   x (not real<u>a</u>tor)
- wintry   x (not wint<u>e</u>ry)

2. Sound sometimes left unpronounced:

- arctic
- candidate
- probably
- quantity
- sophomore
- surprise
- temperament
- temperature
- veteran

3. Sounds sometimes wrongly reversed:

- jewelry   x (not jewlery)
- modern   x (not modren)
- nuclear   x (not nucular)
- perform   x (not preform)
- professor   x (not perfessor)
- perspiration   x (not prespiration)

32d   Review other commonly misspelled words.

A good way to begin your private spelling list (p. 388, 32a) is to look through the following commonly misspelled words, along with those already mentioned above, and pick out the ones that trouble you. (The letters *C/B* indicate Canadian and British forms wherever they differ from American.)

absence	allege
accidentally	all right
accommodate	a lot
acknowledgment	altogether
across	always
actually	analysis, analyses *(plural)*
address	analyze
adolescence, adolescent	anesthesia
aggravate, aggravated,	annihilate
aggravating	apparent
aggress, aggressive, aggression	appearance

sp
32d

appreciate, appreciation
aquatic
argument
assassin, assassination
assistant, assistance
attendance
bachelor
balloon
beggar
benefit, benefited; *C/B:*
   benefitted
besiege
bigoted
bureau
bureaucracy, bureaucratic
burglar
bus
cafeteria
calendar
camouflage
category
ceiling
cemetery
changeable
commit, commitment
committee
competent
concomitant
conscience
conscious
consensus
consistent, consistency
consummate
control, controlled, controlling
controversy
convenience, convenient
coolly
corollary

correlate
correspondence
corroborate
counterfeit
criticism, criticize
decathlon
deceive
defendant
defense; *C/B:* defence
definite, definitely
deity
dependent
desirable
despair
desperate, desperation
destroy
develop, development
diarrhea
dilapidated
dilemma
disastrous
discipline
dispensable
divide
divine
drunkenness
duly
ecstasy
eighth
emanate
embarrass, embarrassed,
   embarrassing
equip, equipped, equipment
evenness
exaggerate
exceed
excellent, excellence
exercise

sp
32d

exhilarate
existence
exorbitant
expel
extraordinary
fallacy
familiar
fascinate
fascist
February
fiend
fiery
finally
forehead
foresee, foreseeable
forfeit
forty
fourth
friend
fulfill
fulsome
futilely
gases
gauge
glamour, glamorous
grammar, grammatically
greenness
grievance, grievous
gruesome
guarantee
guard
handkerchief
harangue
harass
heroes
hindrance
hoping
idiosyncrasy

imagery
immediate
impel
inadvertent
incidentally
incredible
independent, independence
indestructible
indispensable
infinitely
innuendo
inoculate
interrupt
irrelevant
irreparable, irreparably
irreplaceable, irreplaceably
irresistible, irresistibly
jeopardy
judgment; *C/B:* judgement
knowledge, knowledgeably
laboratory
legitimate
leisure
length
library
license; *C/B:* licence
loneliness
lying
maintenance
maneuver
manual
marriage
marshal *(verb and noun),*
    marshaled, marshaling
mathematics
medicine
millennium, millennial
mimic, mimicked

sp
32d

mischief, mischievous
missile
more so
naive (*or* naïve)
necessary
nickel
niece
noncommittal
noticeable, noticing
occasion
occur, occurred, occurring,
   occurrence
omit, omitted, omitting,
   omission
opportunity
optimist, optimistic
paid
pajamas
parallel, paralleled
paralysis, paralyze
parliament
pastime
perceive
perennial
perfectible, perfectibility
permanent
permissible
phony
physical
physician
picnic, picnicked,
   picnicking
playwright
pleasant
pleasurable
possess, possession
practically
practice; *C/B:* practice *(noun),*
   practise *(verb)*

prairie
privilege
probably
pronunciation
propaganda
propagate
psychiatry
psychology
pursue, pursuit
putrefy
quizzes
rarefied
realize
receipt
receive
recipe
recognizable
recommend
refer, referred, referring
regretted, regretting
relevant, relevance
relieve
remembrance
reminisce, reminiscence
repellent
repentance
repetition
resistance
restaurant
rhythm
ridiculous
roommate
sacrilegious
said
schedule
secretary
seize
sergeant
sheriff

sp
32d

shining
shriek
siege
significance
similar
smooth *(adjective and verb)*
software
solely
soliloquy
sovereign, sovereignty
specimen
sponsor
stupefy
subtlety, subtly
succeed, success
succumb
suffrage
superintendent
supersede
suppress
surprise
symmetry
sympathize
tariff
tendency
terrific
than
therefore
thinness

thorough
threshold
through
traffic, trafficked, trafficking
tranquil, tranquillity
transcendent, transcendental
transfer, transferred,
  transferring
tries, tried
truly
unconscious
unmistakable, unmistakably
unnecessary
unshakable
unwieldy
vacillate
vacuum
vegetable
vengeance
venomous
vice
vilify, vilification
villain
wield
withhold
woeful
worldly
writing
yield

sp
32e

SPELLING RULES

**32e Note how words change their spelling when certain
suffixes are added to them.**

A **suffix** is one or more letters that can be added at the end of a word to
make a new word (*-ship, -ness,* etc.) or a new form of the same word

(*-ed, -ing,* etc.). Since many spelling mistakes are caused by uncertainty over whether and how the root word changes when the suffix is tacked on, you should go over the following rules. (If a rule is hard to follow, you can get the point by studying the sample words that follow it.)

1. **Beauty →Beautiful.** Change a final *-y* preceded by a consonant to *-i* when adding suffixes other than *-ing.*

easy	easily
happy	happier, happiest
hurry	hurries
imply	implies
ordinary	ordinarily
salty	saltier
tyranny	tyrannical
ugly	ugliness

2. **Hurry →Hurrying.** Do not drop the final *-y* of a word adding *-ing.*

embody	embodying
gratify	gratifying
study	studying

3. **Desire →Desirable.** When adding a suffix that begins with a vowel, usually drop a final *-e.*

drive	driving
future	futuristic
hope	hoping
impulse	impulsive
mate	mating
sincere	sincerity
suicide	suicidal

sp 32e

Exceptions: In words ending in *-ce* or *-ge,* retain the "s" or "j" pronunciation by keeping the *-e* before a suffix that begins with *a* or *o.*

notice	noticeable
peace	peaceable
courage	courageous
manage	manageable

And note two further exceptions:

acre	acreage
mile	mileage

4. **Advance→Advancement.** Usually keep the final *-e* of a word when adding a suffix that begins with a consonant.

precise	precisely
safe	safely
tame	tameness

Exceptions: Look out for a few words that drop the *-e* before adding a suffix beginning with a consonant.

argue	argument
judge	judgment (in American English)
nine	ninth
true	truly

5. **Beg→Begging.** In a one-syllable word having a final consonant that is preceded by a single vowel, double the consonant before adding a suffix beginning with a vowel.

sp
32e

chop	chopper
clip	clipped
fun	funnier
thin	thinnest

6. In a word of more than one syllable having a final consonant that is preceded by a single vowel, follow these suffix rules.

   a. **Prefer→Preferring.** If the word is accented on its last syllable, double the consonant before adding a suffix that begins with a vowel.

begín	begi<u>nn</u>ing
detér	dete<u>rr</u>ent
contról	contro<u>ll</u>ed
occúr	occu<u>rr</u>ence
regrét	regre<u>tt</u>able

b. **Differ→Difference.** If the accent does not fall on the last syllable, do not double the final consonant.

ópen	ope<u>n</u>er
shórten	shorte<u>n</u>ed
stámmer	stamme<u>r</u>ing
trável	trave<u>l</u>er (in American English)

c. **Prefer→Preference.** If, when you add the suffix, the accent shifts to an earlier syllable, do not double the final consonant.

confér	cónfe<u>r</u>ence
infér	ínfe<u>r</u>ence
refér	réfe<u>r</u>ence

32f Remember the old jingle for *ie/ei*.

sp
32f

i before *e*	(achieve, believe, friend, grieve)
except after *c*	(deceive, ceiling, receive)
or when sounded like *a*	
as in *neighbor* and *weigh*	(freight, neighbor, vein, weigh)

Exceptions:

ancient	leisure
conscience	science
efficient	seize
foreign	weird

32g Overcome the confusion between *-cede*, *-ceed*, and *-sede*.

ac<u>cede</u> con<u>cede</u> inter<u>cede</u> pre<u>cede</u> re<u>cede</u> se<u>cede</u>	Several words end in *-cede*.
ex<u>ceed</u> pro<u>ceed</u> suc<u>ceed</u>	Only three words end in *-ceed*.
super<u>sede</u>	This is the only word that ends in *-sede*.

33 Hyphenation

33a Observe the conventions for dividing words at line endings.

In a manuscript or typescript, where right-hand margins are normally uneven, you can avoid breaking words at line endings. Just finish each line with the last word you can complete. A word processing program (Chapter 42) will do this for you automatically unless you specify otherwise.

When you do choose to hyphenate, follow these conventions:

1. Divide words at syllable breaks as marked in your dictionary. Spaces or heavy dots between parts of a word indicate such breaks: *en•cy•clo•pe•di•a.*

2. Never divide a one-syllable word, even if you might manage to pronounce it as two syllables *(rhythm, schism).*

3. Do not leave one letter stranded at the end of a line *(o-ver, i-dea),* and do not leave a solitary letter for the beginning of the next line *(Ontari-o, seed-y).*

4. If possible, avoid hyphenating the last word on a page.

5. If a word is already hyphenated, divide it only at the fixed hyphen. Avoid x *self-con-scious, ex-pre-mier.*

6. You can anticipate what your dictionary will say about word division by remembering that:

   a. Double consonants are usually separated: *ar-rogant, sup-ply.*

   b. When a word has acquired a double consonant through the adding of a suffix, the second consonant belongs to the suffix: *bet-ting, fad-dish.*

   c. When the root of a word with a suffix has a double consonant, the break follows both consonants: *stall-ing, kiss-able.*

33b Use a hyphen in terms like *ex-wife* to separate certain prefixes from the root words to which they are attached.

A **prefix** is a letter or a group of letters that can be placed *before* a root word to make a new word. (Compare **suffix,** p. 395, 32e.) Dictionaries do not always agree with each other about hyphenation after a prefix, but the following guidelines will enable you to be consistent in your practice.

All-, ex-, self-

Words beginning with *all-, ex-,* and *self-,* when these are prefixes, are hyphenated after the prefix:

- all-powerful
- ex-minister
- self-motivated

Note that in words like *selfhood, selfish, selfless,* and *selfsame,* the accented syllable *self* is not a true prefix; no hyphen is called for.

Prefixes with names

Prefixes before a name are always hyphenated:

- pre-Whitman
- un-American
- anti-Soviet

Words like anti-intellectual and preempt

Prefixes ending with a vowel usually take a hyphen if that same vowel comes next, or if a different following letter would make for an awkward or misleading combination:

hyph
33b

- anti-intellectual
- semi-independent

- pro-organic
- co-worker

But prefixed terms that are very common are less likely to be misconstrued, and many double vowels remain unhyphenated:

- cooperate
- coordinate

- preempt
- reentry

Some dictionaries recommend a dieresis mark over the second vowel to show that it is separately pronounced: *reëntry*. In contemporary prose, however, you will not come across many instances of the dieresis.

Constructions like <u>post-heart surgery</u>

When a prefix applies to two or more words, attach it to the first one with a hyphen:

- a pre-aurora borealis phenomenon
- the anti-status quo faction

Constructions like <u>pre- and postwar</u>

When a modifier contains compound prefixes, the first prefix usually stands alone with a hyphen, whether or not it would take a hyphen when joined directly to the root word:

- There was quite a difference between *pre-* and postwar prices.
- *Pro-* and antifascist students battled openly in the streets of Rome.

hyph
33c

33c Follow your dictionary in deciding whether to hyphenate words like *bull's-eye* and *skydive*.

Many compound words (formed from more than one word) are hyphenated in most dictionaries: *bull's-eye, secretary-treasurer, spring-cleaning, water-ski* (verb only), and so forth. Many others, however, are usually written as separate words (*fire fighter, head start, ice cream, oil spill,* etc.) or as single unhyphenated words (*earring, scofflaw, scoutmaster, skydive,* etc.). To make matters more confusing, practice is always in flux; as compound terms become more familiar, they tend to lose their hyphens. All you can do, then, is be alert to the compound words you see in print and consult an up-to-date dictionary whenever you are in doubt.

33d Study the guidelines for hyphenating compound modifiers.

Compound modifiers (containing more than one word) such as *light sensitive* and *second-hand* pose especially tricky problems of hyphenation. The rules (below) are hard to remember and are not always observed by otherwise careful writers. You will often have to call on your assessment of the case at hand. If an expression would be ambiguous (uncertain in meaning) without a hyphen, include it; but omit the hyphen if you see that your reader can get along without it.

Before modified term: a well-trained philosopher

A compound modifier is usually hyphenated if it meets two conditions:

1. it comes before the term it modifies; and

2. its first element is itself a modifier.

These two conditions are met in the following examples:

MOD
- a *high-school* teacher

MOD
- a *short-tempered* umpire

MOD
- some *deep-ocean* drilling

MOD
- *nineteenth-century* art

MOD
- an *out-of-work* barber

In such phrases the hyphens sometimes prevent confusion. Consider what would happen, for example, if you wrote:

- a short tempered umpire
- some deep ocean drilling

Is the umpire short in stature but tempered in judgment? Is it the drilling rather than the ocean that is deep? When hyphens are added, a reader can see at once that *short* is part of the compound modifier *short-tempered* and that *deep* is part of the compound modifier *deep-ocean.* In such a case the hyphen tells us not to take the next word to be the modified term.

If the first word in a compound modifier is a noun, as in *school program administrator,* do not put a hyphen after it. A noun generally runs a low risk of being mistaken for a modifier of the next word. The following phrases are correct:

MOD
- the *ocean salinity* level

MOD
- a *barbecue sauce* cookbook

MOD
- a *mercury vapor* lamp

But do use a hyphen if the initial noun is followed by a modifier:

MOD
- a *picture-perfect* landing

MOD
- that *time-honored* principle

hyph
33d

> Here the hyphens are needed to show that the initial noun does not stand alone; it is part of a compound modifier.

Even when the first part of a compound modifier is itself a modifier, leave it unhyphenated if it forms a familiar pair with the following word and if there is no danger of confusion:

MOD
- the *Modern Language* Association

MOD
* an *electric typewriter* store

MOD
* the *happy birthday* card

After modified term: a philosopher well trained in logic

When a compound modifier *follows* the modified term, the hyphen usually disappears:

* A barber *out of work* resents people who cut their own hair.

Modifiers like barely suppressed

When a compound modifier contains an adverb in the *-ly* form, it does not have to be hyphenated in any position. There is no danger of ambiguity, since the adverb, clearly identifiable *as* an adverb, can only modify the next word:

* a *barely suppressed* gasp
* an *openly polygamous* chieftain
* a *hypocritically worded* apology

Modifiers like fast-developing

Adverbs lacking the *-ly* form do run the risk of ambiguity. Whether they come before or after the modified term, you should always hyphenate them:

* a *fast-developing* crisis
* a *close-cropped* head of hair
* The traffic was *slow-moving.*

**hyph
33d**

Modifiers with fixed hyphens

If you find that a modifier is hyphenated in the dictionary, keep it hyphenated wherever it occurs:

* She was an *even-tempered* instructor.
* She was *even-tempered.*

33e   Study the guidelines for hyphenating numbers.

Numbers <u>twenty-one</u> to <u>ninety-nine</u>

Always hyphenate these numbers, even when they form part of a larger number:

- Two hundred *seventy-five* years ago, religious toleration was almost unknown.

Number as part of a modifier

If the number and the term it modifies work together as a modifier, place a hyphen after the number:

- A *twelve-yard* pool is hardly long enough for swimming.

Noun formed from a number

Hyphenate all such nouns:

- Two *eighty-year-olds* were sitting on the bench.
- Three *sixty-five-year-olds* were standing nearby.

Fractions with and without hyphens

Hyphenate a fraction only if you are using it as a modifier.

AS MODIFIER:
- The luggage compartment was *five-eighths* full.

NOT AS MODIFIER:
- *Five eighths* of the space had already been taken.

  In the first sentence, *five-eighths* modifies the adjective *full.* In the second, *five-eighths* is the subject of the verb.

Some good writers, however, overlook this distinction. In your reading you will find that the more common fractions such as *one quarter* and *two thirds* are sometimes left unhyphenated even when they serve as modifiers. When in doubt, you would still do well to follow the rule.

33f   Use a hyphen to connect numbers expressing a range, as in *1987-1991.*

- pages 37-49 [the pages 37 through and including 49]
- September 11-October 4 [from September 11 through October 4]
- 1987-1991 [from 1987 through 1991]

34 Capitals

34a Capitalize the first letter of every sentence or intentional sentence fragment.

- *She* will need help when she moves.
- *Count* on me.
- *Will* you be able to come over on Sunday?
- *With* pleasure!

34b Learn when to capitalize within a quotation.

First letter of the quotation

Capitalize the first letter of a quotation if (1) it begins your own sentence, (2) it begins the sentence of a speaker or thinker whose words you are representing, (3) it is capitalized in the original and it doesn't help to complete a clause or phrase of your own, or (4) it is a customary capital beginning a line of poetry.

BEGINNING OF THE WRITER'S OWN SENTENCE:
- *"When* to stop" is the crucial lesson a dieter must learn.

BEGINNING OF A SPEAKER'S OR THINKER'S SENTENCE:
- Leslie told Mark, *"After* you dismantle the stereo, bring the truck around to the back."
- Mark thought, *Let's* hope she saved the original packing boxes.

CAPITALIZED IN THE ORIGINAL:
- As Ben Jonson remarked, *"Talking* and eloquence are not the same: to speak, and to speak well, are two things."

Notice how the sentence from Ben Jonson stands apart from the language introducing it. But when a passage beginning with a capital letter does help to complete a clause or phrase of your own, change the capital to lower case:

- Ben Jonson believed that "*talking* and eloquence are not the same: to speak, and to speak well, are two things."

    Here, *talking* is part of the quoter's subordinate clause (p. 201, 16c) already under way, *that talking and eloquence are not the same.*

INITIAL CAPITAL IN LINE OF POETRY:
- One would have thought, writes Spenser, that nature had imitated "*Art,* and that Art at nature did repine."

    Here, although the quotation helps to complete the quoter's own clause *(that nature had imitated art),* the capital *A* is retained because it begins a poetic line.

Significant capital in the quoted passage

- Spenser fancies that "*Art* at nature did repine."

    Even though this *Art* is not the first word in the line of poetry, its capitalization seems to be important in the original passage and thus is retained.

34c Learn when to capitalize after a colon.

cap
34c

As a rule, leave the next letter after a colon uncapitalized.

UNCAPITALIZED:
- Home was never like this: *twenty-four* roommates and a day starting at 5:00 A.M.
- I finally understood how the Air Force makes a pilot of you: *after* the crowded barracks, every cadet yearns for the solitude of flight.

Do use a capital letter, however, if (1) you are quoting a passage that begins with such a letter, (2) you want to make an especially formal effect, or (3) the element following your colon consists of more than one sentence.

CAPITALIZED:
- At Antony's death, Cleopatra speaks her unforgettable lament: "*And* there is nothing left remarkable / Beneath the visiting moon."
- The sign at the gate left no room for misunderstanding: *Trespassers* would be shot.
- Jacqueline was left with two nagging questions: *To* whom could she turn for help? And would anyone believe her story?

34d   Capitalize the first word of a sentence in parentheses only if the parenthetic sentence stands between complete sentences.

CAPITALIZED:
- In the Air Force we learned to fly. (*We* also learned a good deal about life on the ground.) I would not have traded the experience for any other.

UNCAPITALIZED:
- Life in the Air Force (*the* Army and Navy never attracted me) was just what the doctor ordered for a lazy, smart-aleck eighteen-year-old.

**cap
34e**

34e   Capitalize the first, the last, and all other important words in a title or subtitle.

If an article, a coordinating conjunction, or a preposition does not occur in the first or last position, leave it in lowercase:

- *The House of the Seven Gables*
- *The Closing of the American Mind*
- *For Whom the Bell Tolls*

Do capitalize the first letter of a subtitle:

- *Peasants into Frenchmen: The Modernization of Rural France, 1870-1914*
- "Male Gymnasts: The Olympic Heights"

34f Capitalize both parts of most hyphenated terms in a title.

The Modern Language Association recommends that you capitalize both parts of a hyphenated term in a title:

- *Fail-Safe*
- *Through the Looking-Glass*
- *Self-Consuming Artifacts*

When an obviously minor element is included in a hyphenated term, however, leave it uncapitalized:

- "A Guide to Over-*the*-Counter Medications"

34g Capitalize the name of a person, place, business, or organization.

- Joyce Carol Oates
- Western Hemisphere
- New Canaan, Connecticut
- Lifeboat Associates
- Canadian Broadcasting Corporation
- Xerox Corporation

**cap
34h**

34h Capitalize an adjective derived from a name.

- Shakespearean
- Malthusian
- the French language
- Roman numerals

But note the use of lowercase in *roman type* and *french fries.*

34i Capitalize a word like *father* only if you are using it as a name or part of a name.

NAME OR PART OF NAME (CAPITALIZED):
- Everyone has seen posters of *Uncle* Sam.
- Oh, *Mother,* I miss you!

NOT PART OF NAME (UNCAPITALIZED):
- My *uncle* Sam bought me my first baseball mitt.
- I cabled my *mother* when I reached Athens.

34j Capitalize a rank or title only when it is joined to a name or when it stands for a specific person.

CAPITALIZED:
- General Dwight D. Eisenhower
- The Colonel was promoted in 1983.

UNCAPITALIZED:
- Two *generals* and a *colonel* attended the parade.
- She was elected *mayor* in 1989.

34k Capitalize the name of a specific institution or its formal subdivision, but not of an unspecified institution.

cap
34k

When you are designating a particular school or museum, or one of its departments, use capitals:

- Museum of Modern Art
- University of Chicago
- the Department of Business Administration
- Franklin High School

Subsequent, shortened references to the institution or department are sometimes left uncapitalized:

- She retired from the *university* last year.

  But *University* would also be correct here.

Do not capitalize a name that identifies only the *type* of institution you have in mind:

- a strife-torn *museum*
- Every *university* must rely on contributions.
- She attends *high school* in the daytime and *ballet school* after dinner.

34l Capitalize a specific course of study but not a general branch of learning.

CAPITALIZED:
- Physics 1A
- Computer Science 142B

UNCAPITALIZED:
- He never learned the rudiments of *physics*.
- Her training in *computer science* won her a job as a programmer.

34m Capitalize a sacred name but not a secular word derived from it.

cap
34m

Whether or not you are a believer, use capitals for the names of deities, revered figures, and holy books:

- the Bible
- God
- the Lord
- Allah
- the Virgin Mary
- Buddha
- the Gospels
- the Koran

But do not capitalize a secular word derived from a sacred name:

- biblical tones
- a godlike grandeur
- her scriptural authority
- the gospel of getting ahead

The pronouns *he* and *him,* when referring to the Judeo-Christian deity, have traditionally been capitalized, but this practice is less common today. You can consider it optional.

34n   Capitalize the name of a historical event, movement, or period.

- the Civil War
- the Depression
- the Romantic poets
- the Bronze Age
- the Roaring Twenties

Note that *the* is uncapitalized in these examples.

34o   Capitalize a day of the week, a month, or a holiday but not a season or the numerical part of a date.

cap
34o

CAPITALIZED:
- next Tuesday
- May 1988
- Christmas
- Passover
- Columbus Day

UNCAPITALIZED:
- next fall
- a winter storm
- July twenty-first
- the third of August

34p Capitalize the name of a group or nationality but not of a looser grouping.

CAPITALIZED:
- Moslem
- Hungarian
- Friends of the Earth

UNCAPITALIZED:
- the upper class
- the underprivileged
- environmentalists

34q Capitalize a word like *south* only if you are using it as a place name.

CAPITALIZED:
- Northwest Passage
- Southeast Asia
- The South and the Midwest will be crucial in the election.

UNCAPITALIZED:
- northwest of here
- Go west for two miles and then turn south.

cap
34r

34r Reproduce a foreign word or title as you find it in the original language.

- *Märchen* [Ger: fairy tale]
- *una cubana* [Sp.: a Cuban woman]
- *La terre* [title of a French novel: *The Earth*]

34s   Notice that a word may have different meanings in its capitalized and uncapitalized forms.

- The Pope is *Catholic*. [He belongs to the Church.]
- George has *catholic* tastes. [His tastes are wide-ranging.]
- He became a *Democrat* after he married Rosa. [He joined the party.]
- Tocqueville saw every American farmer as a *democrat*. [He believed that they all supported the idea of equality.]

cap 34s

35 Italics, Abbreviations, Numbers

ITALICS

Ordinary typeface is known as **roman,** and the thin, slightly slanted typeface that contrasts with it is **italic**—as in *these three words.* In manuscript or typescript, "italics" are indicated by underlining, although with a word processor and an appropriate printer, you can make direct use of italics.

MANUSCRIPT:

TYPESCRIPT:
* The Great Gatsby

PRINT OR WORD PROCESSOR:
* *The Great Gatsby*

35a   Learn which kinds of titles belong in italics.

ITALICS:

One Hundred Years of Solitude	[a book]
Paradise Lost	[a long poem published as a whole volume]

Waiting for Godot	[a play]
Casablanca	[a film]
New York Times	[a newspaper]
Popular Mechanics	[a magazine]
Abused Children	[a pamphlet]
The Firebird	[a long musical work]
The Smithsonian Collection of Classic Jazz	[a record album]
Jazz Matinee	[a radio series]
The Bill Cosby Show	[a television series]
Van Gogh's *Starry Night*	[a painting]
Rodin's *Adam*	[a sculpture]

QUOTATION MARKS:

"Araby"	[a short story]
"To Autumn"	[a poem]
"The Political Economy of Milk"	[a magazine article]
"Magic and Paraphysics"	[a chapter of a book]
"Smoke Gets in Your Eyes"	[a song]

Note the following special conditions:

**ital
35a**

1. In the name of a newspaper, include the place of publication in the italicized title:

   • She read it in the *Philadelphia Inquirer*.

   The article preceding the place name is usually not italicized (or capitalized).

2. The title of a poem, story, or chapter may also be the title of the whole volume in which that smaller unit is found. Use italics only when you mean to designate the whole volume:

   • "The Magic Barrel" [Bernard Malamud's short story]
   • *The Magic Barrel* [the book in which Malamud's story was eventually republished]

3. Some publications, especially newspapers, use italics sparingly or not at all. If you are writing for a specific publication, follow its style. If not, observe the rules given here.

4. Do not italicize or use quotation marks around sacred works and their divisions.

DO:
- the Talmud
- the Vedas
- the Book of the Dead
- the Bible
- the New Testament
- Leviticus

5. When one title contains another title that would normally be italicized, make the embedded title roman. That is, you should not underline it.

- She was reading *The Senses of* Walden to get ideas for her paper.

35b   Italicize a foreign term that has not yet been adopted as a common English expression.

STILL "FOREIGN" (ITALICIZE):
- *la dolce vita*
- *sine qua non*
- *La Belle Époque*
- *Schadenfreude*

FAMILIAR IN ENGLISH (DO NOT ITALICIZE):
- ad hoc
- blitzkrieg
- cliché
- de facto
- guru
- junta
- status quo
- sushi

**ital
35b**

Latin abbreviations

Latin abbreviations are often italicized, but the tendency is now to leave them in roman. For example, according to the general practice these may be left in roman:

| cf. | et al. | i.e. | viz. |
| e.g. | f., ff. | q.v. | vs. |

See pages 422–423, 35g, for the meanings of these and other abbreviations used in documentation.

Translating a foreign term

When translating into English, put the foreign term in italics and the English one in quotation marks:

- The Italian term for "the book" is *il libro;* the French term is *le livre.*

The Modern Language Association also allows a translation to be placed within single quotation marks without intervening punctuation:

- *ein wenig* 'a little'
- They called the Fiat 500 *Topolino* 'little mouse.'

35c Italicize the name of a ship, aircraft, or spacecraft.

- *Queen Elizabeth II*
- *Cristoforo Colombo*
- *Air Force One*
- *Voyager 2*

But do not italicize abbreviations such as *SS* or *HMS* preceding a ship's name:

- SS *Enterprise*

ital
35d

35d Use italics or quotation marks to show that you are treating a word *as* a word.

- When Frank and Edith visited the rebuilt neighborhoods of their youth, they understood the meaning of the word *gentrified.*

    It would be equally correct to keep *gentrified* in roman type and enclose it in quotation marks: "gentrified."

35e To add emphasis to part of a quoted expression, italicize the key element.

If you want to emphasize one part of a quotation, put that part in italics. And to show that the italics are your own rather than the author's, follow the quotation with a parenthetical acknowledgment such as *emphasis added* or *emphasis mine:*

- The author writes mysteriously of a *"rival* system of waste management" (emphasis added).

35f Use italics sparingly to emphasize a key element in your own prose.

To distinguish one term from another or to lend a point rhetorical emphasis, you can italicize (underline) some of your own language:

- No doubt she can explain where she was in the month of June. *But what about July?* This is the unresolved question.

Beware, however, of relying on emphatic italics to do the work that should be done by effective sentence structure and diction. Prose that is riddled with italics creates a frenzied effect.

DON'T

x The hazard from *immediate radiation* is one issue—and a *very important* one. But the *long-term* effects from *improper waste storage* are *even more crucial,* and *practically nobody* within the industry seems to take it seriously.

This passage would inspire more confidence if it lacked italics altogether.

**abbr
35g**

ABBREVIATIONS

35g Use abbreviations in parenthetical citations, notes, reference lists, and bibliographies.

For purposes of documentation (Chapter 37), you can use the following abbreviations.

ABBREVIATION	MEANING
anon.	anonymous
b.	born
bibliog.	bibliography
©	copyright
c. or ca.	about [with dates only]
cf.	compare [not *see*]
ch., chs.	chapter(s)
d.	died
diss.	dissertation
ed., eds.	editor(s), edition(s), edited by
e.g.	for example [not *that is*]
esp.	especially
et al.	and others [people only]
etc.	and so forth [not interchangeable with *et al.*]
f., ff.	and the following [page or pages]
ibid.	the same [title as the one mentioned in the previous note]
i.e.	that is [not *for example*]
introd.	introduction
l., ll.	line(s)
ms., mss.	manuscript(s)
n., nn.	note(s)
N.B.	mark well, take notice *[nota bene]*
n.d.	no date (in a book's imprint)
no., nos.	number(s)
p., pp.	page(s)
pl., pls.	plate(s)
pref.	preface
pt., pts.	part(s)
q.v.	see elsewhere in this text [literally *which see*]
rpt.	reprint

ABBREVIATION	MEANING
rev.	revised, revision; review, reviewed by [beware of ambiguity between meanings; if necessary, write out instead of abbreviating]
sc.	scene
sec., secs., sect., sects.	section(s)
ser.	series
st., sts.	stanza(s)
tr., trans.	translator, translation, translated by
v.	versus [legal citations]
viz.	namely
vol., vols.	volume(s)
vs.	versus [ordinary usage]

Note that *passim,* meaning "throughout," and *sic,* meaning "thus," are not to be followed by a period; they are complete Latin words. For the function of *sic,* see page 351, 28r.

35h Learn which abbreviations are allowable in your main text.

Allowed in main text

Some abbreviations are considered standard in any piece of writing, including the main body of an essay:

1. *Mr., Ms., Mrs., Dr., Messrs., Mme., Mlle., St.,* etc., when used before names. Some publications now refer to all women as *Ms.,* and this title has rapidly gained favor as a means of avoiding designation of marital status.

2. *Jr., Sr., Esq., M.D., D.D., D.D.S., M.A., Ph.D., LL.D.,* etc., when used after names: *Olivia Martinez, M.D.*

3. abbreviations of, and acronyms (words formed from the initial letters in a multiword name) for, organizations that are widely

abbr
35h

known by the shorter name: CIA, FBI, ROTC, NOW, NATO, UNESCO, and so on. Note that very familiar designations such as these are usually written without periods between the letters.

4. *B.C., A.D., A.M., P.M., mph.* These abbreviations should never be used apart from numbers (not x *I use the computer in the P.M.* but *I use the computer between 8 and 11 P.M.*). *B.C.* always follows the year, but *A.D.* usually precedes it: *252 B.C.,* but *A.D. 147.*

5. places commonly known by their abbreviations: *U.S., D.C., USSR,* etc. One writes *in the U.S.,* not *in U.S.* Do not use *D.C.* alone as a place name: x She commutes into *D.C.* Prefer *Washington.*

Inappropriate in main text

		DON'T	DO
1.	titles	x the Rev., the Hon., Sen., Pres., Gen.	• the Reverend, the Honorable, Senator, President, General
2.	given names	x Geo., Eliz., Robt.	• George, Elizabeth, Robert
3.	months, days of the week, and holidays	x Oct., Mon., Vets. Day	• October, Monday, Veterans Day
4.	localities, cities, counties, states, provinces, and countries	x Pt. Reyes Natl. Seashore, Phila., Sta. Clara, N.M., Ont., N.Z.	• Point Reyes National Seashore, Philadelphia, Santa Clara, New Mexico, Ontario, New Zealand
5.	roadways	x St., La., Ave., Blvd.	• Street, Lane, Avenue, Boulevard
6.	courses of instruction	x Bot., PE	• Botany, Physical Education
7.	units of measurement	x ft., kg, lbs., qt., hr., mos., yrs.	• feet, kilogram, pounds, quart, hour, months, years

**abbr
35h**

Technical versus nontechnical prose

In general, you can do more abbreviating in technical than in non-technical writing. See the following examples.

TECHNICAL WRITING	OTHER PROSE
km	kilometer(s)
mg	milligram(s)
sq.	square

Even in general-interest prose, however, abbreviation of a much-used term can be a convenience. Give one full reference before relying on the abbreviation:

- Among its many services, the Harvard Student Agency (HSA) sponsors the *Let's Go* series of travel books for students. HSA also functions as a custodial agency, rents photographic equipment and linens, acts as an employment clearinghouse, and caters parties.

35i   Be consistent in capitalizing or not capitalizing abbreviations following times.

Authorities disagree over *A.M.* and *P.M.* versus *a.m.* and *p.m.* Either form will do, but do not mix them.

abbr
35i

DON'T:

x She was scheduled to arrive at 11 a.m., but we had to wait for her until 2 P.M.

DO:

- She was scheduled to arrive at 11 a.m., but we had to wait for her until 2 p.m.

or

- She was scheduled to arrive at 11 A.M., but we had to wait for her until 2 P.M.

35j   Learn which kinds of abbreviations can be written without periods.

Good writers differ in their preference for periods or no periods within an abbreviation. Practice is shifting toward omission of periods. In general, you can feel safe in omitting periods from abbreviations written in capital letters, provided the abbreviation does not appear to spell out another word. Thus *USA* needs no periods but *U.S.* does, since otherwise it might be mistaken for a capitalization of the pronoun *us*. Other typical abbreviations without periods are:

- JFK
- USSR
- IOU
- NJ

Note that *N.J.*, with periods, is an option for abbreviating *New Jersey* but not for supplying a mail code before a ZIP number: *NJ 08540*.

But most abbreviations that end in a lowercase letter still require periods:

- Ont.
- Chi.
- Inc.
- i.e.

Note that there are commonly recognized exceptions such as *mph* and *rpm*. Also, abbreviations for metric measures are usually written without periods: *ml, kg*, etc.

35k   Leave single spaces between the initials of a name, but close up all other abbreviations and acronyms, including postal abbreviations for states.

abbr
35k

SPACED:
- T. S. Eliot
- E. F. Hutton
- A. J. P. Taylor

UNSPACED:
- e.g.
- A.M. (or a.m.)
- Ph.D
- CIA

POSTAL ABBREVIATIONS FOR STATES

Alabama	AL	Montana	MT
Alaska	AK	Nebraska	NE
Arizona	AZ	Nevada	NV
Arkansas	AR	New Hampshire	NH
California	CA	New Jersey	NJ
Colorado	CO	New Mexico	NM
Connecticut	CT	New York	NY
Delaware	DE	North Carolina	NC
District of Columbia	DC	North Dakota	ND
		Ohio	OH
Florida	FL	Oklahoma	OK
Georgia	GA	Oregon	OR
Hawaii	HI	Pennsylvania	PA
Idaho	ID	Rhode Island	RI
Illinois	IL	South Carolina	SC
Indiana	IN	South Dakota	SD
Iowa	IA	Tennessee	TN
Kansas	KS	Texas	TX
Kentucky	KY	Utah	UT
Louisiana	LA	Vermont	VT
Maine	ME	Virginia	VA
Maryland	MD	Washington	WA
Massachusetts	MA	West Virginia	WV
Michigan	MI	Wisconsin	WI
Minnesota	MN	Wyoming	WY
Mississippi	MS		
Missouri	MO		

abbr
35k

NUMBERS AND FIGURES

35l Know which circumstances call for written-out numbers.

Technical versus nontechnical prose

In scientific and technical prose, figures *(67)* are preferred to written-out numbers *(sixty-seven)*, though very large multiples such as *million, billion,* and *trillion* are written out. Newspapers customarily spell out only numbers *one* through *nine* and such round numbers as *two hundred* and *five million.* In your nontechnical writing, prefer written-out numbers for the whole numbers *one* through *ninety-nine* and for any of those numbers followed by *hundred, billion,* and so on.

TECHNICAL PROSE	NONTECHNICAL PROSE
3/4	three-quarters
4	four
93	ninety-three
202	202
1500 (or 1,500)	fifteen hundred
10,000	ten thousand
38 million	thirty-eight million
101 million	101 million
54 billion	fifty-four billion
205 billion	205 billion

**num
35l**

Special uses for written-out numbers

1. In nontechnical prose, write out a concise number between one thousand and ten thousand that you can express in hundreds: not *1600* but *sixteen hundred.* This rule does not apply to dates, however.

2. Write out round (approximate) numbers that are even hundred thousands:

   • Over six hundred thousand refugees arrived here last year.

3. Always write out a number that begins a sentence.

   • *Eighty-four* students scored above grade level.

     But if the number would not ordinarily be written out, you would usually do better to recast the sentence.

   • The results were less encouraging for *213* other takers of the test.

     It would have been awkward to begin the sentence with *Two hundred thirteen.*

4. Write out a whole hour, unmodified by minutes, if it appears before *o'clock, noon,* or *midnight: one o'clock, twelve noon, twelve midnight.* Do not write *twelve-thirty o'clock* or *12:30 o'clock.*

Special uses for figures

1. Use figures with abbreviated units of measure:

   • 7 lbs.
   • 11 g
   • 88 mm

2. If you have several numbers bunched together, use figures regardless of the amounts:

   • Harvey skipped his birthday celebrations at ages 21, 35, and 40.

3. When two or more related amounts call for different styles of representation, use figures for all of them:

**num
35l**

- The injured people included 101 women and 9 children.

4. Use figures for all of the following:

    a. apartment numbers, street numbers, and ZIP codes:

        - Apt. 17C, 544 Lowell Ave., Palo Alto, CA 94301.

    b. tables of statistics.

    c. numbers containing decimals: *7.456, $5.58, 52.1 percent.*

    d. dates (except in extremely formal communications such as wedding announcements): *October 25, 1989; 25 October 1989.*

    e. times, when they precede A.M. or P.M. (a.m. or p.m.): *8 A.M., 6 P.M., 2:47 P.M.*

    f. page numbers: *p. 47, pp. 341–53.*

    g. volumes *(vol. 2),* books of the Bible *(2 Corinthians),* and acts, scenes, and lines of plays *(Macbeth I.iii.89–104).*

35m Use Roman numerals only where convention requires them.

num
35m

In general, **Roman numerals** *(XI, LVIII)* have been falling into disuse as **Arabic numerals** *(11, 58)* have taken over their function. But note the following exceptions.

1. In some citation styles, upper and lowercase Roman numerals are still used in combination with Arabic numerals to show sets of numbers in combination. Thus *Hamlet III.ii.47* refers to line 47 in the second scene of the play's third act.

2. Use Roman numerals for the main divisions of an outline (p. 43, 4b).

3. Use lowercase Roman numerals to cite pages at the beginning of a book that are so numbered:

- (Preface v)
- (Introduction xvi-xvii)

4. Use Roman numerals as you find them in the names of monarchs, popes, same-named sons in the third generation, ships, and so forth:

- George III
- Leo IV
- Orville F. Schell III
- Queen Elizabeth II

The following list reminds you how to form Roman numerals.

1 I	10 X	50 L	200 CC
2 II	11 XI	60 LX	400 CD
3 III	15 XV	70 LXX	499 CDXCIX
4 IV	19 XIX	80 LXXX	500 D
5 V	20 XX	90 XC	900 CM
6 VI	21 XXI	99 XCIX	999 CMXCIX
7 VII	29 XXIX	100 C	1000 M
8 VIII	30 XXX	110 CX	1500 MD
9 IX	40 XL	199 CXCIX	3000 MMM

num
35n

35n Distinguish between the uses of cardinal and ordinal numbers.

Numbers like *one, two,* and *three (1, 2, 3)* are called **cardinal numbers;** those like *first, second,* and *third (1st, 2d, 3d;* note the shortened spelling) are called **ordinal numbers.** The choice between cardinal and ordinal numbers is usually automatic, but there are several differences between spoken and written convention:

SPEECH	WRITING
Louis the Fourteenth	Louis XIV
July seventh, 1989	July 7, 1989 *or* 7 July 1989
But: July seventh [no year]	July 7th *or* July seventh

Note that the rules of choice between written-out numbers and figures are the same for cardinal as for ordinal numbers (35l).

Terms like firstly

The word *firstly* is now rarely seen; *first* can serve as an adverb as well as an adjective.

ADJECTIVE:
- The *first* item on the agenda is the budget.

ADVERB:
- There are several items on the agenda. *First, . . .*

When you begin a list with *first,* you have the option of continuing either with *second, third,* or with *secondly, thirdly.* For consistency of effect, drop all the *-ly* forms:

- Let me say, *first,* that the crisis has passed. *Second,* I want to thank all of our employees for their extraordinary sacrifices. And *third, . . .*

**num
35n**

But as soon as you write *secondly,* you have committed yourself to *thirdly, fourthly,* and so on.

Finally, beware of mixing cardinal and ordinal forms.

DON'T:
- x *One,* a career as a writer presents financial hardship. *Second,* I am not sure I have enough emotional stamina to face rejection. *Third, . . .*

For consistency, change *One* to *First.*

VIII
RESEARCH
PAPERS

Research Papers

When assigned a research paper, some students feel they must set aside everything they have learned about writing essays and concentrate instead on showing how much library reading they can do. The result may be a paper crammed with references but lacking a clear point or concern for the reader's patience. A research paper is above all an essay—one that happens to be based in part on library materials (Chapter 36), duly documented (Chapter 37). The advice that follows should be regarded not as a self-sufficient unit but as a supplement to Chapters 1–5. If you are undertaking a research paper and have not gone through those chapters, it would be good to do so now.

36 Finding and Mastering Sources

A college library is in essence an information retrieval system. As with a computer, the knack of using it successfully consists in knowing the right questions to present it with. Searching through the stacks without any questions at all would be as senseless as trying to browse in the computer's memory bank; you have to be looking for something from the outset. And the more specific your question, the more short-cuts you can take. Experienced researchers do not run through all the ways of seeking information described in this chapter. Rather, they find a few key works as early as possible and then allow those works—especially those containing a **bibliography,** or list of further books and articles on the topic—to suggest how to proceed.

36a   Get acquainted with the parts of your library.

Perhaps your college library strikes you as mysterious or even vaguely threatening. If so, bear in mind that you do not have to understand the whole system—just some procedures for retrieving the books and articles you need. Watch for free library tours and information packets, and do not hesitate to ask a *reference librarian* for help in getting an efficient start on your project.

No two libraries are quite alike, and your own may be much simpler than the model we summarize here. Even so, you will find the same functions met within a more consolidated floor plan. Here, then, are the key rooms and services found in an ample college library:

1. *Stacks.* These are shelves on which most books and bound periodicals are stored. In the "open stack" system, all users can enter the stacks, find materials, and take them to a check-out desk. If your library has "closed stacks," access to the stacks is limited by status; see the next item.

2. *Circulation desk.* You can check out a book or bound periodical by submitting a *call slip*—a card identifying what you need—to the *circulation desk,* to which a clerk will return either with the book or with an explanation that it is on reserve (see item 5), out to another borrower, or missing. If it is out to another borrower, you can "put a hold" on it—that is, indicate that you want to be notified as soon as the book has been returned. Since you may have to wait as long as two weeks for some items, it is important to begin your research early.

3. *Catalog.* Near the circulation desk you will find cabinets full of alphabetically filed cards, listing all the library's printed holdings (books, periodicals, pamphlets, and items on microfilm, but no manuscripts, records, or tapes). This is the *card catalog.* Its listings are by author, title, and subject. In some libraries the card catalog has been supplemented or replaced by a *microfiche catalog,* consisting of miniaturized photographic entries on plastic cards that can be read when placed in a microfiche reader, available nearby. Your library may also have an *on-line catalog*—that is, a continually updated computer file. If so, you will see computer terminals, accompanied by appropriate instructions, near the circulation desk. Whatever its form, the catalog is your master key to the stacks, for it gives you call numbers enabling you or a clerk to locate the books you need.

4. *Reference room.* In the *reference room* (or behind the reference desk) are stored sets of encyclopedias, indexes, dictionaries, bibliographies, and similar multipurpose research tools. You cannot check out reference volumes, but you can consult them long enough to get the names of promising-looking books and articles that you *will* be able to get from the main collection. The reference room usually doubles as a *reading room,* enabling you to do much of your reading near other sources of information.

5. *Reserve desk.* Behind the *reserve desk* (or in the reserve book

room) are kept multiple copies of books that are essential to current courses. The distinctive feature of reserved books is that they must be returned quickly, usually within either an hour or a day or a week. When you learn that a book is "on reserve," even for a course other than your own, you can be reasonably sure of finding an available copy.

6. *Periodical room.* In the *periodical room* you can find magazines and journals too recent to have been bound as books. Thus, if you do research on a topic of current interest, you are certain to find yourself applying to the periodical room for up-to-date articles.

7. *Newspaper room.* Take your call slips to this room to get a look at newspaper articles and editorials. Most newspapers are stored on *microfilm,* which can be read only with a microfilm reader. Ask a clerk to show you how the machine works.

Thus your research is likely to take you back and forth between various sites:

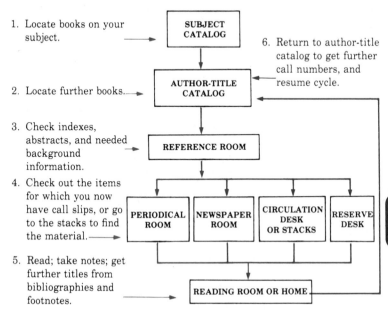

1. Locate books on your subject.

SUBJECT CATALOG

6. Return to author-title catalog to get further call numbers, and resume cycle.

AUTHOR-TITLE CATALOG

2. Locate further books.

3. Check indexes, abstracts, and needed background information.

REFERENCE ROOM

4. Check out the items for which you now have call slips, or go to the stacks to find the material.

PERIODICAL ROOM | **NEWSPAPER ROOM** | **CIRCULATION DESK OR STACKS** | **RESERVE DESK**

5. Read; take notes; get further titles from bibliographies and footnotes.

READING ROOM OR HOME

libr 36a

At some point, obviously, this cycle has to be interrupted; the first draft beckons. But even as you write successive drafts, you may find yourself dipping back into library sources to check new leads and follow up ideas that now look more fruitful than they did at first.

36b Learn the most efficient ways to search for books.

Subject catalog

If you are searching for a topic within a general subject area, the first thing you want to do is check your library's holdings within that area. You can do so by consulting the *subject catalog,* which is arranged not by authors and titles of books but by fields of knowledge, problems, movements, schools of thought, and so forth. Once you locate an array of relevant titles, you should fill out call slips for the most recent appropriate-looking works. If you get hold of just one recent book that has a *bibliography*—a list of consulted works—in the back, you may discover that you already have the names of all the further books and articles you will need.

Guide to subject headings

But how do you know which headings your subject catalog uses to classify the entries you will want to review? You can try your luck, sampling a number of alternative phrases, or you can take a more systematic and reliable approach. Your subject catalog follows the headings adopted by the Library of Congress in Washington, D.C. Ask your reference librarian where a book called *Library of Congress Subject Headings* is to be found. That book is heavily *cross-indexed;* in other words, if you look up a plausible-sounding phrase, you will not only learn whether it constitutes a Library of Congress subject heading, you will also be directed to other phrases that do serve as headings.

libr
36b

Thus the student who wanted to investigate U.S.-Chinese business relations for his research paper (pp. 492–507) began by going to the *Library of Congress Subject Headings* pages referring to *Technology transfer.* There he found the following headings and symbols:

Technology transfer *(Indirect) (T174.3)* ——————— 1
>> Subdivided by the region or country re-
>> ceiving the technology. Where appli-
>> cable, also make an additional entry
>> under this heading with subdivision for —— 2
>> the region or country transferring the
>> technology.
> 3 —————— *sa* Agriculture—Technology transfer
>> Foreign licensing agreements
>> New products
>> Nuclear nonproliferation
>> Technological forecasting
>> Technical innovations
>> Technology—international cooperation
> 4 —————— *x* Technological transfer
>> Transfer of technology
> 5 —————— *xx* Diffusion of innovations
>> Foreign licensing agreements
>> Inventions

Observe that:

1. The entry provides the Library of Congress call number of a key
   work on the subject. Armed with this number, the reader can
   consult the Library's *shelf list*—a catalog arranged in order of
   call numbers—and be sure of finding relevant material near
   card T174.3

2. Special instructions show the reader how to break the subject
   down by nationality—for example, by doing a subject search
   under *Technology transfer—China.*

3. The symbol *sa* ("see also") introduces seven related headings
   that can be consulted to locate titles not covered under *Technology transfer.*

libr
36b

4. The symbol *x* tells the reader not to bother looking up *Technological transfer* or *Transfer of technology;* since these are not
   Library of Congress headings, they will not be headings in the
   campus library catalog, either.

5. The symbol *xx* introduces three *broader* headings that will cover further works on technology transfer. By doing a subject search using these headings, the reader can see the chosen topic in a wider perspective.

Author-title catalog

When you conduct a subject search using Library of Congress headings (above), you won't necessarily be consulting a separate subject catalog (p. 438 above). In many libraries, subject entries are interfiled within the *author-title catalog.*

If you know that your paper will deal with a certain author or public figure, you can bypass a subject search and go directly to the author-title catalog, which lists works alphabetically by both author and title. The last entries in your author's listing, after his or her own works, may be useful books of biography, criticism, and commentary. Thus the author-title catalog is itself a kind of subject catalog, with the treated figures as subjects.

The most important piece of information in any catalog entry is the *call number* in the upper left corner; it tells exactly where the book or bound journal is shelved. But you can also get several other kinds of information from a card, as did a student who was doing research for a paper on computer crime. The cards she consulted are shown on the opposite page. In addition to some coded information chiefly of interest to librarians, the author card contains six potentially useful kinds of knowledge:

1. The author's name.

2. The call number, enabling someone to apply for the book at the circulation desk or to locate it in the stacks.

3. The title of the book, the author's name as it appears on the title page, the fact that this is a first edition, the place of publication, the publisher, and the date of copyright. A researcher would want to get all this information (except "1st edition") recorded on a bibliography card (p. 452, 36e).

4. Physical features of the book. It contains 164 pages, is illustrated, and is 21 centimeters in height. The key point here is the

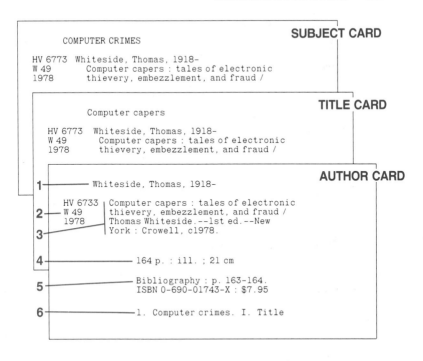

length; this book will be more worth looking into than, say, a forty-page pamphlet would be.

5. Notes on the contents of the book. In this case we are promised a bibliography—that is, a list of other related materials—which could prove extremely helpful for a research paper.

6. A list of all the headings under which this book is filed in the library's catalogs. By going to "Computer crimes" in the subject catalog, a researcher might find several items of related interest.

libr
36b

Once in a while you may come across a reference to an apparently indispensable book that is unlisted in your library's catalog. Since there are some sixty thousand new volumes published each year in English alone, no library but the Library of Congress itself could acquire more than a minority of them. You can get essential information about the book's author, title, publisher, and date of publication from the *National Union Catalog,* which reproduces the Library of Congress Catalog and includes titles from other libraries as well. If you cannot visit a library that has the book, you can probably borrow it through *interlibrary loan.* The same holds for journals as well. By consulting the *Union List of Serials in Libraries of the United States and Canada,* you can discover which libraries own sets of hard-to-find journals.

On-line catalog

Most card catalogs are now being supplemented or replaced by *on-line* (computer) *catalogs* that serve the same function, but with greater efficiency for both catalogers and users. The writer of the research paper on Chinese-American business relations, for example, guided by the *Library of Congress Subject Headings* (p. 438 above), used a library terminal to run a subject search on "China—Economic conditions— 1976– ." This is what came up on the screen:

```
Your search for the Subject: CHINA ECONOMIC CONDITIONS 1976—
retrieved multiple records.

Title List

 1. China trade:a guide to doing business with the People's Re
 2. China's economy in global perspective/A. Doak Barnett
 3. China takes off:technology transfer and modernization/E.E.
 4. The second economy of rural China/Anita Chan and Jonathan
 5. China's allocation of authority and responsibility in ener
 6. China's economic development:growth and structural change/
 7. Mainland China:why still backward?/by Cheng Chu-Yuan
 8. China among the nations of the Pacific/edited by Harrison
 9. China and Southeast Asia:contemporary politics and economi
10. China, economic structure in international perspective.
11. China in transition:papers/Kenneth Lieberthal . . . [et al
```

**libr
36b**

By requesting further information about item 3, the student was shown the equivalent of a catalog card for a book that eventually proved useful to him:

```
 Call #:  HC430.T4.B381 1986 Chinese Stdy, Main Stack,
          Business/SS

 Author:  Bauer, E. E.

  Title:  China takes off : technology transfer and
          modernization / E.E. Bauer ; introduction by
          Michel Oksenberg. Seattle : University of
          Washington Press, © 1986. xvi, 227 p. :
          ill. ; 25 cm.

  Notes:  Includes bibliographical references.

Subjects: Technology transfer--China.
          China--Economic conditions--1976-
```

For more information about on-line searching, see page 447.

36c Learn how to find recent articles and reviews.

If you have chosen a topic of current interest—the spread and control of a new disease, say, or the changing American family structure—you will want to review the latest available information. You cannot find it in even the most recently published books, which will necessarily be a year or two behind the times. Newspaper articles will be best for following events as they occur. Magazine articles, such as those in *Harper's* or *The Atlantic,* will give you a general perspective that may be just right for the audience and level you have in mind. And in professional journals—specialized scholarly periodicals such as the *New England Journal of Medicine* or the *Bulletin of the Atomic Scientists*—you will get access to detailed knowledge and theory that may not yet have appeared in hard cover. You may also want to check expert reviews of books you hope to use. Digests of reviews (p. 445) can show you how much trust you should place in a given book.

Indexes and abstracts

Obviously, you would be wasting your time poring over the handiest newspapers, magazines, and journals in the hope of finding relevant items. The efficient thing is to consult indexes and abstracts, which you will find shelved together in your library's reference room. *Indexes* are books, usually with a new volume each year, containing alphabetically ordered references to articles on given subjects. And *abstracts* are summaries of articles, allowing you to tell whether or not a certain article is important enough to your project to be worth tracking down. It is the reference room, then—not the newspaper room or the periodical room—that holds the key to your search for pertinent articles and reviews.

1. *To Newspapers.* The only newspaper index you may ever need to consult is the *New York Times Index* (1913–   ), which covers a vast array of news and commentary having national or international importance. Since it is issued every two weeks before being bound into annual volumes, you can be sure of staying current with developments in your subject. For coverage of newspapers in Chicago, Los Angeles, New Orleans, and Washington, D.C., try the *Newspaper Index* (1972–   ). And for international and especially British coverage, consult the *Index to the* [London] *Times* (1906–   ).

2. *To Magazines.* If you want to find an article in a general-interest magazine, go to the *Reader's Guide to Periodical Literature* (1900–   ), which covers about 160 magazines on a twice-monthly basis. Indeed, the *Reader's Guide* is so useful for the typical research essay that many students begin their investigation there, saving the subject catalog until they have seen whether their topic has engaged the public lately. Browsing through the headings in the *Reader's Guide* may help you focus your topic better. If you draw a blank from the *Reader's Guide,* ask yourself whether your topic is too broad, too narrow, too specialized, or too outdated to merit pursuing.

A typical segment of a column in the *Reader's Guide* looks like the one shown on the facing page. There you see:

a. *An entry listed by subject.* The article about heme proteins appeared in the journal *Science,* volume 233, August 29, 1986, on pages 948 through 952, and it contained a bibliography, footnotes, and illustrations.

b. *An entry listed by the author's name.*

c. *Two entries listed by the individuals who are discussed.*

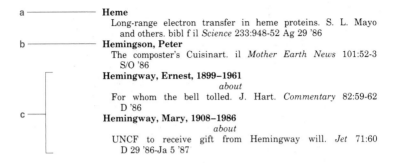

a — **Heme**
    Long-range electron transfer in heme proteins. S. L. Mayo and others. bibl f il *Science* 233:948-52 Ag 29 '86

b — **Hemingson, Peter**
    The composter's Cuisinart. il *Mother Earth News* 101:52-3 S/O '86

Hemingway, Ernest, 1899–1961
    about
    For whom the bell tolled. J. Hart. *Commentary* 82:59-62 D '86

c — **Hemingway, Mary, 1908–1986**
    about
    UNCF to receive gift from Hemingway will. *Jet* 71:60 D 29 '86-Ja 5 '87

3. *To Journals.* While the *Reader's Guide* gives you good access to such popular magazines as *Time* and *Psychology Today,* it does not cover journals such as *Science* and *Modern Language Quarterly.* Journals are issued less often than magazines and are far more technical in nature. Although you probably want to keep a general-interest focus in your paper, an important piece of information may be accessible to you only in a journal. The key indexes for access to journal articles in a variety of fields are the *Humanities Index* (1974–) and the *Social Sciences Index* (1974–). The *Humanities Index* should be your first choice for post-1973 articles in archaeology, area studies, classics, folklore, history, language and literature, literary criticism, performing arts, philosophy, religion, and theology. Use the *Social Sciences Index* for post-1973 articles in anthropology, economics, environmental science, geography, law and criminology, medicine, political science, psychology, public administration, and sociology. For years before 1973, consult the *International Index* (1907–1965) and the *Social Sciences and Humanities Index* (1965–1974); the latter was the parent of the now separate *Humanities Index* and *Social Sciences Index.*

4. *To Book Reviews.* If you want to know how reliable a certain book is, you can quickly learn what some of the book's original reviewers had to say by consulting *Book Review Digest* (1905–). Thus, for example, the writer of the paper on doing business with China wanted to know whether Orville Schell's *To Get Rich Is Glorious: China in the Eighties* would be useful to his research. Looking in *Book Review Digest* for 1985, he found the following synopsis:

libr
36c

SCHELL, ORVILLE. To get rich is glorious; China in the eighties. 210p $15.95 1985 Pantheon Bks.

    951.05   1. China—Description   and   travel
    2. China—Social conditions
    ISBN 0-394-53952-4   LC 84-42697

"Schell divided his book into two parts, 'The Wind of Wanting to Go It Alone' and 'The New Open Door.' Wanting to go it alone refers to China's new private enterprise incentives in agriculture and business. . . . As he narrates his travels throughout China, Schell analyzes what the long-range consequences of China's new economic style might mean." (America)

————

"[Schell is] a gifted writer with a Vermeer eye. . . . The author is certain of the main line of his argument; China is rapidly changing. He, however, like those with whom he talks, hesitates to draw even the most tentative of conclusions as to the long-range effects of China's new style."

    America 153:36 Jl 27 '85. Peter Fleming (900w)

"We can now add a third volume to Schell's In the People's Republic [BRD 1977], and 'Watch Out for the Foreign Guests!' [BRD 1981], his ongoing chronicle of the PRC's post-Mao development. Like those works, this new title, most of which appeared originally in the New Yorker, is an informed and literate travelogue, reliable and of lasting value. . . . Highly recommended for most libraries."

    Libr J 110:161 F 15 '85. Charles W. Hayford (90w)

"Orville Schell has traveled in China repeatedly since the later days of the Cultural Revolution. 'To Get Rich Is Glorious' puts his most recent, vivid impressions into the perspective of one who reads the Chinese press and has seen these places before. His book aims to be more than a simple travelogue. . . . [This book] does not ultimately succeed even on its own terms. Mr. Schell has tried to make this more than a visitor's account, but his writing rarely goes beyond the 'gee whiz' level. Numerous minor factual errors (such as his having Soviet advisers leave China in 1959 instead of 1960), moreover, contribute to the sense that this is not a volume that has met its full potential. Even Mr. Schell's beautifully crafted prose and eye for telling detail do not, in the final analysis, make this book more than an interesting set of experiences and impressions."

    N Y Times Book Rev p8 F 17 '85. Kenneth Lieberthal
    (600w)

Taken together, the reviews suggested that Schell's book, though fascinating, was more concerned with everyday life in China than with joint business ventures. The student thus decided to rely on other sources.

For other guides to book reviews, consult *Book Review Index* (1965–), *Current Book Review Citations* (1976–), and *The New York Times Book Review Index* (1896–1970).

On-line searching

In increasing numbers, printed indexes, abstracts, reports, conference proceedings, and government documents are being gathered in the alternative form of *databases*—that is, computer files that can be instantly scanned. If your library has an on-line catalog (p. 442), then that catalog is itself a database. But that is just the beginning. If your library subscribes to such databases as, say, *Pharmaceutical News Index, Population Bibliography,* and *Pollution Abstracts,* you can instruct the computer to retrieve every relevant article from one or more of those sources.

Such *on-line searching* can save time, unearth very recent references, and ferret out specific topics that do not constitute subject headings in the index itself. Suppose, for example, you are interested in the connection between child abuse and alcoholism. Instead of asking for all items within each of those large subjects, you can tell the computer to display only those items whose titles refer to *both* problems. The outcome will be a relatively short but highly efficient list, fairly free of "dumb mistakes" on the computer's part.

On-line searching can produce dramatic results if you have a well-defined topic in mind. But there are serious disadvantages as well:

libr 36c

1. You will be charged a fee—possibly a steep one—for the search.

2. You will need the assistance of a trained technician.

3. It is hard to "browse" in computer files; if your chosen keywords do not appear in the title of a relevant article, the computer will probably overlook that title.

On the whole, then, for the purposes of a college essay it is better to do your searching in printed sources. But remember that on-line searching is available if you should need it. A reference librarian can tell you whether your project is one that lends itself readily to a computer search.

36d   Consult background sources as necessary.

The steps we have already covered should be enough to give you all the information you need for a typical research essay. Sometimes, however, you may want an out-of-the-way bit of knowledge or a broad introduction to the field you are going to treat. Where should you turn? Most of the works mentioned below can be found in the reference room.

If you know an author's name but not the title of the book, if you have the title but not the author, or if you want to know when a certain book appeared, try consulting *Books in Print* (1948–   ), *Cumulative Book Index* (1898–   ), *Paperbound Books in Print* (1955–   ), or *Subject Guide to Books in Print* (1957–   ). The last of these volumes can give you a quick idea of what you could hope to find under a given subject heading of your card catalog. If you see an essential item in the *Subject Guide* that is missing from your catalog, you may be able to send for it through interlibrary loan.

Reference works—books that survey a field and tell you how to find materials within that field—are now so numerous that you may need to consult an even more general book that lists reference works and explains their scope. Try especially Eugene P. Sheehy, *Guide to Reference Books* (1976, with later supplements), which can lead you to the most appropriate bibliographies and indexes to articles.

libr
36d

For a college research paper, however, you will probably need at the most one survey of your field and one guide to sources. Here is a representative sample of titles to consult:

ART
Encyclopedia of World Art (1959–83)
Art Index (1947–   )

BUSINESS AND ECONOMICS
Dictionary of Economics and Business, ed. Erwin E. Nemmers (1978)

DRAMA
McGraw-Hill Encyclopedia of World Drama (1984)
How to Locate Reviews of Plays and Films, by Gordon Samples (1976)

EDUCATION
A Dictionary of Education, by Derek Rowntree (1982)
Education Index (1929–   )

FILM
The World Encyclopedia of the Film (1972)
Film Literature Index (1973–   )

FOLKLORE AND MYTHOLOGY
Funk & Wagnalls Standard Dictionary of Folklore, Mythology, and Legend (1972)
Motif-Index of Folk-Literature, by Stith Thompson (1955–58)

HISTORY
An Encyclopedia of World History, ed. William L. Langer (1972)
Historical Abstracts (1955–   )

LITERATURE
A Handbook to Literature, by C. Hugh Holman (1986)
Literary Research Guide, by Margaret C. Patterson (1983)

MUSIC
The New Oxford Companion to Music (1983)
Music Index (1949–   )

PHILOSOPHY
The Encyclopedia of Philosophy, ed. Paul Edwards (1972–   )
Philosopher's Index (1967–   )

PSYCHOLOGY
Encyclopedia of Psychology, ed. Raymond J. Corsini (1984)
Annual Review of Psychology (1950–   )

RELIGION
A Reader's Guide to the Great Religions, ed. Charles J. Adams
(1977)
Religious and Theological Abstracts (1958–   )

SCIENCE AND TECHNOLOGY
McGraw-Hill Encyclopedia of Science and Technology (1982)
Applied Science and Technology Index (1913–   )

SOCIAL AND POLITICAL SCIENCE
International Encyclopedia of the Social Sciences, ed. David L. Sills
(1977–79)
Social Sciences Citation Index (1969–   )

WOMEN'S STUDIES
Handbook of International Data on Women (1976)
Women's Studies Abstracts (1972–   )

**libr
36d**

When you need to draw on a particular fact—the population of
a country, an event in someone's life, the origin of an important
term, the source of a quotation—you can go to one of the following
sources:

GENERAL ENCYCLOPEDIAS
Encyclopaedia Britannica (1985)
Encyclopedia Americana (revised annually)

COMPILATIONS OF FACTS
Facts on File (1940–   )
The World Almanac and Book of Facts (1868–   )

ATLASES
National Geographic Atlas of the World (1981)
The Times Atlas of the World (1985)

DICTIONARIES (See p. 161 for college dictionaries.)
A Comprehensive Etymological Dictionary of the English Language,
by Ernest Klein (1979)

A New English Dictionary on Historical Principles (more commonly
known as *The Oxford English Dictionary*) (1888–1985)

BIOGRAPHY
Who's Who in the World (1976–   )
The McGraw-Hill Encyclopedia of World Biography (1973)

QUOTATIONS
Familiar Quotations, by John Bartlett and E. M. Beck (1980)
The Oxford Dictionary of Quotations (1980)

36e   Take full and careful notes from your reading.

A typical library book or journal will be available to you for a few
hours or days or weeks, depending on its importance to other borrow-
ers. When you try to get it again, you may find that it is on loan to
someone else, or has been sent to the bindery or even misplaced or
stolen. Thus you have to be sure to get everything you need from the
work on your first try, and your notes must be clear and full enough to
be your direct source when you write. Although it is always a good
idea to keep the work before you and recheck it for accurate quotation
and fair summary, you should assume that this will not be possible.
Your notes should contain all the information necessary for full citations (Chapter 37), and you should make sure your notes are error-free
before you let the book or article out of your hands.

libr
36e

Bibliography cards and content cards

The notes you take from your reading will serve two distinct purposes: to keep an accurate list of the works you have consulted and to record key information you have found in them. Sooner or later most researchers understand that these purposes demand different kinds of notecards. To compile a *bibliography* or list of works consulted, one card per entry is ideal; but *content* (or informational) notes may run through many cards. To avoid confusion use 3"×5" bibliography cards to identify the works you have consulted, and larger (usually 4"×6") content cards for quotations, summaries, and miscellaneous comments. Or, if you prefer, use cards of different colors.

You may choose to jot down ideas on sheets of paper rather than on cards. For quoting and summarizing published statements, however, cards are easier to keep track of and to rearrange as the organization of your essay takes shape.

Observe the following sample cards. (Note that once a separate bibliography card has been prepared, the researcher can give the briefest of references on a content card: *Wang, p. 4.*)

BIBLIOGRAPHY CARD:

HF 5001
C 635

Wang, N.T.
"United States and China : Business Beyond Trade - an Overview."
Columbia Journal of World Business
Spring 1986 : 3-11

(Surveys trends and prospects from a general perspective, offering suggestions to American entrepreneurs.)

CONTENT CARD:

Wang. p. 4   U.S. Chinese trade imbalance

"US exports account for about one-fifth of
China's total market and it (sic) ranks third
among all suppliers. US exports to China are,
however, only a little more than one percent
of the United States total, while US imports
from China are even less important except
in the case of a few categories such as textiles."

(Note opportunities for expansion!)

Form of notecards

The more systematic you are about note taking, the less likely you will
be to misquote, summarize unfairly, or supply inaccurate references.
Here are some tips about form:

1. Use cards of one uniform size or color for all bibliography notes,
   and cards or sheets of another uniform size or color for all your
   content notes. This will make for easy filing and reshuffling.

2. Write in ink. Penciled notes smudge when pressed against other notes.

3. Never put entries from different sources on one card or page,
   and never write on the reverse side. Otherwise you will probably lose track of some of your work.

libr 36e

4. Include the call number of any book or magazine you have found in the library. You never know when you may want to retrieve it for another look.

5. Quote exactly, including the punctuation marks in the original, and check each quotation as soon as you have copied it.

6. Use quotation marks only when you are actually quoting verbatim, and check to see that the marks begin and end exactly where they should. Use the dots known as ellipses (p. 348, 28o) to indicate where you have skipped some material within a quotation. If you have inserted any of your own words into the quoted passage, enclose them in brackets, as in the content card on page 453.

7. Be attentive to oddities of spelling and punctuation in quoted material. If, for instance, the original text omits a comma that you would have included, you can place a bracketed [*sic*], meaning *this is the way I found it,* at the questionable point in your notes; this will remind you not to improve the quotation illegitimately when reproducing it in your essay. But do not retain the [*sic*] in your paper unless it refers to an obvious blunder.

8. Supply page references not only for all quotations but for paraphrases and summaries as well.

9. Do not allow any ambiguities in your system of abbreviations. If two of your symbols mean the same thing, change one of them.

10. Distinguish between your own comments and those of the text you are summarizing. Use slashes, brackets, or your initials to show that the following remarks are yours, not those of the author.

11. When copying a passage that runs from one page to another, mark on your notecard where the first page ends: *"One other point might be noted, in view of the White / House concern over the military implications of lasers."* If you finally quote only a portion of the excerpt in your paper, you will want to know where it ended in the original.

12. Use a portion of the card or page to evaluate the material and to remind yourself of possibilities for further study. You might say, for example, *This looks useless—but reconsider chapter 13 if discussing astrology.*

13. Leave some space in the margin or at the top for an indexing symbol, so that you can easily keep related items together.

36f Summarize or paraphrase relevant passages that you do not intend to quote.

The most accurate way of noting what you have read is to quote it exactly (Chapter 28) or to photocopy it. But in your notes you can only quote a fraction of the important material you have seen, and once you have photocopied many pages, you still face the task of drawing from them what is essential to your own purpose. Here is where *summary,* or brief restatement, and *paraphrase,* or more ample restatement, can come to your aid. Remember that summary and paraphrase require the same accurate documentation that quotation does. You must cite the source of someone else's ideas, even when you express those ideas in your own words (see p. 458, 37a).

A **summary** of a text concisely presents the author's key ideas, omitting examples and descriptive detail. Insofar as possible you should use your own language, though some repetition of the author's terms may be inevitable. The knack of efficient summary is to strip away everything but the essential content.

ORIGINAL TEXT:
The modern world began on 29 May 1919 when photographs of a solar eclipse, taken on the island of Principe off West Africa and at Sobral in Brazil, confirmed the truth of a new theory of the universe. It had been apparent for half a century that the Newtonian cosmology, based upon the straight lines of Euclidean geometry and Galileo's notions of absolute time, was in need of serious modifications. It had stood for more than two hundred years. It was the framework within which the European Enlightenment, the Industrial Revolution, and the vast expansion of human knowledge, freedom and prosperity which characterized the nineteenth century, had taken place. But increasingly powerful telescopes were revealing anomalies. In particular, the motions of the planet

Mercury deviated by forty-three seconds of arc a century from its predictable behaviour under Newtonian laws of physics. Why?

In 1905, a twenty-six-year-old German Jew, Albert Einstein, then working in the Swiss patent office in Berne, had published a paper, "On the electrodynamics of moving bodies," which became known as the Special Theory of Relativity. Einstein's observations on the way in which, in certain circumstances, lengths appeared to contract and clocks to slow down, are analogous to the effects of perspective in painting. In fact the discovery that space and time are relative rather than absolute is comparable, in its effect on our perception of the world, to the first use of perspective in art, which occurred in Greece in the two decades c. 500–480 B.C.

The originality of Einstein, amounting to a form of genius, and the curious elegance of his lines of argument, which colleagues compared to a kind of art, aroused growing, world-wide interest. In 1907 he published a demonstration that all mass has energy, encapsulated in the equation $E=mc^2$, which a later age saw as the starting point in the race for the A-bomb. Not even the onset of the European war prevented scientists from following his quest for an all-embracing General Theory of Relativity which would cover gravitational fields and provide a comprehensive revision of Newtonian physics. In 1915 news reached London that he had done it. The following spring, as the British were preparing their vast and catastrophic offensive on the Somme, the key paper was smuggled through the Netherlands and reached Cambridge, where it was received by Arthur Eddington, Professor of Astronomy and Secretary of the Royal Astronomical Society.

—PAUL JOHNSON, *Modern Times:*
The World from the Twenties to the Eighties

SUMMARY:

Johnson dates "the modern world" from the solar eclipse observations of 29 May 1919, confirming Albert Einstein's General Theory of Relativity. The world had already shown great interest in Einstein after his 1905 publication of the Special Theory of Relativity, indicating that space and time are relative categories, and his 1907 demonstration that mass possesses energy ($E=mc^2$). The General Theory, embracing gravitational fields, completed the overthrow of Newtonian physics, based in its turn on Euclid's geometry and Galileo's absolute time. The Einsteinian revolution affected our perception of the world as radically as the ancient Greek discovery of perspective in art.

A **paraphrase** is a running restatement of the original passage in your own words. You should follow the order of the text and include important detail. Since a paraphrase is closer to the original than a summary, you must be careful not to repeat the author's wording without quotation marks; that practice could lead you into accidental **plagiarism** (p. 459, 37a), or the presentation of someone else's words (or ideas) as your own.

PARAPHRASE:

Johnson dates "the modern world" from the 29 May 1919 observations of a solar eclipse, taken in Africa and Brazil, confirming Einsteinian cosmology. For fifty years the existing Newtonian conception, based on Euclid's geometry and Galileo's absolute time, had been in trouble. It had been the set of assumptions behind the Enlightenment, the Industrial Revolution, and nineteenth-century progress in learning, democracy, and wealth, but it had been placed in doubt by unaccountable telescopic data such as the deviated motion of Mercury.

The new universe began to take shape with Albert Einstein's 1905 paper, "On the electrodynamics of moving bodies" (the Special Theory of Relativity), showing how in some conditions time and space are variable. This discovery affected our way of seeing the world as profoundly as did the Greeks' use of artistic perspective in the fifth century B.C.

In 1907 Einstein proposed that all mass has energy ($E=mc^2$), an idea later seen as having begun the race to develop the atomic bomb. Not even the outbreak of World War I could stop scientists from participating in his search for a General Theory of Relativity that would include gravitational fields. Word of Einstein's having completed that theory arrived in London in 1915, and in 1916, at the height of the awful war, the key paper reached Arthur Eddington, Secretary of the Royal Astronomical Society, in Cambridge.

libr
36f

37 Documenting Sources

DOCUMENT A SOURCE IF . . .

you quote the passage verbatim
you paraphrase the passage
you summarize the passage
you include obscure information
you borrow someone else's opinion

37a Learn where documentation is called for.

If you have done research for a paper, there are several reasons why you should cite your sources, using a standard form of documentation. You want credit for your efforts, and your documentation will help to show a reader that your ideas are consistent with facts and expert judgments that have already appeared in print. In some cases you may even want to pose a challenge to received views, showing that you know what those views are and where they can be found. And documentation is also a courtesy to your readers, who ought to be able to check your sources either to see if you have used them responsibly or to pursue an interest in your topic.

Avoiding plagiarism

A further reason for providing documentation is to avoid **plagiarism**—the serious ethical violation of presenting other people's words or ideas as your own. Plagiarism does tempt some student writers who feel too rushed or insecure to arrive at their own conclusions. Yet systematic dishonesty is only part of the problem. For every student who buys a term paper or copies a whole article without acknowledgment, there are dozens who indulge in "little" ethical lapses through thoughtlessness, haste, or a momentary sense of opportunity. Though nearly all of their work is original, they too are plagiarists—just as someone who robs a bank of $2.39 is a bank robber.

Unlike the robber, however, some plagiarists fail to realize what they have done wrong. Students who once copied encyclopedia articles to satisfy school assignments may never have learned the necessity of using quotation marks and citing sources. Others may think that by *paraphrasing* a quotation or *summarizing* an idea (p. 455, 36f)—that is, by putting it into their own words—they have turned it into public property. Others acknowledge the source of their idea but fail to indicate that they have borrowed words as well as thoughts. And others plagiarize through sloppy note taking (p. 451, 36e). Since their notes do not distinguish adequately between personal observations and the content of a consulted book or article, their papers repeat the oversight. And finally, some students blunder into plagiarism by failing to recognize the difference between fact and opinion. They may think, for example, that a famous critic's opinion about a piece of literature is so authoritative that it belongs to the realm of common facts—and so they paraphrase it without acknowledgment. All these errors are understandable, but none of them constitutes a good excuse for plagiarism.

What to acknowledge

Consider the following source and three ways that a student might be tempted to make use of it.

doc
37a

SOURCE:
The joker in the European pack was Italy. For a time hopes were entertained of her as a force against Germany, but these disappeared under

Mussolini. In 1935 Italy made a belated attempt to participate in the scramble for Africa by invading Ethiopia. It was clearly a breach of the covenant of the League of Nations for one of its members to attack another. France and Great Britain, as great powers, Mediterranean powers, and African colonial powers, were bound to take the lead against Italy at the league. But they did so feebly and half-heartedly because they did not want to alienate a possible ally against Germany. The result was the worst possible: the league failed to check aggression, Ethiopia lost her independence, and Italy was alienated after all.

—J.M. ROBERTS, *History of the World*

VERSION A:

Italy, one might say, was the joker in the European
deck. When she invaded Ethiopia, it was clearly a
breach of the covenant of the League of Nations; yet
the efforts of England and France to take the lead
against her were feeble and halfhearted. It appears
that those great powers had no wish to alienate a possible ally against Hitler's rearmed Germany.

Comment: Clearly plagiarism. Although the facts cited are public knowledge, the stolen phrases are not. Note that the writer's interweaving of his own words with the source does *not* make him innocent of plagiarism.

VERSION B:

Italy was the joker in the European deck. Under Mussolini in 1935, she made a belated attempt to participate in the scramble for Africa by invading Ethiopia.
As J.M. Roberts points out, this violated the covenant
of the League of Nations (Roberts 845). But France
and Britain, not wanting to alienate a possible ally
against Germany, put up only feeble and halfhearted
opposition to the Ethiopian adventure. The outcome,
as Roberts observes, was "the worst possible: the
league failed to check aggression, Ethiopia lost her
independence, and Italy was eliminated after all"
(Roberts 845).

**doc
37a**

Comment: Still plagiarism. The two correct citations of Roberts serve as a kind of alibi for the appropriating of other, unacknowledged phrases.

VERSION C:

```
Much has been written about German rearmament and mil-
itarism in the period 1933-1939. But Germany's domi-
nance in Europe was by no means a foregone conclusion.
The fact is that the balance of power might have been
tipped against Hitler if one or two things had turned
out differently. Take Italy's gravitation toward an
alliance with Germany, for example. That alliance
seemed so very far from inevitable that Britain and
France actually muted their criticism of the Ethiopian
invasion in the hope of remaining friends with Italy.
They opposed the Italians in the League of Nations, as
J.M. Roberts observes, "feebly and half-heartedly be-
cause they did not want to alienate a possible ally
against Germany" (Roberts 845). Suppose Italy,
France, and Britain had retained a certain common in-
terest. Would Hitler have been able to get away with
his remarkable bluffing and bullying in the later
thirties?
```

Comment: No plagiarism. The writer has been influenced by the public facts mentioned by Roberts, but he has not tried to pass off Roberts's conclusions as his own. The one clear borrowing is properly acknowledged.

There *is* room for disagreement about what to acknowledge; but precisely because this is so, you ought to make your documentation relatively ample. Provide citations for all direct quotations and paraphrases, borrowed ideas, and facts that do not belong to general knowledge.

Ask yourself, in doubtful cases, whether the point you are borrowing is an opinion or a fact. Opinions are by definition ideas that are not yet taken for granted; document them. As for facts, do not bother to document those that could be found in any commonly used source—for example, the fact that World War II ended in 1945. But give references for less accessible facts, such as the numbers of operational submarines that Nazi Germany still possessed at the end of the war. The harder it would be for readers to come across your fact through their own efforts, the more surely you need to document it.

If you are quoting, paraphrasing, or making an **allusion** to statements or literary passages that are not generally familiar, cite the source. A phrase from Lincoln's Gettysburg Address could get by with-

**doc
37a**

out a citation, but a remark made in a presidential news conference
could not.

DO NOT DOCUMENT	DOCUMENT
the population of China	the Chinese balance of payments in 1987
the existence of a disease syndrome called AIDS	a possible connection between AIDS and the virus that carries cat leukemia
the fact that Dickens visited America	the supposed effect of Dickens's American visit on his subsequently written novels
the fact that huge sums are wagered illegally on professional football games	an alleged "fix" of a certain football game
a line from a nursery rhyme	a line from a poem by Yeats

37b Observe the differences between parenthetic citation form and footnote/endnote form.

In your reading you will encounter many documentation styles, but
every version will belong to one of two general schemes. In *parenthetic
citation form,* citations within parentheses in the main text are keyed
to a list of "Works Cited" or "References" appearing at the end of the
paper, article, chapter, or book. In *footnote/endnote form,* raised numbers in the main text—usually at the ends of sentences—are keyed to
notes appearing either at the foot of the page (**footnotes**) or at the end
of the whole text (**endnotes**). Both forms allow for **substantive** or
bibliographic notes (p. 489, 37f) that make comments or mention
further references.

**doc
37b**

PARENTHETIC CITATION FORM	FOOTNOTE/ENDNOTE FORM
No note numbers are used (except for supplementary notes.)	Raised numbers appear in text.

PARENTHETIC CITATION FORM	FOOTNOTE/ENDNOTE FORM
No notes are used to cite works.	Notes appearing at foot of page or at end of text give citations corresponding to note numbers in text.
All references are made through parenthetic citations within text.	Parenthetic citations within text are used only for "subsequent references" to frequently cited works.
Substantive and bibliographic notes, if any, appear after main text but before reference list.	Substantive and bibliographic notes, if any, are integrated into footnotes or endnotes.
A reference list, identifying only works cited or consulted, appears at the end. The listed works match the parenthetic citations in the text.	A bibliography, identifying both works cited and works consulted, may appear after all the notes.

Until recently, parenthetic citation form has generally prevailed in the physical and social sciences and footnote/endnote form in the humanities. Today, however, parenthetic citation form is gaining ground in the humanities as well; it is recommended, for example, by the Modern Language Association. But if your instructor prefers footnote/endnote form, you should know how it works; see page 483, 37e.

In some disciplines—for example, mathematics, chemistry, physics, biology, and engineering—the textual citations are Arabic numerals that correspond to numbered items in the reference list. A numbered item may mention any number of works.

doc
37b

SENTENCE IN TEXT:
It appears that female choice is frequently involved in the evolution of the conspicuous acoustic signals that precede mating (2, 3).

ITEMS IN REFERENCE LIST:
2. L. Fairchild, *Science 212,* 950 (1981); R. D. Howard, *Evolution 32,* 850 (1978); M. J. Ryan, *Science 209,* 523 (1980).

3. R. D. Alexander, in *Insects, Science, and Society,* D. Pimentel, Ed. (Academic Press, New York, 1975), p. 35; P. D. Bell, *Can. J. Zool. 58,* 1861 (1980); W. Cade, *Science 190,* 1312 (1975); in *Sexual Selection and Reproductive Competition in Insects,* M. S. Blum and N. A. Blum, Eds. (Academic Press, New York, 1979); A. V. Popov and V. F. Shuvalov, *J. Comp. Physiol. 119,* 111 (1977); S. M. Ulagaraj and T. J. Walker, *Science 182,* 1278 (1973).

        —CHRISTINE R. B. BOAKE and ROBERT R. CAPRANICA,
"Aggressive Signal in 'Courtship' Chirps of a Gregarious Cricket"

In other disciplines—for example, botany, geology, zoology, economics, psychology, and sociology—the parenthetic citations include the author(s) and date of publication *(Comstock & Fisher, 1975),* and the reference list is ordered alphabetically.

If you are writing for publication in any field, look at a relevant journal and adopt its conventions. You can also consult one of the following style manuals if it corresponds to your subject matter.

BIOLOGY:
Council of Biology Editors Style Manual: A Guide for Authors, Editors, and Publishers in the Biological Sciences (1983)

BUSINESS:
Report Writing for Business, by Raymond V. Lesikar (1986)

CHEMISTRY:
Handbook for Authors of Papers in American Chemical Society Publications (1978)

EDUCATION:
NEA Style Manual for Writers and Editors (1974)

doc
37b

GEOLOGY:
Guide to Authors: A Guide for the Preparation of Geological Maps and Reports, by Robert G. Blackadar et al. (1980)

HISTORY:
Historical Journals: A Handbook for Writers and Reviewers, by Dale R. Steiner (1981)

JOURNALISM:
The UPI Stylebook: A Handbook for Writers and Editors (1977)

LAW:
A Uniform System of Citation, ed. Harvard Law Review Association (1986)

LIBRARY SCIENCE:
A Style Manual for Citing Microform and Nonprint Media, by Eugene B. Fleisher (1978)

LINGUISTICS:
LSA Bulletin, Dec. issue, annually

MATHEMATICS:
A Manual for Authors of Mathematical Papers, ed. American Mathematical Society (1984)

MEDICINE:
Manual for Authors and Editors: Editorial Style and Manuscript Preparation, by William R. Barclay et al. (1981)

PHYSICS:
Style Manual for Guidance in the Preparation of Papers, ed. Publication Board, American Institute of Physics (1978)

37c Learn how to present a reference list according to MLA or APA style.

Most research papers for composition courses are now written in parenthetic citation form, following the style of either the Modern Language Association **(MLA style)** or the American Psychological Association **(APA style).** We present the essential features of both styles here and in 37d. For further detail, see Joseph Gibaldi and Walter S. Achtert, *MLA Handbook for Writers of Research Papers* (3rd ed., 1988) and *Publication Manual of the American Psychological Association* (3rd ed., 1983).

doc
37c

For an extended sample of the MLA style, see the sample research paper on pages 492–507 below. To get a quick idea of the differences between MLA and APA reference lists, compare the MLA "Works Cited" on page 506 with the APA "References" on page 508.

Place your "Works Cited" or "References" after your main text and any substantive or bibliographic notes (p. 489, 37f). Start on a new page, consecutively numbered with the foregoing ones. Space your list like the relevant sample below (either p. 506 or p. 508).

Order of entries

Order your reference list alphabetically by authors' last names or, when no author appears, by the first significant word of the title (omitting *A, An,* and *The*). If the author is an institution—for example, SRI International—list it by the first letter in the corporate name's first significant word (in this case *S*).

If you are citing more than one work by a given author, note that:

1. In MLA style, follow the alphabetical order of that author's *titles.* In APA style, follow the order of that author's *dates of publication* (earliest first).

2. If a cited author is also the coauthor of another cited work, put the single-author work first.

3. If a cited author has different coauthors for two cited works, place the works according to the alphabetical order of the coauthors' last names.

4. In APA style, if you are citing two works showing the same author(s) and date, follow the alphabetical order of the titles and add lowercase letters to the dates:

   Mauldin, C., & Valle, R. (1988a). Apple-Growing . . .
   Mauldin, C., & Valle, R. (1988b). Bee-Keeping . . .

**doc
37c**

Order within entries

In MLA style, present information (where relevant) within each entry in the following order. The arrows indicate how that order varies in APA style.

BOOKS	ARTICLES
1. Author's name **APA**	1. Author's name **APA**
2. Title of part of book	2. Title of article
3. Title of book	3. Name of periodical
4. Name of editor, translator, or compiler	4. Series number or name
5. Edition used	5. Volume number
6. Number of volumes	6. Date of publication
7. Name of series	7. Page numbers
8. Place of publication, shortened name of publisher, date of publication	
9. Page numbers	

Here are sample entries covering typical kinds of works that might appear in your reference list.

Books

A BOOK BY A SINGLE AUTHOR:

MLA   Gay, Peter. <u>Freud: A Life for Our Time</u>. New
           York: Norton, 1988.

APA   Gay, P. (1988). <u>Freud: A life for our time</u>.
           New York: Norton.

Note that MLA uses full first names while APA uses initials, and note the different conventions for capitalization of titles. Observe also that APA leaves one space, not two, after a period.

TWO OR MORE BOOKS BY THE SAME AUTHOR:

MLA   Michaels, Leonard. <u>I Would Have Saved Them
           If I Could</u>. New York: Farrar, 1975.

           ---. <u>The Men's Club</u>. New York: Farrar,
           1981.

**doc
37c**

APA   Michaels, L. (1975). <u>I would have saved them</u>
            <u>if I could</u>. New York: Farrar, Straus & Gi-
            roux.

            Michaels, L. (1981). <u>The men's club</u>. New
            York: Farrar, Straus & Giroux.

A BOOK BY TWO AUTHORS:
MLA   Liehm, Mira, and Antonin J. Liehm. <u>The Most</u>
            <u>Important Art: Soviet and Eastern Euro-</u>
            <u>pean Film after 1945</u>. Berkeley: U of
            California P, 1977.

APA   Liehm, M., & Liehm, A. J. (1977). <u>The most</u>
            <u>important art: Soviet and eastern European</u>
            <u>film after 1945</u>. Berkeley: University of
            California Press.

A BOOK BY THREE AUTHORS:
MLA   Burns, James MacGregor, J. W. Peltason, and
            Thomas E. Cronin. <u>Government by the</u>
            <u>People</u>. 12th ed. Englewood Cliffs:
            Prentice-Hall, 1984.

APA   Burns, J. M., Peltason, J. W., & Cronin, T.
            E. (1984). <u>Government by the people</u>.
            (12th ed.). Englewood Cliffs, NJ: Pren-
            tice-Hall.

A BOOK BY MORE THAN THREE AUTHORS:
MLA   Lauer, Janice, M., et al. <u>Four Worlds of</u>

doc
37c

```
Writing.  2nd ed.  New York: Harper,
1985.
```

APA
```
Lauer, J. M., Montague, G., Lunsford, A., &
Emig, J. (1985). Four worlds of writing.
(2nd ed.). New York: Harper & Row.
```

Observe that APA requires that all authors, no matter how many, be named. Compare the MLA's preference for *et al.* (Latin 'and others').

A BOOK BY A CORPORATE AUTHOR:

MLA
```
American Society of Hospital Pharmacists.
    Consumer Drug Digest.  New York: Facts
    on File, 1982.
```

APA
```
American Society of Hospital Pharmacists.
    (1982). Consumer drug digest. New York:
    Facts on File.
```

AN ANONYMOUS BOOK:

MLA
```
Chicago Manual of Style.  13th ed.  Chicago:
    U of Chicago P, 1982.
```

APA
```
Chicago manual of style. (1982). (13th ed.).
    Chicago: University of Chicago Press.
```

A WORK IN AN ANTHOLOGY:

MLA
```
Herbert, George.  "The Pulley."  The Bedford
    Introduction to Literature.  Ed. Michael
    Meyer.  New York: St. Martin's, 1987:
    790-91.
```

doc
37c

APA   Herbert, G. (1987). The pulley. In M. Meyer
            (Ed.), The Bedford introduction to liter-
            ature (pp. 790–791). New York: St. Mar-
            tin's.

If you are citing more than one work from an anthology, provide an entry for the anthology itself, and cite
it along with the references to the separate works, as
follows. Note that APA uses no quotation marks
around the titles of items within an anthology.

THE ANTHOLOGY ITSELF:

MLA   Meyer, Michael, ed. The Bedford Introduction
            to Literature. New York: St. Martin's,
            1987.

APA   Meyer, M. (Ed.). (1987). The Bedford intro-
            duction to literature. New York: St. Mar-
            tin's.

WORK FROM A COLLECTION BY ONE AUTHOR:

MLA   Mill, John Stuart. On Liberty. Three Es-
            says: On Liberty, Representative Gov-
            ernment, The Subjection of Women. New
            York: Oxford UP, 1975. 1–141.

APA   Mill, J. S. (1975). On liberty. In Three es-
            says: On liberty, Representative govern-
            ment, The subjection of women (pp. 1–
            141). New York: Oxford University Press.
            (Original work published 1859).

THE EDITED WORK OF AN AUTHOR:

MLA   Plato. The Collected Dialogues of Plato: In-
            cluding the Letters. Ed. Edith Hamilton
            and Huntington Cairns. Princeton:
            Princeton UP, 1961.

APA   Plato. (1961). The collected dialogues of
            Plato: Including the letters. (E. Hamil-
            ton & H. Cairns, Eds.). Princeton:
            Princeton University Press.

A BOOK EDITED BY TWO OR THREE PEOPLE:

MLA   White, George Abbott, and Charles Newman,
            eds. Literature in Revolution. New
            York: Holt, 1972.

APA   White, G. A., & Newman, C. (Eds.). (1972).
            Literature in revolution. New York: Holt.

A BOOK EDITED BY MORE THAN THREE PEOPLE.

MLA   Kermode, Frank, et al., eds. The Oxford An-
            thology of English Literature. 2 vols.
            New York: Oxford UP, 1973.

APA   Kermode, F., Hollander, J., Bloom, H.,
            Price, M., Trapp, J. B., & Trilling, L.
            (Eds.). 1973. The Oxford anthology of En-
            glish literature. (Vols. 1-2). New York:
            Oxford University Press.

doc
37c

A TRANSLATION:

MLA   Soseki, Natsume. <u>The Miner</u>. Trans. Jay Rubin. Stanford: Stanford UP, 1988.

APA   Soseki, N. (1988). <u>The miner</u>. (J. Rubin, Trans.). Stanford: Stanford University Press.

A REPUBLISHED BOOK:

MLA   Conroy, Frank. <u>Stop-time</u>. 1967. New York: Penguin, 1977.

APA   Conroy, F. (1977). <u>Stop-time</u>. New York: Penguin. (Original work published 1967).

Articles in journals, magazines, and newspapers

AN ARTICLE IN A JOURNAL WITH CONTINUOUS PAGINATION:

MLA   Cooper, Arnold M. "Psychoanalysis at One Hundred: Beginnings of Maturity." <u>Journal of the American Psychoanalytic Association</u> 32 (1984): 245–67.

APA   Cooper, A. M. (1984). Psychoanalysis at one hundred: Beginnings of maturity. <u>Journal of the American Psychoanalytic Association</u>, <u>32</u>, 245–267.

**doc
37c**

AN ARTICLE IN A JOURNAL THAT DOES NOT IDENTIFY THE EXACT DATE OF EACH ISSUE:

MLA   Langford, Larry L. "How Many Children Had Molly Bloom? Sons and Lovers in <u>Ulys-</u>

ses." Literature and Psychology 34.2
(1988): 27–40.

APA   Langford, L. L. (1988). How many children
had Molly Bloom? Sons and lovers in Ulysses. Literature and Psychology, 34 (2),
27–40.

**AN ARTICLE IN A MAGAZINE WITH SEPARATE PAGINATION
FOR EACH ISSUE:**

MLA   Lowenstein, Frank. "Mastering Winter." Sierra, Jan.-Feb. 1988: 124–28.

APA   Lowenstein, F. (1988, January-February).
Mastering winter. Sierra, pp. 124–128.

A REVIEW:

MLA   Singer, Brett. "Husbands at Bay." Rev. of
Only Children, by Rafael Yglesias. New
York Times Book Review 17 July 1988:
19.

APA   Singer, B. (1988, July 17). Husbands at bay.
[Review of Only children, by R. Ygle-
sias]. New York Times Book Review, p. 19.

AN UNSIGNED MAGAZINE ARTICLE:

MLA   "Hard-Sell Shopping Carts." Newsweek 18 July
1988: 46.

APA   Hard-sell shopping carts. (1988, July 18).
Newsweek, p. 46.

doc
37c

A SIGNED NEWSPAPER ARTICLE:

MLA   Kershner, Vlae. "Prime Rate Raised to 9.5%."

San Francisco Chronicle 15 July 1988,

five-star ed.: A1+.

APA   Kershner, V. (1988, July 15) Prime rate

raised to 9.5%. San Francisco Chronicle,

sec. A, pp. 1, 24.

AN UNSIGNED NEWSPAPER ARTICLE OR EDITORIAL:

MLA   "Insider Trading: A Matter of Trust." New

York Times 23 Nov. 1986, national ed.:

E5.

APA   Insider trading: A matter of trust. (1986,

November 23). New York Times, sec. E, p.

5.

Other written works

AN ENCYCLOPEDIA ENTRY:

MLA   L[ustig], L[awrence] K. "Alluvial Fans."

Encyclopaedia Britannica: Macropaedia.

1985.

doc 37c

The author's initials appear at the end of the entry; they are identified elsewhere. Note that volume and page numbers are unnecessary when items appear in alphabetical order. But since the *Britannica* from 1974 onward has three sets of contents, the note should indicate which one is intended—in this case the "Macropaedia."

APA   L[ustig], L. K. (1985). Alluvial fans. <u>Ency-</u>
            <u>clopaedia Britannica: Macropaedia</u>.

A PAMPHLET OR MANUAL:

MLA   Wiggins, Robert R., and Steve Brecher, with
            William P. Steinberg. <u>Suitcase User's</u>
            <u>Guide</u>. Sunnyvale: Software Supply,
            1987.

APA   Wiggins, R. R., & Brecher, S., with Stein-
            berg, W. P. (1987). <u>Suitcase User's</u>
            <u>Guide</u>. Sunnyvale, CA: Software Supply.

A DISSERTATION:

MLA   Boudin, Henry Morton. "The Ripple Effect in
            Classroom Management." Diss. U of
            Michigan, 1970.

APA   Boudin, H. M. (1970). <u>The ripple effect in</u>
            <u>classroom management</u>. Unpublished doctor-
            al dissertaton, University of Michigan,
            Ann Arbor.

A PUBLIC DOCUMENT:

MLA   United States Dept. of Agriculture. "Ship-
            ments and Unloads of Certain Fruits and
            Vegetables, 1918–1923." <u>Statistical</u>
            <u>Bulletin</u> 7 (Apr. 1925).

**doc
37c**

APA   United States Dept. of Agriculture. (1925,
             April). Shipments and unloads of certain
             fruits and vegetables, 1918–1923. Statis-
             tical Bulletin, 7.

A PUBLISHED LETTER:

MLA   McFann, Winfried S. Letter. Popular Photog-
             raphy Aug. 1988: 8.

APA   McFann, W. (1988, August). [Letter to the
             editor]. Popular Photography, p. 8.

AN UNPUBLISHED LETTER:

MLA   Graff, Gerald. Letter to the author. 18
             Jan. 1989.

APA   Graff, G. (1989, January 18). [Letter to the
             author].

Nonwritten works

A THEATRICAL PERFORMANCE:

MLA   Broadway Bound. By Neil Simon. Dir. Gene
             Saks. With Joan Rivers. Broadhurst
             Theatre, New York. 10 July 1988.

doc
37c

APA   Saks, G. (Director). (1988, July 10). Broad-
             way bound. Broadhurst Theatre, New York
             City.

A FILM:

MLA   A Handful of Dust. Dir. Charles Sturridge.
With Anjelica Huston. New Line Cinema,
1988.

APA   Sturridge, C. (Director). (1988). A handful
of dust. New Line Cinema.

A RADIO OR TELEVISION PROGRAM:

MLA   Knocking on Armageddon's Door. Prod. and
dir. Torv Carlsen and John R. Magnus.
PBS. 19 July 1988.

APA   Carlsen, T., & Magnus, J. R. (Producer & Director). (1988, July 19). Knocking on Armageddon's door. PBS.

A RECORDING:

MLA   Beethoven, Ludwig van. Symphony no. 8 in F,
op. 93. Cond. Pierre Monteux. Vienna
Philharmonic Orch. Decca, STS 15238,
1964.

MLA requires that names of musical works be under-
lined except when (as here) the work is identified by
its form, number, and key rather than by a title.

APA   [No form specified]

**doc
37c**

A LECTURE:

MLA   Hirsch, E. D., Jr. "Frontiers of Critical
Theory." Wyoming Conference on Freshman

```
                    and Sophomore English, U of Wyoming.
                    Laramie, 9 July 1979.
```

APA   Hirsch, E. D., Jr. (1979, July). <u>Frontiers
             <u>of critical theory</u>. Paper presented at
             the Wyoming Conference on Freshman and
             Sophomore English, University of Wyoming,
             Laramie.

Note that APA omits the precise day of a lecture.

AN INTERVIEW:
MLA   Collier, Peter, and David Horowitz. Personal
             interview. 5 Nov. 1988.

APA   Collier, P., & Horowitz, D. (1988, November
             5). [Interview with the author].

COMPUTER SOFTWARE:
MLA   <u>Word</u>. Computer Software. Microsoft, 1988.
             Macintosh, Version 4.0, disk.

APA   <u>Word</u>. (1988). [Computer program]. Microsoft,
             Macintosh, Version 4.0.

---

doc
37d
37d   Learn how to present parenthetic citations according to MLA or APA style.

The idea behind all parenthetic citations is to give the minimum of
information that will send a reader to the correct item in the reference
list (37c) and, where applicable, to the cited portion of the work. As you
might expect, MLA citations rely on authors' *names* and, if necessary

for clarity, the *titles* of their works, whereas APA citations rely on *names* and *dates*.

MLA parenthetic citations

If you are referring to a whole work and if the author's name appears in your sentence, MLA does not require you to supply any further information:

```
Cooper's presidential address struck a gloomy note.
```

But the same sentence would require a parenthetic page reference— without repeating the author's name—if you had in mind only part of the item:

```
Cooper's presidential address struck a gloomy note

(249-52).
```

Where the author's name does not appear in your sentence, supply it in the citation:

```
One prominent authority has expressed serious doubt

about the current health of the profession (Cooper

249-52).
```

For an indented quotation (p. 343, 28h), place your end-punctuation before rather than after the parenthesis.

The following sample MLA citations cover a variety of features in the cited works:

A MULTIVOLUME WORK:
```
In "An Apology for Poetry," Sidney shows a healthy

distrust of what he calls "that honey-flowing matron

Eloquence" (Abrams et al. 1:503).
```

A WORK LISTED BY TITLE:
```
The word "Saint" is disregarded in the alphabetizing

of saints' names (Chicago Manual 18.103).
```

**doc
37d**

Note the shortened title; compare page 469 above. No edition number is needed, since the reference list contains only one entry under this name. Note, too, the citing of a section, rather than a page, of a reference work thus ordered.

A WORK BY A CORPORATE AUTHOR:

```
The American Society of Hospital Pharmacists considers
methicillin "particularly useful" in treating hospital-
acquired infections (89).
```

"Corporate" names are usually too long to be inserted into a parenthetic citation without distracting the reader. Make an effort to get the name into the main part of your sentence. Here the remark about methicillin is attributed to page 89 of the book in the reference list named under *American Society of Hospital Pharmacists.*

TWO OR MORE WORKS BY THE SAME AUTHOR:

```
"I feel you're feeling anger," says Kramer after his
wife has clobbered him with an iron pot (Michaels,
Men's Club 172).
```

The title of the work is included in the citation when two or more works by the same author appear in the reference list (p. 467).

AN INDIRECT SOURCE:

```
Writing in Temps Modernes in 1957, Woroszylski ex-
pressed surprise at "how much political nonsense we
allowed ourselves to be talked into" (qtd. in Liehm
and Liehm 116).
```

doc
37d

If you have no access to the original text, use *qtd. in* to show that your source for the quotation is another work.

A CLASSIC VERSE PLAY OR POEM:

"I prithee, daughter," begs Lear, "do not make me mad"

(II.iv.212).

> Cite acts, scenes, and lines instead of pages. The capital and lowercase Roman numerals here help to distinguish the act and scene from the line number; however, *2.4.212* would also be acceptable.

MORE THAN ONE WORK IN A CITATION:

The standard view of "scientific method" has come under

concentrated attack in recent years (Kuhn; Lakatos;

Laudan).

> But if your parenthetic citation becomes too cumbersome, consider replacing it with a bibliographic note (37f).

APA parenthetic citations

In a first APA citation, include the date of publication:

Cooper (1984) struck a gloomy note in his address.

> Observe that in APA style the parenthetic date comes immediately after the author's name. In this example the whole work is being cited. If, on the other hand, you wanted to cite a specific passage, you would put the page numbers into a separate, later, parenthesis:

Bercovitch (1986) mentions a growing sense among crit-

ics that race, class, and gender are essential catego-

ries of textual analysis (p. viii).

> The following examples show further APA rules in action:

"I feel you're feeling anger," says Kramer after his

**doc
37d**

```
wife has clobbered him with an iron pot (Michaels, 1981,
p. 172).
```

Even though the reference list may contain more than one work by Michaels, the date alone suffices to show which one is meant.

```
Karsh (1987b) has proposed a rival explanation.
```

The date-plus-letter shows which work is meant among two or more by the same author in the same year.

```
Preston and Martini (1988) examined the backgrounds of
234 schizophrenic patients.
```

If there are two authors, always mention both.

```
A study of 234 patients produced no support for the
idea that schizophrenia is caused by unusual family
tensions (Preston & Martini, 1967).
```

Note the use of the ampersand ("&") within the parenthetic citation but not in the main sentence (previous example).

```
Lauer, Montague, Lunsford, and Emig (1985) emphasize
that writers must make their evaluative standards
known to their readers (p. 200).
```

**doc
37d**

```
Writers must make their evaluative standards known to
their readers (Lauer, Montague, Lunsford, & Emig, 1985,
p. 200).
```

In a first citation, APA requires that all coauthors, no matter how many, be mentioned.

```
Lauer et al. (1985) acknowledge their debt to Kinneavy
(1971) for key rhetorical terms.
```

```
The authors acknowledge their debt to Kinneavy (1971)
for key rhetorical terms (Lauer et al., 1985, p. 21).
```

> Both of these sentences illustrate a "subsequent citation"; that is, the four coauthors have already been named. Consequently, the *et al.* ("and others") formula can now be used to save space. Note also how each of these sentences efficiently cites *two* items from the writer's reference list.

```
According to Nietzsche, Greek tragedy arose "out of
the spirit of music" (cited in Merquior, p. 83).
```

This sentence shows how to cite a quotation from an indirect source.

37e   Observe the features of "alternative MLA" footnote/endnote style.

If your instructor prefers the "alternative MLA" style of citation, you will use either **footnotes** or **endnotes** instead of parenthetic citations and a reference list. A footnote appears at the bottom of the page on which its corresponding number appears within the text; see page 485 for a sample of text and notes together. Endnotes, by contrast, appear in sequence at the end of the paper, article, chapter, or book.

    Wherever you decide to put your notes, you should follow these rules for handling the note numbers within your text:

1. Number all the notes consecutively (1, 2, 3, . . .).

2. Elevate the note numbers slightly, as here.[8]

3. Place the numbers after, not before, the quotations or other information being cited: not x As Rosenhan says,[11] "the evidence is simply not compelling," but As Rosenhan says, "the evidence is simply not compelling."[11]

doc
37e

4. Place the numbers after all punctuation except a dash; even parentheses, colons, and semicolons should precede note numbers.

Endnotes versus footnotes

Type endnotes on a new page after your main text, but before a bibliography if you are supplying one. Here is the standard form for endnotes.

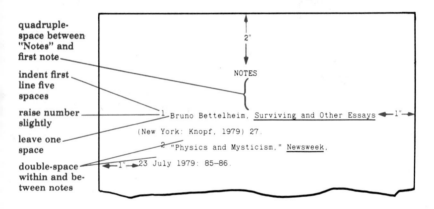

quadruple-space between "Notes" and first note

indent first line five spaces

raise number slightly

leave one space

double-space within and between notes

2"

NOTES

1 Bruno Bettelheim, Surviving and Other Essays ◄—1"—►

(New York: Knopf, 1979) 27.

2 "Physics and Mysticism," Newsweek,

◄—1"—►23 July 1979: 85–86.

when only 1" remains at the bottom of the page, continue notes on the following page

Handle footnotes just like endnotes except for these differences:

1. On each page where you will have notes, stop your main text high enough to leave room for the notes.

2. Quadruple-space between the end of the text and the first note on a page.

3. Single-space within the notes, but double-space between them.

4. If you have to carry a note over to the next page, type a solid line a full line below the last line of text on that new page, quadru-

ple-space, and continue the note. Then continue any new notes.

Thus, footnotes at the bottom of a page look like this.

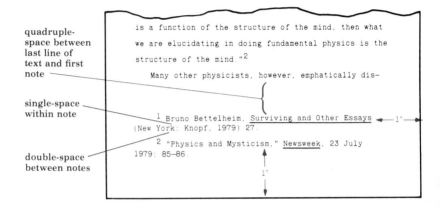

quadruple-space between last line of text and first note

single-space within note

double-space between notes

And here is a footnote carried over from a preceding page.

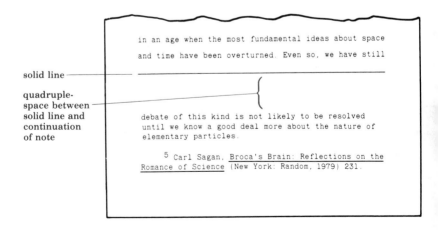

solid line

quadruple-space between solid line and continuation of note

First notes

To see how notes differ from reference list entries, compare the following sample notes with the corresponding entries on pages 467–468. Notes 1–18 include references to specific parts of the cited works.

1 Peter Gay, Freud: A Life for Our Time (New York: Norton, 1988) 48.

2 Mira Liehm and Antonin J. Liehm, The Most Important Art: Soviet and Eastern European Film after 1945 (Berkeley: U of California P, 1977) 234–45.

3 American Society of Hospital Pharmacists, Consumer Drug Digest (New York: Facts on File, 1982) 107.

4 Chicago Manual of Style, 13th ed. (Chicago: U of Chicago P, 1982) 18.103.

5 George Herbert, "The Pulley," The Bedford Introduction to Literature, ed. Michael Meyer (New York: St. Martin's, 1987) 790–91.

6 Plato, The Collected Dialogues of Plato: Including the Letters, ed. Edith Hamilton and Huntington Cairns (Princeton: Princeton UP, 1961) 327.

7 Frank Kermode et al., eds., The Oxford Anthology of English Literature, 2 vols. (New York: Oxford UP, 1973) 1:209–11.

8 Natsume Soseki, The Miner, trans. Jay Rubin (Stanford: Stanford UP, 1988) 99–103.

9 Frank Conroy, Stop-time (1967; New York: Penguin, 1977) 8.

doc
37e

[10] Arnold M. Cooper, "Psychoanalysis at One Hundred: Beginnings of Maturity," Journal of the American Psychoanalytic Association 32 (1984): 250.

[11] Larry L. Langford, "How Many Children Had Molly Bloom? Sons and Lovers in Ulysses," Literature and Psychology 34.2 (1988): 27–28.

[12] Brett Singer, "Husbands at Bay," rev. of Only Children, by Rafael Yglesias, New York Times Book Review 17 July 1988: 19.

[13] "Hard-Sell Shopping Carts," Newsweek 18 July 1988: 46.

[14] Vlae Kershner, "Prime Rate Raised to 9.5%," San Francisco Chronicle 15 July 1988, five-star ed.: A24.

[15] L[awrence] K. L[ustig], "Alluvial Fans," Encyclopaedia Britannica, 1985, Macropaedia.

[16] Henry Morton Boudin, "The Ripple Effect in Classroom Management," diss., U of Michigan, 1970, 78–93.

[17] United States, Dept. of Agriculture, "Shipments and Unloads of Certain Fruits and Vegetables, 1918–1923," Statistical Bulletin 7 (Apr. 1925): 208.

[18] Winfried S. McFann, letter, Popular Photography Aug. 1978: 8.

[19] Neil Simon, Broadway Bound, dir. Gene Saks, with Joan Rivers, Broadhurst Theatre, New York, 10 July 1988.

doc
37e

²⁰ A Handful of Dust, dir. Charles Sturridge, with Anjelica Huston, New Line Cinema, 1988.

²¹ Knocking on Armageddon's Door, prod. and dir. Torv Carlsen and John R. Magnus, PBS, 19 July 1988.

²² Ludwig van Beethoven, Symphony no. 8 in F, op. 93, cond. Pierre Monteux, Vienna Philharmonic Orch., Decca, STS 15238, 1964.

²³ Peter Collier and David Horowitz, personal interview, 5 Nov. 1988.

Subsequent references

After you have provided one full endnote or footnote, you can be brief in citing the same work again:

²⁴ Gay 197.

If you refer to more than one work by the same author, add a shortened title:

²⁵ Michaels, Men's Club 45.

²⁶ Michaels, I Would Have Saved Them 89–91.

If you cite the same work a third time, do not use the obsolete abbreviations *ibid.* or *op cit.;* repeat the identifying information given in your first shortened reference. If the title of the whole work is cumbersome, abbreviate it.

**doc
37e**

FIRST NOTE:

²⁷ The McGraw-Hill Encyclopedia of World Biography. 12 vols. (New York: McGraw-Hill, 1973) 6: 563; hereafter cited as MEWB.

SUBSEQUENT NOTE:
   28 MEWB 8: 354.

If the same work comes up repeatedly in your notes, provide one full reference and then shift to parenthetic citations.

FIRST NOTE:
   29 William Shakespeare, The Merchant of Venice,

ed. Louis B. Wright and Virginia LaMar (New York:

Washington Square, 1957) II.iii.43.

SUBSEQUENT PARENTHETIC REFERENCE:
Portia tells Nerissa that she will do anything "ere I

will be married to a sponge" (I.ii.90—91).

Bibliography

A bibliography is a list of works that you have consulted or that you recommend to your readers for further reference. Research papers, dissertations, and scholarly books that do not follow a parenthetic citation style of documentation (37b–d) typically contain bibliographies at the end. If you are supplying endnotes or footnotes, you can decide whether or not to include a bibliography by asking whether your notes have given a sufficient idea of your sources.

   For bibliographical form, follow the conventions specified for an MLA reference list of "Works Cited" (p. 465). In practice, the only differences between a bibliography and a reference list are that (a) parenthetic citations are not keyed directly to a bibliography, and (b) a bibliography may include some works that were consulted but are not actually cited in the text.

**doc
37f**

37f   Learn the uses of substantive and bibliographic notes.

If you are using parenthetic citations (pp. 462–483, 37b–d), you will not be routinely supplying footnotes or endnotes. But you may nevertheless want to include some notes—usually endnotes, placed between the final paragraph of your main text and the beginning of your reference list—to make substantive comments (**substantive notes**) or to supply more references than you could gracefully fit into one set of parentheses (**bibliographic notes**). Although APA generally discourages use of such supplementary notes, MLA does not.

SUBSTANTIVE NOTE:

¹ According to Jalby, the peasants of Languedoc dressed lightly on the whole, but on feastdays, regardless of the heat, they wore their best winter clothes <u>over</u> their best summer ones to demonstrate their sense of luxury (194).

BIBLIOGRAPHIC NOTE:

² See also E. R. Dodds, <u>The Greeks and the Irrational</u> (Berkeley: U of California P, 1951) 145–62; Richard Stillwell, "The Siting of Classical Greek Temples," <u>Journal of the Society of Architectural Historians</u> 13 (1954): 5; and Robert Scranton, "Group Design in Greek Architecture," <u>Art Bulletin</u> 31 (1949): 251.

If the words cited in this note appeared in the reference list, the note could be briefer:

² See also Dodds 145–62; Stillwell 5; Scranton 251.

**doc
37f**

If you have been following a footnote/endnote form, your substantive and bibliographic notes should be integrated with the others. But whichever form you use, beware of demoting important points from your main text to your notes. Remember that readers would be annoyed by having to lurch back and forth between text and notes in order to follow your reasoning.

38 A Sample Research Paper

38a Note the features of a research paper following MLA parenthetic citation style.

To illustrate the fruits of library research, here is an analytic student paper about the prospects for joint Chinese-American business ventures.

"THE GREAT WALL: DOING BUSINESS WITH CHINA"	
Mode	Analysis
Title page	Page 492
Thesis statement and outline	Page 493
Documentation style	MLA parenthetic citation
List of sources	"Works Cited" reference list (pp. 506–507)
Sample reference list in APA style	Pages 508–509
Sample page in "alternative MLA" footnote style	Page 510

About ⅓ down page {

The Great Wall: Doing Business with China

} **2″**

by

Ely Tsern

Double-space

} **2″**

English 144, Section 2

Mr. Crews

TA: John McBratney

May 6, 1988

<u>Thesis:</u> Although Americans seeking to do business with China face formidable obstacles, efforts to reduce misunderstanding on both sides already show promise of excellent long-term results.

Outline

The writer uses a topic outline (p. 46).

  I. Introduction: Difficulties to Be Overcome

 II. Problem #1: Negotiating across Cultural Barriers

     A. The Crucial Importance of Negotiations

     B. Cultural Misunderstandings

         1. Contractual language versus personal trust

         2. Different conceptions of entertainment

     C. The Rewards of Patience

III. Problem #2: Managing Chinese Workers

     A. Relatively Untrained, Unmotivated Labor Force

         1. Political disruption of the economy under Mao Zedong

         2. A noncompetitive tradition in the workplace

     B. Remedies Being Taken

 IV. Problem #3: The Plague of Bureaucracy

     A. Interference with Management

     B. A Drain on Profitability

     C. Remedies Being Taken

  V. Conclusion: A Brighter Future

     A. Political Stability and Pragmatism

     B. Mutual Efforts to Overcome Misunderstanding

For a sample
first page when
a title page is
not supplied,
see page 73.

2″

The Great Wall: Doing Business with China

4 spaces

The writer begins with striking anecdotes that arouse interest.

American business executives coming back from China have many arresting stories to tell. In one instance, a Chinese adviser refused to do business with Procter and Gamble because he believed the company dealt in "gambling" (Wang 8). In another, an American official stunned Chinese artisans by giving them miniature replicas of the Liberty Bell as parting gifts. The words "Liberty Bell," when translated into Chinese, sound the same as "death" (Tung 22).

Parenthetic citations are keyed to the "Works Cited" on page 9.

Since China opened its doors to the West in 1979, hundreds of American companies have eagerly pursued business relationships with the Chinese, hoping to capture the potential market of 1.2 billion people. But the road to joint-venture success has proved bumpy thus far. Western investors "complain of soaring costs, arbitrary tax and tariff levies, inadequate labor and numerous other annoyances" (Sterba 1). And

Tsern 2 **Numbering begins on the second page.**

beyond the immediate obstacles, American executives have been made aware of more profound differences between the two peoples--differences in culture, political ideology, and social background. As I will suggest, however, we have every reason to expect that such problems will become less serious as Chinese and Americans get better acquainted and pursue their common welfare.

The thesis is stated.

Negotiations are the first step in any business venture. They form the agreement upon which all subsequent transactions will be based, while also establishing a personal relationship between future partners. A delicate process, negotiating is a major hurdle for American and Chinese companies because the two sides must overcome long-standing cultural differences to establish a working relationship.

Problem #1: negotiations

In the United States, the fundamental concept behind every business deal is that the written contract, backed by a strong legal system, settles any disputes that may arise between partners. In China, however, according to Lucian W. Pye, a political scientist at

Tsern 3

MIT and a specialist on Asian affairs, this concept is

not invoked:

> The Chinese see stability [of a business re-
> lationship] not in the power of the law but
> in the strength of human relationships. A
> contract establishes what is essentially a
> personal relationship. . . . Their culture
> still reflects a philosophy that governance
> is more by people than by laws. (79)

Essentially, the Chinese believe that no contract or

set of laws can anticipate all the problems that might

arise, but that disputes, no matter how large, can be

resolved by people working together in a trusting re-

lationship.

The Chinese approach negotiations in this spirit.

To establish a long-term business relationship based

on trust, they usually present a letter of understand-

ing which outlines the general principles of the rela-

tionship (Pye 76). Furthermore, whereas Americans

prefer elaborate contracts which they believe will

eliminate misunderstandings, the Chinese prefer sim-

ple, informal contracts. Fred Clark, successful in

negotiating a venture between Orlando Airways and the

For a prose quotation of more than four typed lines, use the block form, indenting by ten spaces and omitting quotation marks. (See p. 63 for single versus double spacing.)

Tsern 4

Canton Machine Company, has recommended that American negotiators "not be too formal and hard with the contract. . . . If you go in there with your attorneys in tow and want every 'i' dotted and every 't' crossed, you'll have trouble. You have to keep the contract simple . . ." (Bertrand 68).

In an effort to build trust with potential partners, Chinese executives, playing the role of hosts, also spend time away from the bargaining table entertaining their American guests. Unfortunately for the Americans, this social process takes a great deal of time. Fred Clark of Orlando Airways said that he "drank a lot of tea, had a lot of banquets and took a lot of sightseeing trips" during negotiations which lasted two years (Bertrand 68). The Chinese believe that such social interactions are a critical part of negotiations.[1] E. E. Bauer, a Boeing engineer who

---

[1] Chinese social customs often put Americans in uncomfortable situations. Many U.S. executives reported that Chinese hosts served them favorite native delicacies, such as "smiling fish" (partially live fish) and poultry with its head on, expecting their guests to indulge themselves (Tung 23).

Substantive footnotes can be combined with reference list documentation.

Tsern 5

spent four years assisting the Civil Aviation Administration in China, explained it this way: "Chinese banquets were far more than mere dinners, more even than
significant social events--indeed, they formed the ve-
nue for serious business discussions" (29). Unfortunately, many Americans, unaware of the importance of
these events, frequently grow frustrated with them.

Solving
problem #1

Ultimately, American executives who understand
Chinese social customs and the Chinese concept of a
business relationship usually succeed in negotiations.
For example, recognizing their Chinese partners' concern to establish a long-term relationship, the Otis
Elevator Company committed itself to a thirty-year
"marriage arrangement" with a company in Tianjin, and
now enjoys a solid relationship with its Chinese coun-
terpart (Pye 76). Another company, Orlando Airways,
underwent two full years of negotiations before finally reaching a helicopter manufacturing agreement with
the Canton Machine Company. Patience eventually paid
off for Orlando, which generated annual sales of $4
million in 1985 (Bertrand 68).

Tsern 6

The heart of any industrial economy is its human **Problem #2: managing Chinese workers** capital, and China, with its 1.2 billion people, possesses workers in abundant supply. Thus, labor shortages have not been a problem for U.S. businesses in China. In comparison with their American counterparts, however, Chinese workers appear relatively untrained and unmotivated. Reasons for this condition can be traced to China's recent turbulent history. While initiating sweeping political and social reforms, such as the Cultural Revolution, Chairman Mao Zedong failed during his thirty-year reign to develop the country's greatest economic resource, its human capital. When Mao died in 1976, China's economy was

> primarily a collectivist agricultural system
> that could barely produce enough food for a
> burgeoning population. A generation of
> younger people had been denied university
> education, resulting in a terrible shortage
> of scientists, engineers, and managers.
> (Phillips 53)

Today, over three quarters of China's total population still lives in the countryside ("China" 60), and the urban labor force of 125 million remains

Tsern 7

"largely unskilled and undereducated" (De Keijzer 35).

A general lack of motivation among workers can be traced more specifically to the concept of the "iron rice bowl," introduced by Mao Zedong in the early years of the Chinese Communist party and by now a habitual part of Chinese thinking. The "iron rice bowl" guarantees all Chinese secure jobs without drastic disparities in pay (Bronson 182+). Understandably, then, American managers have found it difficult to motivate their Chinese employees to work hard and care about their job performance.

Solving problem #2   The current Chinese regime, under the pragmatic leadership of Deng Xiaoping, recognizes these labor problems and has turned to foreign industrial nations, particularly the United States, for assistance. By requiring that U.S. companies hire native workers and middle managers, Deng's government has made use of American managers to teach technical skills and positive work attitudes. For American managers, this task often means completely retraining Chinese employees.

Tsern 8

In coping with untrained labor, some companies have
even sent Chinese workers to be schooled in the United
States. Westinghouse Electric, for instance, has sent
approximately five hundred Chinese engineers to the
U.S. for advanced training over the last five years
(Bronson 182).

Chinese bureaucracy has also affected American **Problem #3:**
bureaucratic
managers' ability to manage Chinese employees. During **interference**
Chairman Mao's leadership, the Chinese government established tight controls over all domestic businesses.
Today, Chinese workers must still report directly not
only to their corporate supervisors but also to government officials in "municipal functional bureaus."
Steven Hendryx, director of China operations for Otis
Elevator Company, explains the Chinese bureaucracy in
this way:

> The company's labor, materials, engineering,
> production, and finance departments report
> not only to the general manager of the plant
> but also to their respective municipal func-
> tional bureaus, which supervise all corre-
> sponding departments of all the companies in
> the city. Each local bureau reports to its
> corresponding ministry in Beijing. The labor

Tsern 9

department of Tianjin-Otis, for example, is
responsible to the Tianjin Labor Bureau,
which reports to the labor ministry in Beij-
ing. It's just as if the treasurer of IBM
reported through state channels to the Secretary of the Treasury in Washington. (81)

Because these bureaus have the authority to hire

and fire Chinese employees, many American managers

find themselves powerless to implement their manage-

ment strategies. The goals of Chinese officials often

clash with management's efforts to maintain profit-

ability, product quality, and factory efficiency.

Typically, for example, "Squibb China President John

McCoy . . . found his plant periodically invaded by

Shanghai officials who would march into the plant and

twirl dials on equipment in hopes of boosting output"

(Bronson 182).

**Solving
problem #3**

Recognizing the burden of bureaucracy, both Amer-

ican businesses and the Chinese government have made

efforts to establish more autonomy for joint venture

management. Some American managers have succeeded in

reducing government contact with their Chinese employ-

ees. One manager, according to Hendryx, established a

Tsern 10

company policy requiring that all on-site government
visits be cleared with him, thus limiting the contact
between workers and officials (82). The Chinese government also passed several reforms in October 1986
which gave foreign managers the authority to hire and
fire workers and provide employee incentive programs
(Bronson 185). Although the pervasive bureaucracy
will continue to pose resistance to free-enterprise
businesses in China, foreign companies will gradually
gain more autonomy as Deng Xiaoping and his followers
in the Communist party continue pushing for greater
incentives for foreign investors.

The future is still bright for Chinese-American
relations. According to most experts, the pragmatic
leadership currently in control of the Chinese government will remain in power for some time:

> Today, Deng and his chosen lieutenants appear
> to be in firm control and to have the support
> of most of the top leadership, both in their
> pursuit of goals, and in their choice of tac-
> tics to attain these goals. In fact, it is
> fair to say that today there is greater sta-
> bility within China's leadership than there
> has been at any time since the 1950s. The

**Conclusion:
reasons for
optimism**

Tsern 11

> new policies appear to have widespread popu-
> lar support. The Chinese people, extremely
> fed up with the political ferment and ideo-
> logical excesses of the past, are now begin-
> ning to see tangible improvements in living
> standards. It would probably take a major
> disaster to turn the clock back. (Phillips
> 56)

With a stable Chinese government eager to implement

modernization reforms and U.S. companies eager to es-

tablish a foothold in the enormous Chinese market,

both sides have strong motivation to improve mutual

business relationships.

Improvements will come, however, only if special

efforts are made by both the Americans and the Chi-

nese. American executives must develop an apprecia-

tion for Chinese culture and customs. Moreover, they

must adapt their management styles to accommodate the

mammoth Chinese bureaucracy and largely untrained Chi-

nese labor and management. In turn, Chinese officials

and managers must become more open to Western concepts

of management and free enterprise. Such mutual ef-

forts will not only improve business relationships but

also help to bring the Americans and Chinese closer

Tsern 12

together, breaking down the great wall of misunderstanding which has always stood between the two
peoples. It shouldn't be too difficult, after all,
to prove that "Liberty Bell" does not mean "death."

To complete his essay on a lively note, the writer calls on both his title and a phrase from his opening paragraph.

A reference list according to MLA style

Works Cited

Bauer, E. E. China Takes Off: Technology Transfer and Modernization. Seattle: U of Washington P, 1986.

Bertrand, Kate. "Learning a 'Different Ball Game.'" Business Marketing Jan. 1986: 68+.

Bronson, Gail. "The Long March." Forbes Magazine 15 Dec. 1986: 182+.

"China." Worldmark Encyclopedia of the Nations: Asia and Oceania. N.p.: 1984.

De Keijzer, Arne J. "Cracking the China Market." Industry Week 17 Feb. 1986: 35+.

Hendryx, Steven R. "The China Trade: Making the Deal Work." Harvard Business Review July-Aug. 1986: 75+.

Phillips, Christopher H. "China in Transition." Columbia Journal of World Business Twentieth Anniversary Issue 1985: 53–56.

Pye, Lucian W. "The China Trade: Making the Deal." Harvard Business Review July-Aug. 1986: 74+.

Tsern 14

Sterba, James P. "Firms Doing Business in China Are
     Stymied by Costs and Hassles." Wall Street Jour-
     nal 17 July 1986, 1+.

Tung, Rosalie L. "Corporate Executives and Their Fam-
     ilies in China: The Need for Cross-Cultural Un-
     derstanding in Business." Columbia Journal of
     World Business Spring 1986: 21–25.

Wang, N. T. "United States and China: Business beyond
     Trade--an Overview." Columbia Journal of World
     Business Spring 1986: 3–11.

38b   Note how the reference list would look in APA style.

References

Bauer, E. E. (1986). China takes off: Technology
    transfer and modernization. Seattle: University of
    Washington Press.

Bertrand, K. (1986, January). Learning a "different
    ball game." Business Marketing, pp. 68, 72, 74, 76.

Bronson, G. (1986, December 15). The long march.
    Forbes Magazine, pp. 182, 184–185.

China. (1984). Worldmark encyclopedia of the nations:
    Asia and Oceania.

De Keijzer, A. J. (1986, February 17). Cracking the
    China market. Industry Week, pp. 35, 38–39.

Hendryx, S. R. (1986, July-August). The China trade:
    Making the deal work. Harvard Business Review, pp.
    75, 81–84.

Phillips, C. H. (1985). China in transition. Columbia
    Journal of World Business, pp. 53–56.

Pye, L. W. (1986, July-August). The China trade: Mak-
    ing the deal. Harvard Business Review, pp. 74, 76–
    80.

Sterba, J. P. (1986, July 17). Firms doing business in
    China are stymied by costs and hassles. Wall Street
    Journal, pp. 1, 11–13.

Tung, R. L. (1986, Spring). Corporate executives and
    their families in China: The need for cross-cultur-
    al understanding in business. Columbia Journal of
    World Business, pp. 21–25.

Wang, N. T. (1986, Spring). United States and China:
    Business beyond trade--an overview. Columbia Jour-
    nal of World Business, pp. 3–11.

38c Learn how the sample paper would look in "alternative MLA" footnote style.

If you go in there with your attorneys in tow and want every 'i' dotted and every 't' crossed, you'll have trouble. You have to keep the contract simple. . . ."[5]

In an effort to build trust with potential partners, Chinese executives, playing the role of hosts, also spend time away from the bargaining table entertaining their American guests. Unfortunately for the Americans, this social process takes a great deal of time. Fred Clark of Orlando Airways said that he "drank a lot of tea, had a lot of banquets and took a lot of sightseeing trips" during negotiations which lasted two years.[6] The Chinese believe that such social interactions are a critical part of negotiations.[7] E. E. Bauer, a Boeing engineer who spent four years assisting the Civil Aviation Administration in

[5] Kate Bertrand, "Learning a 'Different Ball Game,'" Business Marketing Jan. 1986: 68.

[6] Betrand 68.

[7] Chinese social customs often put Americans in uncomfortable situations. Many U.S. executives reported that Chinese hosts served them favorite native delicacies, such as "smiling fish" (partially live fish) and poultry with its head on, expecting their guests to indulge themselves. See Rosalie L. Tung, "Corporate Executives and Their Families in China: The Need for Cross-Cultural Understanding in Business," Columbia Journal of World Business Spring 1986: 23.

IX
APPLIED
WRITING

Applied Writing

Most of the skills you have developed for the writing of essays will serve you well in answering examination questions. At the same time, it is vital to understand the ways in which the in-class situation limits your options and calls for a more direct and emphatic style of writing (Chapter 39). And to operate successfully beyond the classroom, you must familiarize yourself with some new conventions. Chapter 40 indicates several standard ways of writing a business letter. Following one of those forms, you can make an impression of competence and confidence as you apply for a job, order merchandise, reply to correspondence, state a claim, or request information. And Chapter 41 gives you a model for your résumé—a summary of your background that will show your accomplishments to best advantage in the eyes of potential employers.

39 Examination Answers and In-Class Essays

39a Be prepared for the special conditions of an examination.

Here are eleven points of advice for improved examination taking, the first of which you can put into operation weeks before the exam.

1. *Try to anticipate questions.* Listen and take notes throughout the term. Attend especially to topics and theories that keep coming up week after week, so that you arrive at the exam with ideas that tie together the assigned material.

2. *Read through all instructions and questions before beginning any answer.* Determine whether you must answer all the questions. If you have a choice, decide which questions you can answer best. Re-

513

sponding to more than the required number may take time from your strong area to answer an unnecessary question in a weaker area, and the grader will usually be under no obligation to count "extra credit" answers.

3. *Gauge your available time.* Translate the point value of a question into a time value. A 30-point question in a 50-minute, 100-point exam should not take much more of your time than 15 minutes (30 percent of 50). If you find yourself running over, stop and leave some blank space while you get something written on *all* other questions.

4. *Note the key instruction in each question.* Always pause and study the wording of each question. Be aware that most questions begin with a key word that tells you what to do: *compare, contrast, discuss, analyze, classify, list, define, explain, summarize, describe, justify, outline.* Let that word guide the writing of your answer. If you are asked to *describe* how lasers are used to unblock obstructed arteries, do not waste time *explaining* possible causes of the obstruction. And do not be tempted into writing prepared answers to questions that were not asked. If you are to contrast *X* with *Y,* be sure you are not setting out to give 90 percent of your emphasis to *X.* If you are to state the relationship between *A* and *B,* do not throw in *C* for good measure. And if the question tells you to analyze the content and style of a quoted passage, do not suppose that a double effort on content alone will gain you full credit. Break the question into its parts and attend to all of them.

5. *Plan your answer.* For longer answers, draw up a scratch outline (p. 44, 4b), and check the outline against the question to make sure it covers the required ground.

6. *Do not waste time restating the question.* A grader can only be annoyed by a hollow introductory paragraph that merely announces your willingness to address the question. Your grader will already be looking for ideas.

7. *Begin with a clear statement of your thesis in the opening paragraph.* Use your first paragraph to announce your main point and to

establish the structure of everything that will follow. Do not fear that your strategy will be made too obvious. There is no such thing as being too obvious about your thesis in an examination answer. The danger, on the contrary, is that a harried grader will miss it.

8. *Highlight your main points.* Remember that your grader will be reading rapidly and will appreciate signals that make the structure of your answer clear. Consider enumerating key points, either with actual numbers (*1, 2, 3*) or with words (*First, Second, Third*); you can even underline the most essential statements to ensure that they will come to the grader's notice.

9. *Support your generalizations with specific references.* Most essay questions are broad enough to allow for a variety of "right" answers. Give your grader evidence that you have done the reading and have thought about it carefully. Your own ideas, backed by examples drawn from the assigned reading, will be much more impressive than unsupported statements taken directly from lectures and textbooks.

10. *Keep to the point.* In an examination answer you have no time for digressions—passages that stray from the case being made. You should not, for example, try to befriend your grader with humorous asides or pleas for sympathy.

11. *Read through your completed answer.* Try to leave time to go over your answer. Read it as if you were the grader, and try to catch inconsistencies, incoherent sentences, illegible scribbles, and unfulfilled predictions about what follows. Do not hesitate to cross out whole paragraphs if necessary or to send your grader, through an inserted arrow and a boldly printed note, to an extra page in the back of the blue book.

A sample answer

For a further idea of the way an examination answer typically goes straight to the point and reveals its structure, read this answer to a question on an American history final.

exam 39a

Question:

Summarize and explain the importance of Jefferson's reforms in the Virginia Legislature after 1776.

Answer:

Thesis first → Jefferson's purpose in revising the laws of Virginia was to get rid of all traces of aristocracy and to lay the foundations for democratic government. There were four key reforms—governing inheritance, education, and religion—that helped to change Virginia from a royal colony to a republican state.

Preview of supporting points →

First, the abolition of primogeniture. This ancient practice meant that the firstborn son inherited all the father's wealth. The importance of the reform was that wealth could now be distributed among several surviving offspring, thereby breaking down the holdings of large landowners and distributing ownership to a wider number of Virginians.

Second, the repeal of the laws of entail. These laws provided that a landowner who had inherited an entailed estate had to leave it whole to a fixed line of heirs. Jefferson's reform allowed an owner to divide up his property and leave it to whomever he liked. The importance, again, was that the repeal broke the power of a landed aristocracy, a sure threat to a young democracy.

Each numbered point receives a paragraph of its own. Each paragraph both summarizes and explains the importance of its point.

Third, the establishment of a system of general education. Jefferson felt it was the duty of the state to provide education and libraries for the poor. He felt that free education was the only guarantee against tyranny—that only educated people could become useful citizens by participating in the drafting of sound laws, thereby insuring the well-being and happiness of all citizens.

And fourth, the disestablishment of the state church and the guarantee of freedom of conscience. A deist himself, Jefferson supported the ethical teachings of religion but rejected a church/state alliance, which he felt unavoidably led to favoritism and tyranny. He proposed that Virginians be free of statutory taxation in support of a state church. Jefferson's legislation went beyond mere tolerance to guarantee freedom of religion for all by law.

A brief concluding paragraph emphasizes that the → **terms of the question have been met.**

These four reforms broke down a landed aristocracy, educated a democratic citizenry to participate in government, and guaranteed for all a separation of church and state, thereby eradicating all traces of hereditary rank and privilege in Virginia.

exam
39a

516

39b Modify your composing method to suit the conditions of the in-class essay.

Nearly all the advice in this book applies to the writing of in-class as well as at-home essays. But an in-class essay resembles an examination (39a) in requiring you to make the "first draft" fully adequate. As in an exam, you must carefully gauge your available time, be absolutely sure you are meeting the terms of the questions, and foreshorten your planning and revision.

If you are given an hour to produce an essay, do not feel that you have been directed to write for exactly sixty minutes. Take out about ten minutes for planning, and try to finish in time to read through the whole essay and make emergency corrections. The key period is the beginning: you must not start writing until you have a clear idea of your thesis. If you search for ideas as you go along, your essay will probably show a meandering structure or even a self-contradictory one.

To guide your writing, make a scratch outline (p. 44, 4b) indicating the anticipated order of your points. Steer clear of elaborate or highly unusual structures that could turn out to be unworkable. Get your thesis into the first or second paragraph, and then concentrate on backing it with important points of evidence.

Your instructor will make allowances for the time constraint when judging your essay. Remember as you write, however, that it *is* an essay—one that should show such virtues as clear statement, coherent paragraph development, and variety of sentence structure. Do not, then, write like someone who has crammed for a test and who must now hastily spill out page after page of sheer information. The length of your in-class essay will be less crucial than the way it hangs together as a purposeful structure controlled by a thesis.

In your remaining time, check first to see that you have adequately developed your thesis, and insert any needed additions as neatly as you can (see p. 511, point 11). Then check for legibility and correctness of usage, punctuation, spelling, and diction, making needed changes as you go. Your instructor will not object to a marked-up manuscript if it remains reasonably easy to read.

exam
39b

40 Business Letters

40a Master the standard features of the business letter.

Customary elements

Examine the business letter on page 524. There you see:

1. *The heading.* It contains your address and the date of writing. Notice the absence of end punctuation.

2. *The inside address.* Place this address high (or low) enough so that the body of the letter will appear centered on the page. Include the name of the addressee, that person's title or office, the name of the company or institution, and the full address:

```
Joan Lacey, M.D.            Mr. Kenneth Herbert
Pioneer Medical Group       Director of Personnel
45 Arrow Avenue             Cordial Fruit Cooperative
Omaha, NE 68104             636 Plumeria Boulevard
                            Honolulu, HI 96815
```

3. *The salutation.* This formal greeting appears two lines lower than the inside address:

```
Dear Dr. Lacey:            Dear Ms. Diaz:

Dear Mr. Herbert:          Dear Reverend Melville:
```

Ms. is now the preferred form for addressing a woman who has no title such as *Dr.* or *Professor.* Use *Miss* or *Mrs.* only if your correspondent has put that title before her own typed name in a letter to you: (*Mrs.*) *Estelle Kohut.* And unless you see otherwise, you should assume that a woman wishes to be known by her own first name, not her husband's.

When writing to an institution or a business, you can avoid the possibly offensive *Dear Sir* or *Sirs* by choosing a neutral salutation:

```
Dear Personnel Manager:      Dear Editor:
Dear Sir or Madam:           Dear Macy's:
Dear Bursar:                 To Whom It May Concern:
```

Note that business salutations end with a colon. Only if the addressee happens to be a friend should you strike a more informal note: *Dear Estelle, Dear Andy, ...*

4. *The body.* Use the body of your letter to explain the situation and to make your request or response in a straightforward, concise way. You can write briefer paragraphs than you would use in an essay. Prefer middle-level diction, avoiding both slang and legalese: not ˣ *You really put one over on me* or ˣ *The undersigned was heretofore not apprised of the circumstances cited hereabove* but *I was not aware of the problem.*

Single-space the paragraphs of your letter, but leave a double space between one paragrah and the next.

5. *The complimentary close.* Type the complimentary close two lines below the last line of the body. The most common formulas are:

```
Sincerely,                   Yours sincerely,
Sincerely yours,             Very truly yours,
Yours truly,                 Cordially,
```

Of these tags, *Cordially* is the only one that hints at actual feeling.

6. *Your typed name.* Leave four lines between the complimentary close and your typed name as you intend to sign it. If you have a professional title or role that is relevant to the purpose of the letter, add it directly below your name:

```
Nicole Pinsky               Jackson Marley
Assistant Manager           Lecturer
```

In general, such titles are appropriate when you are using letterhead stationery.

7. *Your signature.* Always use blue or black ink. Match your signature and your typed name; a briefer signature is a sign of impatience.

bus
40a

8. *Special notations.* Lowest on the page, always flush left, come notations to indicate the following circumstances if they are applicable:

NOTATION	MEANING
cc: A. Pitts F. Adler	"Carbon copies" (probably photocopies) are being simultaneously sent to interested parties Pitts and Adler.
encl.	The mailing contains an enclosure (always mentioned in the body of the letter).
att.	A document has been attached to the letter.
BR: clc *or* BR/clc	The writer (initials *BR*) has used the services of a typist (initials *clc*).

Alternative formats

There are three recognized ways of handling the arrangement of a business letter's elements on the page. You can choose any of the three, but they make somewhat different impressions. For extreme impersonality, the *block format* works best. A middle style, very commonly used, is the *modified block format.* And if you want your business letter to have some of the flavor of a personal letter, the *indented format* is available.

Here are the specifications for all three formats:

	BLOCK FORMAT	MODIFIED BLOCK FORMAT	INDENTED FORMAT
Heading	Flush left	Toward right margin	Toward right margin
Inside Address	Flush left	Flush left	Flush left
First Lines of Paragraphs	Flush left	Flush left	Indented 5–10 spaces
Complimentary Close, Name, and Signature	Flush left	Toward right margin	Toward right margin

bus
40a

	BLOCK FORMAT	MODIFIED BLOCK FORMAT	INDENTED FORMAT
Special Notations	Flush left	Flush left	Flush left

("Flush left" means that the lines begin at the left margin. "Toward right margin" means they should end at or near the right margin.)

These differences may sound complicated, but they are easy to see:

BLOCK FORMAT: page 523
MODIFIED BLOCK FORMAT: pages 524, 525
INDENTED FORMAT: page 526

Note that indented format is simply modified block format plus indentions for the first lines of paragraphs.

Form of envelope

Make the address on your envelope identical to the inside address. In the upper left corner, type your address as it appears in the heading:

```
Kevin Oppenheimer
2264 N. Cruger Avenue
Milwaukee, WI 53211

                Mr. Robert F. Stone
                Customer Relations
                Kaiser Appliances, Inc.
                834 La Salle Street
                Chicago, IL 60632
```

40b Recognize the main purposes of the business letter.

Asking for information

Make your inquiry brief, and limit your request to information that

**bus
40b**

can be sent in an available brochure or a brief reply. Be specific, so that there can be no doubt about which facts you need.

Stating a claim

Take a courteous but firm tone, setting forth the facts so fully and clearly that your reader will be able to act on your letter without having to ask for more information. If you are complaining about a purchase, supply the date of purchase, the model and serial number, and a brief description. If you have been mistakenly billed twice for the same service or product, state what that service or product is, the date of your payment, and the check number if you paid by check. If possible, enclose a photocopy of the canceled check (both sides). In a second paragraph, calmly and fairly state what adjustment you think you are entitled to. (See page 524 for a sample claim letter.)

Ordering merchandise

Begin by stating which items you are ordering, using both product names and stock or page numbers. Tell how many units of each item you are ordering, the price per item, and the total price. If you want to receive the shipment at a different address, say so. Mention that you are enclosing payment, ask to be billed, or provide a credit card name and number and expiration date. (See page 523 for an example of a letter ordering merchandise.)

Making an application

Tailor your letter to the particular job, grant, or program of study you are applying for. Name the opening precisely. If you are asking to be considered for a job, explain how you heard about it. If a person in authority recommended that you apply, say who it was. Tell how you can be reached, and express your willingness to be interviewed.

When applying for a job, include your **résumé** (Chapter 41) and mention that you have included it. Emphasize those elements in the résumé that qualify you for *this* position. Avoid boasting and false modesty alike. The idea to get across is that the facts of your record make such a strong case for your application that no special pleading is necessary.

**bus
40b**

The letters on pages 525 and 526 illustrate how an applicant can state qualifications in different ways for different opportunities. Both letters pertain to the résumé appearing on page 529. Notice how each letter brings out "job-related" elements in the writer's background.

SAMPLE LETTERS

[BLOCK FORMAT]

```
36 Hawthorne Hall
University of the North
Bridgewater, CT 06413
January 15, 1989

NF Systems, Ltd.
P. O. Box 76363
Atlanta, GA 30358

Dear NF Systems:

Please send me the following software items for
use on the IBM Personal Computer, as described on
page 40 in the December 1988 issue of Softalk mag-
azine:

    1 "Household Aids," a group of six
      programs, total package,              $49.95
    1 "Check Register," includes 40 ledger/
      budget headings,                        39.95

Kindly ship this merchandise to the address shown
above.  I enclose my check #186 for $89.90.  Since
your advertisement does not specify shipping
costs, please bill me for them separately if they
are not included in the prices.

Sincerely yours,

Lily Marks
Lily Marks
```

[MODIFIED BLOCK FORMAT]

2264 N. Cruger Avenue
Milwaukee, WI 53211 —— **1. heading**
February 22, 1989

Mr. Robert F. Stone
Customer Relations
Kaiser Appliances, Inc. ———————————— **2. inside address**
834 La Salle Street
Chicago, IL 60632

Dear Mr. Stone: ———————————————— **3. salutation**

The Kitchen-Aid dishwasher I purchased in your
store on February 14 was installed yesterday. Unfortunately, the installation was complete before
the plumber and I noticed a large chip on the edge
of the white front panel. Since the panel was
still in its carton when the plumber arrived, it
was probably defective upon delivery. The serial
number of the dishwasher is T53278004; I enclose a
copy of the bill, already paid.

4. body

In my phone conversation with you yesterday, I
agreed to put this complaint in writing. I would
like you to send a representative here to replace
the damaged panel. To fix a time, please call me
at home after 5:30 P.M. at (414) 565-9776.

Thank you for your prompt attention to this
matter.

Sincerely, ——— **5. complimentary close**

Kevin Oppenheimer ——— **7. signature**
Kevin Oppenheimer —— **6. typed name**

KO: sms ———————————————— **8. special notations**
enc.

[MODIFIED BLOCK FORMAT]

137-20 Crescent Street
Flushing, NY 11367
August 17, 1989

F 1384
New York Times
New York, NY 10018

Dear Personnel Manager:

I am applying for the position of "Accounting Aide to CPA firm," which was advertised in yesterday's Times. I have completed my second year at Queens College as an Accounting major and plan to take a year off to supplement my education with relevant work.

From my enclosed résumé, you can see that I have been working in the business offices of Gristede's Food Stores, where I have assisted the bookkeeper in auditing procedures, including applications to computerized systems. My work requires strong mathematics skills and some familiarity with the Lotus 1-2-3 and Excel spreadsheets.

As a prospective accountant, I am especially interested in spending next year with a CPA firm. I can send you the names of references both at Queens College and at Gristede's and would be grateful for the chance to be interviewed. Please write to me at the above address or call me at (718) 317-1964 after 5:30 P.M.

Sincerely yours,

Janet Madden

Janet Madden

encl.

[INDENTED FORMAT]

137-20 Crescent Street
Flushing, NY 11367
August 17, 1989

Ms. Charlotte DeVico
Rock of Ages Health Related
   Facility
7481 Parsons Boulevard
Flushing, NY 11367

Dear Ms. DeVico:

   Mr. Gene Connelly of the Flushing YMCA has
suggested I write to you about working as a recreation assistant or bookkeeper in your facility beginning this fall. I am an Accounting major with a
minor in Communications, and I plan to take a year
off from school to supplement my education with
relevant work.

   From my enclosed résumé you can see that, in
addition to a business background, I have experience in working with people. At the Flushing "Y" I
have helped stage the annual talent show, held informal "chat" sessions, and presented films. I enjoy this work and find the elderly full of ideas
and a willingness to make themselves happy.

   Mr. Connelly has offered to write you about
my work at the "Y," and I can also send you the
name of my supervisor at Gristede's. I would be
grateful for the chance to be interviewed. Please
write to me at the above address or call me at
(212) 975-1122 between 9:00 A.M. and 4:30 P.M.

                              Sincerely yours,

                              Janet Madden

                              Janet Madden

encl.

41 Résumés

41a Recognize the standard features of the résumé.

Your résumé is a brief (usually one-page) record of your career and qualifications. Along with your letter of application (p. 522, 40b), it can land you a job interview. To that end it should be clear, easy on the eye, and totally favorable in emphasis. Have your résumé typed by a professional if your typewriter or word processor cannot create a polished, near-printed look. Divide your résumé into the following sections:

1. *Personal information.* Provide only what is necessary: name, present address, permanent address, phone numbers. Add your age, marital status, and condition of health only if you know they are relevant to the job you want.

2. *Career objective.* Include a statement of your career goals. Avoid being so specific that you exclude reasonable opportunities or so broad as to be uninformative. Cite two goals if necessary, and mention any geographical limitations.

3. *Education.* Begin with the college you currently attend or have attended most recently, and work backward to high school. (If you

have already graduated from college, omit high school.) Give dates of attendance, degrees attained, major and minor areas of study, and memberships in special societies. Briefly explain any outstanding projects or courses. Include your grade-point average only if it happens to be high.

4. *Work experience.* Begin with your current or most recent employment, and list all relevant jobs since high school. Try not to leave suspicious-looking gaps of time. Give the name and address of each employer, the dates of employment, and a brief description of your duties. Include part-time or volunteer work that may be relevant. Remember that you can mention relevant skills learned on a job that seems unrelated. If you are seeking a teaching position, consider beginning this part of your résumé with a section called *Teaching Experience* and following it with another called *Other Work Experience.*

5. *Special skills, activities, and honors.* Include special competencies that make you a desirable candidate, such as proficiency in a foreign language, ability to operate equipment, or skill in unusual procedures or techniques. Mention any honors, travel, or community service.

6. *References.* Supply the address of your college placement office, which will send out your dossier (dáhss-ee-ay) upon request. The dossier is a complete file of your credentials, including all letters of recommendation and transcripts. You may wish to give the names, positions, and addresses of three people you can trust to write strong letters in your behalf. Be sure you have their permission, however.

Further advice:

1. *Keep the format clear and the text concise.* Single-space within each section, and double-space between sections. Try to keep your résumé to one page; do not exceed two pages.

2. *Do not mention the salary you want.* You will be considered for more openings if you stay flexible on this point.

3. *Update your résumé periodically.* Do not hesitate to ask for new letters of recommendation.

4. *Rewrite your résumé for a particular job opening.* Rewriting allows you to highlight those elements of your background and goals that will suit the job you are aiming for.

JANET MADDEN

Current Address: Permanent Address:
  137-20 Crescent Street   28 Pasteur Drive
  Flushing, NY 11367   Glen Cove, NY 11542
  (718) 317-1964   (516) 676-0620

CAREER   Position as accountant or assis-
OBJECTIVE: tant accountant in an accounting
                firm. (Temporary position as a
                recreation assistant or bookkeeper
                in a recreational facility.)

EDUCATION: Queens College (CUNY)
                B. A. expected June 1992
                Majoring in Accounting
                Minoring in Communications

                Pratt High School, Glen Cove, New
                York
                Received Regents Diploma, June
                1987

EXPERIENCE:

Summers:
1989   Assistant bookkeeper, Gristede
                Brothers Food Stores, Bronx, New
                York

1988   Dramatics Counselor, Robin Hill
                Day Camp, Glen Cove, New York

1987   Volunteer, Flushing YMCA. Worked
                with elderly. Assistant director,
                annual "Y" talent show.

SKILLS: Type 65 wpm.
                Use Lotus 1-2-3 and Excel spread-
                sheets.

REFERENCES: Placement Office
                Queens College
                Flushing, NY 11367

X
TOOLS

Tools

Have you made the leap from typing (or handwriting) to word processing? Sooner or later, you almost certainly will. Chapter 42 offers some orientation to this important aid to composing. In Chapter 43, we present an alphabetical listing of troublesome expressions that make for confusion of meaning and/or spelling. One way to discover where you have been misconstruing the language is simply to check each item in that Index of Usage. Finally, Chapter 44, the Glossary of Terms, explains all the concepts that appear in boldface type throughout this book. You can use the Glossary of Terms to " brush up on grammar" as well as for spot consultation.

42 Writing with a Word Processor

DEVICE	ADVANTAGES
Typewriter:	
Manual or electric	type only
Electronic	some memory and display some formatting options may have spelling checker and thesaurus
Computer with **word processing program:**	
Microcomputer	full memory and display revise whole document on screen many formatting options graphics, computations may have spelling checker, thesaurus, and other aids to composition connection to printer modem access to databases

Mainframe and "dumb"
terminals
	same as microcomputer, plus larger
	  memory, greater speed, and direct
	  access to databases

Like it or not, you already live in a society that depends heavily on electronic information storage and retrieval. As a college-educated person, you will inevitably have to become familiar with computers in your work. As a college writer, meanwhile, you probably have access to word processing facilities on your campus. At many colleges and universities, a writing center or computer center houses a bank of *microcomputers* (such as Macintoshes or IBM PCs) or terminals connected to a *mainframe computer* that serves many functions on a time-sharing basis. Even if your instructor doesn't require that you make use of a word processor, you should take advantage of scheduled demonstrations and get acquainted with this remarkable aid to composition.

As the chart above suggests, the silicon revolution has extended downward to the (electronic) typewriter as well as upward to the vastly powerful mainframe. In this chapter, however, we assume that you will be working either with a freestanding microcomputer or a "dumb" mainframe terminal, both of which go far beyond what a "smart" typewriter can do.

42a   Learn the functions of a word processor.

ESSENTIAL TERMINOLOGY	
Central processing unit (CPU)	the "motherboard" of circuitry through which all instructions to the computer are routed
Monitor	the box housing the screen on which your text is displayed
Cursor	a blinking light on the screen that shows "where you are " in your document. By moving the cursor with keystrokes or a "mouse" (pointing device), you can make changes at different points in the text.
Software	a program, stored on a disk, that allows the computer to do a certain kind of work: word processing, graphics, spreadsheets, etc.
Disk	a storage device containing a program and/or space for filing your documents. A *floppy disk* is a plastic record that you insert into the computer's *disk drive.* A *hard disk,* with vastly greater capacity, serves the function of many floppies.

ESSENTIAL TERMINOLOGY	
Document	one essay, chapter, chart, letter, etc., that you create and display on the monitor screen.
Edit	a mode that allows you to insert, delete, and move letters, words, or blocks of text in a document you are composing or revising on the screen.
File	a document that you have saved under a specific name, so that you can retrieve it for further editing or printing. You can save your drafts as separate files or, more usually, replace each discarded draft by keeping its file name for the new version.
Save	an instruction that the computer make a record of your document in its memory (or on a disk). You should periodically "save" while creating the document, so that an unexpected power failure cannot erase your work.
Backup	a second copy of your file. Always make backups of important documents; if you lose or botch one copy, you can easily switch to the other.
Formatting	your instructions about margins, tabs, typeface and size, italics, etc.
Hard copy	a printed version of what you have created on the screen

Think of a word processor as an electronic chalkboard on which you can scribble, erase, and move text from one spot to another until you are satisfied. Then—presto!—with a keystroke or two, you can get unsmudged "hard copy" of your work from an adjacent printer. The chart at the top of the following page indicates what several kinds of printers can do.

KIND OF PRINTER	SPEED	QUALITY
Dot matrix:		
"draft" mode	fast	looks dotted
"near letter quality" mode	slower	closer to print
Daisy wheel	very slow	comparable to typewriter
Laser	very fast	superior, approaching typeset clarity

Since you will never have to retype a page, a paragraph, or even a line that is already in final form, word processing will save you much time and trouble. (With "word wrap"—the computer's knack of going automatically to the next line and readjusting all the prior spaces in an altered paragraph—every change will leave the whole text looking like new.) Thus, by making small and large changes so painless, the word processor will dissolve much of your reluctance to revise. Once you have effortlessly moved a whole block of paragraphs from one section of an essay to another in half a minute, you will wonder how you ever got along without one of these superb machines.

Many writers, especially older ones, concede the marvels of a word processor but feel most comfortable when writing on a legal pad or marking up a crudely typewritten draft. You will quickly find, however, that you needn't make a final choice of medium. You can start in any way that feels right to you and take a break from composing by transcribing your text onto the computer screen for further editing. Then you can quickly get back to hard copy again by ordering a "draft mode" printout at any moment. But you will always need to have your text back on the screen when you are tidying it for a final, flawless-looking version to be handed in.

With a word processing program you can also *format* your essay at the outset, determining what it will look like on the page, including margins, space between lines, tabs, paragraph indents, type size and face, and a "header" or "footer"—for example, the placement of your name and the page number in the upper-right corner of each page. When you pare down a draft or add material to it, the program will continually repaginate for you. And a feature-rich program can do the same for footnotes or endnotes (p. 483, 37e), liberating you from any fuss over renumbering or trying to squeeze extra notes onto a crowded page. If you like, you can even command that the right margin of your document be *justified* (aligned, as on this page) instead of "ragged." But since right-justified margins make for oddly spaced words, you may want to inquire if your instructor prefers ragged ones.

42b Note the unique ways in which a word processor can aid your composing.

Combined with adequate software, any computer can help you as a writer in more specific ways than we have mentioned thus far:

1. *Freewriting* (p. 11, 1f). To keep yourself from pausing to edit when you are freewriting, turn down the brightness control knob on your monitor. Turn it back up again when the prescribed time for freewriting has elapsed. You may also want to use the computer's alarm function as a stopwatch.

2. *Outlining* (p. 44, 4b). If your word processing program allows you to place "windows" on the screen beside your developing draft, fill one window with your outline. Consult the outline as you proceed from paragraph to paragraph. When you see that your essay must deviate from the outline, stop to revise the entire rest of the outline, double-checking it for coherence.

3. *Linking paragraphs* (p. 91, 6h). If your program can highlight the first and last sentences of every paragraph, make use of it. (If not, you can still "select" those sentences and make a document out of them.) Check to see that the connections between last and next (paragraph-opening) sentences are clear, and revise if necessary to make effective use of these naturally strong positions.

4. *Word mastery* (p. 165, 13b). Put your draft papers through a "search all" command for the words that you have previously tended to misuse. With each questionable instance highlighted, you can check to see if you now have the problem under control.

5. *Saving redundant typing.* Instead of tapping out the full title of a work you are discussing at length, use a brief symbol for it—say, *pam* for *A Portrait of the Artist as a Young Man*. As you approach your final draft, instruct the word processor to find all instances of your use of a particular symbol and replace that symbol with the full title.

6. *Accurate quotation* (p. 451, 36e). If you are taking notes from a book or article when the word processor is handy, and you want to record a long quotation, take the trouble to store that passage as a document, first carefully checking for accuracy of wording, punctuation, and citation. Without retyping, you can transfer the quotation (or any part of it) directly into your first draft, reusing it any number of times until you have arrived at your final copy. This procedure will not only save labor but also ensure that you won't introduce errors while retranscribing the passage several times.

42c Take advantage of available accessories.

Some complex word processing programs contain built-in features that you can call on for special kinds of help. In other cases, such aids are separate from but compatible with the main program; to make use of them, you simply insert another disk and "open" them. Find out which features are available to you. They may include:

1. *Aids to invention.* Some programs include tutorial aids such as reporters' questions (p. 14, 1g), designed to stimulate your initial thinking. By responding to the questions and then performing further operations on your answers, you can speed your search for an appropriate topic and thesis.

2. *Aids to organization.* To assist you in outlining, some programs allow you to make an outline of your existing draft by "selecting" a key sentence in each paragraph. Alternatively, you can make the outline and then flesh it out by writing paragraphs around its sentences. When your word processing program is in "outline mode," you can handily rearrange the order of points or assign different levels of subordination (indention) to different ideas.

3. *Thesaurus.* With an on-line thesaurus, you can pause and search for just the word you have been groping for. Be aware, however, that a thesaurus works only for expressions with which you are already familiar (p. 165, 13b).

4. *Spelling checker.* You can request that the checker search your whole document for possible misspellings. Unfortunately, being "suspicious" of every term not included in its resident dictionary, it will query some names and other correctly typed words that it doesn't rec-

ognize; you can simply bypass those queries. The spelling checker will also overlook "invisible" mistakes such as *to* for *too, it's* for *its,* or *cod* for *cog.* But it will alert you to all other typos and some other errors that may be more chronic with you. Thus you can use the spelling checker to add items to your ongoing list of expressions you habitually misspell (p. 388, 32a).

word proc 42c

5. *Style checker.* Some programs can search your document for telltale flaws of usage and punctuation and locate sentences and paragraphs that may be skimpy or wordy. Like other electronic accessories, a style checker cannot discriminate between a mistake and a shrewdly chosen special effect. It is up to you, then, to approve or veto each suggestion that comes up on the screen. But if your instructor has already identified a typical problem in your work—an overreliance, say, on prepositional phrases or on the passive voice—the style checker may be able to flag relevant instances.

6. *Access to databases.* If your terminal is connected to a mainframe or if your microcomputer is accompanied by a *modem*—a telephone that transmits electronic data—you may be able to search databases such as your library's catalog (p. 442, 36b) or an index of articles in a certain field (p. 443, 36c). Thus you can get a start on library research before you even enter the building. Note, however, that you may have to pay for some on-line searching.

43 An Index of Usage

The Index of Usage does not dwell on differences between dialect expressions, slang, and informal usage. It simply labels *colloquial* any terms that are inadvisable for use in college essays and papers.

above (noun, adjective) Stuffy in phrases like x *in view of the above* and x *for the above reasons.* Substitute *therefore* or *for these reasons.*

accept, except The first means *receive,* the second *exclude* or *excluding.*

A.D. Should precede the date: *A.D. 1185.* It is redundant to write x *In the year A.D. 1185,* since *A.D.* already says "in the year of our Lord" (Latin *anno domini*).

adapt, adopt To *adapt* is to *change for a purpose;* to *adopt* is to *take possession. She adapted her plan to the new circumstances; They adopted the baby.*

advice, advise The first is a noun, the second a verb: *He advised that he had no need of further advice.*

affect, effect As a verb, *affect* means to *influence: Rain affected the final score. Affect* may also be used as a noun meaning *feeling* or *emotion.* The verb *effect* means to *bring about* or *cause: She effected a stunning reversal.* When *effect* is a noun, it means *result: The effect of the treatment was slight.*

afraid See *frightened.*

again, back Redundant after *re*-prefixed words that already contain the sense of *again* or *back: rebound, reconsider, refer, regain, resume, revert,* etc. Do not write x *She referred back to her notes* or x *He resumed his work again.*

ain't Colloquial for *is not, are not.*

usage
43

all, all of Use either *all* or *all of* with separable items: either *All the skillets were sold* or *All of the skillets were sold.* When there are no items to be counted, use *all* without *of: All her enthusiasm vanished; He was a hermit all his life.*

all that Colloquial in sentences like x *I didn't like her all that much.* How much is *that much?* Try *I didn't like her very much* or, more straightforwardly, *I disliked her.*

allusion, illusion, delusion An *allusion* is a *glancing reference: an allusion to Shakespeare.* An *illusion* is a *deceptive impression: Shakespeare created the illusion of enormous battlefields.* A *delusion* is a *mistaken belief,* usually with pathological implications: *He suffered from the delusion that he was Shakespeare.*

alot A mistake for *a lot.*

already, all ready The first means *by this or that time,* the second *all prepared. It was already apparent that they were all ready for the trip.*

also Do not use as a coordinating conjunction: x *She owned two cars, also a stereo.* Try *Along with her two cars, she also owned a stereo.* Here *also* serves its proper function as an adverb.

altar, alter The first is for worship: *The priest approached the altar.* The second is a verb meaning *change: He had altered the text of his sermon.*

alternate, alternative (adjectives) *Alternate* means *by turns: on alternate Fridays. Alternative* means *substitutive: Our alternative plan might work if this one fails.*

altogether, all together The first means *entirely,* the second *everyone assembled: I was altogether delighted that we were all together at last.*

A.M., P.M. These abbreviations, which most writers now capitalize, should not be used as nouns: x *at six in the A.M.* And do not accompany

A.M. or P.M. with *o'clock,* which is already implied. Write *six* A.M. or *six o'clock* but not_X *six* A.M. *o'clock.*

among, between *Among* is vaguer and more collective than *between,* which draws attention to each of the items:

- They hoped to find one good person *among* the fifty applicants.
- Agreement was reached *between* management and the union.

Many careful writers also reserve *between* for sentences in which only two items are involved. See also *between.*

amount, number For undivided quantities, use *amount of: a small amount of food.* For countable items, use *number of: a small number of meals.* The common error is to use *amount* for *number,* as in _X *The amount of people in the hall was extraordinary.*

analyzation Always prefer *analysis.*

angry See *mad.*

ante-, anti- The first prefix means *before,* the second *against: In the antebellum period, there was much antiwar sentiment.*

anybody, any body; nobody, no body; somebody, some body The first member of each pair is an indefinite pronoun: *Anybody can see . . .* The others are adjective-noun pairs: *Any body can be dissected.*

anyway, any way, anyways *Anyway* is an adverb: *I am busy on that day, anyway. Any way* is an adjective-noun pair: *I can't find any way to break the date. Anyways* is colloquial.

anywheres Colloquial for *anywhere.*

apt, liable, likely Close in meaning. But some writers reserve *liable* to mean *exposed* or *responsible* in an undesirable sense: *liable to be misunderstood; liable for damages. Likely* means *probably destined: She is likely to succeed. Apt* is best used to indicate habitual disposition: *When you tell those slouchers to work faster, they are apt to complain.*

argue, quarrel These can be synonyms, but *argue* also has a special meaning of *make a case,* without overtones of quarrelsomeness.

around If you mean *about,* it is better to write *about: about five months,* not x *around five months.*

as (conjunction, preposition) In the sense of *because,* the subordinating conjunction *as* is often ambiguous: x *As she said it, I obeyed.* Does *as* here mean *because* or *while*? Use one or the other of those terms. And do not use *as* to mean *whether* or *that:* x *I cannot say as I do.*

as, like Both *as* and *like* can be prepositions: *as a rule; like a rolling stone.* But when you want a conjunction that will introduce a subordinate clause, always prefer *as* to *like:* not x *Like the forecaster warned, it rained all day,* but *As the forecaster warned . . . .*

as, such as Not synonyms. Do not write x *The burglar's bag contained many items, as masks, screwdrivers, and skeleton keys. Such as* would be appropriate.

as far as . . . Be sure to complete this formula with *is/are concerned.* Do not write x *As far as money, I have no complaints.* Try *As far as money is concerned, I have no complaints,* or *As for money, I have no complaints,* or, better, *I have no complaints about money.*

as good as, as much as Colloquial when used for *practically:* x *He as good as promised me the job.*

author (verb) Widely used, but also widely condemned as substandard: x *He authors historical novels.* Prefer *writes,* and keep *author* as a noun.

back of Colloquial for *behind,* as in x *You can find it back of the stove.* Prefer *behind* to both *back of* and *in back of.*

bad Do not use as an adverb meaning *badly* or *severely,* as in x *It hurt him bad.*

bare, bear *Bare* is an adjective meaning *naked* and a verb meaning to *expose: She bared the secret about her bare cupboard.* To *bear* is to *carry* or *endure: Her guilt was hard to bear until she laid it bare.*

before, ago When referring to the past from a present perspective, use *ago: I told you to get ready two hours ago, and you still aren't even* *dressed.* When focusing on a past time and referring to an even more distant past, use *before: She had told him to get ready two hours before, but he still wasn't even dressed.*

being (participle) Often redundant: x *The city is divided into three districts, with the poorest being isolated from the others by the highway.* Either *with* or *being* should be dropped.

bemused Means *bewildered,* not *amused.*

beside, besides The first means *at the side of,* the second *in addition: Besides, she was beside the car when it happened.*

better than Colloquial as a synonym of *more than:* x *Better than half an hour remained.*

between Requires at least two items (see *among*). Do not write either x *Hamlet's conflict is between his own mind* or x *The poems were written between 1983-84.* In the second sentence *1983-84* is one item, a period of time. Try *The poems were written between 1983 and 1984.*

  Between always requires a following *and,* not *or.* Avoid x *The choice is between anarchy or civilization.*

between each, between every Because *between* implies at least two items, it should not be joined to singular adjectives like *each* and *every:* x *He took a rest between each inning.* Try *He rested after every inning* or *He rested between innings.*

between you and I A "genteel" mistake for *between you and me.* As twin objects of the preposition *between,* both pronouns must be objective in case.

bias, biased The first is a noun meaning *prejudice,* the second an adjective meaning *prejudiced.* Do not write x *Some people are bias.*

bored Should be followed by *with* or *by,* not *of.* Avoid x *He was bored of skiing.*

born, borne The first means *brought into the world,* the second *carried: She had borne many sorrows before her baby was born.*

breadth, breath, breathe *Breadth* means *width:* the noun *breath* means *respiration:* the verb *breathe* means to *take breath.*

bring, take These words describe the same action but from different standpoints. You *bring* something *to* a location but *take* something *away* from it. Thus you can write *He took some flowers from the garden,* but you shouldn't write x *He took his mother some flowers.*

broke (adjective) Colloquial in the sense of *having no money* and as the past participle of *break:* x *The faucet was broke.* Prefer *broken* here.

bunch, crowd (noun) A *bunch* is a dense collection of *things; a crowd,* of *people* or *animals.* Avoid x *a bunch of my friends.*

business, busyness The first means *job,* the second *being busy.*

but that, but what These are awkward equivalents of *that* in clauses following an expression of doubt: x *I do not doubt but that you intend to remain loyal.*

buy, by If you write x *I want to by it,* you have confused the verb *buy* with the preposition *by.*

calculate See *figure.*

calculated See *designed.*

can, may Both are now acceptable to indicate permission. *May* has a more polite and formal air: *May I leave?*

can not, cannot Unless you want to underline *not,* always prefer *cannot,* which makes the negative meaning immediately clear.

capital, capitol *Capital* means either *governmental city* or *funds;* a *capitol* is a *statehouse.*

cause, reason Not synonyms. A *cause* is what produces an effect: *The earthquake was the cause of the tidal wave.* A *reason* is someone's *professed motive or justification: He cited a conflict of interest as his reason for not accepting the post.* Note that the actual *cause* of his refusal could have been something quite different.

cause is due to Redundant. Write *The cause was poverty,* not x *The cause was due to poverty.*

censor, censure (noun) A *censor* is an official who judges whether a publication or performance will be allowed. *Censure* is vehement criticism. *The censor heaped censure on the play.*

center around Since a center is a point, *center around* is imprecise. *Center on* or *center upon* would be better: *The investigation centered on tax evasion.*

character Often redundant. x *He was of a studious character* means, and should be written, *He was studious.*

chord, cord The first means *tones,* the second *rope.*

cite, sight, site To *cite* is to *mention.* A *sight* is a *view.* A *site* is a *locale.*

class (verb) *Classify* is preferable. Avoid x *She classed the documents under three headings.*

climactic, climatic The first means *of a climax,* the second *of a climate.*

coarse, course The first means *rough,* the second *direction* or *academic offering.*

commence Usually pompous for *begin, start.*

compare, contrast *Compare* means either *make a comparison* or *liken.* To compare something *with* something else is to make a comparison between them; the comparison may show either a resemblance or a difference. To compare something *to* something else is to assert a likeness between them.

To *contrast* is to emphasize *differences: She contrasted the gentle Athenians with the warlike Spartans.* As a verb, *contrast* should be followed by *with.*

complement, compliment As a noun, *complement* means *accompaniment: The salad was a perfect complement to the main course.* As a verb, *complement* means to *accompany: The salad complemented the main course. Compliment* means *praise: They complimented her on the outstanding meal; She received a compliment.*

comprise, compose, constitute *Comprise* means *embrace, include: The curriculum comprises every field of knowledge. Compose* and *con-*

stitute mean *make up: All those fields together compose* [or *constitute*] *the curriculum.* The most common mistake is to use *comprise* as if it meant *compose:* x *The parts comprise the whole. Is comprised of* is not an adequate solution: x *The whole is comprised of the parts.* Try *The whole comprises the parts* or *The parts compose the whole.*

concept, conception, idea The broadest of these terms is *idea,* and you should prefer it unless you are sure you mean one of the others. A *concept* is an abstract notion characterizing a class of particulars: *the concept of civil rights.* A *conception* is a stab at an idea, possibly erroneous: *She had an odd conception of my motives.* Note that *idea* would have been suitable even in these examples.

concur in, concur with You *concur in* an action or decision: *He concurred in her seeking a new career.* But you *concur with* a person or group: *He concurred with her in her decision.*

conscience, consciousness The first has to do with responsiveness to ideas of right and wrong, the second with mental awareness in general.

conscious, aware Almost synonyms, but you can observe a difference. People are *conscious* of their own perceptions but *aware* of events or circumstances.

consensus Avoid this noun unless you mean something very close to unanimity. And beware of the redundant x *consensus of opinion* and x *general consensus. Opinion* and *general* are already contained in the meaning of *consensus.*

considerable Colloquial in the sense of *many* (items): x *Considerable dignitaries were there.* Use the word to mean *weighty, important: The costs were considerable; The Secretary-General is a considerable figure.*

consist of, consist in Something *consists of* its components: *The decathlon consists of ten events. Consist in* means *exist in* or *inhere in: Discretion consists in knowing when to remain silent.*

contemptible, contemptuous Very different. *Contemptible* means *deserving contempt. Contemptuous* means *feeling or showing contempt. They felt contemptuous of such a contemptible performance.*

continual, continuous *Continual* means *recurring at intervals. Continuous* means *uninterrupted.* A river flows *continuously* but may overflow its banks *continually* through the years.

contrary to Since *contrary* is an adjective, avoid constructions in which *contrary to* serves as an adverbial modifier: x *Contrary to Baldwin, Orwell is not directly concerned with race.* This sentence makes it appear that Orwell is "contrary to Baldwin," whereas the writer means to compare the two authors' *concerns.* Try *Orwell, unlike Baldwin, is not directly concerned with race.* Save *contrary to* for sentences like *The order to surrender was contrary to everything they had been taught.*

convey Do not follow with a *that* clause: x *They conveyed that they were happy.* Choose a noun as object: *They conveyed the impression that they were happy.*

convince, persuade Often treated as synonyms, but you can preserve a valuable distinction by keeping *convince* for *win agreement* and *persuade* for *move to action.* If I *convince* you that I am right, I may *persuade* you to join my cause. Avoid x *He convinced his father to lend him the car.*

could of Always a mistake for *could have.*

council, counsel The first means *committee,* the second *advice* or *attorney: Her counsel sought counsel from the city council.*

couple, pair *Couple* refers to two items that are united. It is colloquial when the items are only casually linked: x *I have a couple of points I want to raise with you.* When you do use *couple of,* be sure not to drop the *of:* x *a couple reasons.*

Pair refers to two things that are inseparably joined in function or feeling: *The Joneses are a couple, but they are not much of a pair.*

Prefer *pairs* to *pair* for the plural: *four pairs of shoes,* not x *four pair of shoes.*

Verbs governed by *couple* or *pair* are generally plural, although a singular verb could be appropriate in a rare case: *A couple becomes a trio when the first child is born.*

criteria Always plural: *these criteria.* The singular is *criterion.*

cursor, curser The first is the blinking line on a computer screen; the second is someone who curses.

data Opinion is divided over the number of *data,* which is technically the plural form of *datum.* The safe course is to continue treating *data* as plural: *The data have recently become available.* Even so, the singular *data* is by now very commonly seen.

deduce, deduct Both form the same noun, *deduction,* but *deduce* means *derive* or *infer* and *deduct* means *take away* or *detract. He deduced that the IRS would not allow him to deduct the cost of his hair dryer.*

depend Do not omit *on* or *upon,* as in x *It depends whether the rain stops in time.* And avoid *it depends* without a following reason: x *It all depends* is incomplete.

descent, dissent The first means *lowering,* the second *disagreement.*

desert, dessert *Desert* means *barren area* or to *abandon; a dessert* is the last course in a meal.

designed, calculated Misused in passive constructions where no designing agent is envisioned: x *The long summer days are designed to expose your skin to too much ultraviolet light.* Try *The long summer days are likely to expose your skin to too much ultraviolet light.* Again, do not write x *This medicine is perfectly calculated to turn you into an addict.* Try *This medicine is likely to turn you into an addict.*

device, devise The first is a noun meaning *instrument;* the second is a verb meaning to *fashion.*

differ from, differ with To *differ from* people is to be *different from* them; to *differ with* them is to *express disagreement with* them: *The Sioux differed from their neighbors in their religious practices; they differed with their neighbors over hunting rights.*

different from, different than Some readers regard *different than* as an error wherever it occurs. But most readers would not object to *different than* when it helps to save words. *The outcome was different than I expected* is more concise than *The outcome was different from what I expected.*

usage 43

discreet, discrete The first means *prudent,* the second *separate: It was discreet of him to put the documents into discrete piles.*

disinterested, uninterested Many writers use both to mean *not interested,* but in doing so they lose the unique meaning of *disinterested* as *impartial: What we need here is a disinterested observer.* Reserve *disinterested* for such uses. Avoid x *She was completely disinterested in dancing.*

doubtless(ly) Since *doubtless* is already an adverb, the *-ly* is excessive: *She will doubtless be ready at eight.*

drastic Once meant *violent,* and still retains a sense of harshness and grim urgency. Avoid x *a drastic improvement.*

dual, duel The first means *double,* the second a *fight.*

dubious, doubtful An outcome or a statement may be *dubious,* but the person who calls it into question is *doubtful* about it. Though some writers overlook the distinction, you would do well to keep *doubtful* for the mental state of harboring doubts.

due to Do not use adverbially, as in x *Due to her absence, the team lost the game.* In such a sentence use *because of* or *owing to,* and save *due to* for sentences like *The loss was due to her absence.*

dying, dyeing The first means *expiring,* the second *coloring.*

effect See *affect.*

e.g., i.e. Often confused. The abbreviation *e.g.* means *for example;* it can be used only when you are *not* citing all the relevant items. The abbreviation *i.e.* means *that is;* it can be used only when you are giving the *equivalent* of the preceding term. In the main text of an essay or paper, it is best to write out *for example* and *that is.*

Once you have written *e.g.,* do not add *etc.,* as in x *See, e.g., Chapters 4, 7, 11, etc.* The idea of unlisted further examples is already present in *e.g.*

elicit, illicit The first means *draw forth,* the second *unlawful.* Don't write x *His business dealings were elicit.*

eminent, imminent The first means *prominent,* the second *about to happen: The arrival of the eminent diplomat was imminent.*

enhance Does not mean *increase,* as in x *I want to enhance my bank account.* It means *increase the value or attractiveness of,* as in *He enhanced his good reputation by performing further generous acts.* In order to be enhanced, something must be already valued.

usage
43

Note that the quality, not the person, gets enhanced. Avoid x *She was enhanced by receiving favorable reviews.*

enormity, enormousness Increasingly treated as synonyms, but many careful writers insist on keeping to the original meaning of *enormity* as *atrocious wickedness.* You would do well to avoid x *the enormity of his feet.*

envelop, envelope The first is a verb meaning to *surround;* the second is for mail.

escape (verb) When used with an object, it should mean *elude,* as in *They escaped punishment.* Avoid x *They escaped the jail.* Make *escaped* intransitive here: *They escaped from the jail.*

especially, specially, special *Especially* means *outstandingly: an especially interesting idea. Specially* means *for a particular purpose, specifically: This racket was specially chosen by the champion.*

Watch for meaningless uses of *special:* x *There are two special reasons why I came here.* This would make sense only if there had been many reasons, only two of which were special ones. Just delete *special.*

et al. Means *and other people,* not *and other things.* It belongs in citations, not in your main text.

etc. Means *and other things,* not *and other people. Et al.* serves that rival meaning. In formal prose, use a substitute expression such as *and so forth.*

Do not use *etc.* after *for example* or *such as:* x *America is composed of many ethnic groups, such as Germans, Poles, Italians, etc.*

eventhough A mistake for *even though.*

everyday, every day The first means *normal,* the second *each day.*

everyone, every one *Everyone* means *everybody; every one* means *each one* of specified items.

everywheres A mistake for *everywhere.*

**usage
43**

exceeding(ly), excessive(ly) *Exceeding* means *very much; excessive* means *too much.* It is not shameful to be *exceedingly rich,* but to be *excessively rich* is a demerit.

except Do not use as a conjunction, as in x *She told him to leave, except he preferred to stay.* Keep *except* as a preposition meaning *excluding: He remembered everything except his toothbrush.*

expect Mildly colloquial in the sense of *suppose, believe:* x *I expect it will snow tomorrow.*

factor A *factor* is an *element helping to produce a given result,* as in *They overlooked several factors in seeking the causes of the riot.* Do not use *factor* simply as a synonym of *item* or *point.* Note that *contributing factor* is always redundant.

fair, fare *Fair* means *just* or *pretty;* a *fare* is what you pay on the bus.

faze, phase To *faze* is to *daunt;* a *phase* is a *period.*

feel, feeling Many careful writers prefer to keep *feel* a verb, saving *feeling* for the noun. Thus they object to x *She had a feel for trigonometry.*

few, little *Few* refers to things or persons that can be counted; *little* refers to things that can be measured or estimated but not itemized. *Few people were on hand, and there was little enthusiasm for the speaker.*

fewer, less, lesser, least *Fewer* refers to numbers, *less* to amounts; *fewer members; less revenue.* Beware of advertising jargon: x *This drink contains less calories.* Since the calories are countable, only *fewer* would be correct here.

    Lesser is an adjective meaning *minor* or *inferior: The lesser emissaries were excluded from the summit meeting. Least* is the superlative of *little.* As an adjective it should be used only when more than two items are involved: *That was the least of her many worries.*

    Note that *fewer in number* is redundant.

figure, calculate Colloquial as synonyms of *think, suppose,* or *believe:* x *They figured she would be too frightened to complain.*

flaunt, flout Widely confused. To *flaunt* is to *display arrogantly: They flaunted their superior wisdom.* To *flout* is to *defy contemptuously: They flouted every rule of proper behavior.* The common error is to use *flout* for *flaunt:* ˣ *The pitcher flouted his unbeaten record.*

usage
43

flunk Colloquial for *fail,* as in ˣ *He flunked Biology 23.*

for example See *e.g.*

forbear, forebear To *forbear* is to *refrain;* a *forebear* is an *ancestor. She forbore to criticize her forebears.*

forward, foreword The first means *ahead;* the second is a *preface.*

fortuitous Means *by chance,* whether or not an advantage is implied. Do not allow *fortuitous* to mean simply *favorable, auspicious,* or *lucky:* ˣ *How fortuitous it was that fate drew us together!*

free, freely *Free* can serve as both an adjective and an adverb, meaning, among other things, *without cost.* But when you write *I give it to you freely,* you mean *I give it to you without mental reservation.*

frightened, scared, afraid You are *frightened* or, more informally, *scared* by an immediate cause of alarm; you are *afraid* of a more persistent danger or worry: *He was frightened [scared] by noises in the middle of the night; he was afraid he would have to buy a watchdog.*

fulsome Does not mean *abundant;* it means *offensively insincere.* Thus it would be wrong to write: ˣ *I love the fulsome scents of early spring.*

fun Colloquial as an adjective, as in ˣ *a fun party.*

good, well *You look good tonight* means that you are attractive. *You look well tonight* means that you do not look sick.

guess Colloquial as a synonym of *suppose:* ˣ *I guess I should give up trying.*

had better Do not shorten to *better,* as in ˣ *You better pay attention.*

half a Do not precede with a redundant *a,* as in x *He was there for a half a day.*

hangar, hanger A *hangar* is for airplanes, a *hanger* for coats.

hanged, hung The usual past participle of *hang* is *hung,* but many careful writers still use *hanged* when referring to capital punishment: *He was hanged for his heinous crimes; his lifeless body hung from the noose.*

hard, hardly Both can be adverbs. Fear of using *hard* as an adverb can lead to ambiguity: x *She was hardly pressed for time.* This could mean either *She was rushed* or, more probably, *She was scarcely rushed.* There is nothing wrong with writing *She was hard-pressed for time.* Note the hyphen, however.

high, highly *High* can be an adverb as well as an adjective. Prefer it to *highly* in expressions like *he jumped high, a high-flying pilot.* An antique vase may be *highly prized* and therefore *high-priced* at an auction.

hopefully Many readers accept this word in the sense of *it is hoped,* but others feel strongly that *hopefully* can mean only *in a hopeful manner.* Keep to this latter meaning if you want to give no offense. Write *He prayed hopefully* but not x *Hopefully, his pains will subside.*

how Avoid in the sense of *that,* as in x *I told her how I wouldn't stand for her sarcasm any more.*

how ever, however Distinct terms. *How ever are you going to untie that knot? You, however, know more about it than I do.*

   However is correct in the sense of *in whatever manner; However you consider it, the situation looks desperate.*

i.e. Means *that is;* see *e.g.*

if not Potentially ambiguous, as in x *There were good reasons, if not excellent ones, for taking that step.* Does this mean that the reasons decidedly were not excellent or that they may indeed have been excellent? Try *but not excellent ones* or *indeed, excellent ones,* depending on the intended sense.

usage 43

ignorant, stupid Often confused. To be *ignorant* of something is simply not to know it: *Newton was ignorant of relativity.* An *ignorant* person is one who has been taught very little. A *stupid* person is mentally unable to learn: *The main cause of his ignorance was his stupidity.*

imbue, instill You *imbue* somebody *with* a quality like courage; you *instill* that quality *into* the person. Don't write x *She imbued courage into him* or x *She instilled him with courage.*

implicit, explicit, tacit *Implicit* can be ambiguous, for it means both *implied* (left unstated) and *not giving cause for investigation.* Consider, e.g., x *My trust in her was implicit.* Was the trust left unstated, beyond question, or both? Try *My trust in her was left implicit* or *My trust in her was absolute.*

    Explicit is the opposite of *implicit* in the sense of *implied: In his will he spelled out the explicit provisions that had previously been left implicit. Tacit* is close to this sense of *implicit,* but it means *silent, unspoken;* its reference is to speech, not to expression in general.

imply, infer Widely confused. To *imply* is to *leave an implication;* to *infer* is to *take an implication. She implied that she was ready to leave the company, but the boss inferred that she was bluffing.* The common error is to use *infer* for *imply.*

in back of See *back of.*

in case Can usually be improved to *if: If* [not *In case*] *you do not like this model, we will refund your money.* Save *in case* for *in the event: This sprinkler is provided in case of fire.*

in connection with See *in terms of.*

in terms of, along the lines of, in connection with Vague and wordy. Instead of writing x *In terms of prowess, Tarzan was unconquerable,* just write *Tarzan was unconquerable.* Similarly, x *He was pursuing his studies along the lines of sociology* should be simply *He was studying sociology.*

include Do not use loosely to mean *are,* as in x *The Marx Brothers included Groucho, Harpo, Chico, and Zeppo.* Use *were* in this instance.

Only when at least one member is omitted should you use *include: The Marx Brothers included Harpo and Zeppo.*

individual (noun) Often pompous for *person:* ˣ *He was a kind-hearted individual.* Use *individual* where you want to draw attention to the single person as contrasted with the collectivity, as in *Our laws respect the individual.*

inside of Widely regarded as colloquial; can always be shortened to *inside.* Write *inside the car,* not ˣ *inside of the car.*

inspite of A mistake for *in spite of.*

is because See *reason is because.*

is when, is where Often involved in faulty predication: ˣ *A war is when opposing countries take up arms;* ˣ *Massage is where you lie on a table and. . . .* Match *when* only with times, *where* only with places: *When she was ready, she went where she pleased.* Most predication problems can be solved by changing the verb: *A war occurs when. . . .*

it's, its The first means *it is,* the second *belonging to it.*

kind of, sort of, type of When used at all, these expressions should be followed by the singular: *this kind of woman.* But *such a woman* is preferable.

    Sort of and *kind of* are awkward in the sense of *somewhat,* and they are sometimes followed by an unnecessary *a:* ˣ *He was an odd sort of a king.* Do not use *sort of* or *kind of* unless your sentence needs them to make sense: *This kind of bike has been on the market for only three months.*

lead, led *Led* is the past tense of the verb *lead.* Avoid ˣ *He lead her astray for years.*

leave, let Have different senses in clauses like *leave him alone* and *let him alone.* The first means *get out of his presence;* the second means *don't bother him* (even if you remain in his presence). Don't write ˣ *leave him go in peace.*

lessen, lesson The first means to *reduce;* the second means *teaching.*

level (noun) Overworked in the vague, colorless sense illustrated by x *at the public level;* x *on the wholesale level.* Use only when the idea of degree or ranking is present: *He was a competent amateur, but when he turned professional he found himself beyond his level.*

lie, lay If you mean *repose,* use the intransitive *lie: lie down.* The transitive *lay* means, among other things, *set* or *put: lay it here.*

All forms of these verbs are troublesome. The following sentences use three common tenses correctly:

PRESENT	PAST	PRESENT PERFECT
I lie in bed.	I lay in bed.	I have lain in bed.
I lay down my cards.	I laid down my cards.	I have laid down my cards.

lightening, lightning The first means *getting lighter;* the second is a flash.

like See *as, like.*

likely Weak as an unmodified adverb: x *He likely had no idea what he was saying.* Some readers would also object to x *Very likely, he had no idea what he was saying.* Try *probably,* and reserve *likely* for adjectival uses: a *likely story.* See also *apt, liable, likely.*

likewise An adverb, not a conjuction. You can write *Likewise, Myrtle failed the quiz,* but not x *Jan failed the quiz, likewise Myrtle.*

literally Means *precisely as stated, without a figurative sense.* If you write x *I literally died laughing,* you must be writing from beyond the grave. Do not use *literally* to mean *definitely* or *almost.* It is properly used in a sentence like *The poet writes literally about flowers, but her real subject is forgiveness.*

loath, loathe The first means *reluctant,* the second to *despise.*

loose, lose *Loose* is usually an adjective meaning *slack* or *free: The door hinge was loose. Lose* means *mislay.* Avoid x *I loose my notes whenever I desperately need them.*

lot, lots Somewhat colloquial in the sense of *many:* x *I could give you lots of reasons. A lot* (note the spelling) and *lots* make colloquial modifiers, too: x *She pleases me lots.* Try *very much.*

mad, angry *Mad* means *insane.* It is colloquial in the sense of *angry:* x *They were mad at me.*

majority Do not use unless you mean to contrast it with *minority: The majority of the caucus voted to disband the club.* In x *the majority of the time,* the term is out of place because *time* does not contain members that could be counted as a majority and a minority.

many, much *Many* refers to countable items, *much* to a total amount that cannot be divided into items (see *amount, number): Many problems make for much difficulty.* Do not write x *There were too much people in the line.*

material, materiel *Material* means *matter* or *pertaining to matter. Materiel* means *military supplies.*

media Increasingly used as a singular term, but many good writers disapprove. Since *media* is the plural of *medium,* you would do well to keep it plural. Don't write x *The media is to blame.*

militate, mitigate Often confused. To *militate* is to *have an adverse effect.* It is followed by *against,* as in *His poor eyesight militated against his becoming a pilot. Mitigate* means *reduce* (an unpleasant effect). It always takes an object, as in *The doctor's cheerful manner mitigated the pain.*

The common error is to use *mitigate* for *militate,* as in x *Their stubborn attitude mitigated against their chances of success.*

miner, minor A *miner* digs coal; a *minor* is not yet an adult.

mislead, misled *Misled* is the past participle of *mislead.* Avoid x *He mislead her several times.*

moreso A mistake for *more so.*

most Colloquial as an adverb meaning *almost:* x *We were most dead by the time we got there;* x *Most all the cows had found their way home.*

much less Avoid x *Skiing is difficult, much less surfing.* The *much less* construction requires an initial negation, as in *He has not even appeared, much less begun his work.*

muchly A mistake for *much.*

myself Do not use this intensive pronoun merely as a substitute for *I* or *me:* x *My friends and myself are all old-timers now;* x *She gave the book to Steve and myself.* Save *myself* for emphatic or reflexive uses: *I myself intend to do it; I have forgiven myself.*

usage 43

naval, navel The first means *nautical,* the second *bellybutton.*

not too, not that Colloquial when used to mean *not very:* x *She was not too sure about that;* x *They are not that interested in sailing.*

nothing like, nowhere near Do not use in place of *not nearly,* as in x *I am nothing like* [or *nowhere near*] *as spry as I used to be.*

nowheres A mistake for *nowhere.*

numerous Properly an adjective. You can write *He still had numerous debts,* but avoid x *Numerous of his debts remained unpaid.*

occur, take place The narrower term is *take place,* which should be used only with scheduled events. Avoid x *The storm took place last Tuesday.*

of Do not try to make this preposition into part of a verb, as in x *She would of helped him if she could of.* Use *have.*

off of Should be either *off* or *from: She jumped off the bridge* or *She jumped from the bridge.* Avoid x *She jumped off of the bridge.*

oftentimes Colloquial for *often.*

old-fashion Colloquial for *old-fashioned.*

on, upon, up on *On* and *upon* mean the same thing, but you should save *upon* for formal effects: *She swore upon her word of honor.* Note that *up on* is not the same as *upon: He climbed up on the ladder.*

on account of Never preferable to *because of.*

only Do not use as a conjunction: x *He tries to be good, only his friends lead him astray.* Keep *only* as an adjective or adverb: *That is his only problem; He only needs some better advice.*

oral, verbal *Oral* means *by mouth; verbal* means *in words,* whether or not the words are spoken. Write *a verbal presentation* only if you have in mind a contrast with some form of communication that bypasses words.

other than that Considered awkward: x *Other than that, I can follow your reasoning.* Try a more definite expression: *except for one point, apart from this objection,* etc.

other times Do not use as an adverb, as in x *Other times she felt depressed.* Use the complete prepositional phrase *at other times.*

otherwise Allowable as an adverb meaning *in other respects* or *differently: Otherwise, I feel healthy; She decided otherwise.* But do not use *otherwise* to replace the adjective *other:* x *He loved old buildings, Victorian and otherwise.*

ourself Should be *ourselves.*

outside of Should be *outside.* And in figurative uses you should prefer *except for:* not x *outside of these reasons* but *except for these reasons.*

part, portion A *part* is a *fraction of a whole;* a *portion* is a *part allotted to some person or use.* Thus you should avoid x *A large portion of the ocean is polluted.*

passed, past Do not mistake the adjective, noun, or preposition *past* for the verb *passed,* as in x *They past the test.* The following sentences are correct: *We passed the tennis courts; The past has passed us by; Past the tunnel lies the railroad station.*

peace, piece The first means *tranquillity,* the second *part.*

persecute, prosecute To *persecute* is to *single out for mistreatment.* To *prosecute* is to *bring to trial. He was prosecuted for persecuting his neighbors.*

personal, personnel The first means *individual,* the second *employees.*

phenomena Not a singular word, but the plural of *phenomenon.*

place Some readers regard terms like *anyplace, no place,* and *someplace* as colloquial. It is safer to write *anywhere, nowhere, somewhere.* Note, in any event, the two-word spelling of *no place.*

plan The verb is best followed by *to,* not *on: He plans to run,* not ˣ *He plans on running.* Note that since *plan* implies a future action, expressions like ˣ *plan ahead* and ˣ *future plans* are redundant.

plus Not a coordinating conjunction or a sentence adverb: ˣ *He was sleepy, plus he hadn't studied.* Keep *plus* as a preposition with numbers: *Two plus two is four.* When no number is involved, avoid *plus:* not ˣ *Her challenging work plus her long vacations made her happy* but *Along with her long vacations, her challenging work made her happy.*

poorly Colloquial in the sense of *ill* or *sick:* ˣ *I feel poorly today.* Keep as an adverb: *I performed poorly in the exam.*

popular Implies favor with large numbers of people. Avoid when you have something smaller in mind: ˣ *The hermit was popular with his three visitors;* ˣ *That idea is not very popular with me.*

possible Do not use as an adverb: ˣ *a possible missing airliner.* Try *possibly.*

pray, prey The first means *implore,* the second *victim.*

precede, proceed To *precede* is to *go ahead of;* to *proceed* is to *go forward. In the preceding announcement, we were instructed to proceed with caution.*

predominant, predominate The first is an adjective, the second a verb. *The Yankees were the predominant team; they predominated for years.*

prejudice, prejudiced The first is a noun meaning *bias;* the second is an adjective meaning *biased.* Do not write ˣ *They were prejudice.*

pressure, press (verbs) Many good writers prefer to keep *pressure* as a noun; they would not be caught writing ˣ *She pressured him to quit his job. Pressed* would raise no objection here.

principal, principle *Principal* is usually an adjective meaning *foremost; principle* is a noun meaning *rule. The principal reason for her success is that she keeps to her principles.* As a noun, *principal* usually refers to the head of a school. Do not write ˣ *He had to go to the principle's office.*

prophecy, prophesy The first is a noun meaning *prediction,* the second a verb meaning to *make predictions.* Write *She prophesied his downfall,* not x *She prophecied his downfall.*

prostate, prostrate The first is the name of a gland; the second means *prone. His prostate pain left him prostrate.*

quote (noun) Often considered colloquial when used to mean *quotation,* as in x *this quote,* or when written in the plural to mean *quotation marks,* as in x *She put quotes around it.* In formal writing, take the trouble to use the full terms *quotation* and *quotation marks.*

rack, wrack The first is a *framework,* the second a *ruin.*

rain, rein, reign *Rain* is precipitation; to *rein* is to *restrain;* to *reign* is to *rule.*

raise, rise (verbs) *Raise* takes an object: *Raise your arm. Rise* does not: *Rise and shine.*

real Colloquial as an adverb, as in x *I am real committed.* Prefer *really.*

reason is because A classic predication error. You can write either *She stayed home because of her health* or *The reason was her health,* but it is redundant to write x *The reason she stayed home was because of her health.*

rebut, refute To *rebut* an argument is to *speak or write against* it; to *refute* an argument is to *disprove* it. The common error is to use *refute* for *rebut:* x *You may be right, but I will refute what you said.*

reckon Colloquial for *suppose, think:* x *I reckon I can handle that.* Use in the sense of *count* or *consider: She is reckoned an indispensable member of the board.*

relation, relationship These overlap in meaning, and some writers use *relationship* in all contexts. But *relation* is preferable when you mean an abstract connection: *the relation of wages to prices.* Save *relationship* for mutuality: *the President's relationship with the press.*

relevant Requires a following prepositional phrase. Do not write x *The course was extremely relevant.* To what? Try *The course was* *extremely relevant to the issues of the hour.* Note, incidentally, that *revelant* is not a word.

replace See *substitute.*

reticent Does not mean *reluctant,* as in x *They were reticent to comply.* It means *disposed to be silent,* as in *Reticent people sometimes become talkative late at night.*

scared See *frightened, scared, afraid.*

set, sit With few exceptions, *set* takes an object: *set the table. Sit* almost never takes an object: *sit down.* Avoid x *She set there sleeping* and x *I want to sit these weary bones to rest.*

similar Means *resembling,* not *same.* Avoid x *Ted died in 1979, and Alice suffered a similar fate two years later.* Try *the same fate.*

Do not use *similar* as an adverb meaning *like:* x *This steak smells similar to the one I ate yesterday.* Try *like the one.*

since An indispensable word, but watch for ambiguity: x *Since she left, he has been doing all the housework.* Here *since* could mean either *because* or *ever since.* Prefer one of these terms.

some Do not use as an adverb meaning *somewhat,* as in x *He worried some about his health.* Try *He was somewhat worried about his health.*

something Avoid as an adverb meaning *somewhat,* as in x *He is something over six feet tall.*

sometime, some time, sometimes *Sometime* is an adverb meaning *at an unspecified time; some time* is an adjective-noun pair meaning *a span of time. Sometime I must tell you how I spent some time in prison. Sometimes* means *at times.* Write *Sometimes I get lonely,* not x *Sometime I get lonely.*

somewheres A mistake for *somewhere.*

sort of See *kind of.*

special, specially See *especially.*

stationary, stationery The first means *still,* the second *paper.*

substitute, replace *Substitute* takes as its object the new item that is supplanting the old one: *He substituted margarine for butter. Replace* takes as its object the item being abandoned: *He replaced the butter with margarine.* Note that these sentences are recounting the same act.

such as See *etc.*

suppose to A mistake for *supposed to,* as in ˣ *We are suppose to watch our manners.*

sure Colloquial as an adverb: ˣ *She sure likes muffins.* Since *surely* would sound stuffy here, try *certainly.*

sympathy for, sympathy with, sympathize with To feel *sympathy for* someone is to experience compassion: *She has sympathy for the people of Ethiopia. Sympathy with* is a feeling of kinship or identity: *Her sympathy with Gloria Steinem made her a feminist.* To *sympathize with,* however, is once again to experience compassion: *She sympathized with the poor.*

tack, tact A *tack* is a nautical course; *tact* is *discretion.*

than, then *Than* is for comparison; *then* means *at that time.* Avoid ˣ *It was later then she thought.*

that Beware of using *that* as an unexplained demonstrative adjective: ˣ *He didn't have that much to say. All that much to say* would not improve matters. Just write *He didn't have much to say.*

that, which In restrictive clauses (p. 254, 19m), most careful writers prefer *that* to *which: Alberta is the province that fascinates me.* Use *that* wherever the clause serves to narrow or identify the term it refers to. Compare: *Alberta, which fascinates me, is my favorite province.*

theirself, theirselves Mistakes for *themselves.*

those kind, type, etc. Should be *that kind, type,* etc. But prefer *such,* which is more concise: *such people.*

thusly A mistake for *thus.*

till, until, til, 'til, 'till *Till* and *until* are interchangeable. The other three forms are inappropriate.

to, too, two *To* means *toward; too* means *also; two* is the number. *Too* is weak when used as a sentence adverb: x *It was dark and cold; too, the rain was heavy.* Try *moreover* or *furthermore.*

Avoid *too* as a synonym of *very:* x *It was too kind of them to come.* Just drop *too* here.

try and Should be *try to:* not x *Try and do better* but *Try to do better.*

type Colloquial in place of *type of:* x *You are a headstrong type person.* But *type of* is itself objectionably wordy; try *You are headstrong.*

usage, use Widely confused. Save *usage* for contexts implying convention or custom: *English usage; the usages of our sect.* Avoid x *They discouraged the usage of cocaine* or x *Excessive usage of the car results in high repair bills.* Substitute *use* in both sentences.

Even *use of* often proves wordy: x *By his use of symbolism Ibsen establishes himself as a modern playwright.* Why not just *By his symbolism Ibsen establishes himself as a modern playwright?*

use (verb), **utilize; use** (noun), **utilization** *Utilize* and *utilization* are almost always jargon for *use.* To *utilize* is properly to *put to use* or to *turn a profit on,* and it makes sense when coupled with an abstraction: *to utilize resources.* But the word has a dehumanizing air; prefer *use* in ordinary contexts. Note that *utilization* is almost four times as long as *use,* which can always stand in its place.

use to In an affirmative past construction, be sure to write *used to,* not *use to:* x *They use to think so;* x *They are not use to the cold.* In addition, certain past negative constructions with *use* always sound awkward: x *Didn't she use to take the bus?* Try *She used to take the bus, didn't she?*

verbal, oral See *oral.*

violently Not a synonym of *strongly,* as in x *I violently oppose your program.* Only thugs and terrorists oppose programs *violently,* causing actual physical damage.

waive, wave To *waive* is to *relinquish.* *Wave* is a verb meaning to *move to and fro* and a noun meaning a *spreading movement.* Avoid x *She waved her right to a jury trial.*

ways Avoid in the sense of *distance:* x *It was only a short ways.* The right form is *way.*

weather, whether *Weather* is the state of the atmosphere; *whether* means *if.*

what ever, whatever Distinct terms. *What ever will we do about the heating bills? Whatever we do, it will not solve the problem.*

where Do not use in place of *whereby,* as in x *T'ai-chi is an exercise regimen where one slowly activates every muscle group. Whereby,* the right word here, means *by means of which.* Save *where* for actual places: *That storefront studio is where we study T'ai-chi.*

where . . . at Redundant and colloquial, as in x *She had no idea where he was at.* Always delete the *at.*

who's, whose *Who's* means *who is; whose* means *of whom. Who's the person whose coat was left behind?*

-wise Acceptable when it means *in the manner of,* as in *clockwise* and *lengthwise,* and when it means *having wisdom: penny-wise and pound-foolish; a ring-wise boxer.* Note the hyphens in this second set of examples.

Avoid *-wise* in the sense of *with respect to:* x *taxwise, agriculture-wise, conflict resolutionwise.* Such terms do save space, but many readers find them ugly. Look for concise alternatives: not x *the situation taxwise* but *the tax situation;* not x *America's superiority agriculture-wise* but *America's superiority in agriculture.*

with See *being.*

would like for Colloquial in sentences like x *They would like for me to quit.* Try *They would like me to quit.*

wreak, wreck To *wreak* is to *inflict: He wreaked havoc.* A *wreck* is a *ruin: a train wreck.*

your, you're The first is a possessive pronoun, the second a contraction of *you are.* Do not write x *Your certain to succeed* or x *Watch you're step!*

44 Glossary of Terms

The Glossary of Terms offers definitions of terms appearing in **bold-face** elsewhere in this book. Within the Glossary itself, words appearing in black boldface have separate entries which you can consult as necessary. The abbreviation *cf.* means "compare"—that is, note the difference between the term being defined and another. And *e.g.* means "for example."

abbreviation (p. 421) A shortened word, with the addition of a period to indicate the omission (*Dr.*).

absolute phrase (p. 249) A **phrase** that, instead of modifying a particular word, acts like an **adverb** to the rest of the sentence in which it appears:

> ABS PHRASE
> - *All struggle over,* the troops laid down their arms.

Absolute phrases are not considered mistakes of usage. Cf. **dangling modifier.**

abstract language (p. 175) Words that make no appeal to the senses: *agree, aspect, comprehensible, enthusiasm, virtuously,* etc. Cf. **concrete language.**

active voice See **voice.**

ad hominem **reasoning** (p. 22) A **fallacy** whereby someone tries to discredit a position by attacking the person, party, or interest that supports that position.

additive phrase (p. 227) An expression beginning with a term like *accompanied by* or *as well as.* It is not strictly a part of a subject, and thus it should not affect the number of a verb.

adjectival clause See **clause.**

adjective (p. 241) A **modifier** of a **noun, pronoun,** or other **nounlike element**—e.g., *strong* in *a strong contender.* Most adjectives can be compared: *strong, stronger, strongest.* See **degree.** See also **interrogative adjective.**

adverb (p. 241) A word modifying either a **verb,** an **adjective,** another adverb, a **preposition,** an **infinitive,** a **participle,** a **phrase,** a **clause,** or a whole **sentence:** *now, clearly, moreover,* etc. Any one-word modifier that is not an adjective or an **article** is sure to be an adverb.

adverbial clause See **clause.**

agreement See **pronoun agreement, subject-verb agreement.**

allusion (p. 461) A passing reference to a work or idea, either by directly mentioning it or by borrowing its well-known language. Thus, someone who writes *She took arms against a sea of troubles* is alluding to, but not mentioning, Hamlet's most famous speech. The sentence *He did it with Shakespearean flair* alludes directly to Shakespeare. Quotation through allusion differs from **plagiarism** in that readers are expected to notice the reference.

"alternative MLA" style (p. 483) A documentation style, formerly preferred by the Modern Language Association, that makes use of **endnotes** or **footnotes** rather than **parenthetic citations.** Cf. **APA style, MLA style.**

analogy (p. 193) In general, a similarity of features or pattern between two things: *The nearest analogy to human speech may be the songs of whales.*

In **rhetoric,** an analogy is an extended likeness purporting to show that the rule or principle behind one thing also holds for the different thing being discussed. Thus, someone who disapproves of people leaving their home towns might devise this analogy: *People, like trees, must find their nourishment in the place where they grow up; to seek it elsewhere is as fatal as removing a tree from its roots.* Like most analogies, this one starts with an obvious resemblance and proceeds to a more debatable one.

analysis (p. 30) In a narrow sense, the breaking of something into its parts or functions and showing how those smaller units go to make up the whole. More broadly, analysis is the application of explanatory strategies to a given problem. In this book, analysis (or *exposition*) is treated as a rhetorical **mode,** along with **description, narration,** and **argument.**

antecedent (p. 236) The word for which a **pronoun** stands:

ANT   PRO
- *Jane* was here yesterday, but today *she* is at school.

anticipatory pattern (p. 149) A structure, such as *both x and y* or *not x but y,* which gives an early signal of the way it will be completed.

APA style (p. 465) The **parenthetic citation** documentation style of the American Psychological Association. Cf. **MLA style, "alternative MLA" style.**

aphorism (p. 152) A memorably concise sentence conveying a very general assertion: *If wishes were horses, beggars would ride.* Many aphorisms show **balance** in their structure.

appositive (p. 257) A word or group of words whose only function is to identify or restate a neighboring **noun, pronoun,** or **nounlike element:**

APP
- Mike *the butcher* is quite a clown.

Arabic numeral (p. 430) A figure such as *3, 47,* or *106,* as opposed to a **Roman numeral** such as *III, XLVII,* or *CVI.*

argument (p. 30) The **mode** of writing in which a writer tries to convince the reader that a certain position on an issue is well-founded. Cf. **description, analysis, narration.**

article An indicator or determiner immediately preceding a **noun** or **modifier.** Articles themselves may be considered modifiers, along with **adjectives** and **adverbs.** The *definite article* is *the;* the *indefinite articles* are *a* and *an.*

attributive noun (p. 167) A **noun** serving as an **adjective:** *beach* in *beach shoes,* or *Massachusetts* in *the Massachusetts way of doing things.*

auxiliary A **verb** form, usually lacking **inflection,** that combines with other verbs to express possibility, likelihood, necessity, obligation, etc.: *She can succeed; He could become jealous.* The commonly recognized auxiliaries are *can, could, dare, do, may, might, must, need, ought, should,* and *would. Is, have,* and their related forms act like auxiliaries in the formation of **tenses:** *He is coming; They have gone.*

baited opener (p. 116) An introductory **paragraph** which, by presenting its early sentences "out of context," teases its reader into taking further interest.

balance (p. 152) The effect created when a whole sentence is controlled by the matching of grammatically like elements, as in *He taught us the intricate ways of the city; we taught him the simple ways of nature.* A balanced sentence typically repeats a grammatical pattern and certain words in order to highlight important differences.

base form of verb (p. 362) An **infinitive** without *to: see, think,* etc. Base forms appear with **auxiliaries** *(should see)* and in the formation of present and future **tenses** *(I see, I will see).*

begging the question (p. 20) The **fallacy** of treating a debatable idea as if it had already been proved. If, in a paper favoring national health insurance, you assert that only the greedy medical lobby could oppose such an obviously needed program, you are begging the question by assuming the rightness of your position instead of establishing it with **evidence.** Also called *circular reasoning.*

bibliographic note (p. 490) A supplementary note directing the reader to further sources of information. Cf. **substantive note.**

bibliography (p. 489) A list of consulted works presented at the end of a book, article, or **essay.** Also, a whole book devoted to listing works within a certain **subject area.**

block quotation See **indented quotation.**

bound element (p. 141) A modifying word, **phrase,** or subordinate **clause** which, because it is **restrictive,** is not set off by commas. Cf. **free element.**

brackets (p. 350) Punctuation marks used to insert an explanatory word or phrase into a sentence, as in *"I voted for [Dianne] Feinstein,"* *she said.* Also called *square brackets.*

brainstorming (p. 12) The process of entertaining many suggestions for a topic without regard for links between them.

cardinal number (p. 431) A number like *four (4)* or *twenty-seven (27),* as opposed to an **ordinal number** like *fourth (4th)* or *twenty-seventh (27th).*

case (p. 262) The **inflection**al form of **nouns** and **pronouns** indicating whether they designate actors *(subjective case: I, we, they),* receivers of action *(objective case: me, us, them),* or "possessors" of the thing or quality modified *(possessive case: his* Toyota, *their* indecision, *Geraldine's* influence). *Personal pronouns* also have "second possessive" forms: *mine, theirs,* etc. Cf. **double possessive.**

choppiness (p. 100) The undesirable effect produced by a sequence of brief sentences lacking pauses marked by punctuation.

circular reasoning See **begging the question.**

circumlocution (p. 178) Roundabout expression, or one such expression—e.g., x *when all is said and done* in place of *finally.*

clause (p. 201) A cluster of words containing a **subject** and a **predicate.** All clauses are either *subordinate* (dependent) or *independent.* (An independent clause is sometimes called a *main clause.*)

**gloss
44**

A subordinate clause cannot stand alone: x *When he was hiding in the closet.* An independent clause, which is considered grammatically complete, can stand alone: *He was hiding in the closet.*

There are three kinds of subordinate clauses:

1. A *relative* clause serves the function of an **adjective:**

REL CLAUSE
- Marty, *who was extremely frightened,* did not want to make a sound.

   The relative clause modifies the **noun** *Marty.*

2. An *adverbial* clause serves the function of an **adverb:**

ADV CLAUSE
- Marty held his breath for forty seconds *when he was hiding in the closet.*

   The adverbial clause modifies the **verb** *held.*

3. And a *noun* clause serves the function of a **noun:**

NOUN CLAUSE
- *That an intruder might slip through his bedroom window* had never occurred to him.

   The noun clause serves as the **subject** of the **verb** *had occurred.*

cliché (p. 182) A trite, stereotyped, overused expression: *an open and shut case; a miss is as good as a mile.* Most clichés contain **figurative language** that has lost its vividness: *a heart of gold; bring the house down,* etc. When two clichés occur together, the effect is usually **mixed metaphor.**

collective noun (p. 229) A **noun** that, though singular in form, designates a group of members: *band, family,* etc.

comma splice (p. 212) A **run-on sentence** in which two independent clauses are joined by a comma alone, without the necessary coordinating conjunction: x *It is raining today, I left my umbrella home.* Cf. **fused sentence.**

common gender (p. 170) The intended sexual neutrality of **pronouns** used to indicate an indefinite party. Traditionally, indefinite *(one)* and masculine personal pronouns *(he)* were used, but the masculine ones are now widely regarded as **sexist language.**

comparative degree See **degree.**

comparison and contrast (p. 109) The analytic strategy of exploring the resemblances and differences between two or more things.

complement (p. 198) Usually, an element in a **predicate** that identifies or describes the **subject.** A single-word complement is either a *predicate noun* or a *predicate adjective:*

PRED NOUN
● He is a *musician.*

PRED ADJ
● His skill is *unbelievable.*

In addition, a **direct object** can have a complement, known as an *objective complement:*

D OBJ   OBJ C
● They consider the *location desirable.*

Infinitives, too, can have complements:

INF   C OF INF
● They beg him *to be* more *cooperative.*

compound, adj. (p. 266) Consisting of more than one word, as in a compound verb (They <u>whistled</u> and <u>sang</u>), a compound noun *(ice cream)*, a compound preposition *(in spite of)*, a compound subject *(<u>He</u> and <u>she</u> were there)*, or a compound modifier *(far-gone)*.

concession (p. 26) In **rhetoric,** the granting of an opposing point, usually to show that it does not overturn one's own **thesis.**

conciseness (p. 176) Economy of expression. Not to be confused with simplicity; conciseness enables a maximum of meaning to be communicated in a minimum of words.

concrete language (p. 175) Words describing a thing or quality appealing to the senses: *purple, car, buzz, dusty,* etc. Cf. **abstract language.**

conjunction (p. 209) An un**inflected** word that connects other words, **phrases,** or **clauses:** *and, although,* etc.

A *coordinating* conjunction—*and, but, for, nor, or, so, yet*—joins grammatically similar elements without turning one into a **modifier** of the other: *You are sad, but I am cheerful.*

A *subordinating* conjunction joins grammatically dissimilar elements, turning one of them into a modifier and specifying its logical relation to the other—e.g., *Although you are sad, I am cheerful; I understand that you like jazz.*

Correlative conjunctions are matched pairs with a coordinating or a disjunctive purpose: *either/or, neither/nor,* etc.

Cf. **preposition.**

connotation (p. 168) An association that a word calls up, as opposed to its **denotation,** or dictionary meaning. Thus, the word *exile* denotes enforced separation from one's home or country, but it connotes loneliness, homesickness, and any number of other, more private, thoughts and images.

continuity (p. 84) The felt linkage between sentences or whole paragraphs, achieved in part by keeping related sentences together and in part by using **signals of relation** to indicate how sentences tie in with the ones they follow.

contraction (p. 386) The condensing of two words to one, with an apostrophe added to replace the omitted letter or letters: *isn't, don't,* etc. Contractions are used primarily in speech and informal writing.

coordinating conjunction See **conjunction.**

coordination (p. 209) The giving of equal grammatical value to two or more parts of a sentence. Those parts are usually joined by a *coordinating conjunction: He tried, but he failed; The lifeguard reached for her megaphone and her whistle.* Cf. **subordination**

correlative conjunction See **conjunction.**

cumulative sentence (p. 156) A sentence that continues to develop after its main idea has been stated, adding **clauses** or **phrases** that **modify** or explain that assertion: *She crumpled the letter in her fist, trembling with rage, wondering whether she should answer the accusations or simply say good riddance to the whole affair.* Cf. **suspended sentence.**

dangling modifier (p. 243) The **modifier** of a term that has been wrongly omitted from the sentence:

DANGL MOD
x *Not wishing to be bothered,* the telephone was left off the hook.

The person who did not wish to be bothered goes unmentioned and is thus absurdly replaced by the telephone.

Cf. **misplaced modifier.**

dead metaphor (p. 191) A **metaphor** that has become so common that it usually does not call to mind an **image:** *a devil of a time, rock-bottom prices,* etc. When overworked, a dead metaphor becomes a **cliché.**

declarative sentence (p. 312) A sentence that presents a statement rather than a question or an **exclamation:** *Lambs are woolly.*

degree (p. 241) The form of an **adjective** or **adverb** showing its quality, quantity, or intensity. The ordinary, uncompared form of an adjective or adverb is its *positive* degree: *quick, quickly.* The *comparative* degree is intermediate, indicating that the modified term surpasses at least one other member of its group: *quicker, more quickly.* And an adjective or adverb in the *superlative* degree indicates that the modified term surpasses all other members of its group: *quickest, most quickly.*

demonstrative adjective (p. 87) A *demonstrative pronoun* form serving as a **modifier,** e.g., *those* in *those laws.*

demonstrative pronoun See **pronoun.**

denotation (p. 161) The primary, "dictionary," meanings of a word. Cf. **connotation.**

dependent clause See **clause.**

description (p. 30) The **mode** of writing in which a writer tries to acquaint the reader with a place, object, character, or group. Cf. **argument, analysis, narration.**

dialogue (p. 345) The direct representation of speech between two or more persons. Cf. **indirect discourse.**

diction (p. 161) The choice of words. Diction is commonly divided into three levels: formal *(deranged)*, middle *(crazy)*, and slang *(nuts)*.

digression (p. 83) A temporary change of topic within a sentence, paragraph, or whole discourse. In an **essay,** an *apparent digression*—one that later turns out to have been pertinent after all—may sometimes serve a good purpose. In general, however, digressions are to be avoided.

direct discourse (p. 303) The use of quotation, as opposed to summary, of a speaker's or writer's words. Cf. **indirect discourse**.

direct object (p. 198) A word naming the item directly acted upon by a **subject** through the activity of a **verb:**

       S   V   D OBJ
- *She hit* the *jackpot.*

Cf. **indirect object.**

direct paragraph (p. 94) A **paragraph** in which the **main sentence** comes at or near the beginning and the remaining sentences support it, sometimes after a **limiting sentence** or two.

disjunctive subject (p. 230) A **subject** containing elements that are alternative to one another, as in *Either you or I must back down.*

distinct expression (p. 129) The forming of sentences in the clearest manner, without causing a reader to guess at the meaning or the relations between elements. Distinct expression is enhanced by effective punctuation, **subordination,** and **conciseness** of phrasing.

double negative (p. 250) The nonstandard practice of conveying the same negative meaning twice: x *They don't want no potatoes.*

double possessive (p. 272) A possessive form using both *of* and *-'s: an idea of Linda's.* Double possessives do not constitute faulty usage.

either-or reasoning (p. 23) The depicting of one's own position as the better of an artificially limited and "loaded" pair of alternatives—e.g., x *If we do not raise taxes this year, a worldwide depression is inevitable.*

ellipsis (p. 348) The three or four spaced dots used to indicate material omitted from a quotation: *"about the . . . story."* A whole row of dots indicates omission of much more material, usually verse.

emotionalism (p. 39) The condition of someone who is too upset to think clearly. Strong emotion can be a valuable aid to writing; emotionalism is always a handicap.

endnote (p. 483) A note placed in a consecutive series with others at the end of an **essay,** article, chapter, or book.

essay (p. 2) A fairly brief (usually between two and twenty-five typed pages) piece of nonfiction that tries to make a point in an interesting way. For the essay **modes,** see **analysis, argument, description, narration.**

euphemism (p. 181) A vague or "nice" expression inadvisedly used in place of a more direct one; e.g., *rehabilitation facility* for *prison,* or *disincentive* for *threat.*

evidence (p. 47) Facts, reasons, and testimony tending to support a **thesis.** One statement can be used as evidence for another only if there is a high likelihood that readers will accept it as true.

exclamation (p. 315) An extremely emphatic statement or outburst: *Get out of here! What a scandal!* Cf. **interjection.**

expletive The word *it* or *there* when used only to postpone a **subject** coming after the verb:

    EXPL V   S
- *There* are many reasons to doubt his story.

exposition See **analysis.**

fallacy (p. 50) A formal error or illegitimate shortcut in reasoning. See **ad hominem reasoning, begging the question, either-or reasoning, faulty generalization,** *post hoc* **explanation,** and **straw man.**

"false start" (p. 156) A device whereby a sentence appears to present its grammatical **subject** first but then breaks off and begins again, thus turning the opening element into an **appositive:** *Elephants, gorillas, pandas—the list of endangered species grows longer every year.* A false start can be a good means of seizing a reader's attention. Cf. **mixed construction.**

faulty generalization (p. 18) The **fallacy** of drawing a general conclusion from insufficient **evidence**—e.g., concluding from one year's drought that the world's climate has entered a long period of change.

figurative language (p. 185) Language that heightens expressiveness by suggesting an imaginative, not a **literal,** comparison to the thing described—e.g., *a man so emaciated that he looked more like an x-ray than a person.* See **metaphor, simile.** Cf. **literal language.**

footnote (p. 483) A note at the bottom of a page. Cf. **endnote.**

fragment See **sentence fragment.**

free element (p. 140) A **modifying** word, **phrase,** or subordinate **clause** that deserves to be set off by commas. Most but not all free elements are **nonrestrictive;** some **restrictive modifiers** at the beginnings of sentences can be treated as free—that is, followed by a comma. Cf. **bound element.**

freewriting (p. 11) The practice of writing continuously for a fixed period without concern for logic or correctness. In *focused freewriting* the writer begins with a specific **topic.**

funnel opener (p. 115) An introductory **paragraph** beginning with a broad assertion and gradually narrowing to a specific **topic.**

fused sentence (p. 213) A **run-on sentence** in which two independent **clauses** are joined without either a comma or a coordinating **conjunction:** ₓ *He is a dapper newscaster I love his slightly Canadian accent.*

gender (p. 274) The grammatical concept of sexual classification determining the forms of masculine *(he),* feminine *(she),* and neuter *(it)* personal pronouns and the feminine forms of certain nouns *(actress)*. Cf. **common gender, sexist language.**

gerund (p. 199) A form derived from a **verb** but functioning as a **noun**—e.g., *Skiing* in *Skiing is dangerous.* Gerunds take exactly the same form as **participles,** and they are capable of having **subjects** (usually possessive in **case**) as well as **objects:**

    S OF GER   GER   OBJ GER
- *Elizabeth's winning* the *pentathlon* was unexpected.

Cf. **participle.**

governing pronoun (p. 34) The prevailing **pronoun** in a piece of writing, helping to establish the writer's **point of view.**

governing tense (p. 298) The prevailing verb **tense** in a piece of writing, establishing a time frame for reported events.

hyperbole (p. 189) **Figurative language** that works by overstatement, as in *I will love you until the sun grows cold.*

idiom (p. 249) A fixed expression whose meaning cannot be deduced from its elements—for example, *come around,* meaning *agree or acquiesce after initial resistance.*

image (p. 185) An expression that appeals to the senses. More narrowly, an example of **figurative language.** In both senses, the use of images is called *imagery.*

imperative mood See **mood.**

implied subject (p. 201) A **subject** not actually present in a **clause** but nevertheless understood: *[You] Watch out!* The customary implied subject, as here, is *you.*

incorporated quotation (p. 338) A quotation placed within quotation marks and not set off from the writer's own prose. Cf. **indented quotation.**

indefinite pronoun See **pronoun.**

indented quotation (p. 343) A quoted passage set apart from the writer's own language. Prose quotations of more than four typed lines and verse quotations of more than two or three lines are customarily indented, without quotation marks. Also known as a *block quotation.* Cf. **incorporated quotation.**

indention (p. 343) The setting of the first word of a line to the right of the left margin, as in a new paragraph (5 spaces) or an **indented quotation** (usually 10 spaces).

independent clause See **clause.**

index (p. 444) A book, usually with a new volume each year, containing alphabetically ordered references to articles (and sometimes books) in a given field. Also, an alphabetical list of subjects and the page numbers where they are treated in a nonfiction book, as on pages 599–636 below.

indicative mood See **mood.**

indirect discourse (p. 303) Reporting what was said, as opposed to directly quoting it. Not *She said, "I am tired,"* but *She said she was tired.* Also called *indirect statement.* Cf. **direct discourse, indirect question.**

indirect object (p. 263) A word designating the person or thing for whom or which, or to whom or which, the action of a **verb** is performed. An indirect object never appears without a **direct object** occurring in the same clause:

- She sent *Fernando* a discouraging *letter.*

    IND OBJ   D OBJ

indirect question (p. 312) The reporting of a question without use of the question form—not *She asked, "Where should I turn?"* but *She asked where she should turn.* Cf. **indirect discourse.**

infinitive (p. 199) The **base form of a verb,** usually but not always preceded by *to: to win; to prove; prove.*

inflection (p. 361) A change in the ending or whole form of a word to show a change in function without creating a new word. Thus *he* can be inflected to *his, George* to *George's, go* to *went,* etc.

intensifier (p. 179) A "fortifying" expression like *absolutely, definitely,* or *very.* Habitual use of intensifiers weakens the force of assertion.

intensive pronoun See **pronoun.**

intentional sentence fragment See **sentence fragment.**

interjection A word that stands apart from other constructions in order to command attention or show strong feeling: *aha, hey, wow,* etc. Cf. **exclamation.**

interrogative adjective An interrogative **pronoun** form that combines with a **noun** to introduce a question—e.g., *Whose* in *Whose socks are these?*

interrogative pronoun See **pronoun.**

interrupting element (p. 238) A word or group of words that interrupts the main flow of a sentence:

INT EL
- You, *I regret to say,* are not the one.

Interrupting elements (also called *parenthetical elements*) should be set off at both ends by punctuation, usually by commas.

intransitive verb (p. 198) A **verb** expressing an action or state without connection to a **direct object** or a **complement**—e.g., *complained* in *They complained.* Cf. **linking verb, transitive verb.**

introductory tag (p. 347) A **clause,** such as *He said* or *Agnes asked,* introducing a quotation. A tag may also interrupt or follow a quotation.

inverted syntax (p. 157) The reversal of the expected order among sentence elements, usually for rhetorical effect: *After many bitter hours came the dawn.*

irony (p. 35) A sharply incongruous or "poetically just" effect—created, for example, when the Secretary of the Treasury has to borrow a coin to make a phone call.

   In **rhetoric,** irony is the saying of one thing in order to convey a different or even opposite meaning: *Brutus is an honorable man* [he really isn't]. Irony can be *broad* (obvious) or *subtle,* depending on the writer's purpose. Cf. **sarcasm.**

irregular verb (p. 364) A **verb** that forms its past **tense** and its past **participle** in some way other than simply adding -*d* or -*ed*: *go* (*went*, *gone*), *swim* (*swam*, *swum*), etc.

italics (p. 417) Thin, slanting letters, *like these*. In handwritten or typewritten work, italics are indicated by underlining. Cf. **roman type.**

jargon (p. 172) Technical language used in inappropriate, nontechnical contexts—e.g., *upwardly mobile* for *ambitious, positive reinforcement* for *praise, paranoid* for *upset.*

leading idea (p. 81) The "point" of a **paragraph,** to which all other ideas in that paragraph should relate. Cf. **main sentence.**

limiting sentence (p. 94) A sentence that addresses a possible limitation, or contrary consideration, to the **leading idea** of a paragraph.

linking verb (p. 198) A **verb** connecting its **subject** to an identifying or modifying **complement.** Typical linking verbs are *be, seem, appear, become, feel, sense, grow, taste, look, sound:*

       S   LV   C
- They *were* Mormons.

       S   LV   C
- She *became* calmer.

Cf. **intransitive verb, transitive verb.**

literal language (p. 185) Words that factually represent what they describe, without poetic embellishment. Cf. **figurative language.**

"literary" present tense (p. 306) The present **tense** form of a verb when it is used to express the ongoing action or meaning of an art work or other text: *Willie Loman tries to hide from reality; The play addresses some of our deepest anxieties.*

main clause See **clause.**

main sentence (p. 81) The sentence in a paragraph that conveys its **leading idea.** Often called *topic sentence.*

metaphor (p. 188) An implied comparison whereby the thing at hand is figuratively asserted to be something else: *His fists were a hurricane of ceaseless assault.* Cf. **simile.**

misplaced modifier (p. 244) A **modifier** whose modified term is present in the sentence but not immediately identifiable as such:

> MISPLACED MOD   MODIFIED TERM?
> x *Laughing* so hard, Nancy was offended by *Ellen's* frivolity in a time of crisis.

Compare:

- Laughing so hard, Ellen offended Nancy by her frivolity in a time of crisis.

Cf. **dangling modifier.**

mixed construction (p. 221) The use of two clashing structures within a sentence, as in x *Even a friendly interviewer, it is hard to keep from being nervous.*

mixed metaphor (p. 189) A **metaphor** whose elements clash in their implications: x *Let's back off for a closer look;* x *He is a straight arrow who shoots from the hip.*

MLA style (p. 465) The **parenthetic citation** style of documentation now favored by the Modern Language Association. Cf. **APA style, "alternative MLA" style.**

mode (p. 30) A type of writing characterized by the purpose of its **rhetoric.** The modes recognized in this book are **analysis, argument, description,** and **narration.** One essay can make use of several modes.

modifier (p. 240) A word, **phrase,** or **clause** that limits or describes another element:

> MOD
- the *gentle* soul

> MOD   MOD
- *When leaving,* turn out the lights *on the porch.*

> MOD
- *Before you explain,* I have something to tell you.

mood (p. 371) The manner or attitude that a speaker or writer intends a **verb** to convey, as shown in certain changes of form. Ordinary statements and questions are cast in the *indicative* mood: *Is he ill? He is.* The *imperative* mood is for commands: *Stop! Get out of the way!* And the *subjunctive* mood is used for certain formulas (*as it were*), unlikely or impossible conditions (*had she gone*), *that* clauses expressing requirements or recommendations (*They ask that she comply*), and *lest* clauses (*lest he forget*).

narration (p. 30) The **mode** of writing in which a writer recounts something that has happened. Cf. **analysis, argument, description.**

nominalization (p. 132) The use of nouns instead of verbs to express action, as in *She made a gesture* as opposed to *She gestured.* Habitual nominalization makes for an indistinct style.

nonrestrictive element (p. 256) A **modifier,** often a **phrase** or a **clause,** that does not serve to identify ("restrict") the modified term and is therefore set off by punctuation, usually commas:

NONR EL

- That woman, *whom I met only yesterday,* already understands my problems.

Cf. **restrictive element.**

noun (p. 200) A word like *Jack, Pennsylvania, house,* or *assessment,* usually denoting a person, place, thing, or idea. A noun can undergo **inflection** for both plural and possessive forms (*houses, house's, houses'*), and it can serve a variety of sentence functions (subject, direct object, etc.).

noun clause See **clause.**

noun phrase See **phrase.**

nounlike element (p. 200) A word or group of words having the same function as a **noun** or **pronoun,** but not the same features of **inflection**—e.g., *what you mean* in *He knows what you mean.* Also called *nominal* or *substantive.*

number (p. 224) In grammar, the distinction between *singular* and *plural* form. The distinction applies to **verbs** (she *drives,* they *drive*), **nouns** (*boat, boats*), and personal **pronouns** (*I, we*).

numeral (p. 430) A number expressed as a figure (*6, 19*) or a group of letters (*VI, XIX*) instead of being written out.

object (p. 198) A **noun, pronoun,** or **nounlike element** representing a receiver of an action or relation. See **direct object, indirect object,** and **object of preposition.** In addition, **infinitives, participles,** and **gerunds** can take objects:

OBJ OF INF
- to chair the *convention*

OBJ OF PART
- Chairing the *convention* impartially, she allowed no disorder.

OBJ OF GER
- Chairing a turbulent *convention* is a thankless task.

object of preposition (p. 265) A **noun, pronoun,** or **nounlike element** following a **preposition** and completing the prepositional **phrase**—e.g., *November* in *throughout November,* or *siesta* in *during a long siesta.*

objective case See **case.**

objective complement See **complement.**

ordinal number (p. 431) A number like *fourth* (*4th*) or *twenty-seventh* (*27th*), as opposed to a **cardinal number** like *four* (*4*) or *twenty-seven* (*27*).

outline (p. 43) A schematic plan showing the organization of a piece of writing. A *scratch outline* merely lists points to be made, whereas a *subordinated outline* shows, through indention and more than one set of numbers, which points are the most important ones. A further distinction is made between the *topic outline,* whose headings are concise **phrases,** and the *sentence outline,* which calls for complete sentences.

paragraph (p. 80) A unit of prose, usually consisting of several sentences, marked by **indention** of the first line (or sometimes by an extra blank line). A well-wrought paragraph of **analysis** or **argument** is expected to provide support for one **leading idea.**

paragraph block (p. 92) A group of paragraphs addressing the same part of a **topic,** with strong continuity from one paragraph to the next.

parallelism (p. 284) The structure or the effect that results from matching two or more parts of a sentence—e.g., the words *Utica, Albany,* and *Rye* in the sentence *He went to Utica, Albany, and Rye,* or the three equally weighted **clauses** that begin this sentence: *That he wanted to leave, that permission was denied, and that he then tried to escape—these facts only became known after months of official secrecy.* Cf. **balance, coordination.**

paraphrase (p. 457) Sentence-by-sentence restatement, in different words, of the meaning of a passage. Cf. **summary.**

parenthetic citation (p. 478) A reference to a work, given not in a **footnote** or **endnote** but in parentheses within a main text—e.g., *(Meyers 241–75).*

parenthetical element See **interrupting element.**

part of speech (p. 163) Any of the major classes into which words are customarily divided, depending on their dictionary meaning and their syntactic functions in sentences. Since many words belong to more than one part of speech, you must analyze the sentence at hand to see which part of speech a given word is occupying. The commonly recognized parts of speech are:

Verb	try, adopts, were allowing
Noun	Cynthia, paper, Manitoba
Pronoun	she, himself, each other, nothing, these, who
Preposition	to, among, according to
Conjunction	and, yet, because, although, if
Adjective	wide, lazier, more fortunate
Adverb	agreeably, seldom, ahead, together, however
Interjection	oh, ouch, gosh
Article	a, an, the
Expletive	it [is], there [were]

participle (p. 199) An **adjectival** form derived from a **verb**—e.g., *Showing* in *Showing fear, he began to sweat*. Participles can be present (*showing*) or past (*having shown*) and active or passive (*having been shown*). Like other **verbals,** they can have **objects** (*fear* in the sentence above), but unlike other verbals, they do not have **subjects.** Cf. **gerund.**

passive voice See **voice.**

past participle See **participle.**

person (p. 224) In grammar, a characteristic of **pronouns** and **verbs** indicating whether someone is speaking (*first* person: *I go, we go*), being spoken to (*second* person: *you go*), or being spoken about (*third* person: *he, she, it goes; they go*).

personal pronoun See **pronoun.**

phrase (p. 203) A cluster of words functioning as a single **part of speech** and lacking a **subject-predicate** combination. Cf. **clause.**

A **noun** and its **modifiers** are sometimes called a *noun phrase* (*the faulty billiard balls*), and a **verb** form consisting of more than one word is sometimes called a *verb phrase* (*had been trying*). But the types of phrases most commonly recognized are *prepositional, infinitive, participial, gerund,* and **absolute.**

A *prepositional phrase* consists of a **preposition** and its **object,** along with any **modifiers** of those words:

<pre>
                              OBJ
    PREP MOD   MOD   MOD   PREP
 • among her numerous painful regrets
                PREP PHRASE
</pre>

An *infinitive phrase* consists of an **infinitive** and its **object** and/or **modifiers:**

<pre>
                                    OBJ
          S INF INF MOD MOD   MOD INF
 • They asked John to hit the almost invisible target.
                        INF PHRASE
</pre>

A *participial phrase* consists of a **participle** and its **object** and/or **modifiers:**

```
                              OBJ
    MOD      PART  MOD MOD    PART
```
• *Quickly reaching the correct decision,* he rang the bell.
                    PART PHRASE

A *gerund phrase* consists of a **gerund** and its **object** and/or **modifiers,** and it may also include a *subject of the gerund:*

```
S GER    GER    OBJ GER MOD
```
• *Their sending Matthew away* was a bad mistake.
       GER PHRASE

An **absolute phrase** (see entry) may contain an **infinitive** or a **participle,** but it always modifies an entire statement.

pivoting paragraph (p. 96) A paragraph that begins with one or more **limiting sentences** but then makes a sharp turn to its **main sentence,** which may or may not be followed by **supporting sentences.**

plagiarism (p. 459) The taking of others' thoughts or words without due acknowledgment. Cf. **allusion.**

positive degree See **degree.**

possessive case See **case.**

post hoc, ergo propter hoc (p. 24) A **fallacy** whereby the fact that one event followed another is wrongly taken to prove that the first event caused the later one. (In Latin, *post hoc, ergo propter hoc* means "after this, therefore because of it.")

predicate (p. 198) In a **clause,** the **verb** plus all the words belonging with it:

```
                PRED
```
• He *had a serious heart attack.*

Cf. **subject.**

predicate adjective See **complement.**

predicate noun See **complement.**

predication (p. 222) The selection of a **predicate** for a given **subject.** The problem of *faulty predication* appears when subjects and predicates are mismatched in meaning: ˣ *The purpose of the film wants to change your beliefs.* **Mixed construction** is a more radical form of faulty predication.

prefix (p. 401) One or more letters that can be attached before the root or base form of a word to make a new word: *pre-, with-,* etc., forming *prearranged, withstand,* etc. Cf. **suffix.**

preposition (p. 265) A function word that introduces a prepositional **phrase**—e.g., *to* in *to the lighthouse.* Other common prepositions include:

about	below	from	since
above	beneath	in	through
across	beside	into	till
after	between	like	under
against	beyond	near	until
along	by	of	up
at	during	off	with
before	except	on	without
behind	for	out	

A preposition consisting of more than one word is **compound:** *along with, apart from,* etc. See also **object of preposition.** Cf. **conjunction.**

present participle See **participle.**

principal parts (p. 364) The **base** or simple **infinitive** form of a **verb,** its past **tense** form, and its past **participle:** *walk, walked, walked; grow, grew, grown.*

process analysis (p. 112) The **analysis** of a series of steps constituting a complete task (cooking a stew, making a candle, testing a product, etc.).

pronoun (p. 262) One of a small class of words mostly used in place of **nouns** for a variety of purposes:

1. A *demonstrative* pronoun (*this, that, these, those*) singles out what it refers to: *This is what we want.*

2. An *indefinite* pronoun (*anybody, each, whoever,* etc.) leaves unspecified the person or things it refers to: *Anyone can see that you are right.*

3. An *intensive* pronoun (*myself, yourself, itself, ourselves,* etc.) emphasizes a preceding noun or pronoun: *She herself is a vegetarian.*

4. An *interrogative* pronoun (*who, whom, whose, which, what*) introduces a question: *Who will win the election?*

5. A *personal* pronoun (*I, you, he, she, it, we, they*) stands for one or more persons or things and is used in the tense formation of verbs: *They are willing to compromise.* Personal pronouns also have objective (*him, them*) and possessive (*his, their*) forms: *We asked her to recognize our rights.*

6. A *reciprocal* pronoun (*each other, each other's, one another, one another's*) expresses mutual relation: *We recognized each other's differences of outlook.*

7. A *reflexive* pronoun (*myself, yourself, itself, ourselves,* etc.) differs from an intensive pronoun in serving as a **direct** or **indirect object.** The reflexive pronoun shows that the **subject** of the **clause** is the same person or thing acted upon by the **verb:** *He hurt himself on the track.*

8. A *relative* pronoun (*who, whom, that, which*) introduces a relative or adjectival clause: *My uncle, who lives next door, slept through the earthquake.* Some grammarians also recognize an "indefinite relative pronoun" (one lacking an antecedent): *She knows what you mean.* See also **relative clause.**

pronoun agreement (p. 274) The correspondence of a **pronoun** to its **antecedent,** which ought to share its **gender, number,** and **person.** Thus, in the sentence *When they saw Bill, they gave him a cool wel-*

come, the pronoun *him* properly agrees with the masculine, singular, third-person antecedent *Bill.* Cf. **pronoun reference, subject-verb agreement.**

pronoun reference (p. 274) The connection in a sentence between a **pronoun** and its **antecedent** whereby the antecedent is explicitly present and the pronoun's relation to it is clear. That is, no other word could be mistaken for the antecedent. Pronoun reference is faulty in a sentence like x *She smelled the cooking shrimp, which made her sick.* What made her sick, the shrimp or smelling them cooking? Cf. **pronoun agreement.**

punctuation marks (Chapters 24–29) Marks used to bring out the meaning of written **sentences.** They are:

. period	**( )** parentheses
? question mark	**[ ]** brackets
! exclamation point	**. . .** ellipsis
, comma	**'** apostrophe
; semicolon	**—** hyphen
: colon	**" "** quotation marks
— dash	**/** slash

racist language (p. 169) **Diction** that can give offense by using a derogatory name for an ethnic group or by perpetuating a demeaning stereotype: *greaser, dumb Pole,* etc.

reciprocal pronoun See **pronoun.**

redundancy (p. 177) The defect of unnecessarily conveying the same meaning more than once. Also, an expression that does so—e.g., *retreat back, ascend up.*

reference See **pronoun reference.**

reference list (p. 466) A list of "Works Cited" or "References," supplied at the end of an **essay,** paper, article, or book, and showing where and when the cited or consulted materials appeared. The **parenthetic citations** within the text refer to items in the reference list.

reflexive pronoun See **pronoun.**

refutation (p. 26) The disproving of a point. By definition, all refutations are successful.

regular verb (p. 364) A **verb** that forms both its past **tense** and its past **participle** by adding *-d: hike (hiked, hiked),* etc. Cf. **irregular verb.**

relative clause (p. 202) A subordinate **clause** that functions like an adjective:

REL CLAUSE

* This is the tomb *that we visited*

See also **clause.**

relative pronoun See **pronoun.**

restrictive element (p. 255) A **modifier,** often a phrase or clause, that "restricts" (establishes the identity of) the modified term. Unless it comes first in the sentence, a restrictive element is not set off by commas:

RESTR EL

* The woman *whom I met* has disappeared.

RESTR EL

* The man *in the black suit* is following you.

RESTR EL

* *On long ocean voyages,* seasickness is common.

(Because it is brief, the initial restrictive element in the last example could also appear without a comma; see page 251.) Cf. **nonrestrictive element.**

rhetoric (p. 28) The strategic placement of ideas and choice of language, as in *His rhetoric was effective* or *His ideas were sound but his rhetoric was addressed to the wrong audience.* Note that *rhetoric* need not mean deception or manipulation.

rhetorical question (p. 157) A question posed for effect, without expectation of a reply: *Who can foretell the distant future?*

Roman numeral (p. 430) A figure such as *III, XLVII,* or *CVI,* as opposed to an **Arabic numeral** such as *3, 47,* or *106.*

roman type (p. 417) Plain letters, like these. Cf. **italics.**

run-on sentence (p. 211) A **sentence** in which two or more independent **clauses** are improperly joined. One type of run-on sentence is the **comma splice:** ˣ*She likes candy, she eats it every day.* The other type is the **fused sentence:** ˣ*She likes candy she eats it every day.* Run-ons are typically corrected either with a semicolon (*She likes candy; she eats it every day*) or with a comma and a coordinating **conjunction** *(She likes candy, and she eats it every day).*

sarcasm (p. 314) Abusive ridicule of a person, group, or idea, as in *What pretty phrases these killers speak!* Cf. **irony.**

scratch outline See **outline.**

sentence (p. 128) A grammatically complete unit of expression, usually containing at least one independent **clause,** beginning with a capital letter and ending with a period, question mark, or exclamation point. See also **sentence fragment.**

sentence adverb (p. 215) An **adverb** that serves to indicate a logical connection between the modified **clause** or whole **sentence** and a previous statement—e.g., *therefore* in *She took the job; therefore, she had to find child care.* Also called *conjunctive adverb.*

sentence fragment (p. 203) A set of words punctuated as a **sentence** but either lacking a **subject-verb** combination (ˣ*A day ago.*) or introduced by a subordinating **conjunction** (ˣ *When they last saw her.*).

In general, sentence fragments are regarded as blunders. But an *intentional sentence fragment*—one whose context shows that it is a shortened sentence rather than a dislocated piece of a neighboring sentence—can sometimes be effective: INT FRAG

• How much longer can we resist? *As long as necessary!*

sentence outline See **outline.**

series (p. 151) A set of more than two **parallel** items within a sentence: SERIES

• They were upset about *pollution, unemployment, and poverty.*

sexist language (p. 169) Expressions that can give offense by implying that one sex (almost always male) is superior or of primary importance or that the other sex is restricted to certain traditional roles:

lady doctor; a man-sized job; Every American pursues his own happiness, etc.

signal of relation (p. 86) A word or phrase, such as *therefore* or *subsequently* or *on the contrary,* that indicates how a sentence relates to the preceding one. Such signals contribute vitally to **continuity** between sentences and between whole paragraphs. A repeated word or a **pronoun** can also serve as a signal of relation.

simile (p. 187) An explicit or open comparison, whereby the object at hand is **figuratively** asserted to be like something else: *His eyes that morning were like an elephant's.* Cf. **metaphor.** Both similes and metaphors are called *metaphorical* or **figurative language.** See also **analogy, image.**

slash (p. 340) The punctuation mark /. A slash is used to separate alternatives *(either/or)* and to indicate line endings in **incorporated quotation** of verse. Sometimes called *virgule.*

split infinitive (p. 247) An **infinitive** interrupted by at least one **adverb:** *to firmly stand.* Some readers consider every split infinitive an error; others object only to conspicuously awkward ones such as x *Jane wanted to thoroughly and finally settle the matter.*

squinting modifier (p. 246) A **modifier** awkwardly trapped between sentence elements, either of which might be regarded as the modified term:

           SQ MOD
  x Why he collapsed *altogether* puzzles me.

    Did he collapse altogether, or is the writer altogether puzzled?

stance (p. 34) The **rhetorical** posture a writer adopts toward an audience, establishing a consistent **point of view.** This book recognizes two stances, *forthright* and *ironic.* A forthright stance implies that the writer's statements are to be taken "straight"; an ironic stance implies that the reader is to "read between the lines" and uncover a different or even opposite meaning.

straw man (p. 21) The **fallacy** of misrepresenting an opponent's position so that it will appear weaker than it actually is. The writer "knocks over a straw man" by attacking and dismissing an irrelevant point.

subject (p. 200) The part of a **clause** about which something is **predicated**:

> SUBJ
> * *Ernest* shot the tiger.

The subject alone is called the *simple subject*. With its **modifiers** included it is called the *complete subject*—e.g., *The only thing to do* in *The only thing to do is compromise.*

Not only **verbs** but also **infinitives, gerunds,** and **absolute phrases** can have "subjects":

> S OF INF   INF
> * They wanted *Alexander* to be king.

> S OF GER   GER
> * *Alexander's* refusing upset them.

> S OF ABS
> PHRASE
> * *The conference having ended,* the diplomats went home.
>   ABS PHRASE

subject area (p. 6) A wide range of related concerns within which the **topic** of an essay or paper may be found. Cf. **thesis, topic.**

subject-verb agreement (p. 224) The correspondence of a **verb** with its **subject** in **number** and **person.** In *I stumble,* e.g., the verb *stumble* "agrees with" the subject *I;* both are singular and first-person in form. Cf. **pronoun agreement.**

subjective case See **case.**

subjunctive mood See **mood.**

subordinate clause See **clause.**

subordinated outline See **outline.**

subordinating conjunction See **conjunction.**

subordination (p. 137) In general, the giving of minor emphasis to minor elements or ideas. In syntax, subordination entails making one element grammatically dependent on another, so that the subordinate element becomes a **modifier** of the other element, limiting or explaining it. Thus, in *They were relieved when it was over,* the subordinate **clause** *when it was over* limits the time to which the **verb** *were relieved* applies.

substantive note (p. 489) A supplementary note which, instead of merely giving a reference for a cited passage or idea, makes further comments. Cf. **bibliographic note.**

suffix (p. 395) One or more letters that can be added at the end of a word's root or base to make a new word or form: *-ed, -ing, -ship, -ness,* etc., as in *walked, singing, membership, weakness.* Cf. **prefix.**

summary (p. 455) A concise recapitulation of a passage. Cf. **paraphrase.**

supporting sentence (p. 94) A **sentence** that restates, elaborates, or provides **evidence** or context for some aspect of a paragraph's **leading idea.**

suspended comparison (p. 291) A comparison proposing two possible relations between the compared items, in which the second item is stated only at the end of the construction: *Taco Bell is as good as, if not better than, Pizza Hut.*

suspended paragraph (p. 98) A paragraph that builds, without a decisive shift of direction, toward a **main sentence** at or near the end. Cf. **direct paragraph, pivoting paragraph.**

suspended sentence (p. 158) A **sentence** that significantly delays completing the statement of its idea while **clauses** and/or **phrases** intervene: *The important thing is not to study all night before the exam, nor to try reading the instructor's mind, nor to butter up the TA, but to keep up with the assignments throughout the term.* Also called *periodic sentence.*

suspended verb (p. 290) A construction in which one subject governs two forms of the same delayed **verb:** *She can, and assuredly will, comply with the law.* Note how the verb *can comply* is "suspended" by the intervening element.

syllogism (p. 49) A chain of deduction from premises to a conclusion:

Premise:	All massive die-offs of fish in Lake Erie are caused by pollution.
Premise:	Last year there was a massive die-off of fish in Lake Erie.
Conclusion:	Last year's massive die-off of fish in Lake Erie was caused by pollution.

gloss 44

tense (p. 361) The time a **verb** expresses: present *(see)*, future *(will see)*, etc.

thesis (p. 6) The point, or one central idea, of an essay, paper, article, book, etc. Cf. **subject area, topic.**

thesis statement (p. 24) A one-sentence statement of the **thesis** or central idea of an essay or paper. In this book, a thesis statement is considered to be full only if it is complex enough to guide the essay's organization.

tone (p. 33) The quality of feeling that is conveyed in a piece of writing. Words like *factual, sober, fanciful, urgent, tongue-in-cheek, restrained, stern, pleading,* and *exuberant* may begin to suggest the range of tones found in **essays.** Cf. **stance, voice.**

topic (p. 6) The specific subject of an essay or paper; the ground to be covered or the question to be answered. Cf. **subject area, thesis.**

topic outline See **outline.**

topic sentence Replaced in this book by the term **main sentence,** since the key sentence in a paragraph is the one stating the **leading idea,** not the one announcing a "topic."

transitional phrase (p. 216) A **phrase** having the same function as a **sentence adverb,** modifying a whole **clause** or **sentence** while showing its logical connection to a previous statement:

TRANS PHRASE

- She says she simply can't bear to be late; *in other words,* she expects the rest of us to show up on time.

transitive verb (p. 198) A **verb** transmitting an action to a **direct object:**

    TR V
- They *cast* the dice.

Cf. **intransitive verb, linking verb.**

trial thesis (p. 16) A possible **thesis,** or central idea, considered before a final thesis has been chosen.

trial topic (p. 13) A tentative **topic** that requires further evaluation before being judged suitable for an essay.

understatement (p. 189) A device of **rhetoric,** often used for **irony,** whereby the writer conveys the importance of something by appearing to take it lightly: *Living near the edge of a runway for jumbo jets is not altogether relaxing.*

verb (p. 197) A word or words like *goes, saw,* or *was leaving,* serving to convey the action performed by a **subject,** to express the state of that subject, or to connect the subject to a **complement.**

verb phrase See **phrase.**

verbal (p. 199) A form derived from, but different in function from, a **verb.** Verbals are either **infinitives, participles,** or **gerunds.** When mistakenly used as verbs, they cause **sentence fragments:**

  VERBAL
x George *going* to the movies tonight.

voice (p. 369) The form of a **verb** indicating whether the **subject** performs the action *(active* voice: *we strike)* or receives the action *(passive* voice: *we are struck).* Also, the "self" projected by a given piece of writing (p. 32). In the latter sense, this book recognizes two voices, the *personal* and *impersonal.*

weaseling thesis (p. 17) A **thesis** that fails to take any definite stand: x *People can be found who oppose gun control;* x *Abortion is quite a controversial topic.*

INDEX

Note: Main entries in **boldface** are defined in the Glossary of Terms (pp. 567–98). Page numbers in *italics* indicate the main discussion of a topic; go to those pages first.

About the Authors

Frederick Crews, Professor of English at the University of California, Berkeley, received the Ph.D. from Princeton University. Throughout a distinguished career he has attained many honors, including a Guggenheim Fellowship, appointment as a Fulbright Lecturer in Italy, an essay prize from the National Endowment for the Arts, and a distinguished teaching award from his campus. His writings include the widely used *Random House Handbook* as well as highly regarded books on Henry James, E. M. Forster, and Nathaniel Hawthorne, the best-selling satire *The Pooh Perplex,* and two volumes of his own essays entitled *Out of My System* and *Skeptical Engagements.* Professor Crews has published numerous articles in *Partisan Review, The New York Review of Books, Commentary, Tri-Quarterly, The American Scholar,* and other important journals. He has twice been Chairman of Freshman Composition in the English Department at Berkeley.

Sandra Schor is Associate Professor of English at Queens College (City University of New York), where she has served as director of the writing program. Her essays and reviews on the theory of composition and the teaching of writing have been collected in *The Writer's Mind, What Makes Writing Good, Audits of Meaning,* and *Linguistics, Stylistics, and the Teaching of Composition,* as well as in the journals *College Composition and Communication* and *College English.* She is also the coauthor, with Judith Summerfield, of the *Random House Guide to Writing.* She has received both a Mellon Fellowship and a grant from the Fund for the Improvement of Postsecondary Education for composition studies. In recognition of her contributions as a teacher of writing, the City University of New York named her a Master Teacher; for her academic writing, she is the recipient of the Mina P. Shaughnessy Writing Award. A fiction writer and poet, Professor Schor has a novel, *The Great Letter* E, published by North Point Press, 1989.

A Note on the Type

The text of this book was set on the Linotronic 300 in Century Schoolbook, one of the several variations of Century Roman to appear within a decade of its creation. The original face was cut by Linn Boyd Benton in 1895 in response to a request by Theodore Low DeVinne for an attractive, easy-to-read type to fit in the narrow columns of his *Century* magazine.

Century Schoolbook was drawn especially for textbooks used by pupils in primary grades, but because of its easy legibility, it quickly gained popularity in varied applications. The Century family remains the only American typeface cut before 1910 still widely in use today.

This book was composed by TSI Graphics, Effingham, Ill., and was printed and bound by Arcata Graphics, Fairfield, Penn.

SYMBOLS FOR COMMENT AND REVISION

When commenting on your written work, your instructor may use some of the following marks. If a mark calls for revision, consult the chapter or section of the *Handbook* printed in boldface type.

✓	Excellent point; well said	dm	Dangling modifier, **19c**
✓ arg	Effective argument	doc	Faulty documentation form, **37**
✓ concr	Good use of concrete language	emp	Weak or inappropriate sentence emphasis, **12a–e**
✓ d	Effective diction	exag	Exaggeration; overstated claim, **2c**
✓ det	Effective supporting detail	fig	Inappropriate figure of speech, **15**
✓ dev	Effective development of the point	frag	Sentence fragment, **16d**
✓ fig	Apt figure of speech	fs	Fused sentence, **17b**
✓ //	Effective parallelism	Gl	Look up this expression in the Glossary of Terms
✓ p	Effective choice of punctuation	hyph	Faulty hyphenation, **33**
✓ trans	Good transition	ital	Use italics (underline), **35a–f**
abbr	Faulty abbreviation, **35a–k**	jarg	Jargon, **13f**
ad	Faulty comparison of adjective or adverb, **19a–b**	lc	Do not capitalize (leave in lowercase), **34**
agr	Faulty subject-verb agreement, **18c–n**	livel	Stale language; rewrite for liveliness, **14**
awk	Awkward expression	log	Faulty logic, **2c–e**
cap	Capitalize this letter, **34**	mis m	Misplaced modifier, **19d**
case	Wrong pronoun case, **20**	mixed	Mixed construction, **18a**
chop	Choppy sequence of sentences, **12f**	ms	Faulty manuscript form, **4j**
cl	Cliché, **14f**	no ¶	Do not begin a new paragraph here, **7d**
coh	Coherence lacking, **10**	num	Inappropriate form for a number, **35l–n**
colloq	Colloquial expression, **13g**	p	Faulty punctuation, **24–28**
comp	Faulty comparison, **22a, 22e**	pass	Inappropriate use of passive voice, **10e**
cs	Comma splice, **17b**	p/form	Faulty form or spacing of punctuation mark, **29**
d	Inappropriate diction (word choice), **13c–g, Index of Usage**		